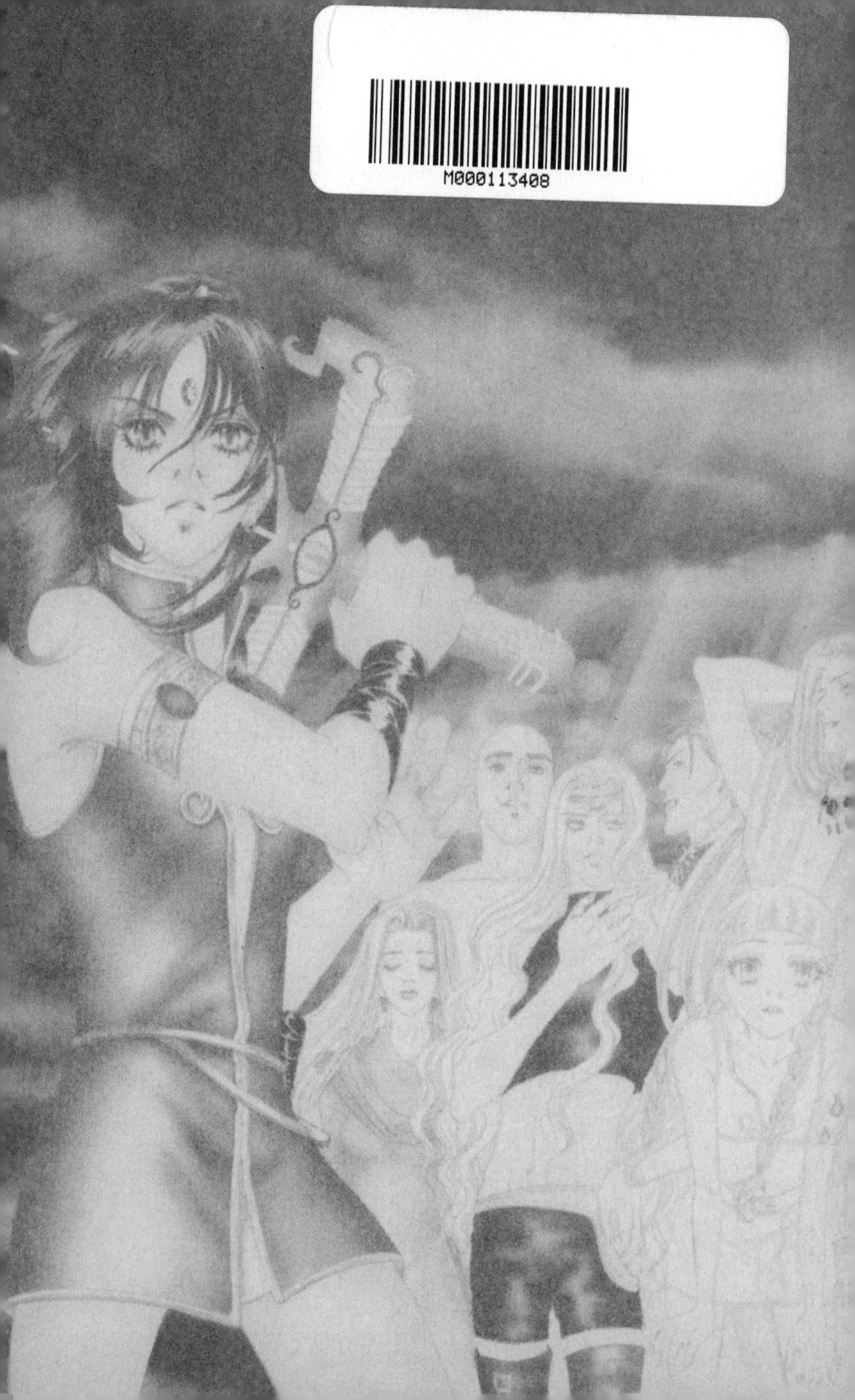

Les Bijoux

Story by
Jo Eun-Ha

Art by
Park Sang-Sun

Volume 5

HAMBURG // LONDON // LOS ANGELES // TOKYO

Les Bijoux Vol. 5
created by DAIWON C.I. INC.
written by Jo Eun-Ha
illustrated by Park Sang-Sun

Translation - Seung-Ah Lee
English Adaptation - Jason Deitrich
Copy Editor - Chrissy Schilling
Retouch and Lettering - Jeanine Han
Production Artist - James Dashiell
Cover Design - Patrick Hook

Editor - Rob Valois
Digital Imaging Manager - Chris Buford
Pre-Press Manager - Antonio DePietro
Production Managers - Jennifer Miller and Mutsumi Miyazaki
Art Director - Matt Alford
Managing Editor - Jill Freshney
VP of Production - Ron Klamert
President and C.O.O. - John Parker
Publisher and C.E.O. - Stuart Levy

A  Manga

TOKYOPOP Inc.
5900 Wilshire Blvd. Suite 2000
Los Angeles, CA 90036

E-mail: info@TOKYOPOP.com
Come visit us online at www.TOKYOPOP.com

ISBN: 1-59182-694-2

First TOKYOPOP printing: October 2004
10 9 8 7 6 5 4 3 2 1
Printed in the USA

LAST TIME IN LES BIJOUX...

The world is divided into 12 *Mines*, each ruled by a tyrannical *Habit*. It is a time of war and oppression, when the *Spars*, the working class, live in mortal fear of the Habits. In the midst of this chaos, in the *Mine of Neige*, a strange thing happened. A miraculous child was born from a union between a dwarf and a hunchback...a child who takes on the form of a male and female.

Now the child, *Lapis Lazuli*, has grown up. After his parents were slaughtered by the Habit *Diamond*, Lapis swore revenge against the Lord of Neige. But Lapis only managed to cut out Diamond's right eye before the Habit escaped. Homeless and friendless, Lapis travels across the continent to the *Mine of Soleil*, where he makes two new friends, *Carnelian*, brother to the Habit, and "Butterfly," a spiritual guide with the ability to transform into a panther.

Lapis gains new allies and new enemies as he faces his role as the one who will overthrow the tyrannical Habits. After steeling his courage, he departs to find the divine sword of Tourmaline. When two of Lapis' friends are slaughtered before his very eyes, Butterfly and Lapis begin a journey to find all of Lapis' guardians.

After Lapis is rescued by Silica, he finds himself recuperating in *Sable Mine*. There, a tyrannical ruler named Pyrope suppresses the people with a heavy water tax and threatens brutality and oppression if they don't pay up. To help the citizens who hunger for change, Lapis comes up with an ingenious plan to quench their thirst for justice.

As the power-hungry Diamond's plans for conquest begin to come to fruition, the one thing he covets most still eludes him--the mysterious Lazuli. In order to get on Diamond's good side, Emerald sets out to capure Lazuli. Meanwhile, although Lapis has vowed to kill Diamond, his female form is beginning to see a softer side of the Lord of the Mine of Niege. Will Diamond become this girl's bestfriend?

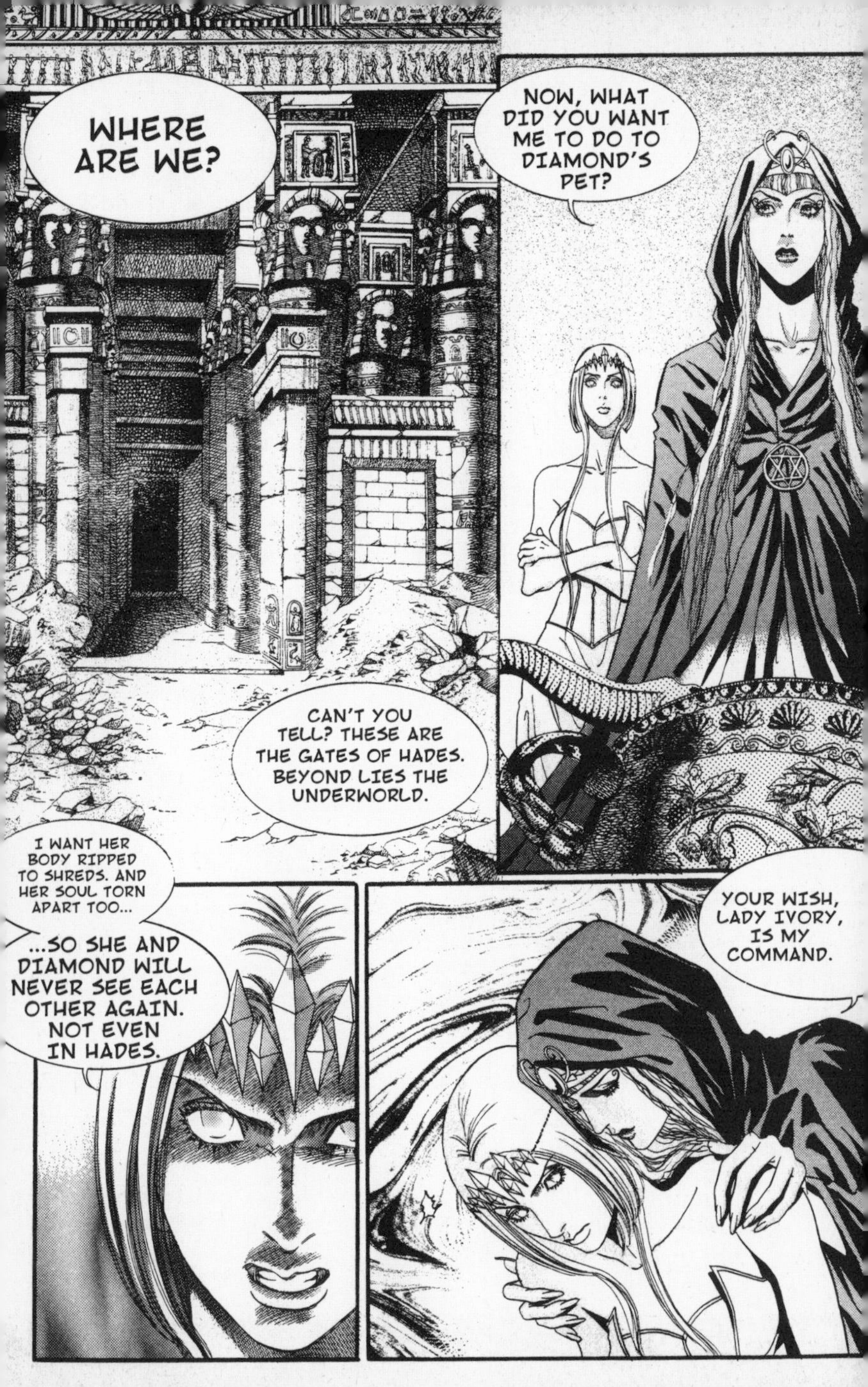
WHERE ARE WE?
NOW, WHAT DID YOU WANT ME TO DO TO DIAMOND'S PET?
CAN'T YOU TELL? THESE ARE THE GATES OF HADES. BEYOND LIES THE UNDERWORLD.
I WANT HER BODY RIPPED TO SHREDS. AND HER SOUL TORN APART TOO...
...SO SHE AND DIAMOND WILL NEVER SEE EACH OTHER AGAIN. NOT EVEN IN HADES.
YOUR WISH, LADY IVORY, IS MY COMMAND.

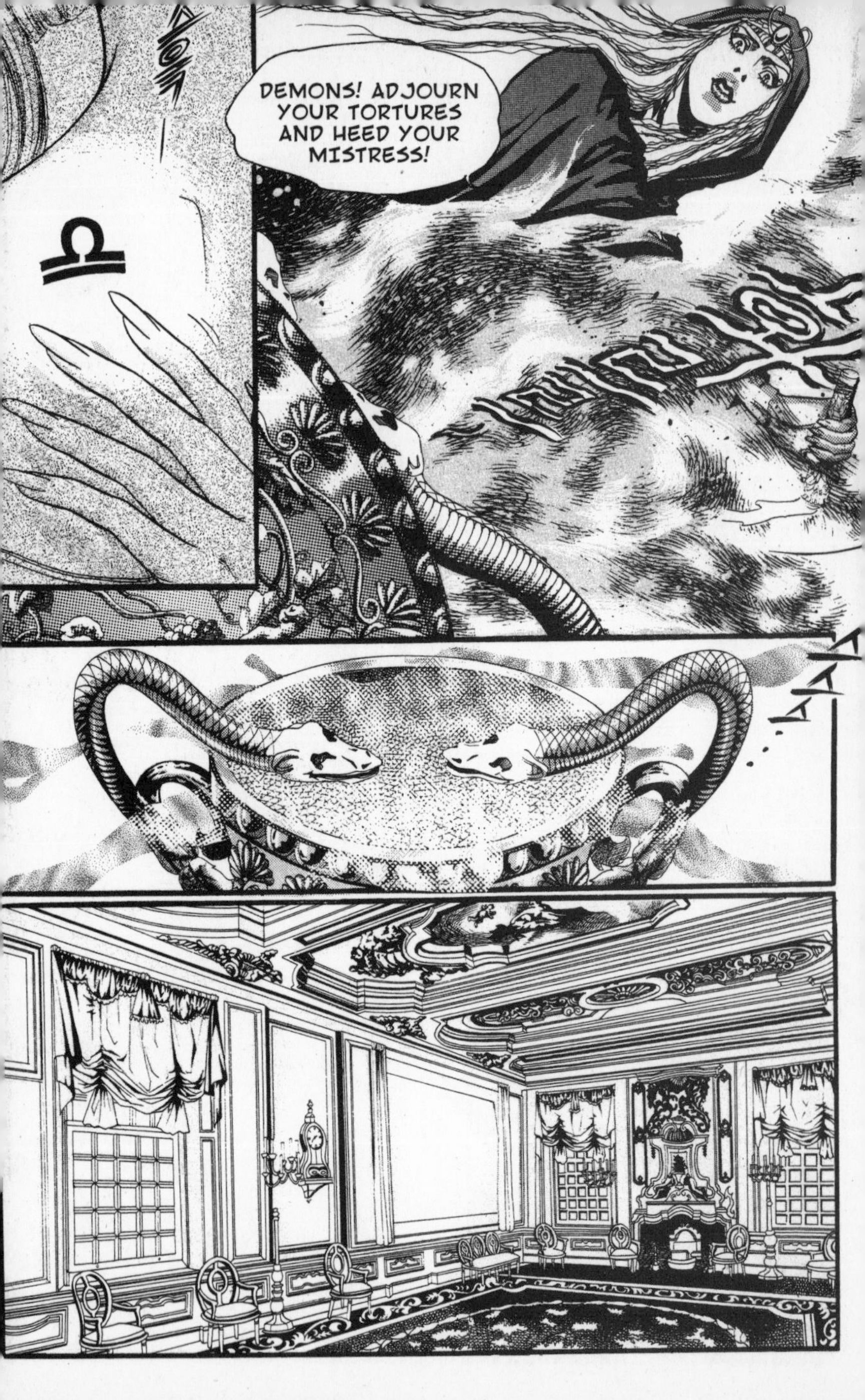
DEMONS! ADJOURN YOUR TORTURES AND HEED YOUR MISTRESS!

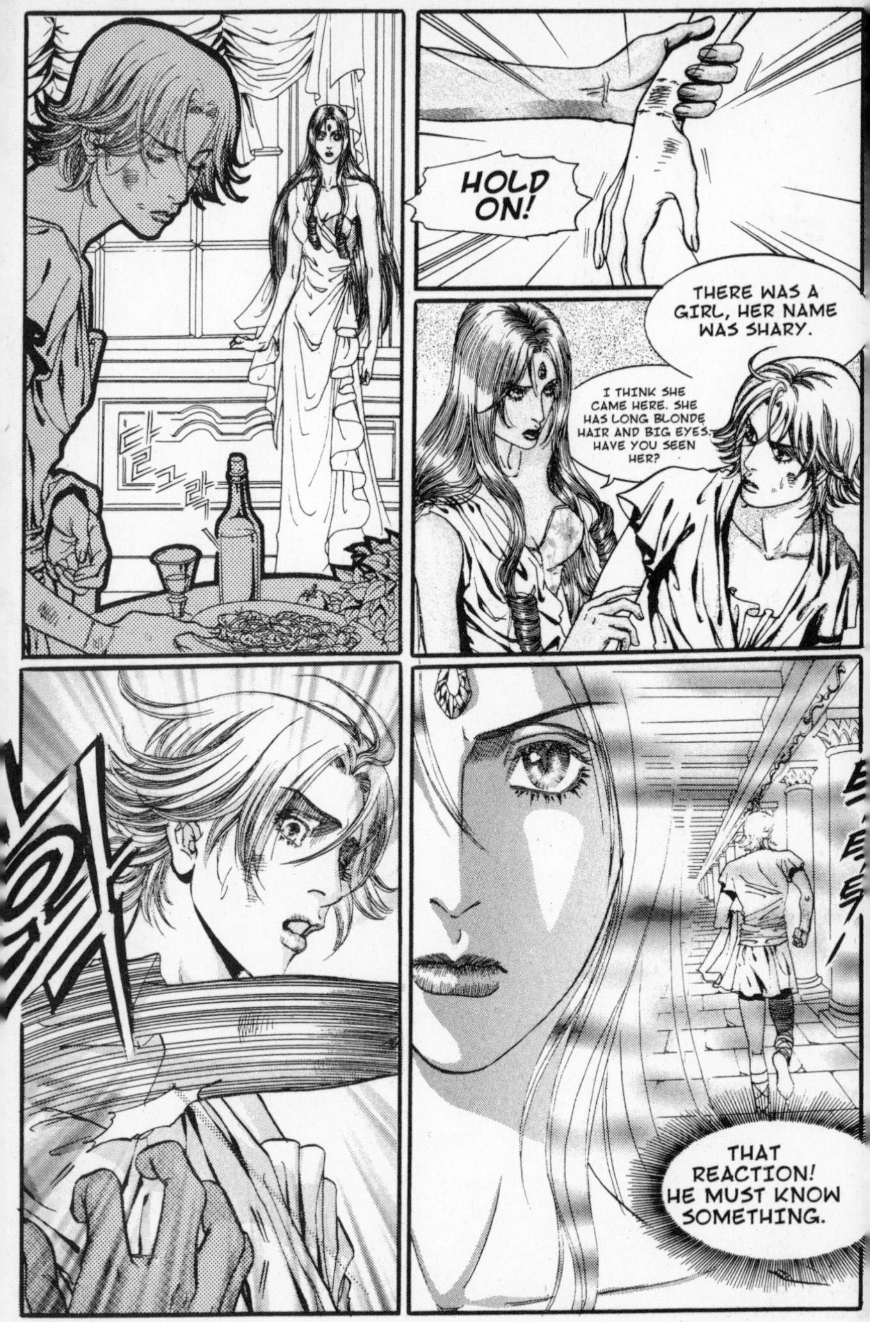
HOLD ON!
THERE WAS A GIRL, HER NAME WAS SHARY.
I THINK SHE CAME HERE. SHE HAS LONG BLONDE HAIR AND BIG EYES. HAVE YOU SEEN HER?
THAT REACTION! HE MUST KNOW SOMETHING.

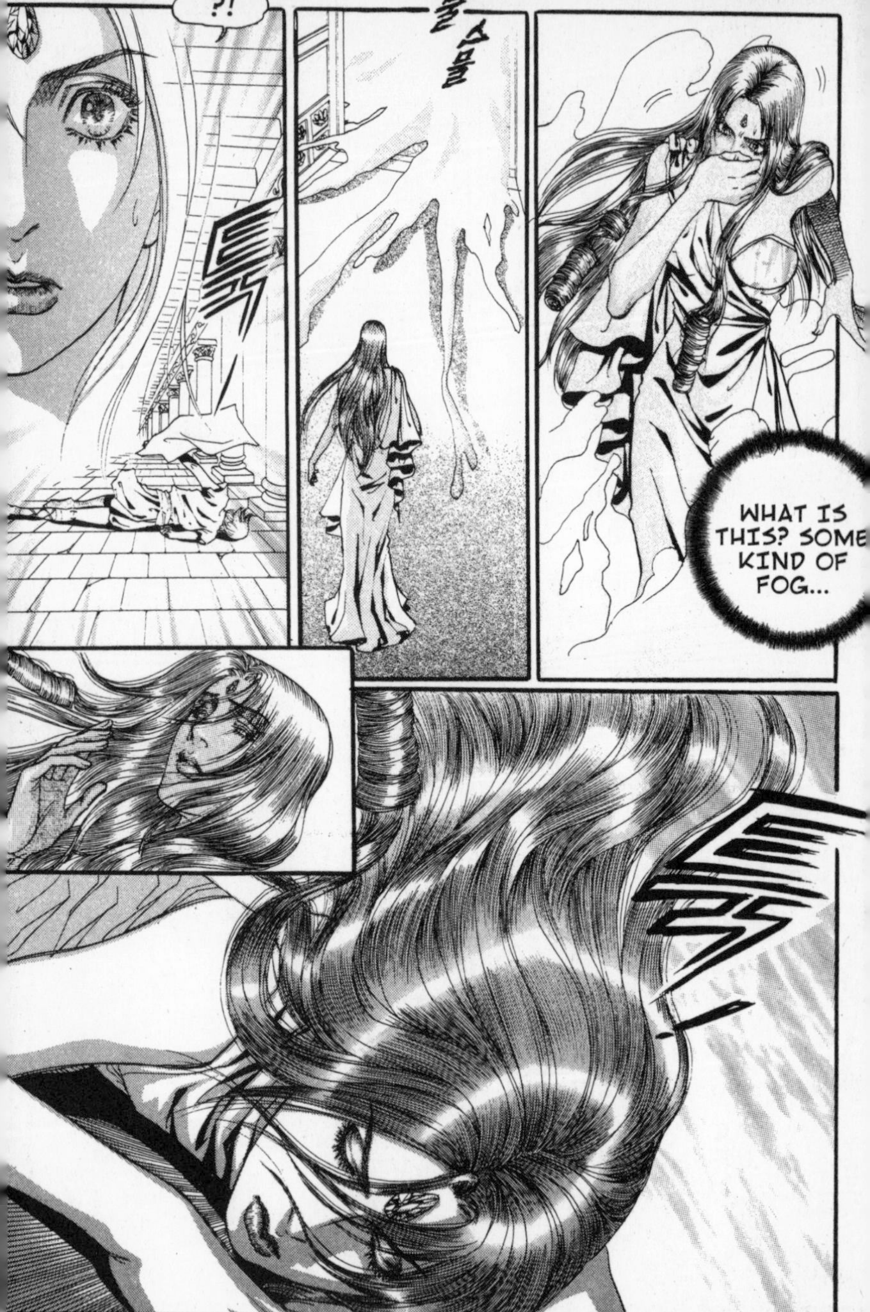
?!
믈스믈
WHAT IS THIS? SOME KIND OF FOG...

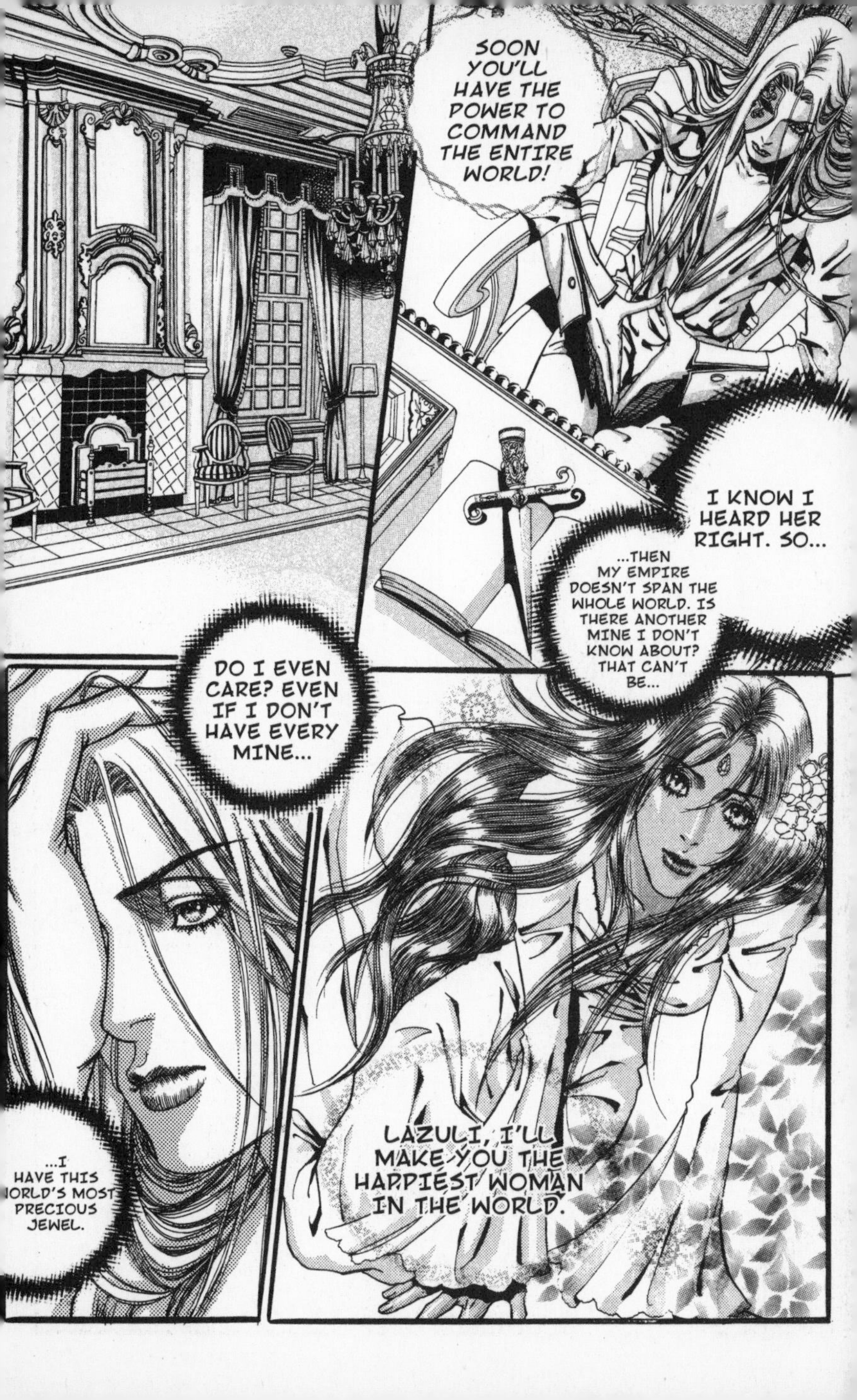
SOON YOU'LL HAVE THE POWER TO COMMAND THE ENTIRE WORLD!
I KNOW I HEARD HER RIGHT. SO...
...THEN MY EMPIRE DOESN'T SPAN THE WHOLE WORLD. IS THERE ANOTHER MINE I DON'T KNOW ABOUT? THAT CAN'T BE...
DO I EVEN CARE? EVEN IF I DON'T HAVE EVERY MINE...
LAZULI, I'LL MAKE YOU THE HAPPIEST WOMAN IN THE WORLD.
...I HAVE THIS WORLD'S MOST PRECIOUS JEWEL.

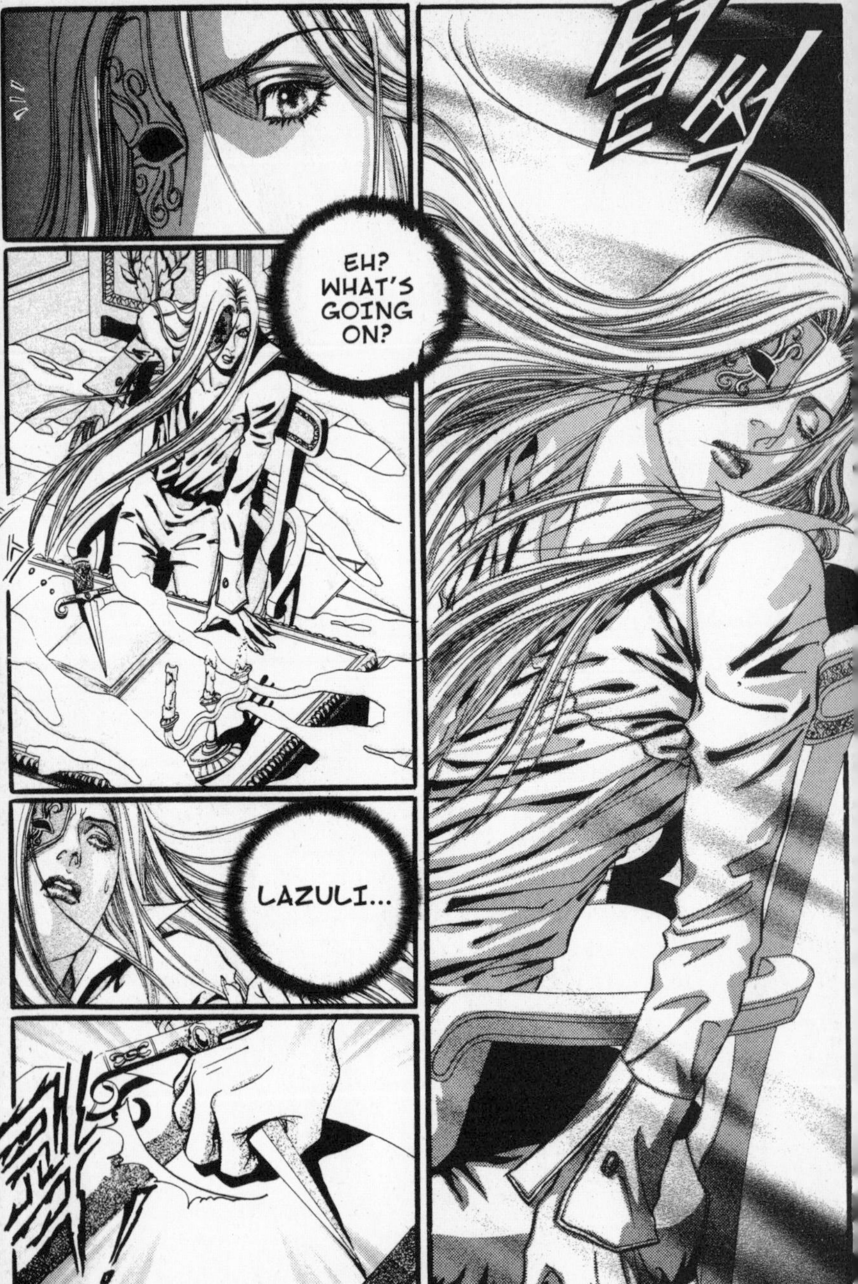
EH? WHAT'S GOING ON?
LAZULI...

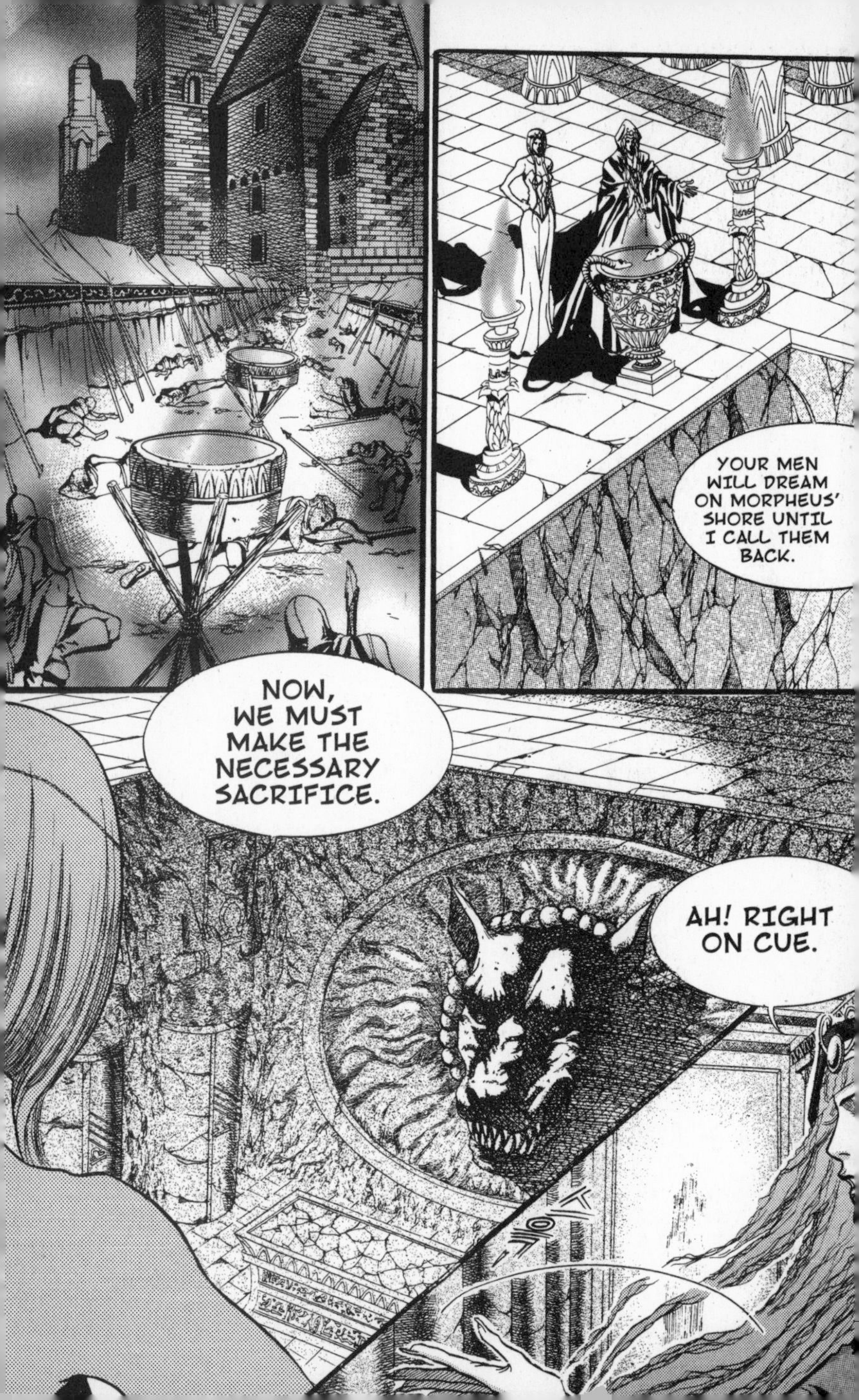
YOUR MEN WILL DREAM ON MORPHEUS' SHORE UNTIL I CALL THEM BACK.
NOW, WE MUST MAKE THE NECESSARY SACRIFICE.
AH! RIGHT ON CUE.

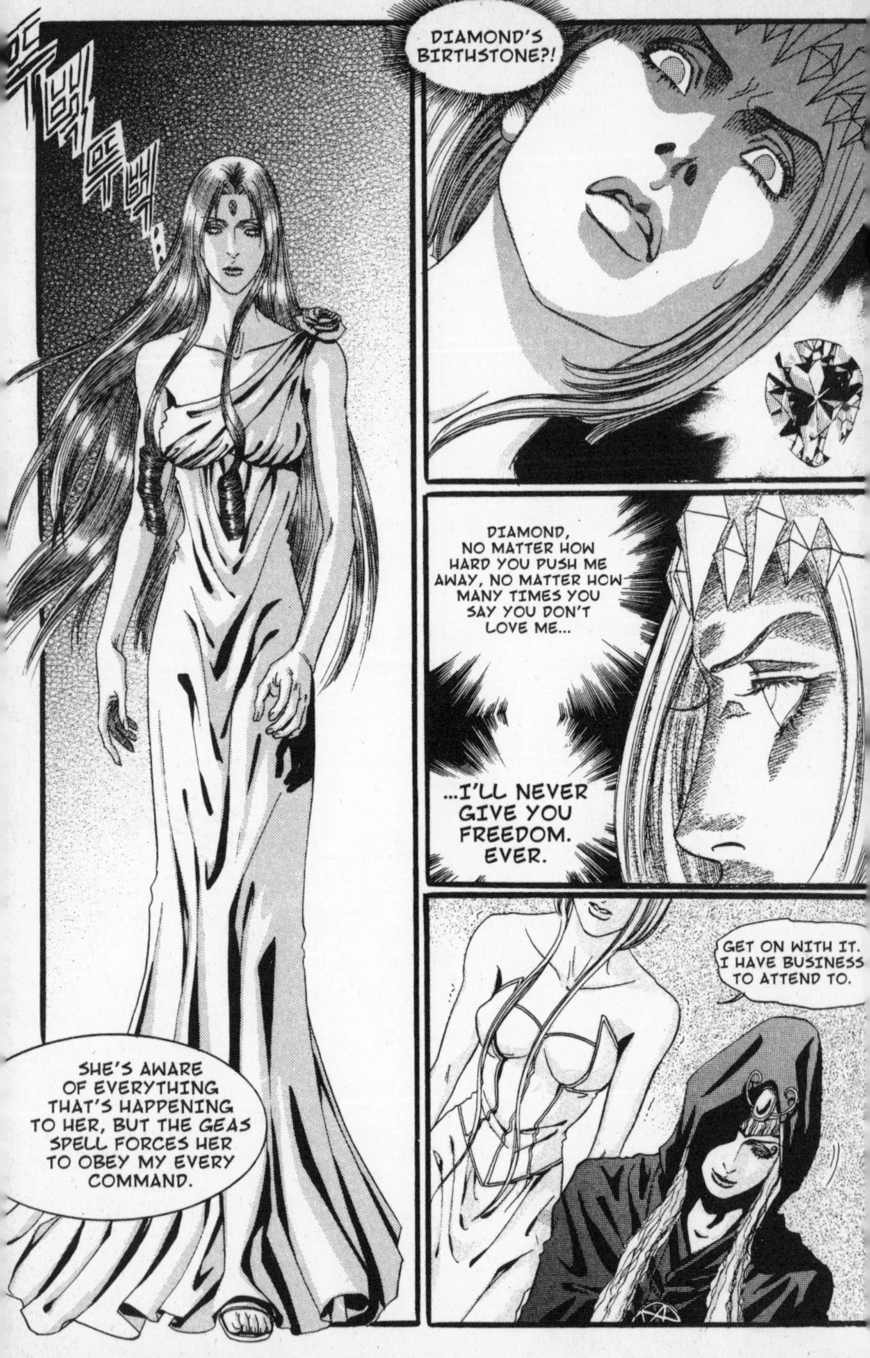

DIAMOND'S BIRTHSTONE?!
DIAMOND, NO MATTER HOW HARD YOU PUSH ME AWAY, NO MATTER HOW MANY TIMES YOU SAY YOU DON'T LOVE ME...
...I'LL NEVER GIVE YOU FREEDOM. EVER.
SHE'S AWARE OF EVERYTHING THAT'S HAPPENING TO HER, BUT THE GEAS SPELL FORCES HER TO OBEY MY EVERY COMMAND.
GET ON WITH IT. I HAVE BUSINESS TO ATTEND TO.

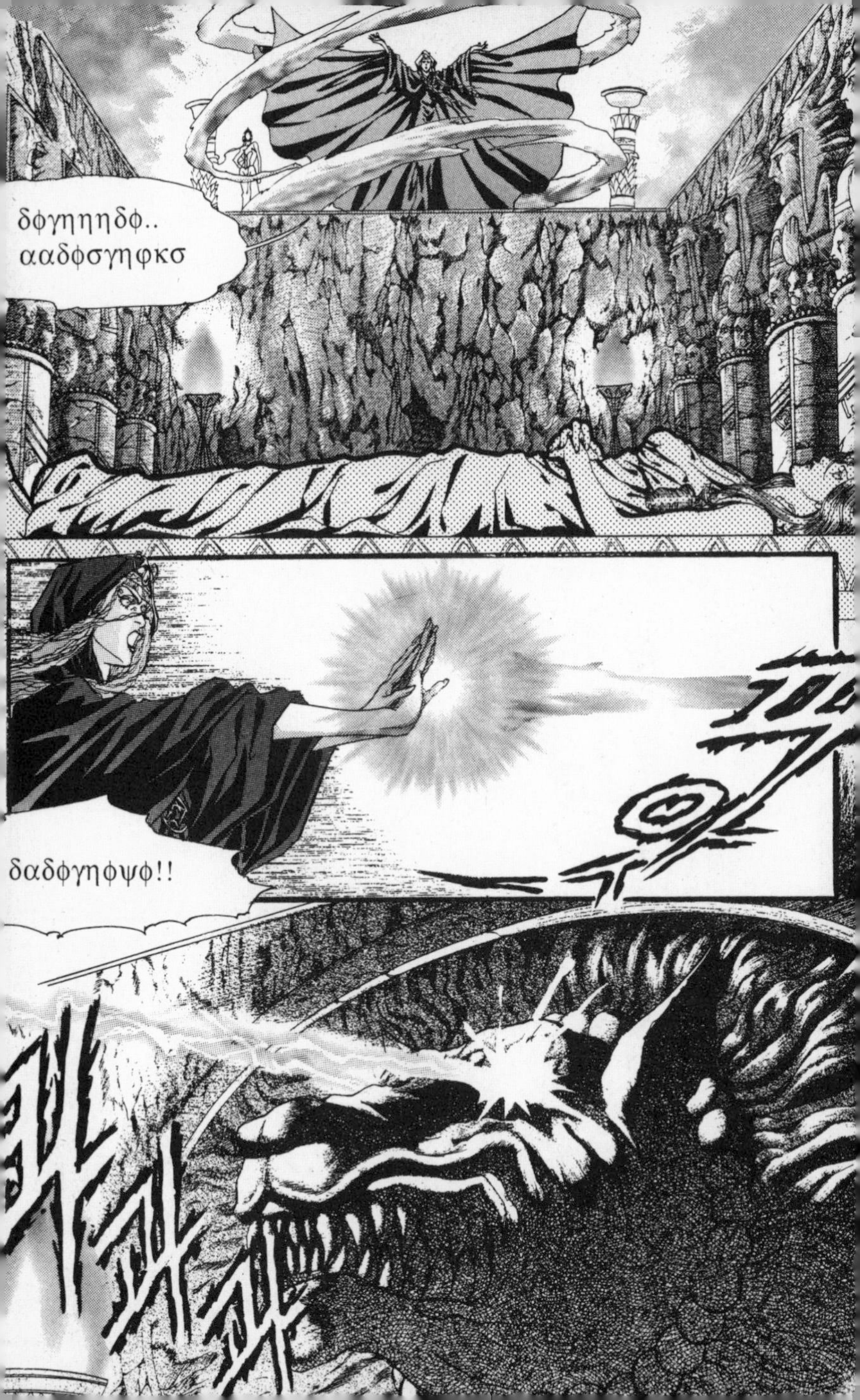
δφγηηηδφ..
ααδφσγηφκσ
δαδφγηφψφ!!

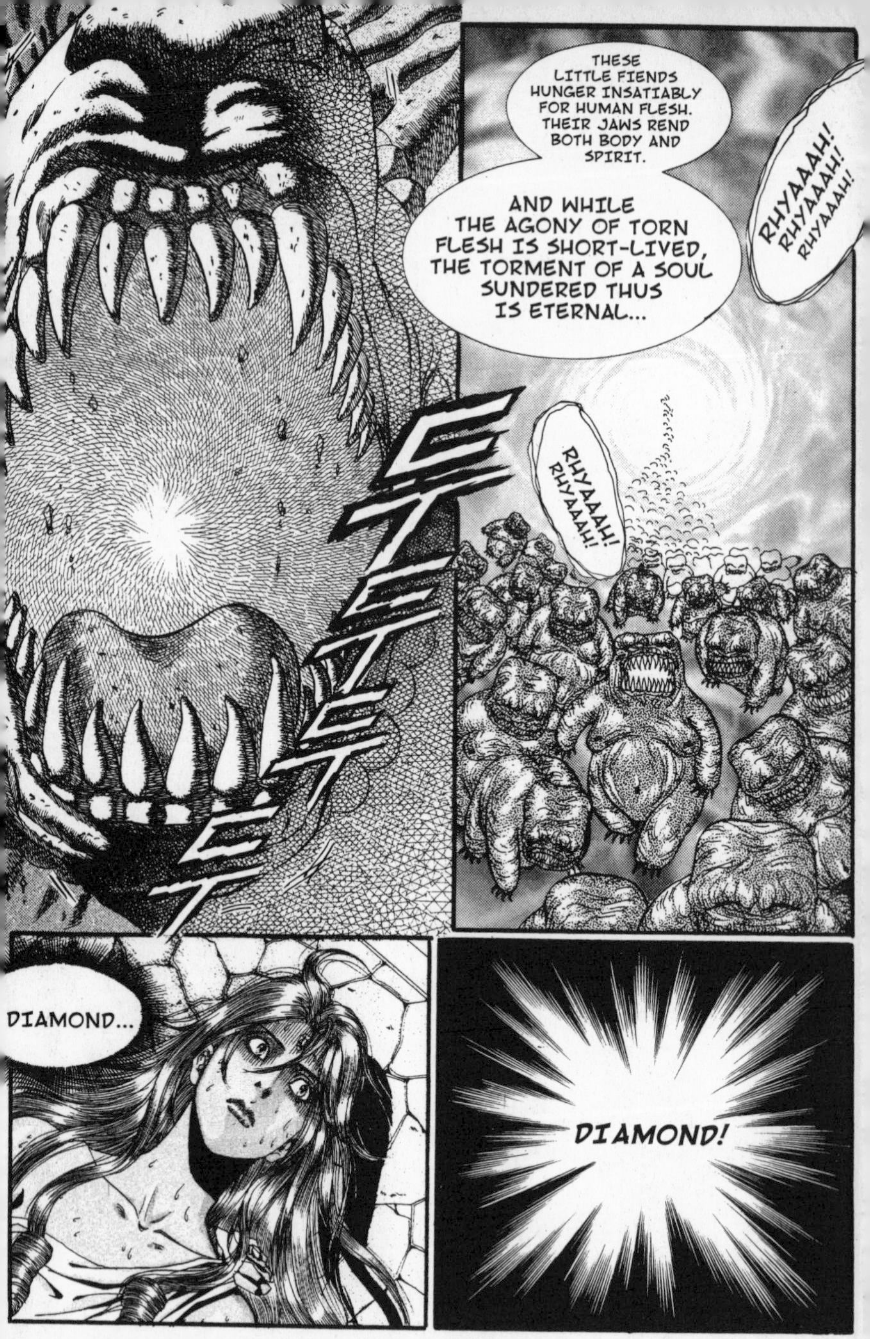

THESE LITTLE FIENDS HUNGER INSATIABLY FOR HUMAN FLESH. THEIR JAWS REND BOTH BODY AND SPIRIT.
AND WHILE THE AGONY OF TORN FLESH IS SHORT-LIVED, THE TORMENT OF A SOUL SUNDERED THUS IS ETERNAL...
RHYAAAH! RHYAAAH! RHYAAAH!
RHYAAAH! RHYAAAH!
DIAMOND...
DIAMOND!

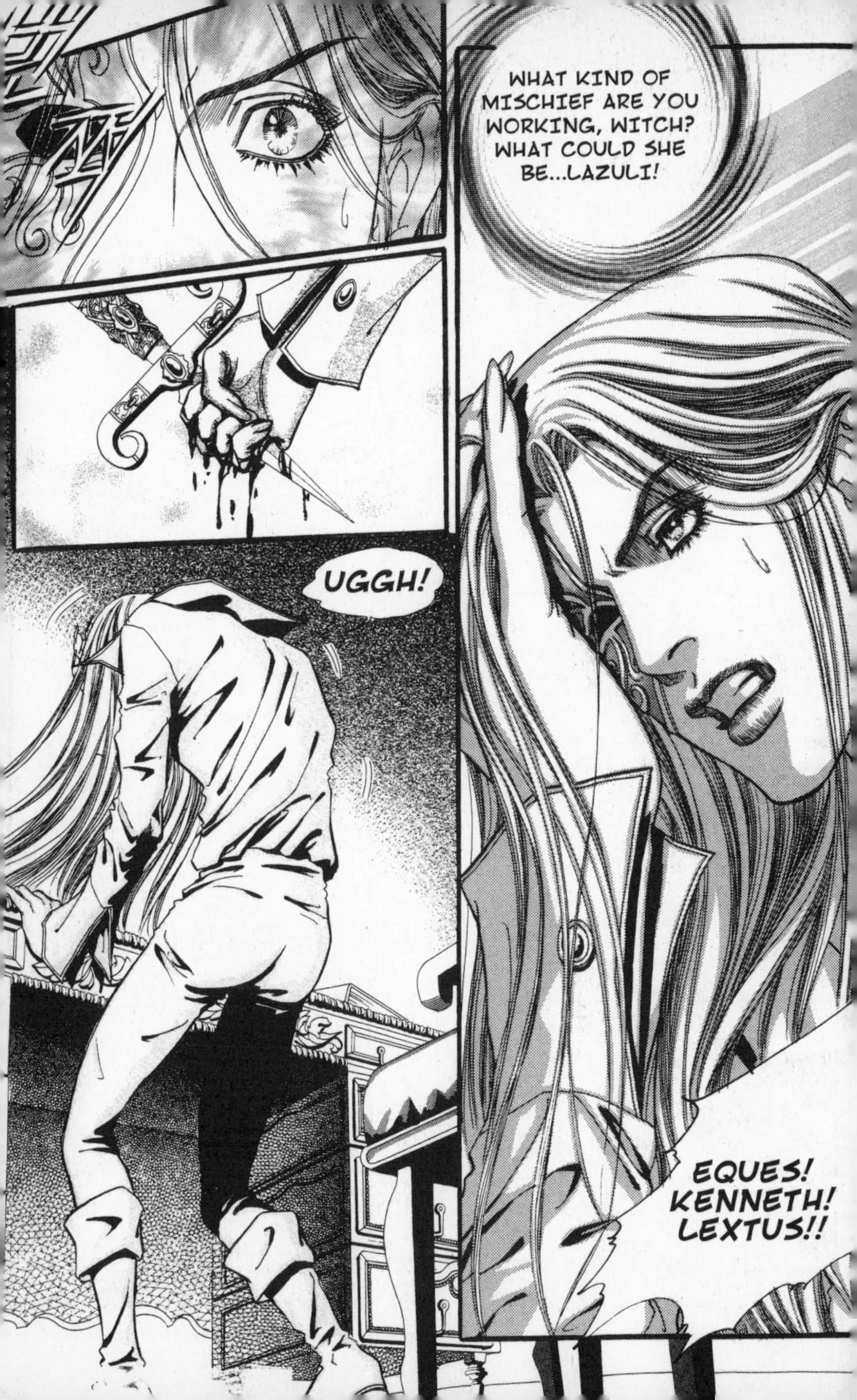
UGGH!
WHAT KIND OF MISCHIEF ARE YOU WORKING, WITCH? WHAT COULD SHE BE...LAZULI!
EQUES! KENNETH! LEXTUS!!

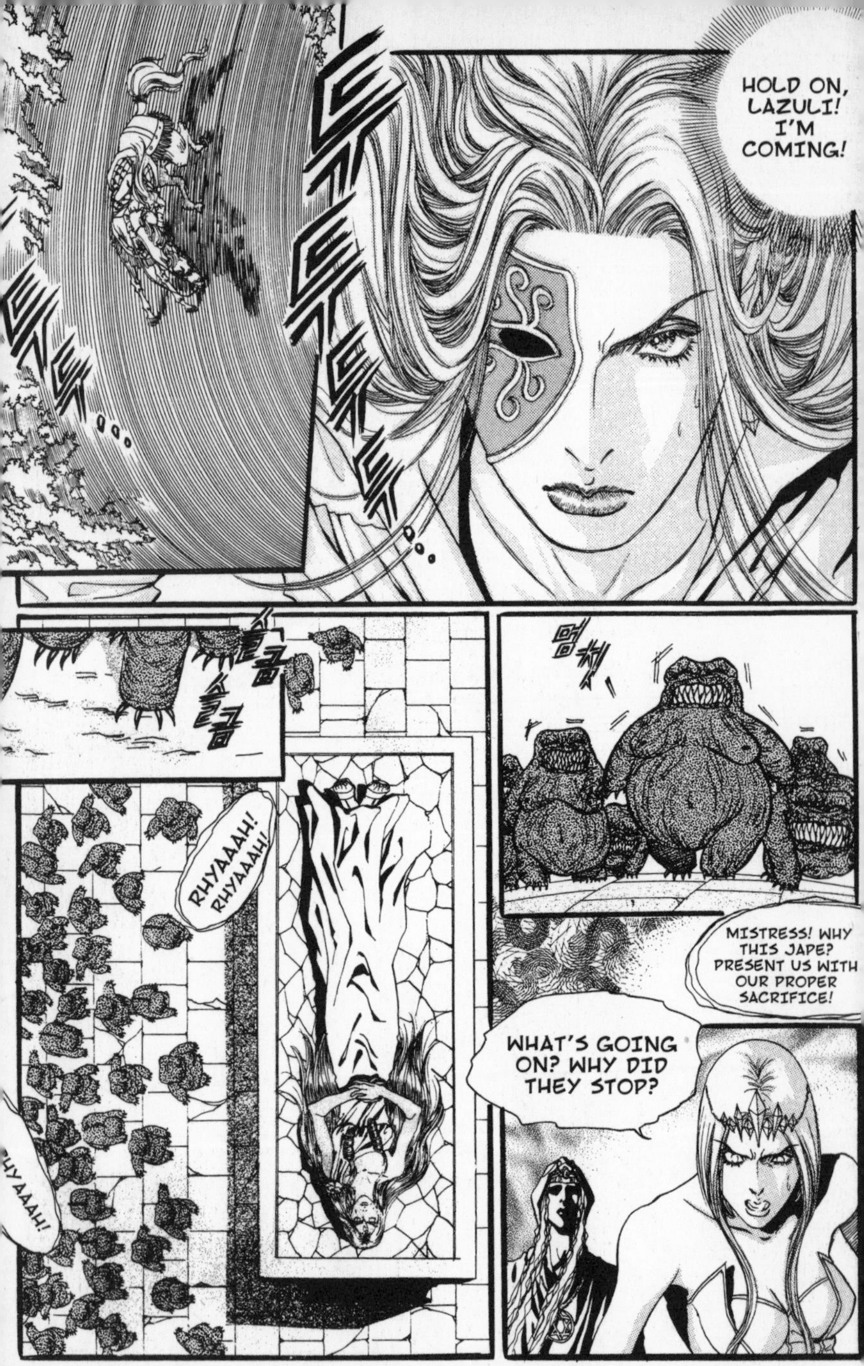
HOLD ON, LAZULI! I'M COMING!
슬금 슬금
멈칫
RHYAAAH! RHYAAAH!
RHYAAAH!
MISTRESS! WHY THIS JAPE? PRESENT US WITH OUR PROPER SACRIFICE!
WHAT'S GOING ON? WHY DID THEY STOP?

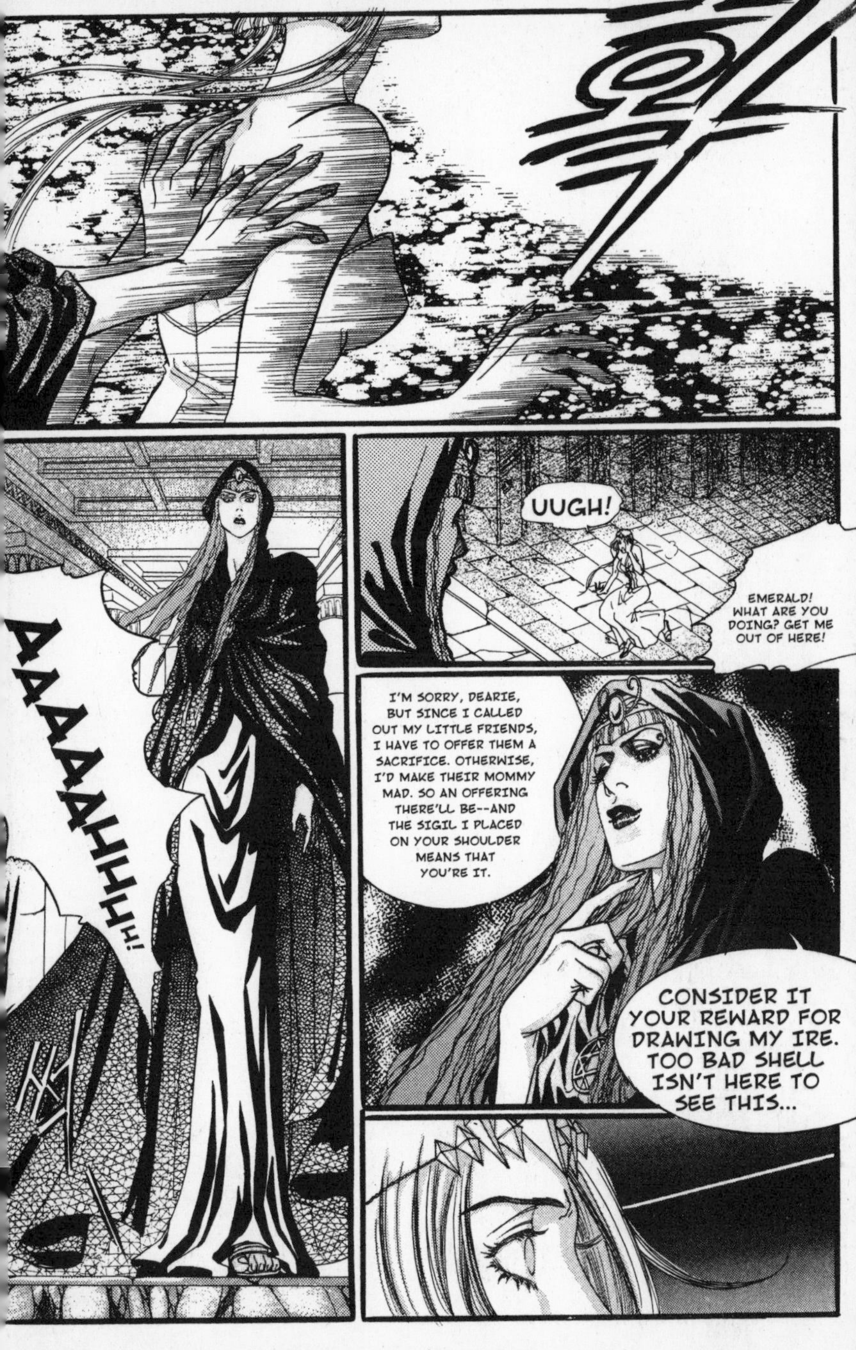

UUGH!
AAAAAHHH!!
EMERALD! WHAT ARE YOU DOING? GET ME OUT OF HERE!
I'M SORRY, DEARIE, BUT SINCE I CALLED OUT MY LITTLE FRIENDS, I HAVE TO OFFER THEM A SACRIFICE. OTHERWISE, I'D MAKE THEIR MOMMY MAD. SO AN OFFERING THERE'LL BE--AND THE SIGIL I PLACED ON YOUR SHOULDER MEANS THAT YOU'RE IT.
CONSIDER IT YOUR REWARD FOR DRAWING MY IRE. TOO BAD SHELL ISN'T HERE TO SEE THIS...

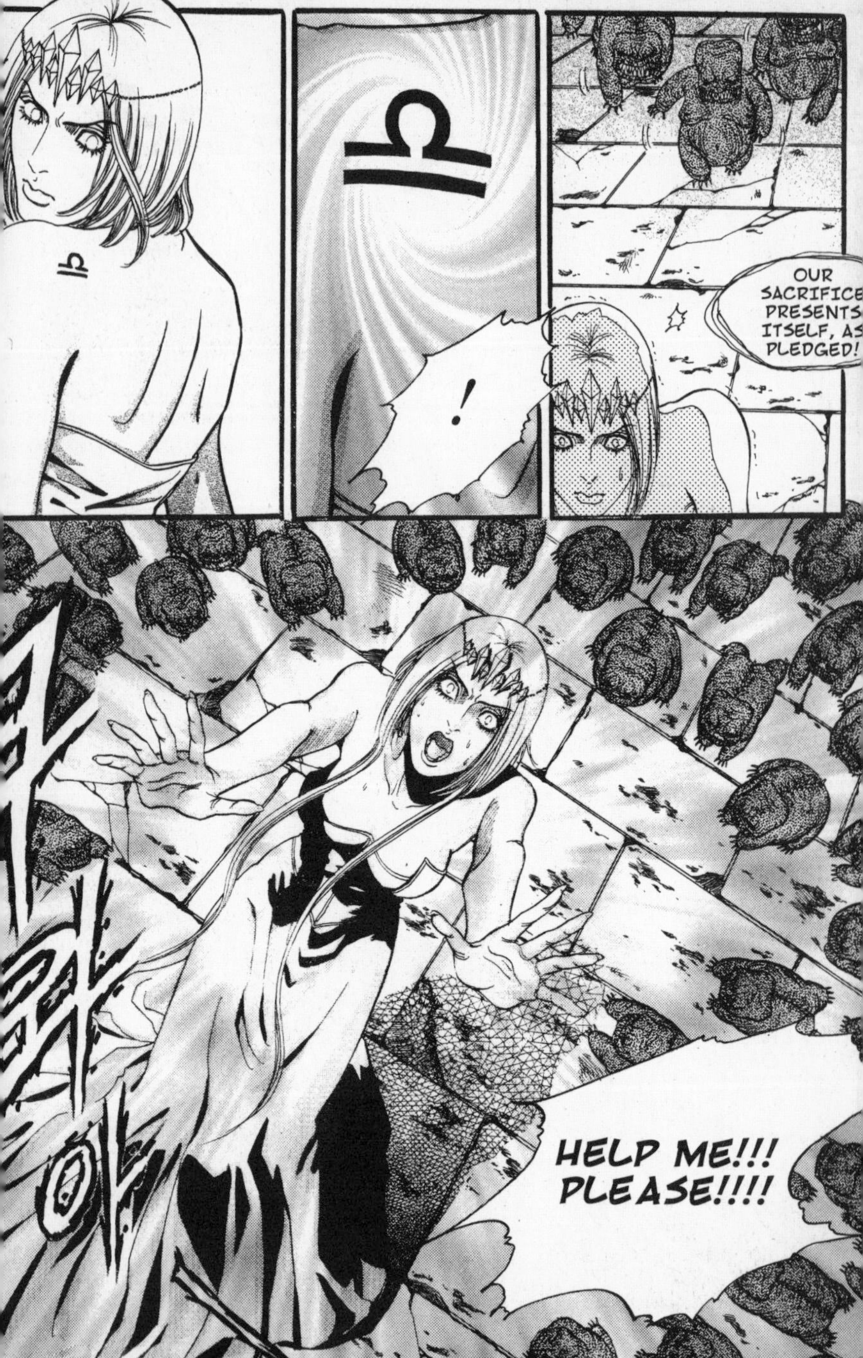

!
OUR SACRIFICE PRESENTS ITSELF, AS PLEDGED!
HELP ME!!! PLEASE!!!!

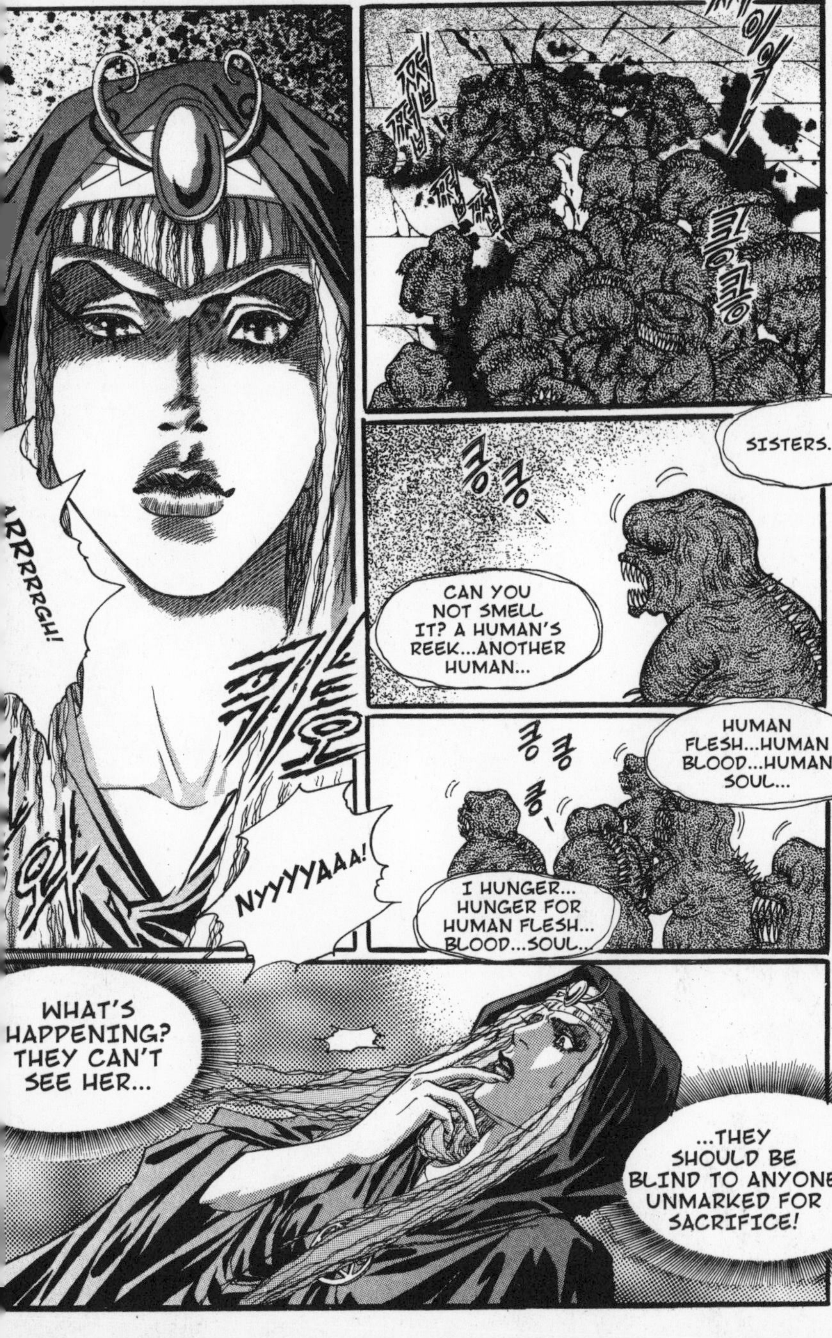

SISTERS...
CAN YOU NOT SMELL IT? A HUMAN'S REEK...ANOTHER HUMAN...
HUMAN FLESH...HUMAN BLOOD...HUMAN SOUL...
I HUNGER... HUNGER FOR HUMAN FLESH... BLOOD...SOUL...
RRRRRRGH!
NYYYYAAA!
WHAT'S HAPPENING? THEY CAN'T SEE HER...
...THEY SHOULD BE BLIND TO ANYONE UNMARKED FOR SACRIFICE!

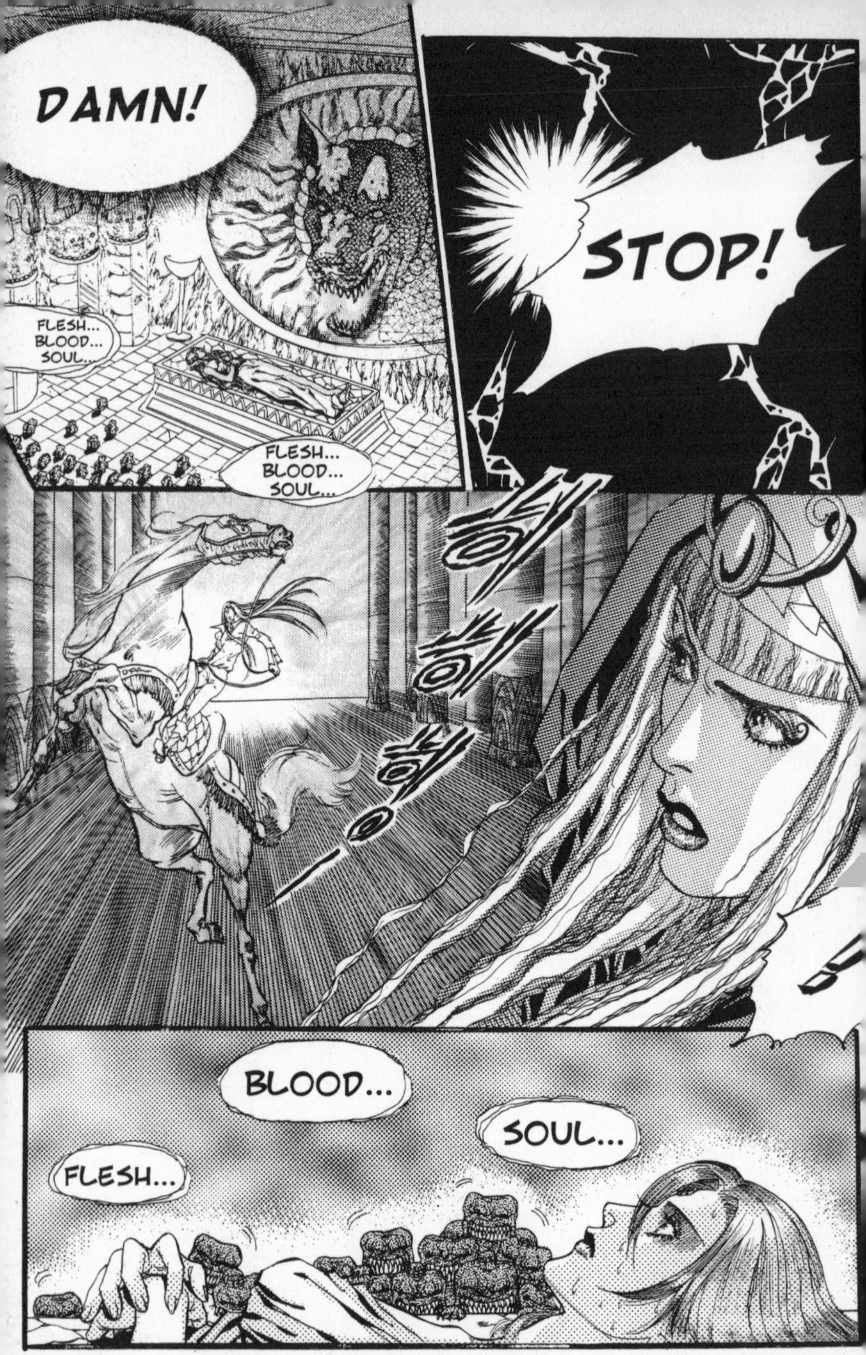
DAMN!
FLESH... BLOOD... SOUL...
FLESH... BLOOD... SOUL...
STOP!
BLOOD...
SOUL...
FLESH...

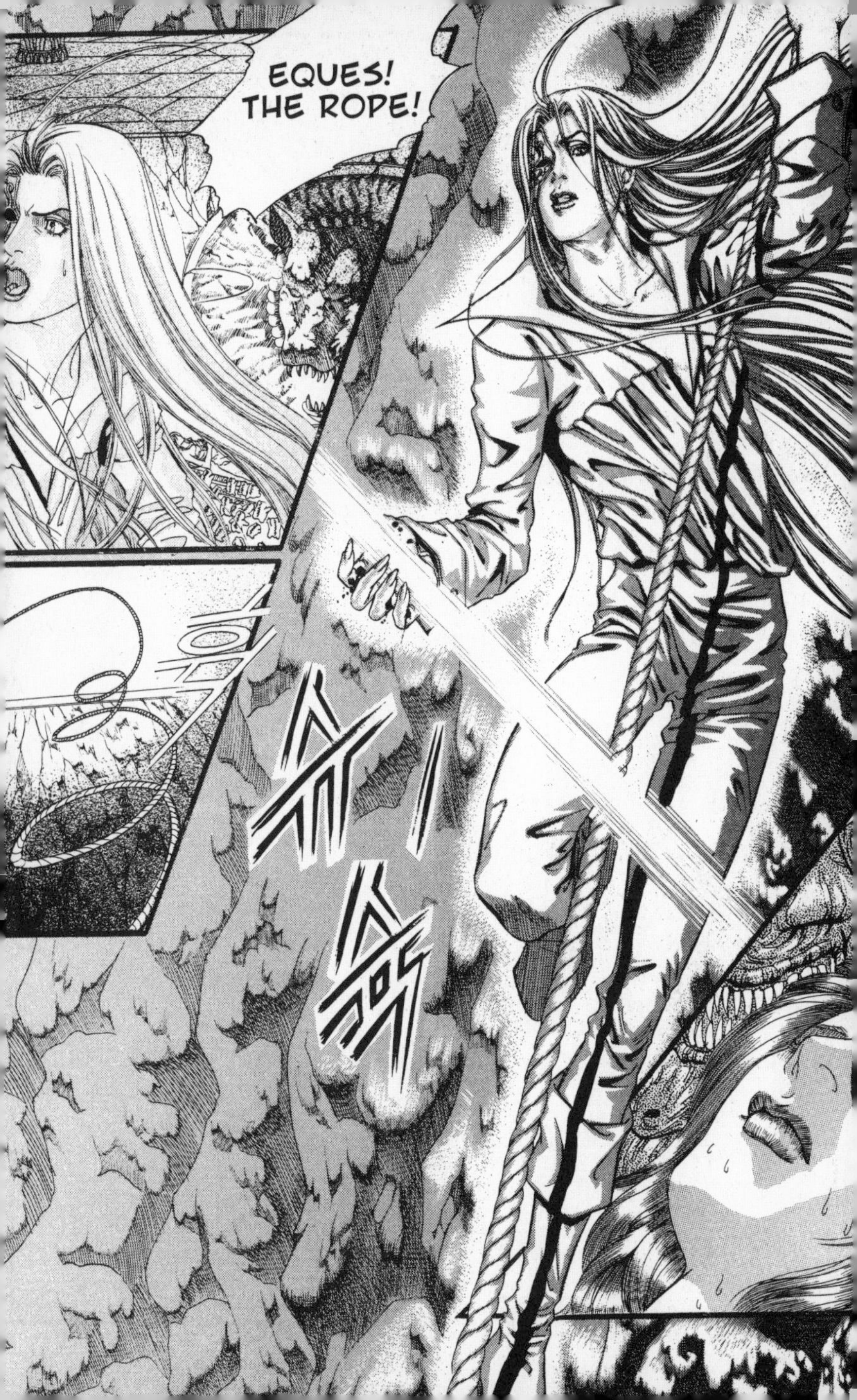
EQUES! THE ROPE!

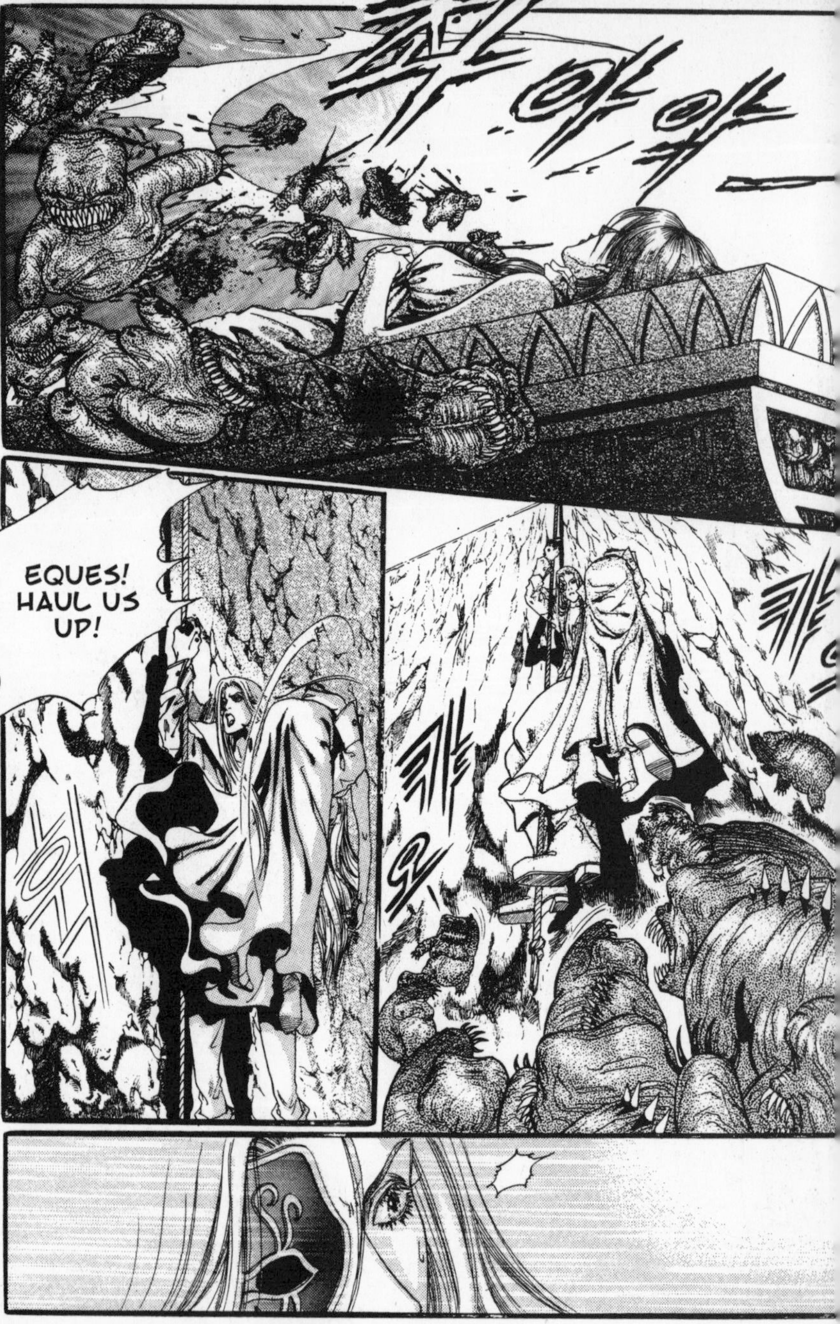
EQUES! HAUL US UP!

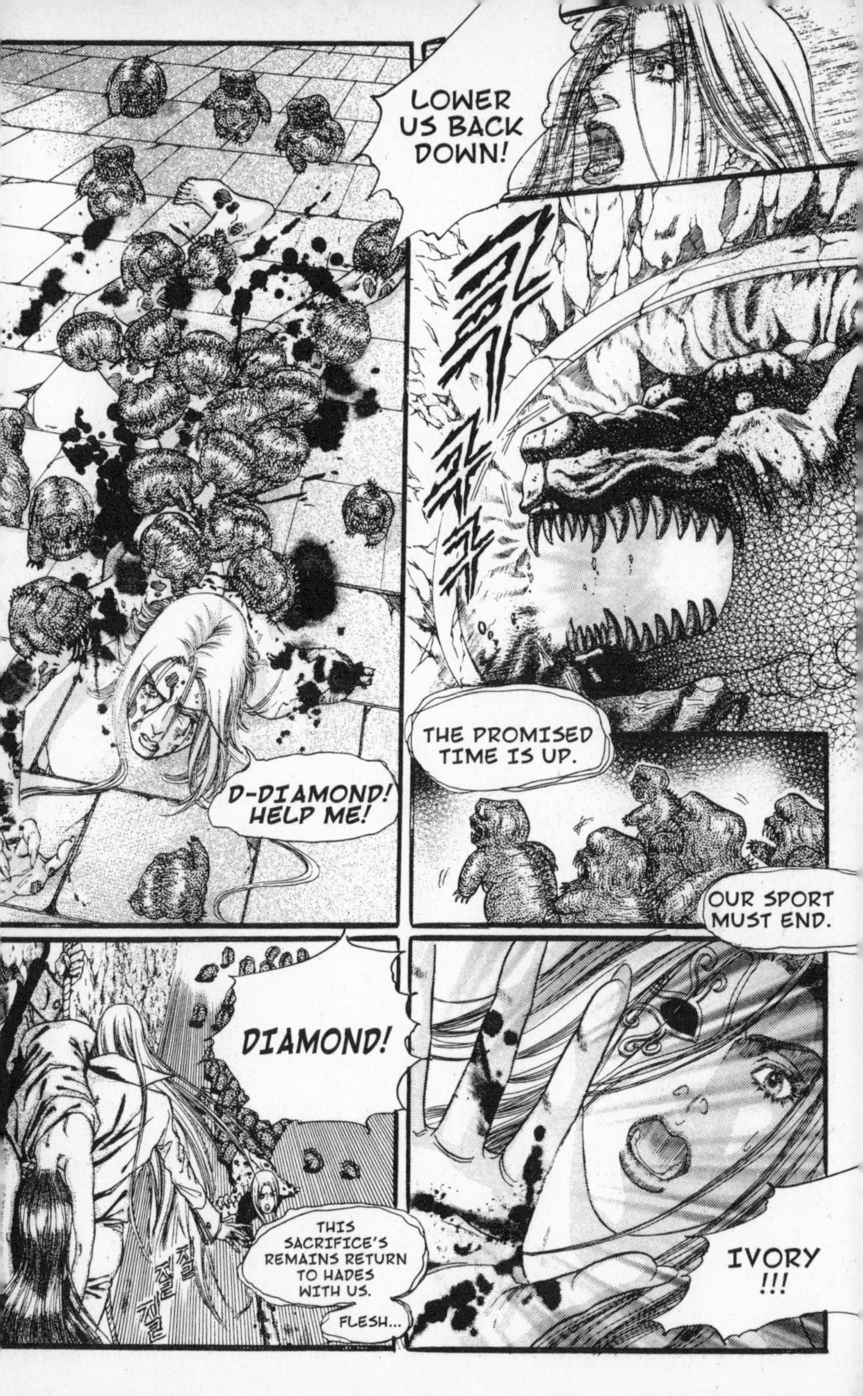
LOWER US BACK DOWN!
D-DIAMOND! HELP ME!
THE PROMISED TIME IS UP.
OUR SPORT MUST END.
DIAMOND!
THIS SACRIFICE'S REMAINS RETURN TO HADES WITH US.
FLESH...
IVORY !!!

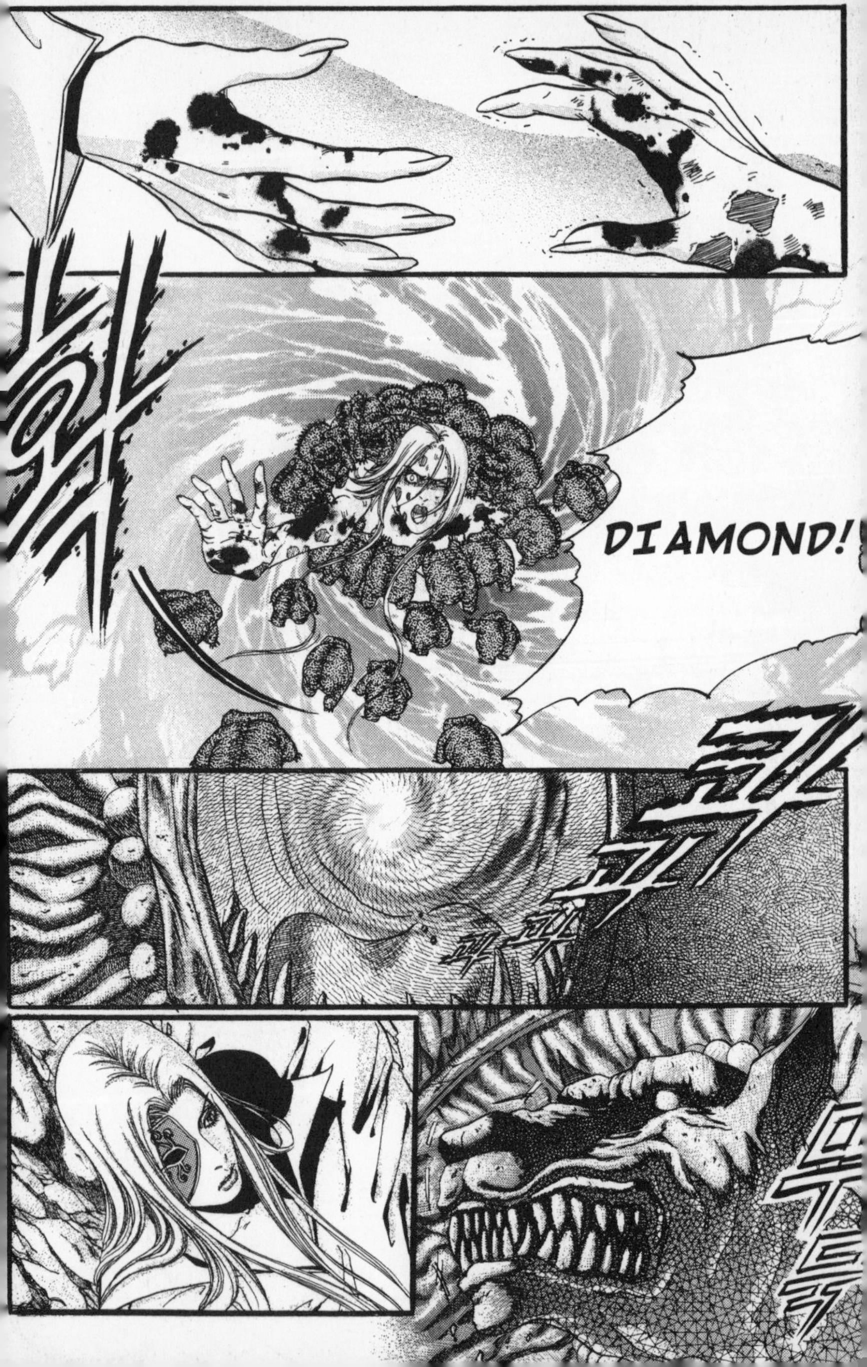
확
DIAMOND!

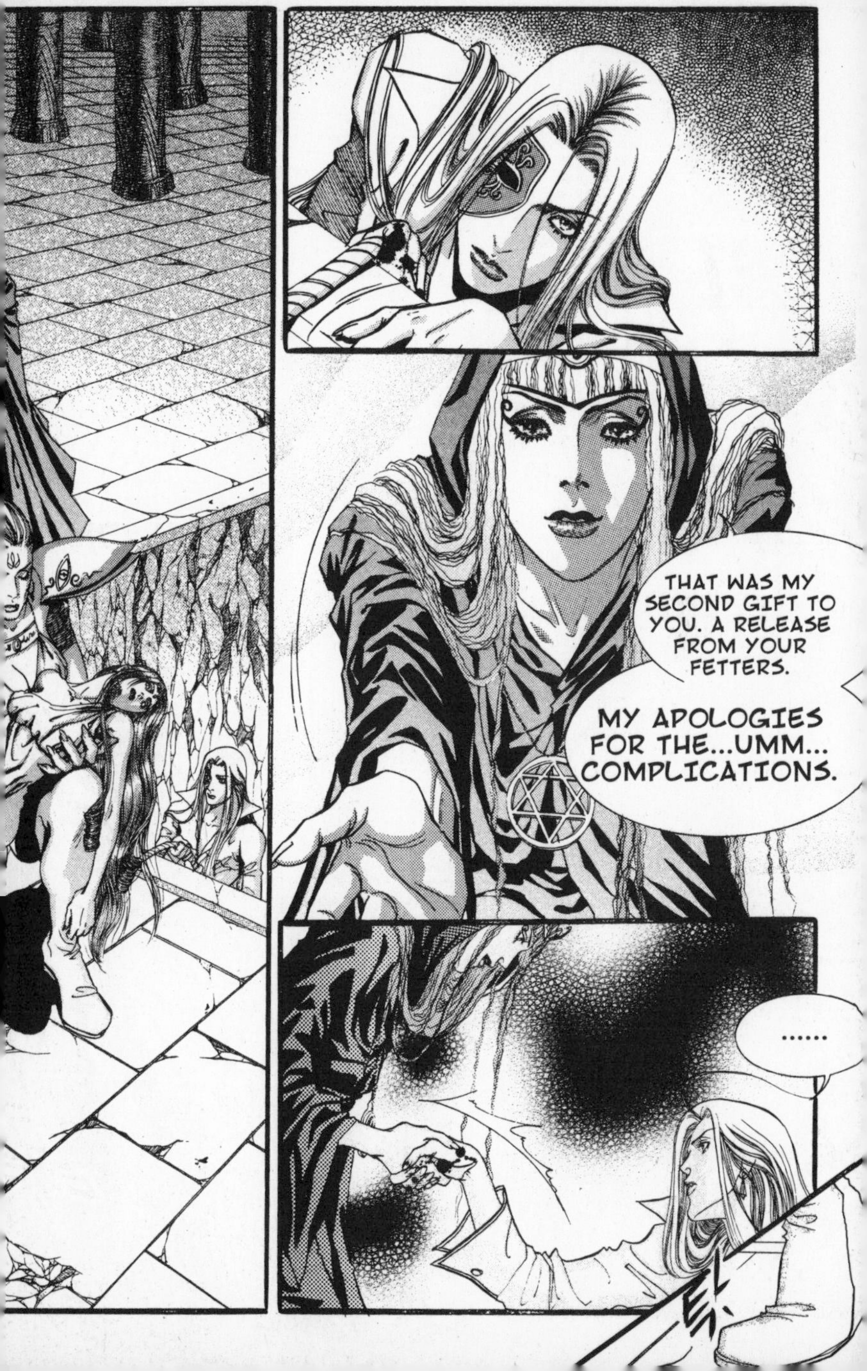
THAT WAS MY SECOND GIFT TO YOU. A RELEASE FROM YOUR FETTERS.
MY APOLOGIES FOR THE...UMM... COMPLICATIONS.
......

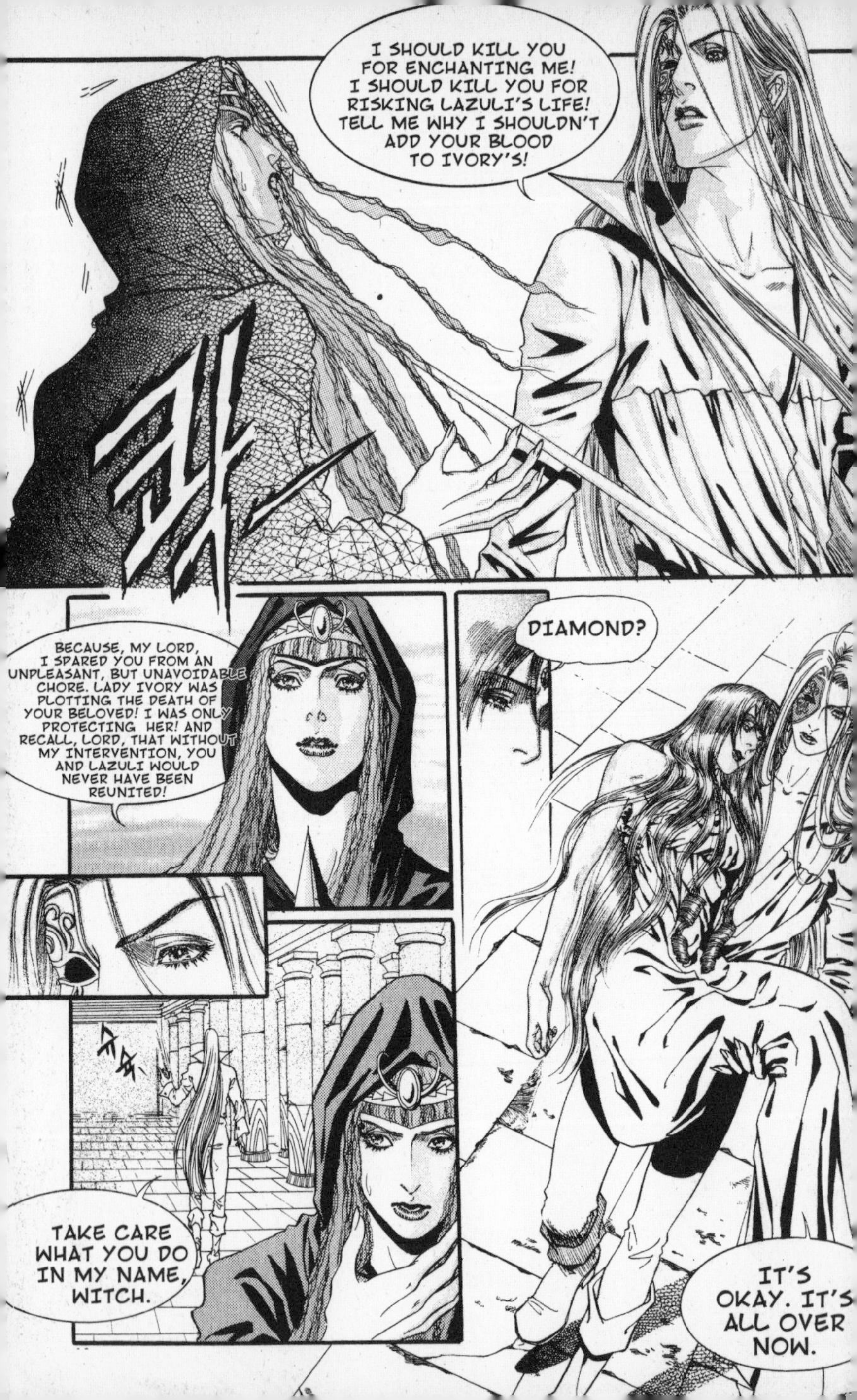
I SHOULD KILL YOU FOR ENCHANTING ME! I SHOULD KILL YOU FOR RISKING LAZULI'S LIFE! TELL ME WHY I SHOULDN'T ADD YOUR BLOOD TO IVORY'S!
BECAUSE, MY LORD, I SPARED YOU FROM AN UNPLEASANT, BUT UNAVOIDABLE CHORE. LADY IVORY WAS PLOTTING THE DEATH OF YOUR BELOVED! I WAS ONLY PROTECTING HER! AND RECALL, LORD, THAT WITHOUT MY INTERVENTION, YOU AND LAZULI WOULD NEVER HAVE BEEN REUNITED!
TAKE CARE WHAT YOU DO IN MY NAME, WITCH.
DIAMOND?
IT'S OKAY. IT'S ALL OVER NOW.

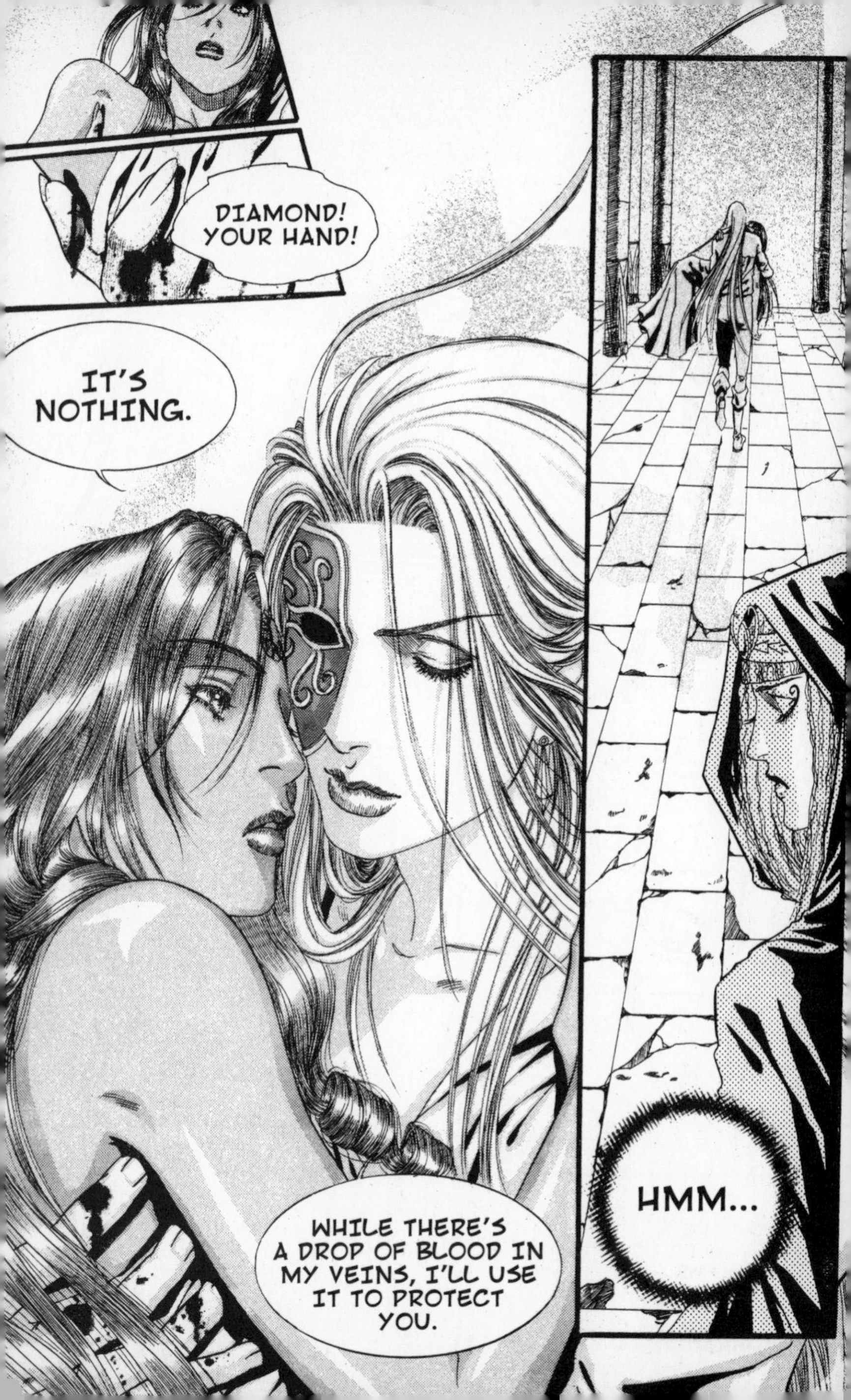
DIAMOND! YOUR HAND!
IT'S NOTHING.
WHILE THERE'S A DROP OF BLOOD IN MY VEINS, I'LL USE IT TO PROTECT YOU.
HMM...

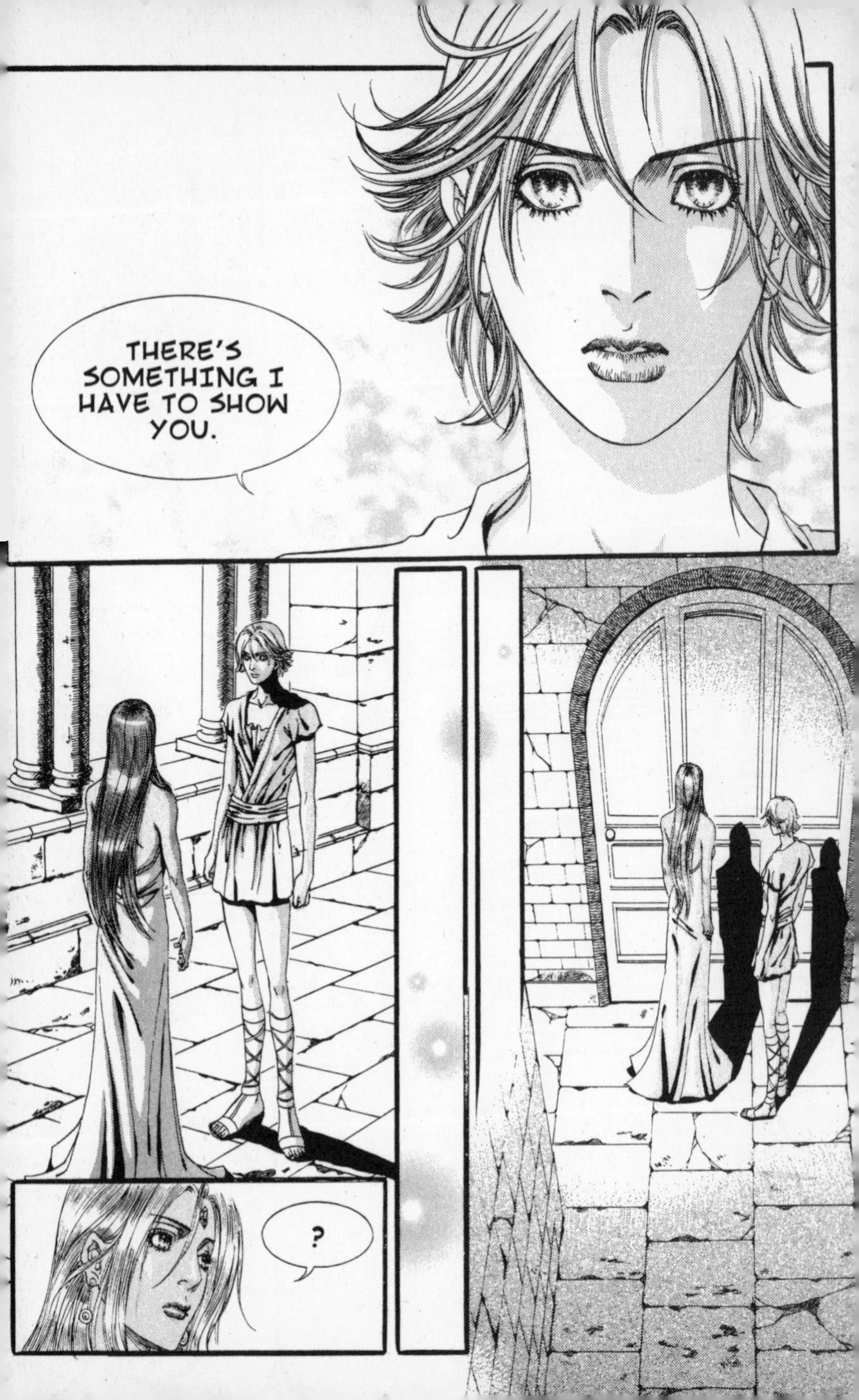
THERE'S SOMETHING I HAVE TO SHOW YOU.
?

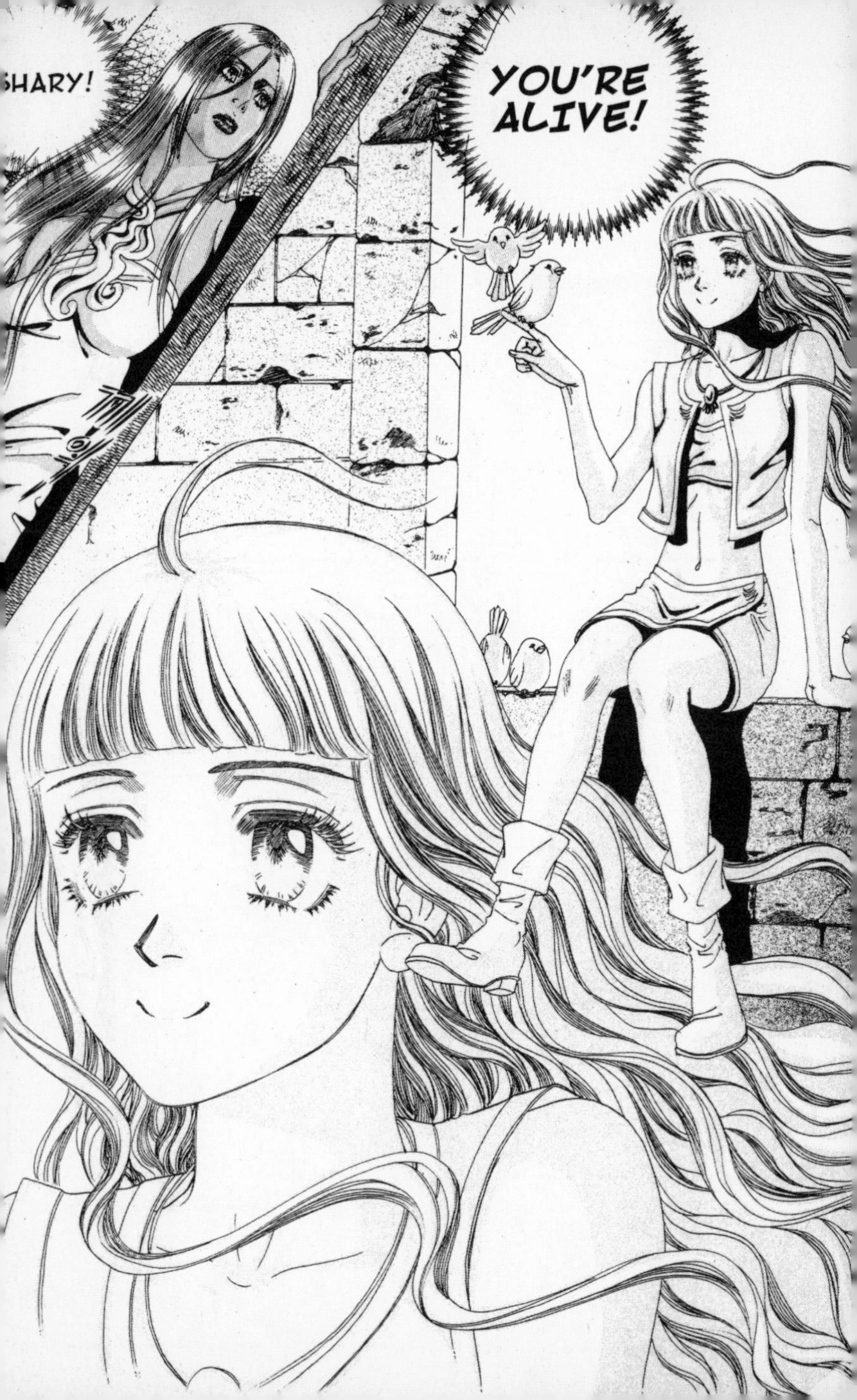

YOU'RE ALIVE!
SHARY!

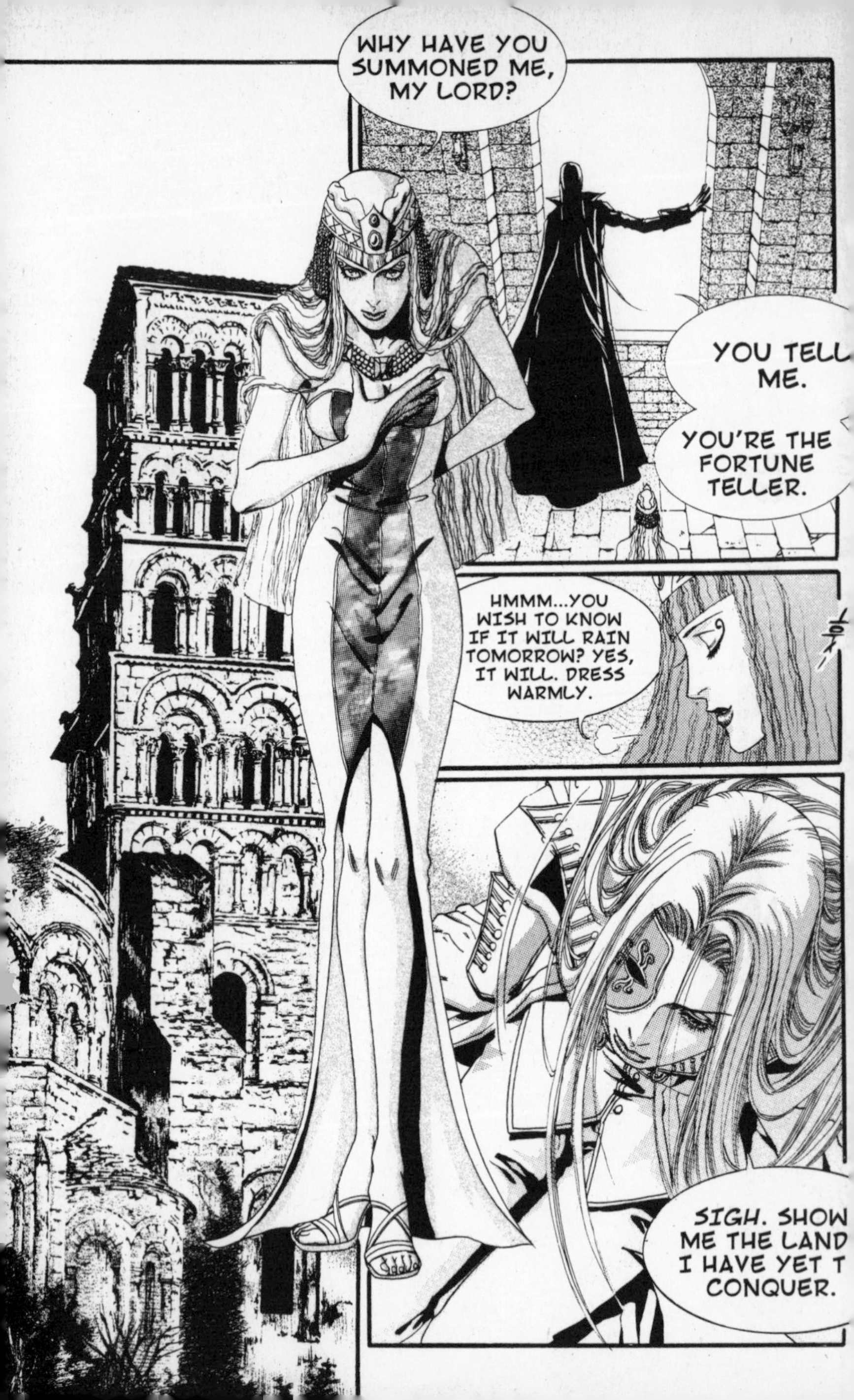
WHY HAVE YOU SUMMONED ME, MY LORD?
YOU TELL ME.
YOU'RE THE FORTUNE TELLER.
HMMM...YOU WISH TO KNOW IF IT WILL RAIN TOMORROW? YES, IT WILL. DRESS WARMLY.
SIGH. SHOW ME THE LAND I HAVE YET T CONQUER.

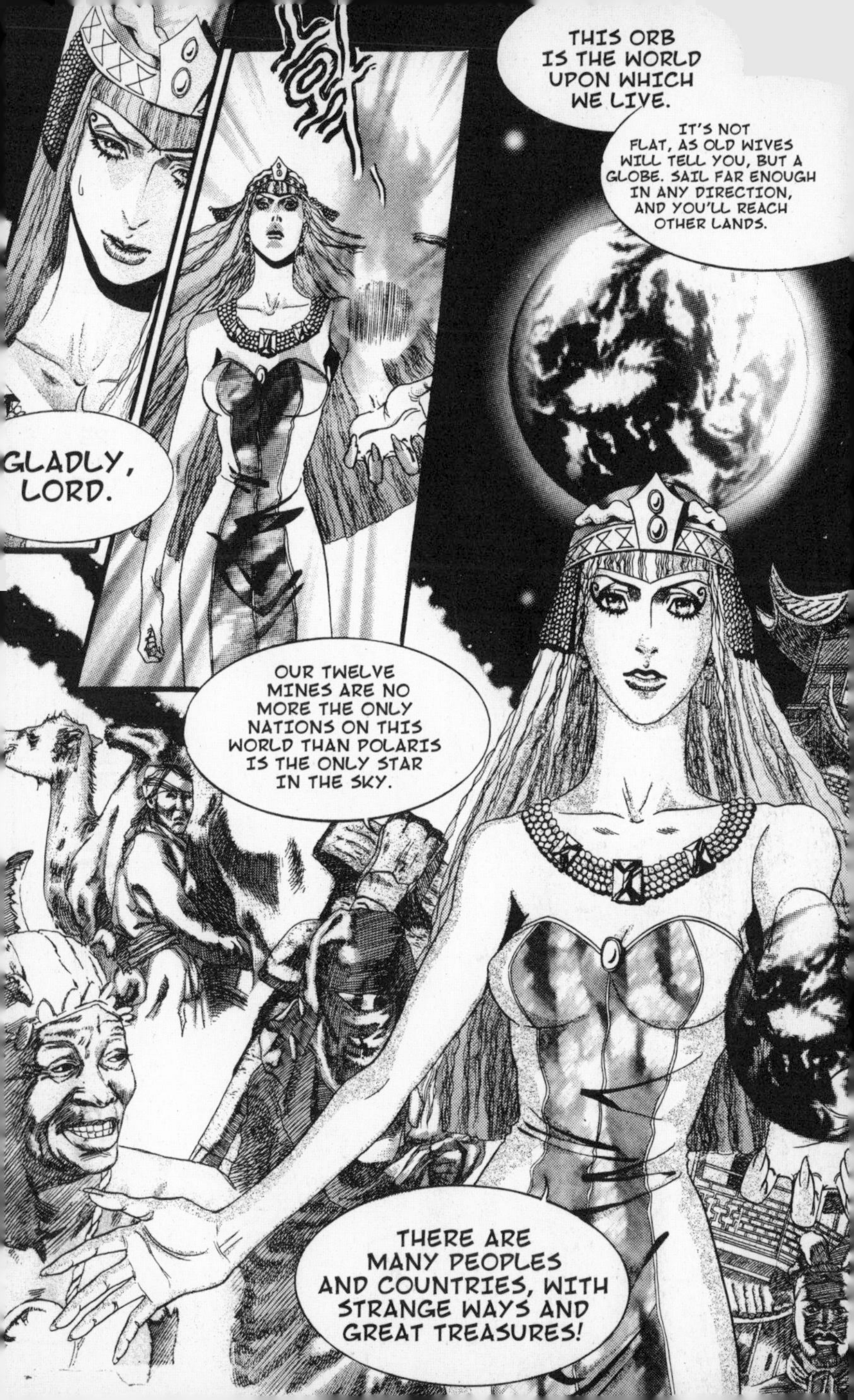
GLADLY, LORD.
THIS ORB IS THE WORLD UPON WHICH WE LIVE.
IT'S NOT FLAT, AS OLD WIVES WILL TELL YOU, BUT A GLOBE. SAIL FAR ENOUGH IN ANY DIRECTION, AND YOU'LL REACH OTHER LANDS.
OUR TWELVE MINES ARE NO MORE THE ONLY NATIONS ON THIS WORLD THAN POLARIS IS THE ONLY STAR IN THE SKY.
THERE ARE MANY PEOPLES AND COUNTRIES, WITH STRANGE WAYS AND GREAT TREASURES!

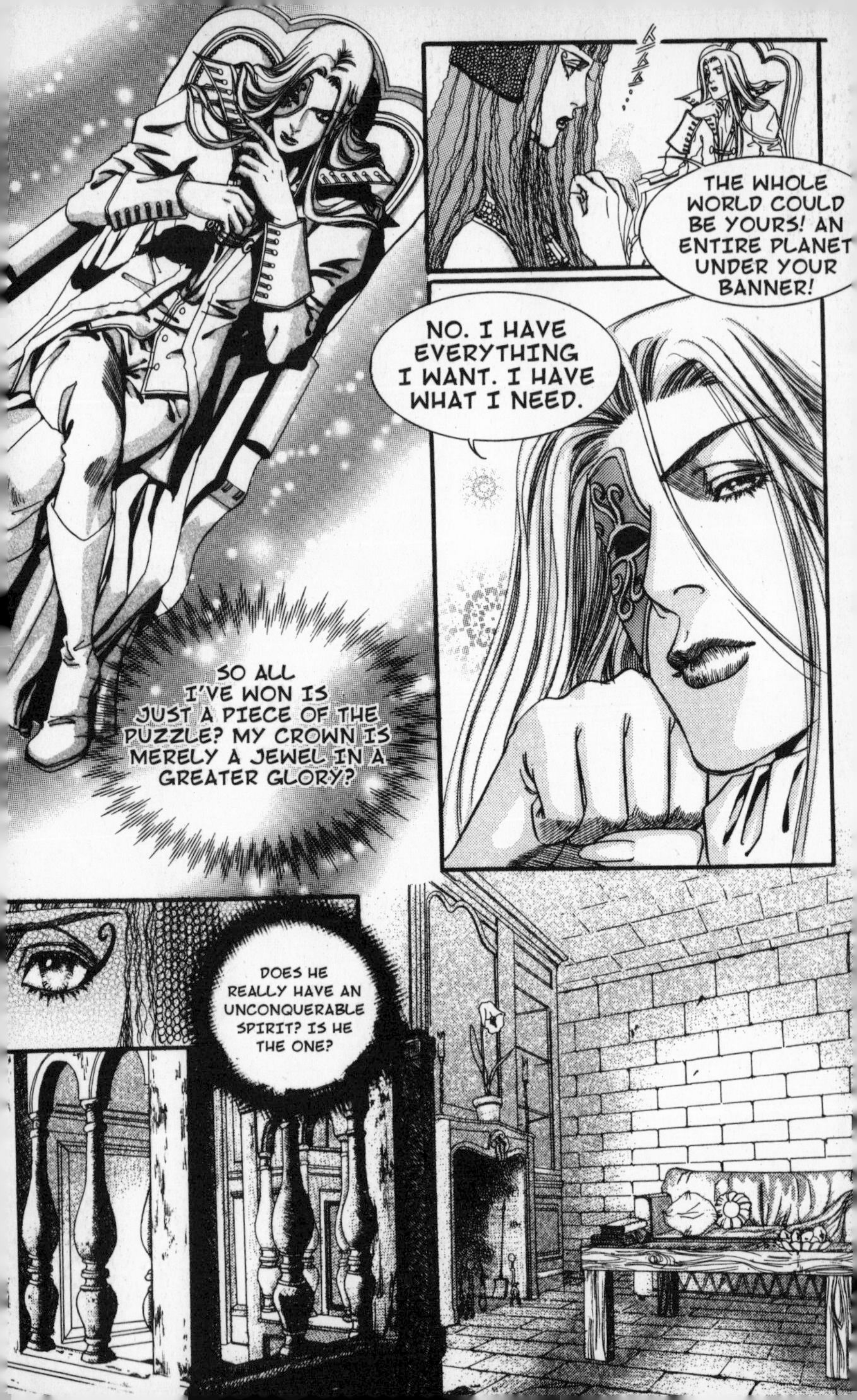
THE WHOLE WORLD COULD BE YOURS! AN ENTIRE PLANET UNDER YOUR BANNER!
NO. I HAVE EVERYTHING I WANT. I HAVE WHAT I NEED.
SO ALL I'VE WON IS JUST A PIECE OF THE PUZZLE? MY CROWN IS MERELY A JEWEL IN A GREATER GLORY?
DOES HE REALLY HAVE AN UNCONQUERABLE SPIRIT? IS HE THE ONE?

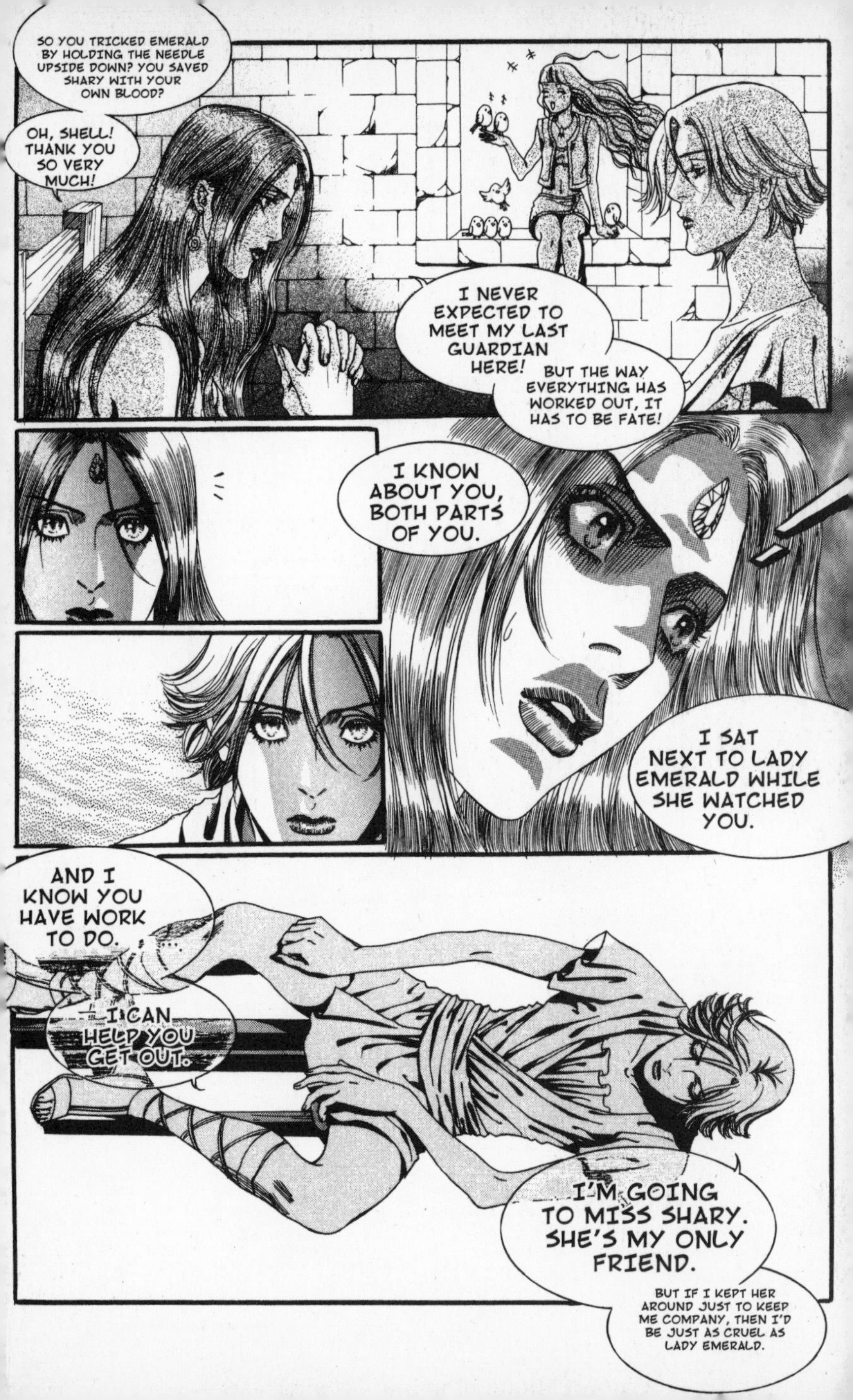
SO YOU TRICKED EMERALD BY HOLDING THE NEEDLE UPSIDE DOWN? YOU SAVED SHARY WITH YOUR OWN BLOOD?
OH, SHELL! THANK YOU SO VERY MUCH!
I NEVER EXPECTED TO MEET MY LAST GUARDIAN HERE!
BUT THE WAY EVERYTHING HAS WORKED OUT, IT HAS TO BE FATE!
I KNOW ABOUT YOU, BOTH PARTS OF YOU.
I SAT NEXT TO LADY EMERALD WHILE SHE WATCHED YOU.
AND I KNOW YOU HAVE WORK TO DO.
I CAN HELP YOU GET OUT.
I'M GOING TO MISS SHARY. SHE'S MY ONLY FRIEND.
BUT IF I KEPT HER AROUND JUST TO KEEP ME COMPANY, THEN I'D BE JUST AS CRUEL AS LADY EMERALD.

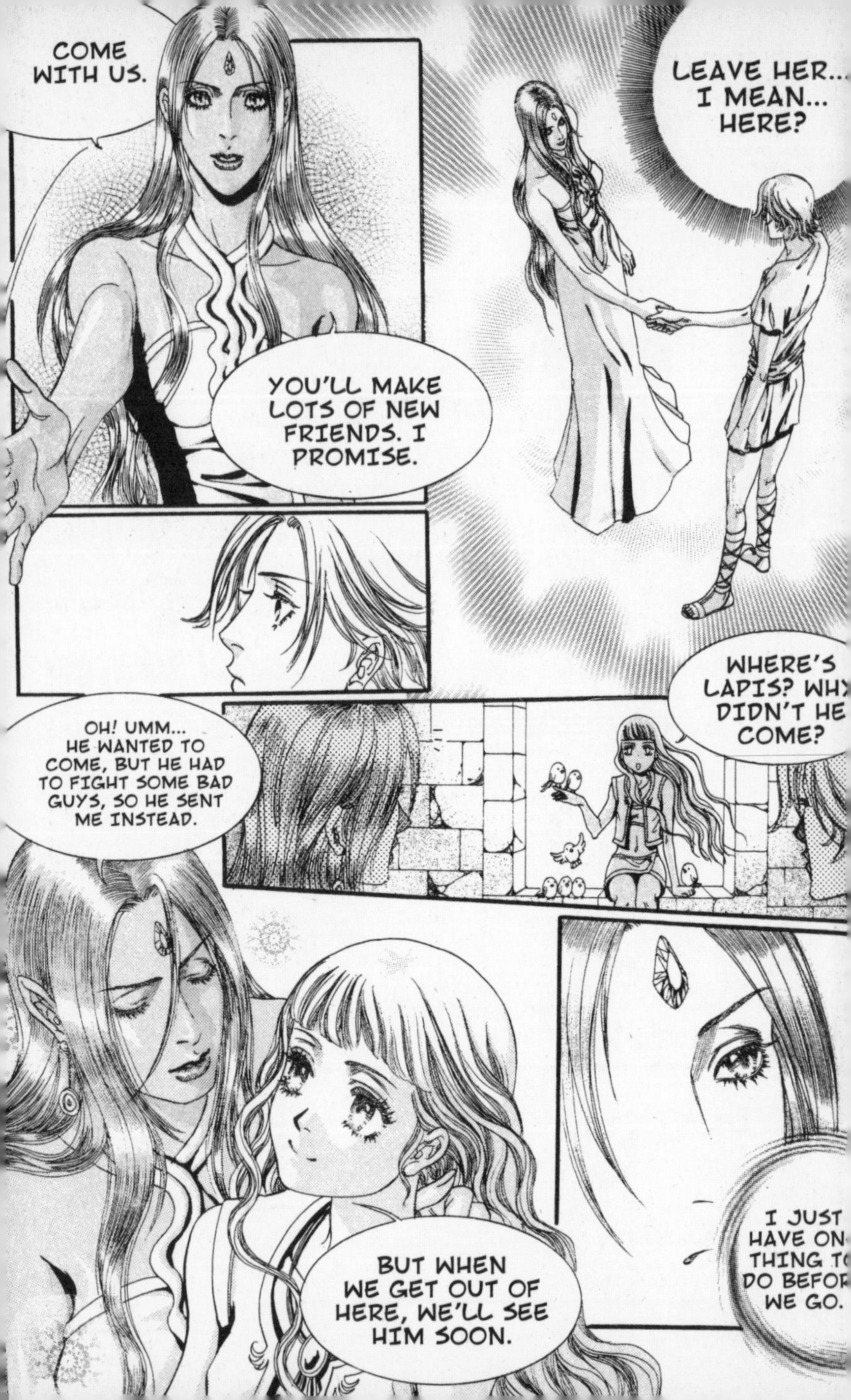
COME WITH US.
YOU'LL MAKE LOTS OF NEW FRIENDS. I PROMISE.
LEAVE HER... I MEAN... HERE?
WHERE'S LAPIS? WHY DIDN'T HE COME?
OH! UMM... HE WANTED TO COME, BUT HE HAD TO FIGHT SOME BAD GUYS, SO HE SENT ME INSTEAD.
BUT WHEN WE GET OUT OF HERE, WE'LL SEE HIM SOON.
I JUST HAVE ONE THING TO DO BEFORE WE GO.

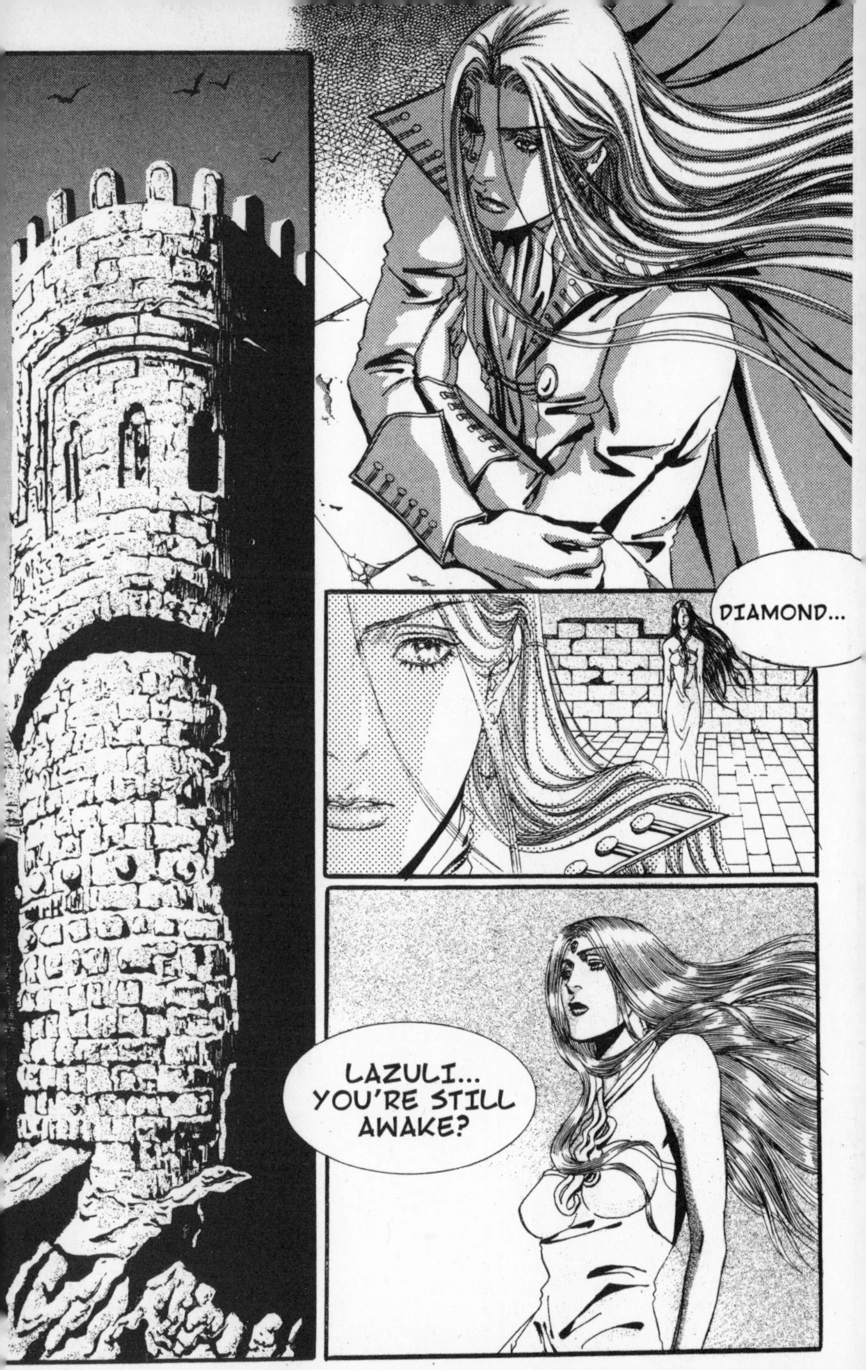
DIAMOND...
LAZULI... YOU'RE STILL AWAKE?

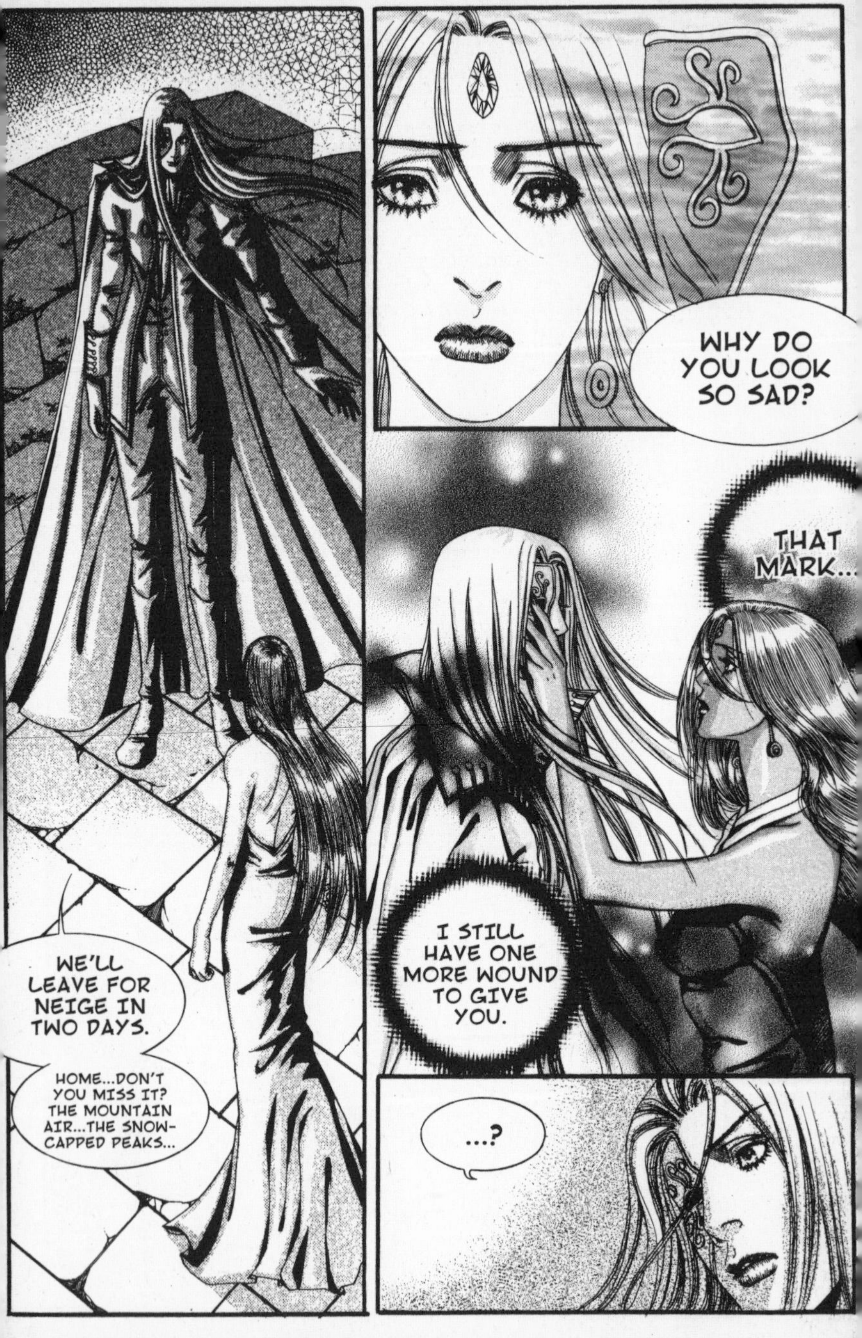
WE'LL LEAVE FOR NEIGE IN TWO DAYS.
HOME...DON'T YOU MISS IT? THE MOUNTAIN AIR...THE SNOW-CAPPED PEAKS...
WHY DO YOU LOOK SO SAD?
THAT MARK...
I STILL HAVE ONE MORE WOUND TO GIVE YOU.
...?

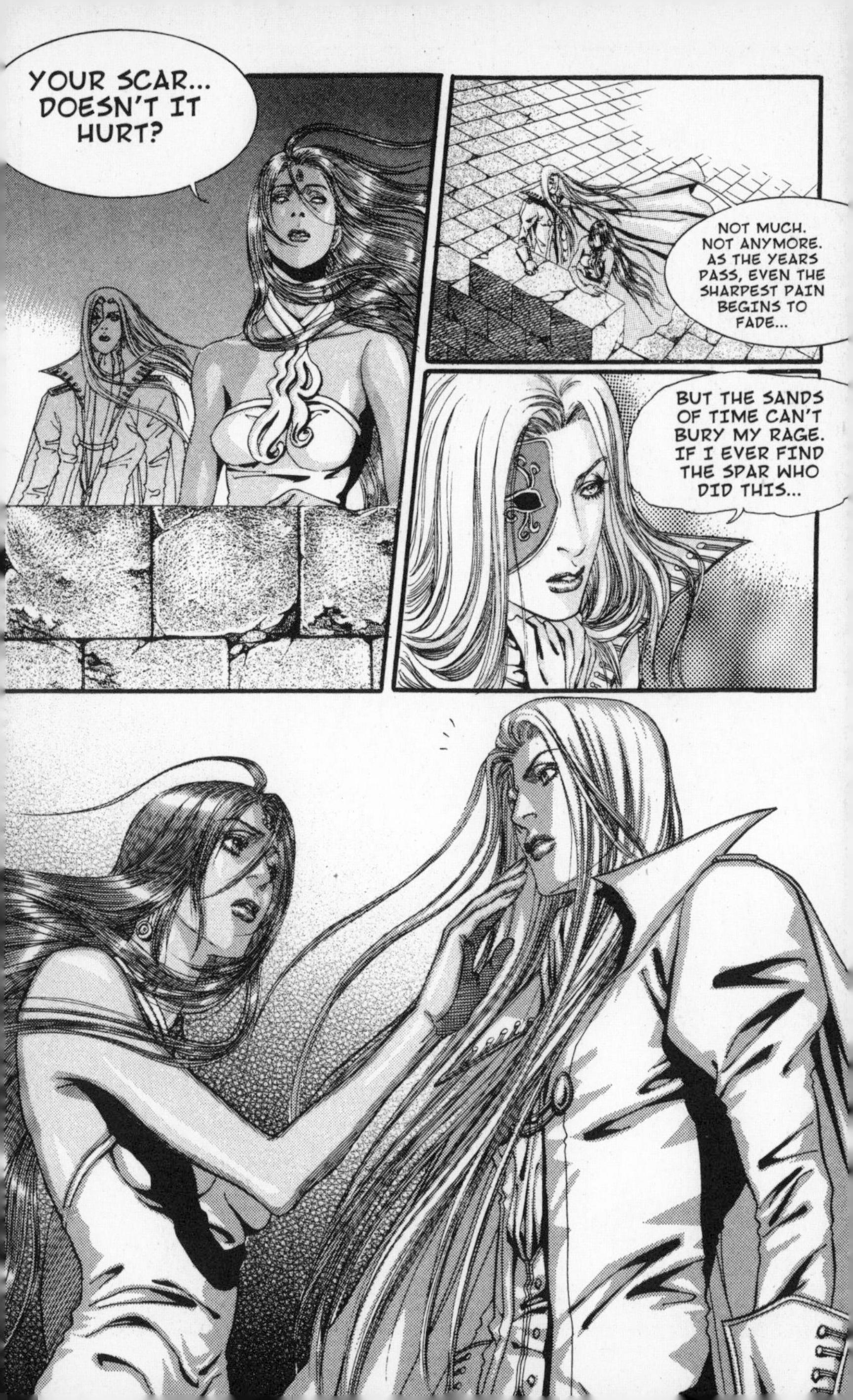
YOUR SCAR... DOESN'T IT HURT?
NOT MUCH. NOT ANYMORE. AS THE YEARS PASS, EVEN THE SHARPEST PAIN BEGINS TO FADE...
BUT THE SANDS OF TIME CAN'T BURY MY RAGE. IF I EVER FIND THE SPAR WHO DID THIS...

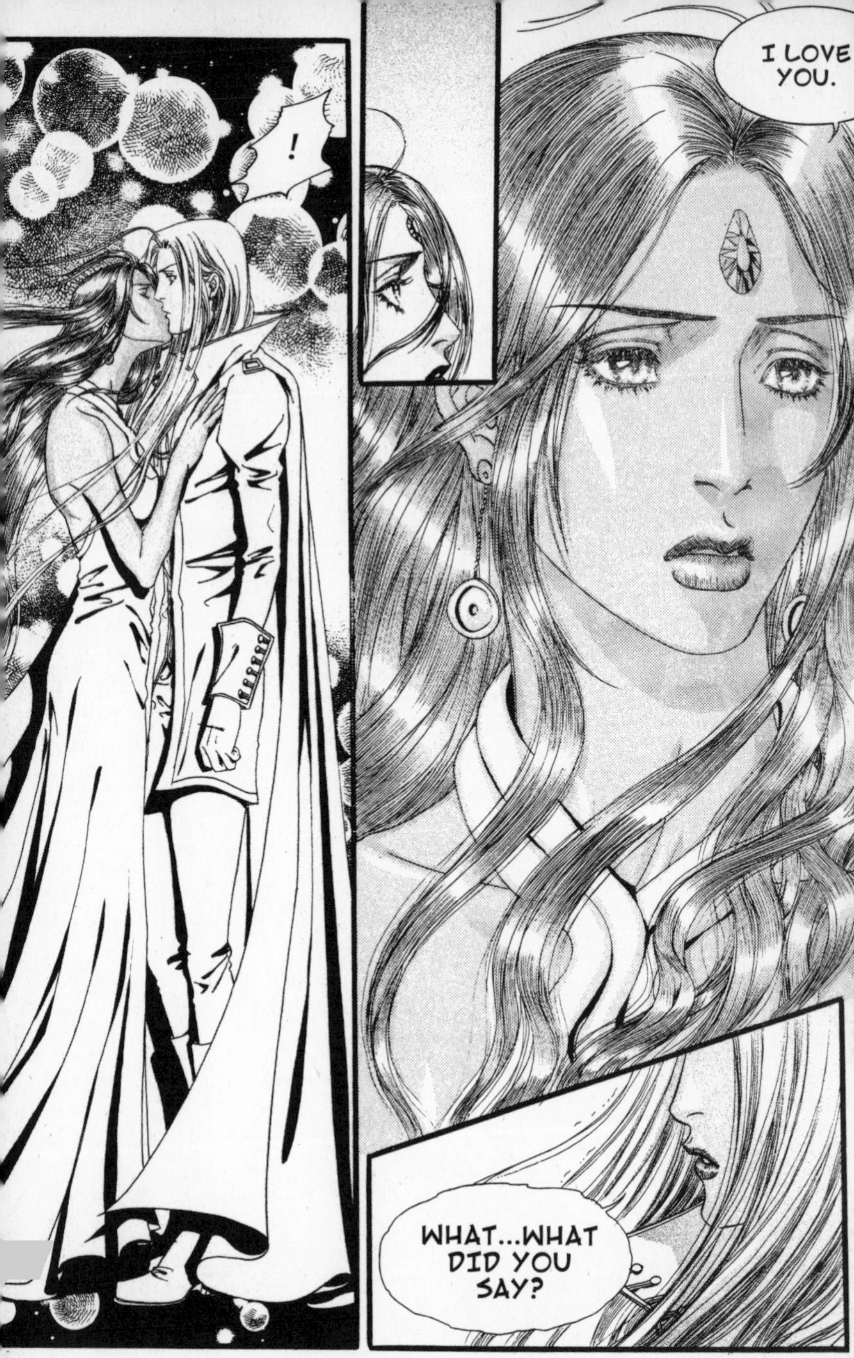
!
I LOVE YOU.
WHAT...WHAT DID YOU SAY?

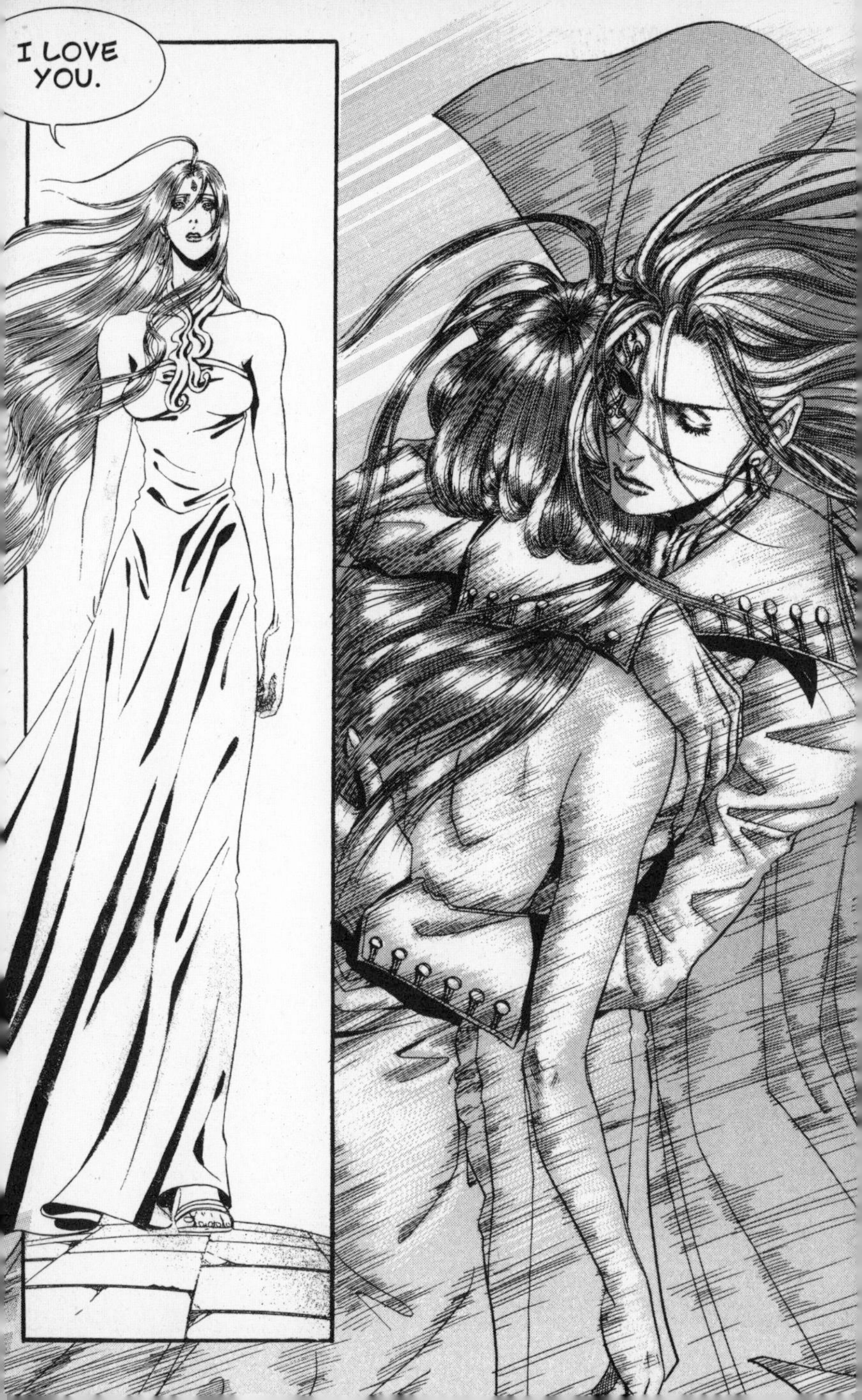
I LOVE YOU.

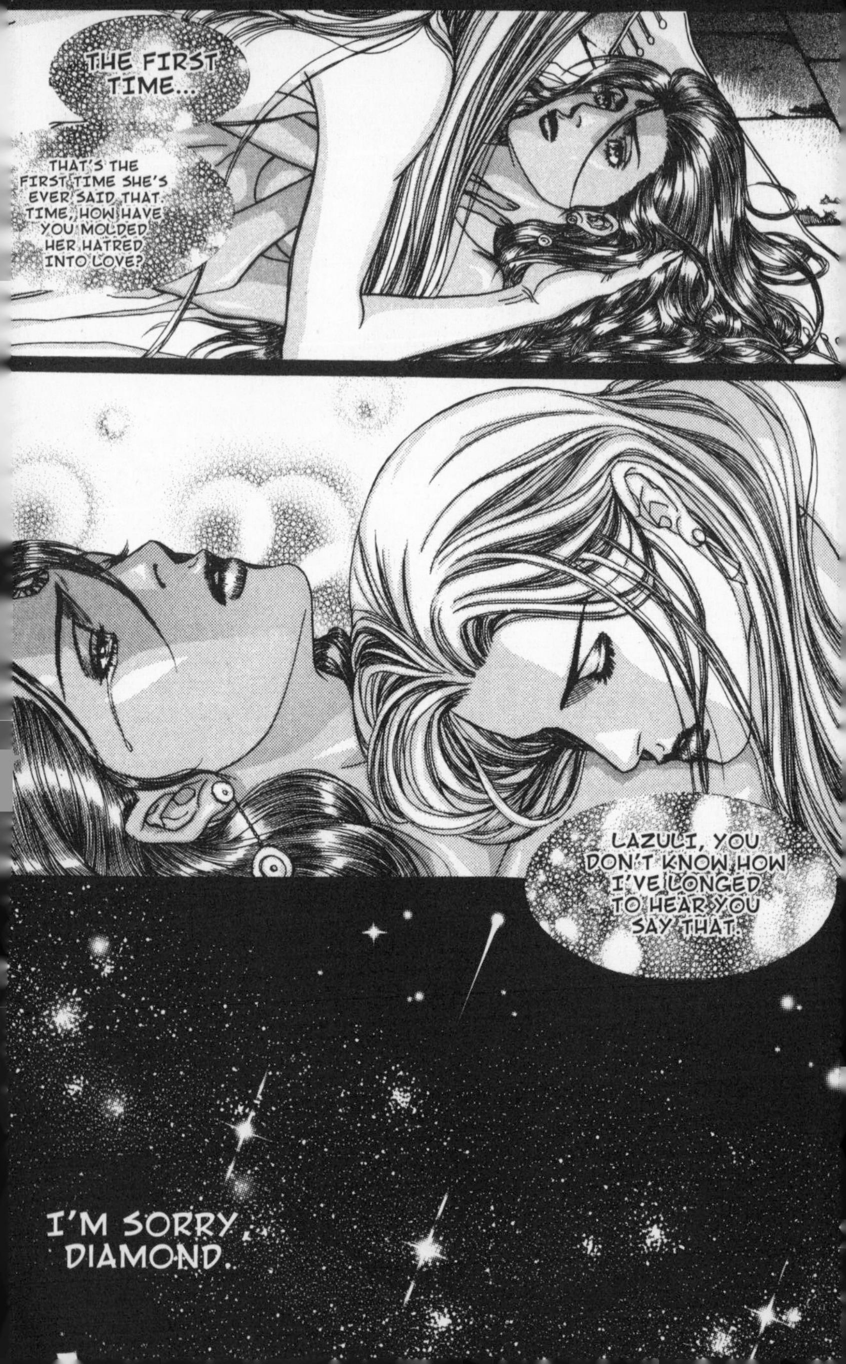
THE FIRST TIME...
THAT'S THE FIRST TIME SHE'S EVER SAID THAT. TIME, HOW HAVE YOU MOLDED HER HATRED INTO LOVE?
LAZULI, YOU DON'T KNOW HOW I'VE LONGED TO HEAR YOU SAY THAT.
I'M SORRY DIAMOND.

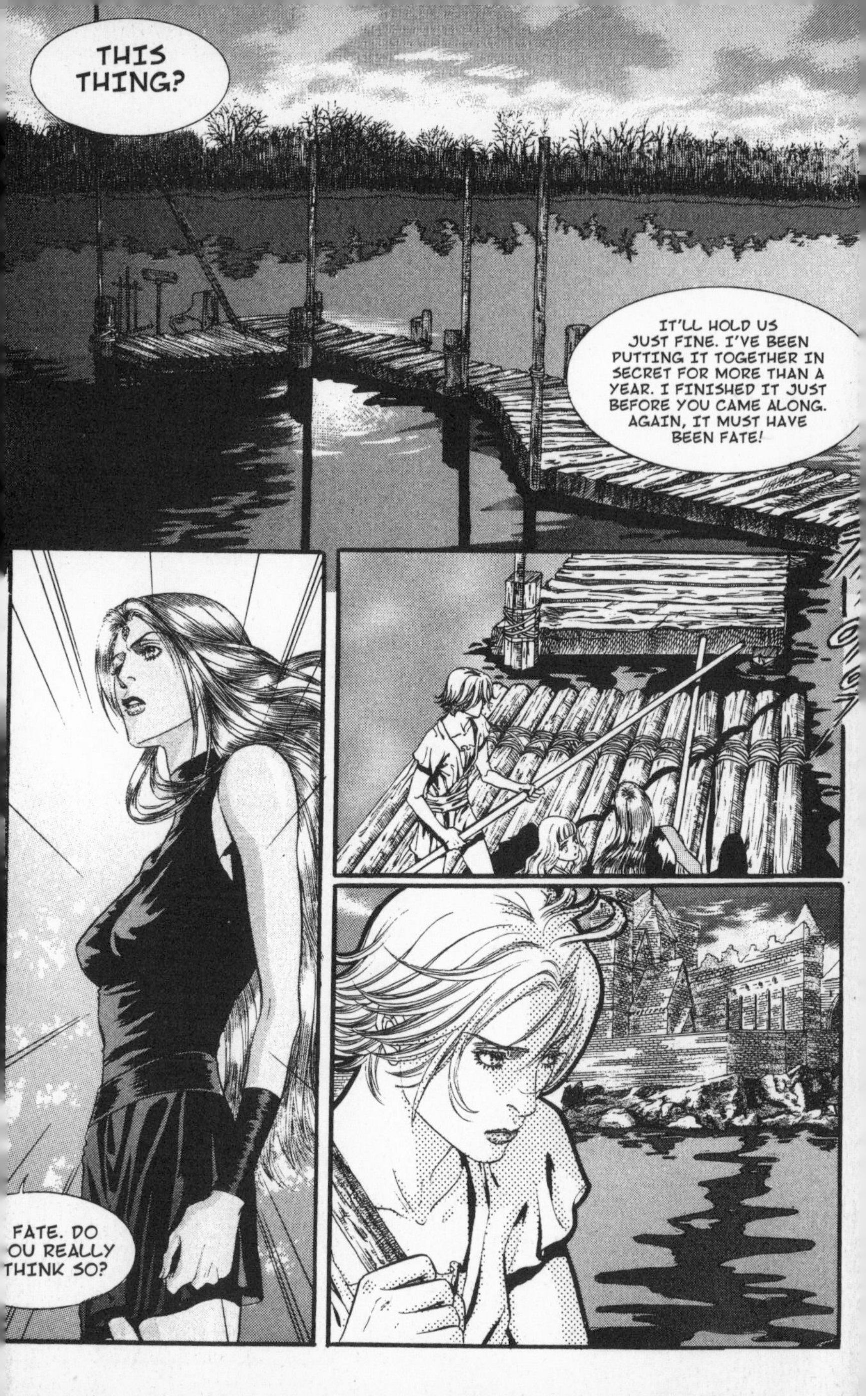
THIS THING?
IT'LL HOLD US JUST FINE. I'VE BEEN PUTTING IT TOGETHER IN SECRET FOR MORE THAN A YEAR. I FINISHED IT JUST BEFORE YOU CAME ALONG. AGAIN, IT MUST HAVE BEEN FATE!
FATE. DO OU REALLY THINK SO?

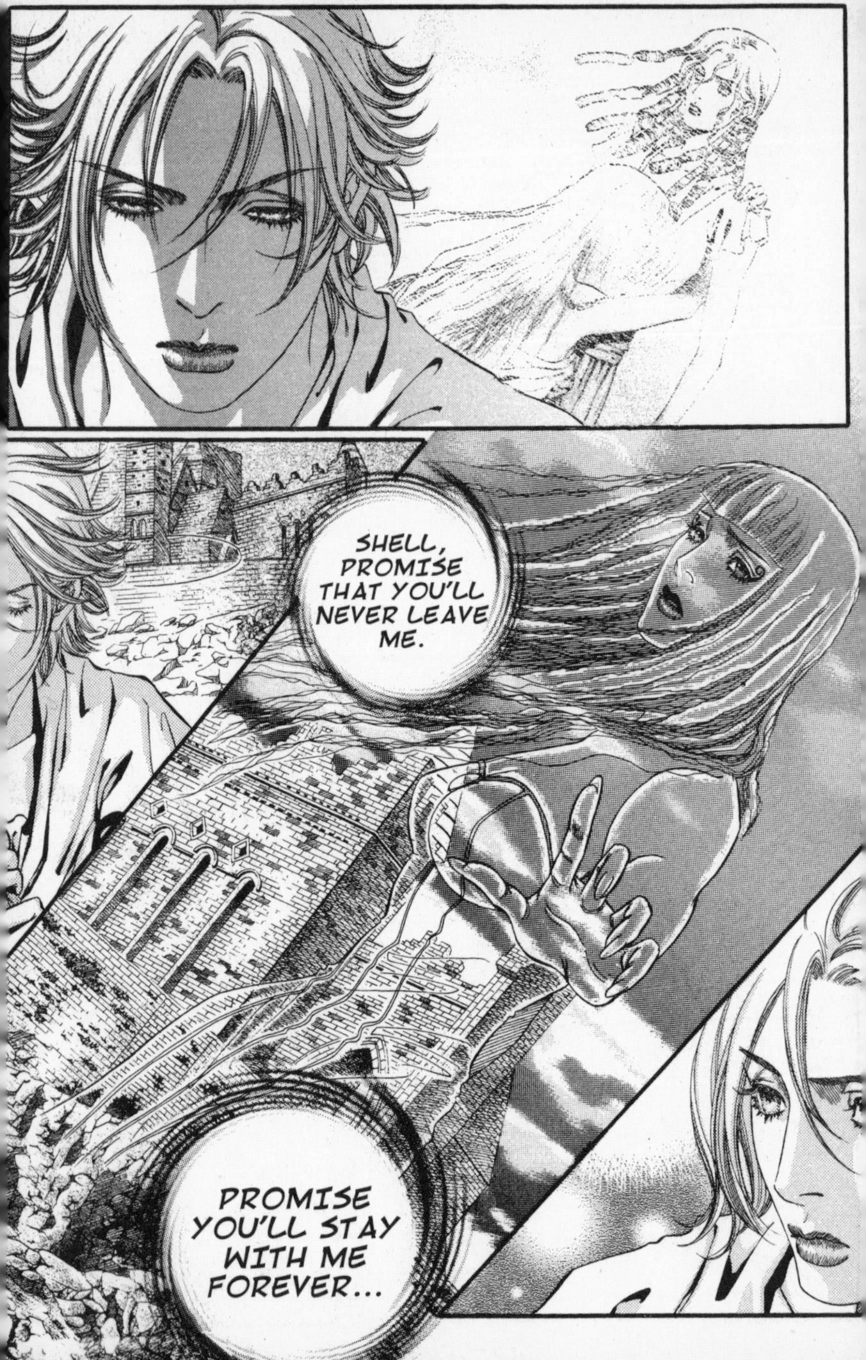
SHELL, PROMISE THAT YOU'LL NEVER LEAVE ME.
PROMISE YOU'LL STAY WITH ME FOREVER...

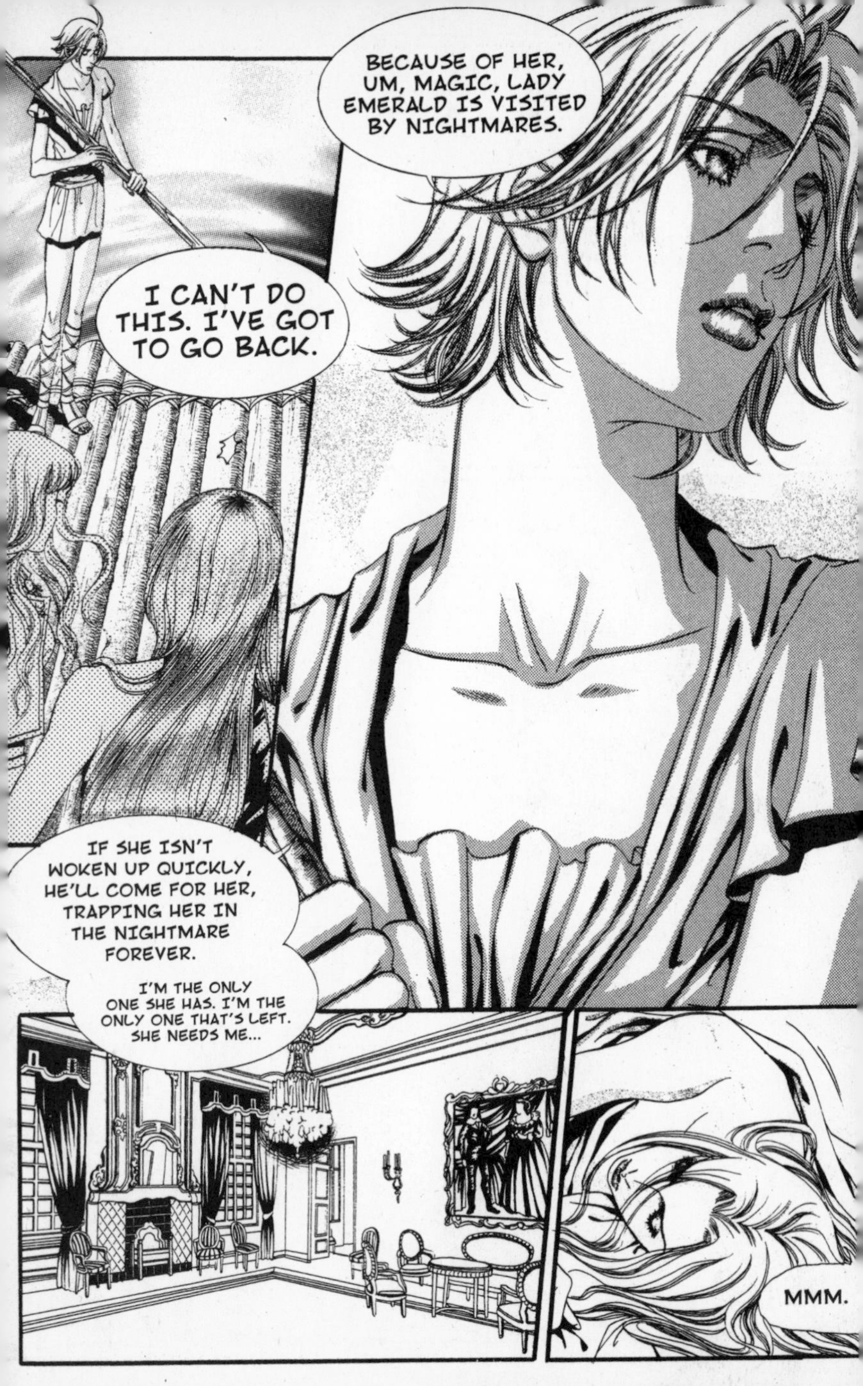
BECAUSE OF HER, UM, MAGIC, LADY EMERALD IS VISITED BY NIGHTMARES.
I CAN'T DO THIS. I'VE GOT TO GO BACK.
IF SHE ISN'T WOKEN UP QUICKLY, HE'LL COME FOR HER, TRAPPING HER IN THE NIGHTMARE FOREVER.
I'M THE ONLY ONE SHE HAS. I'M THE ONLY ONE THAT'S LEFT. SHE NEEDS ME...
MMM.

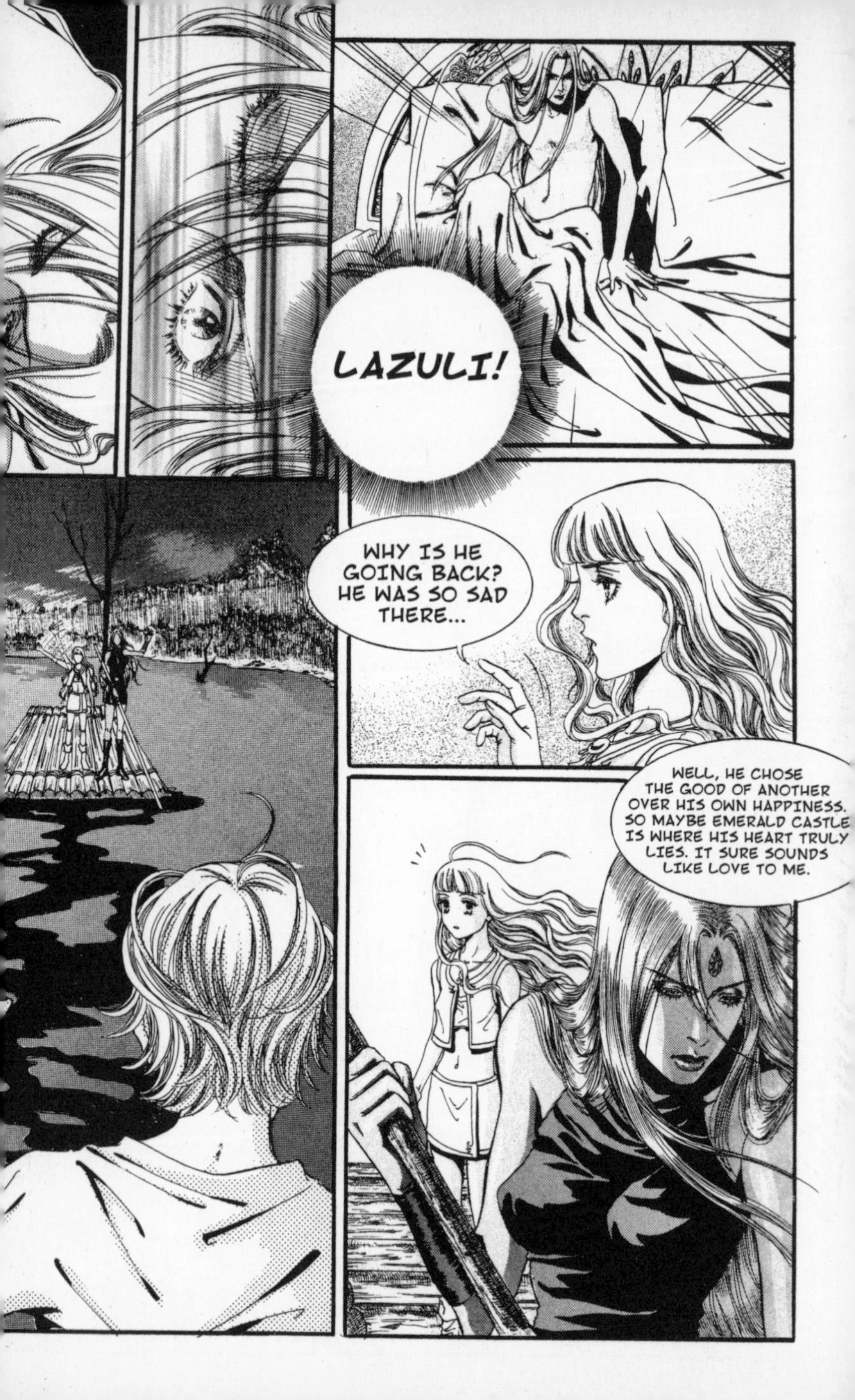
LAZULI!
WHY IS HE GOING BACK? HE WAS SO SAD THERE...
WELL, HE CHOSE THE GOOD OF ANOTHER OVER HIS OWN HAPPINESS. SO MAYBE EMERALD CASTLE IS WHERE HIS HEART TRULY LIES. IT SURE SOUNDS LIKE LOVE TO ME.

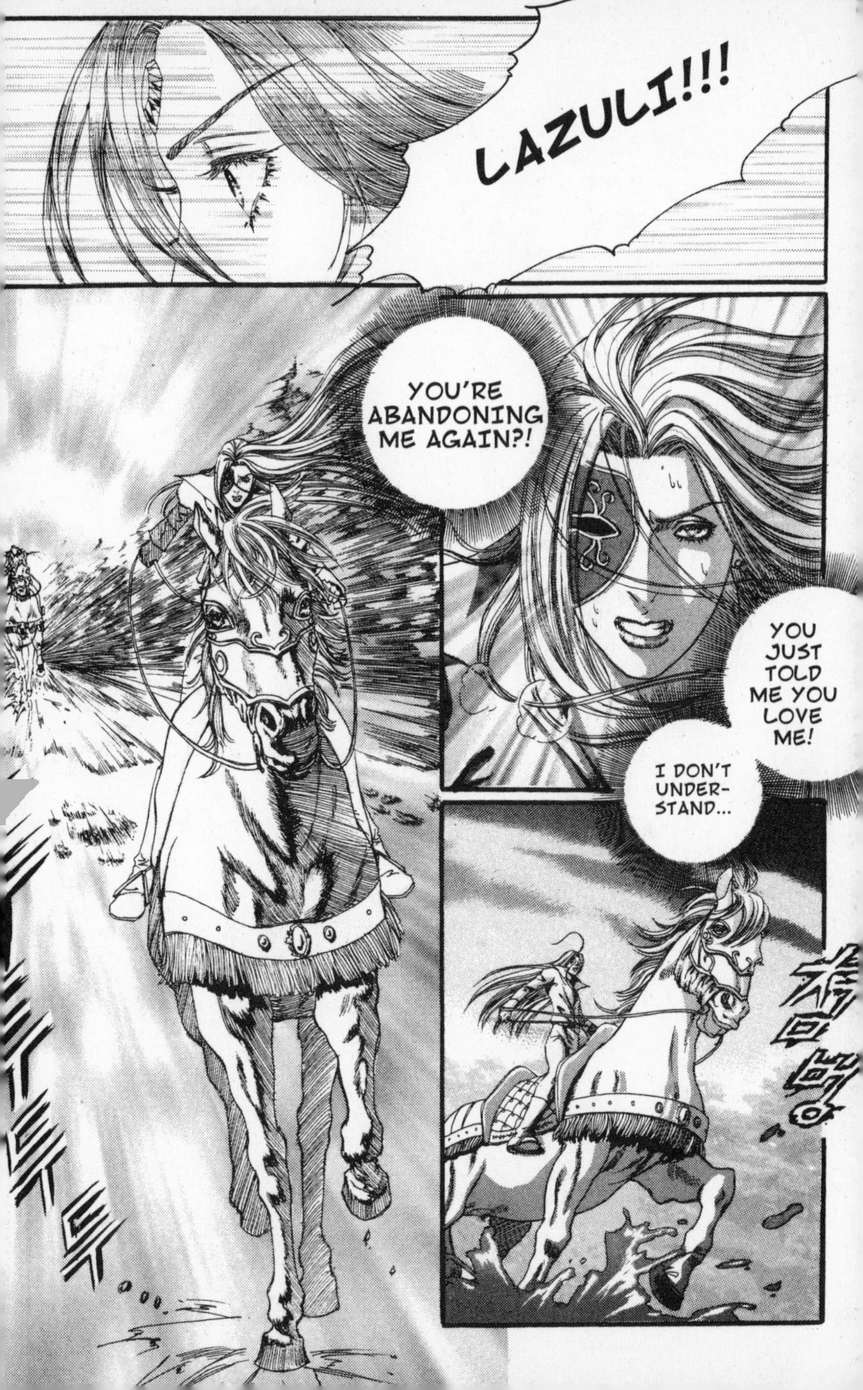
LAZULI!!!
YOU'RE ABANDONING ME AGAIN?!
YOU JUST TOLD ME YOU LOVE ME!
I DON'T UNDER-STAND...

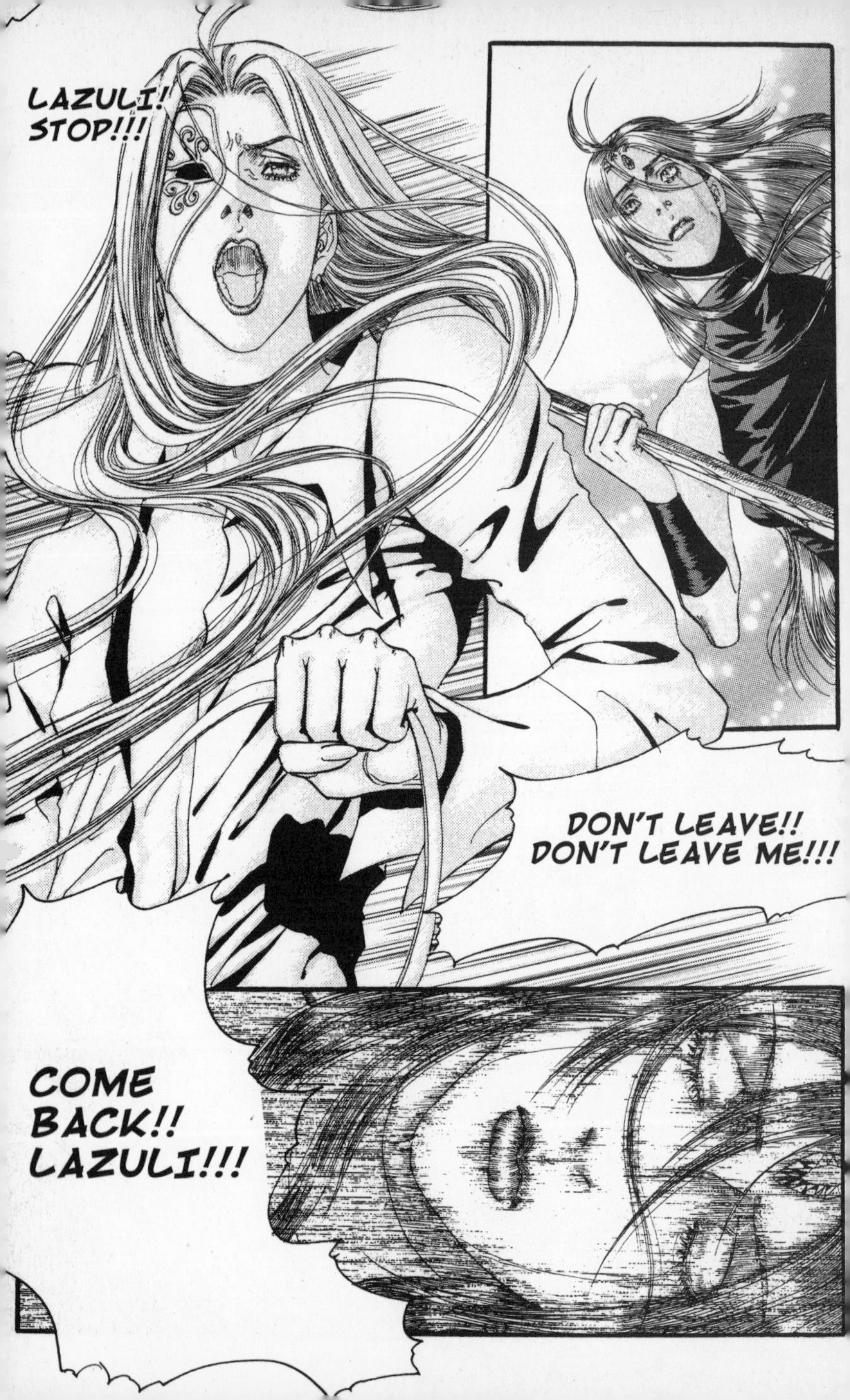
LAZULI!! STOP!!!
DON'T LEAVE!! DON'T LEAVE ME!!!
COME BACK!! LAZULI!!!

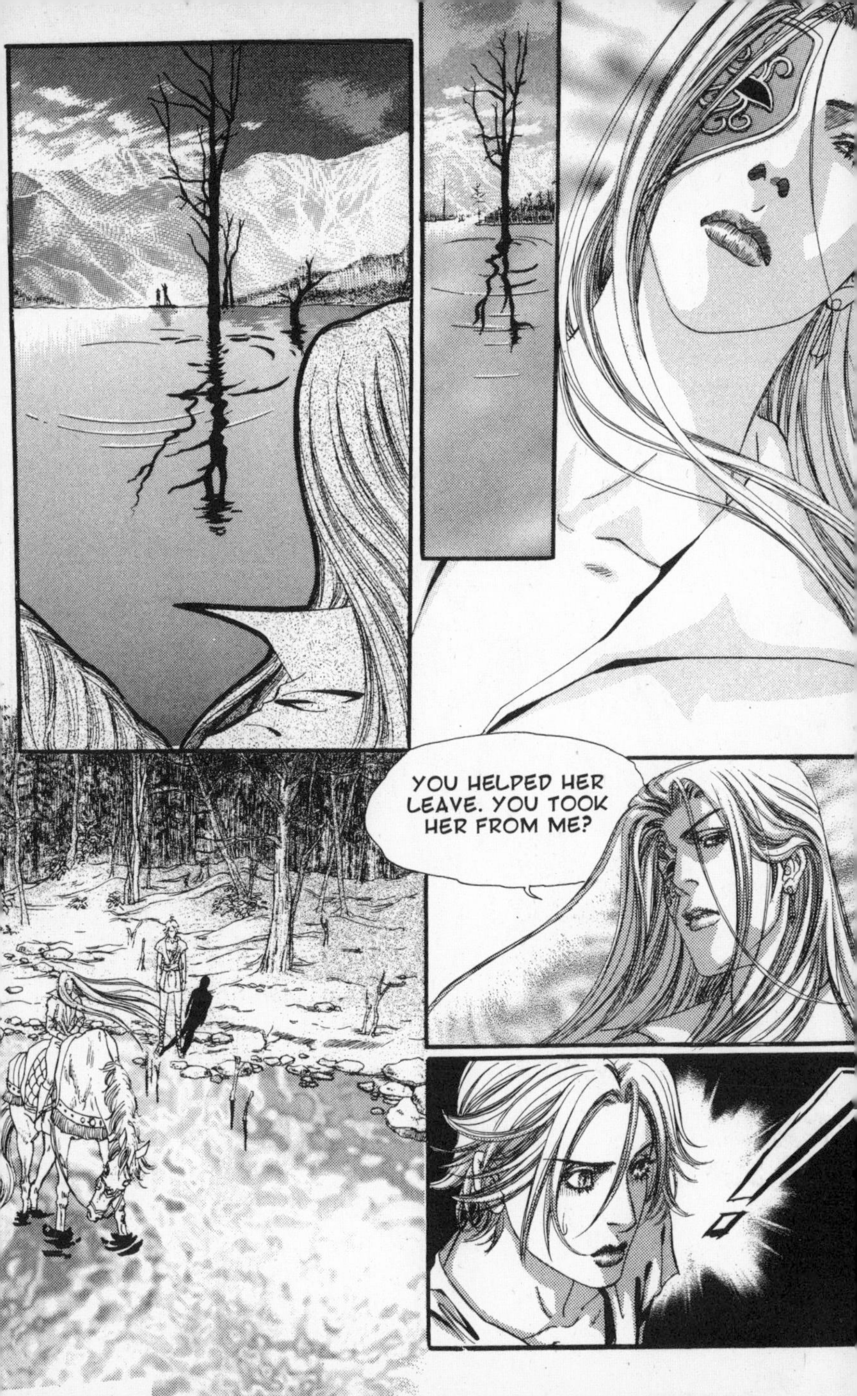
YOU HELPED HER LEAVE. YOU TOOK HER FROM ME?

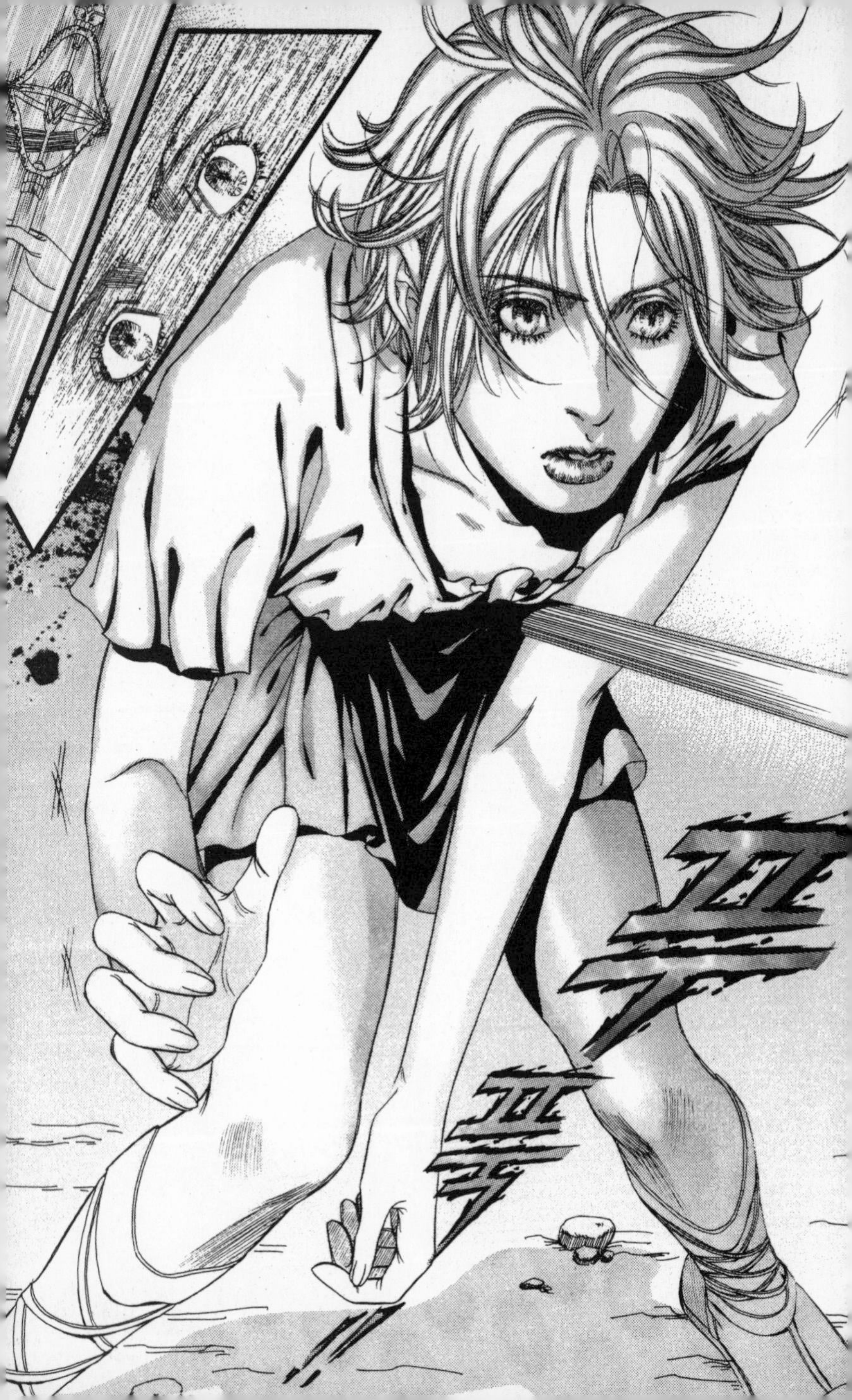

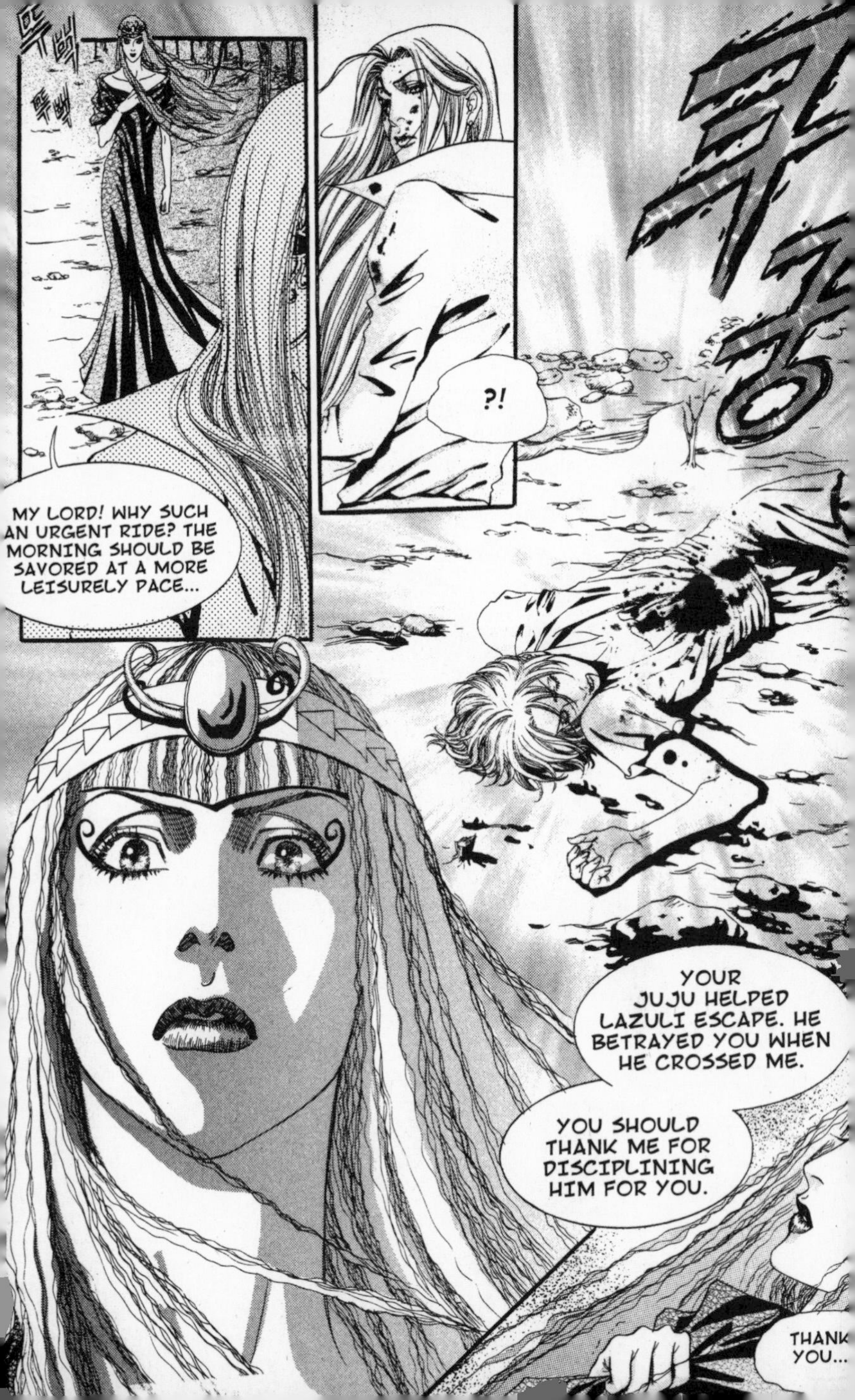

?!
MY LORD! WHY SUCH AN URGENT RIDE? THE MORNING SHOULD BE SAVORED AT A MORE LEISURELY PACE...
YOUR JUJU HELPED LAZULI ESCAPE. HE BETRAYED YOU WHEN HE CROSSED ME.
YOU SHOULD THANK ME FOR DISCIPLINING HIM FOR YOU.
THANK YOU...

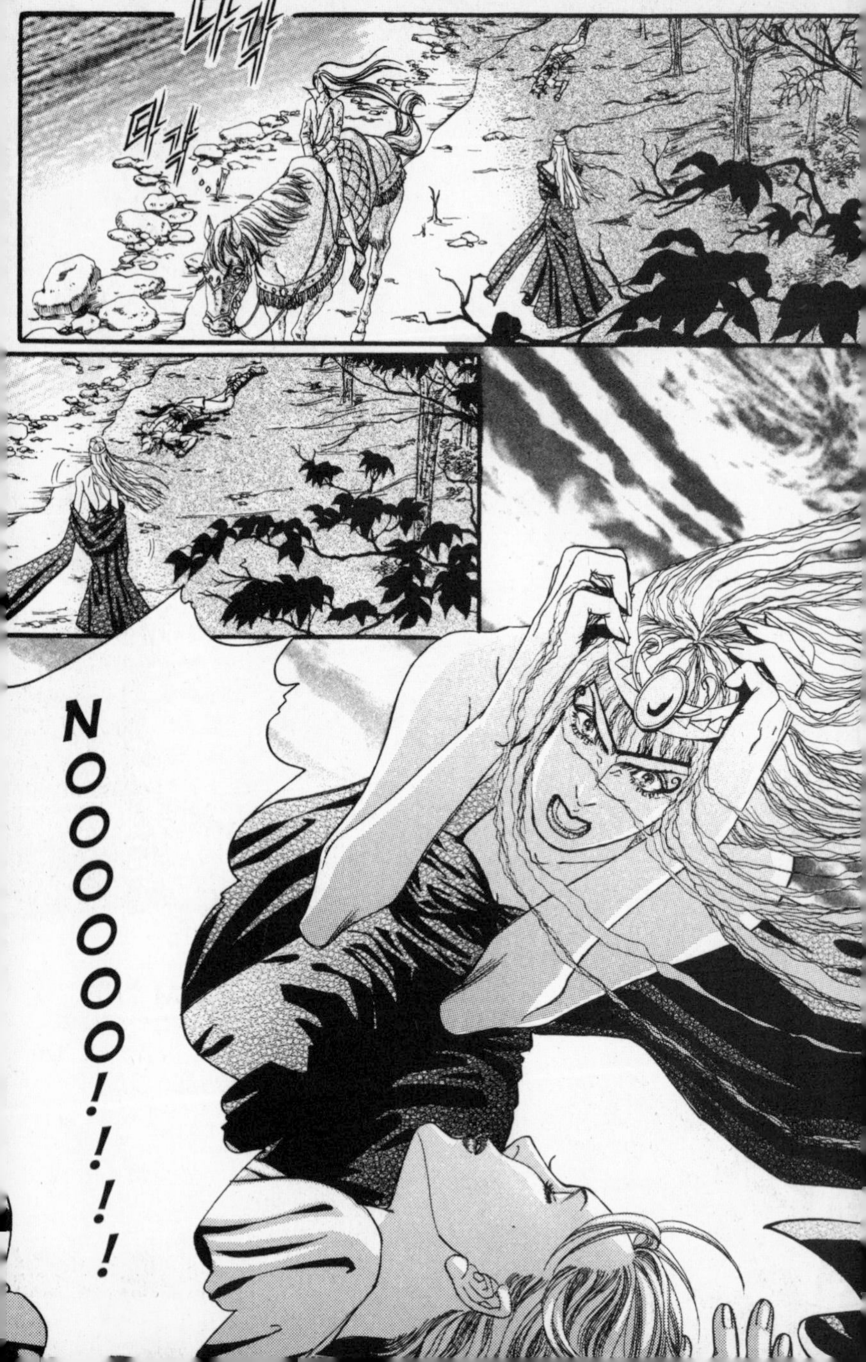
다각
다각
NOOOOOOO!!!!

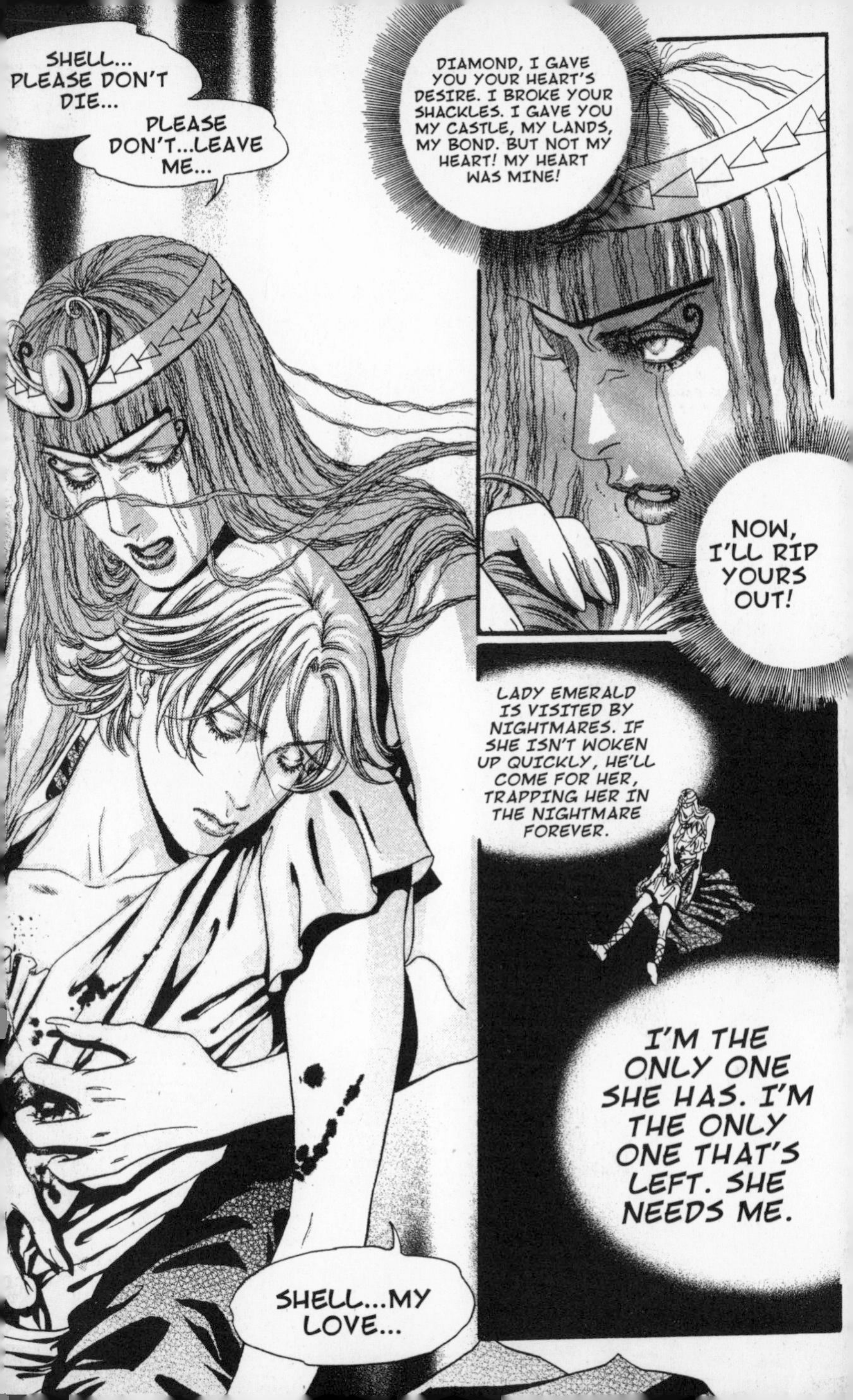
SHELL... PLEASE DON'T DIE...
PLEASE DON'T...LEAVE ME...
DIAMOND, I GAVE YOU YOUR HEART'S DESIRE. I BROKE YOUR SHACKLES. I GAVE YOU MY CASTLE, MY LANDS, MY BOND. BUT NOT MY HEART! MY HEART WAS MINE!
NOW, I'LL RIP YOURS OUT!
LADY EMERALD IS VISITED BY NIGHTMARES. IF SHE ISN'T WOKEN UP QUICKLY, HE'LL COME FOR HER, TRAPPING HER IN THE NIGHTMARE FOREVER.
I'M THE ONLY ONE SHE HAS. I'M THE ONLY ONE THAT'S LEFT. SHE NEEDS ME.
SHELL...MY LOVE...

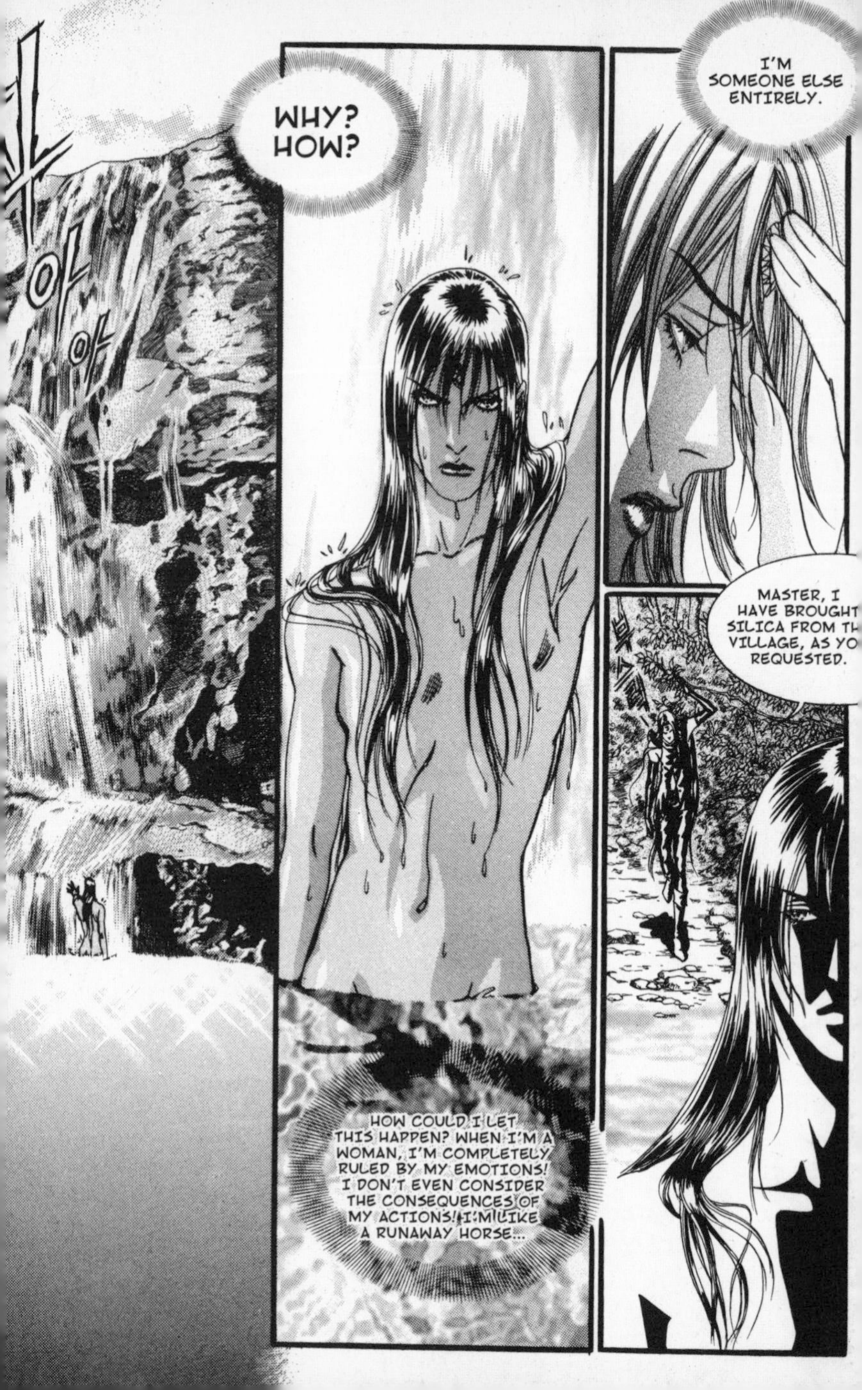
WHY? HOW?
I'M SOMEONE ELSE ENTIRELY.
HOW COULD I LET THIS HAPPEN? WHEN I'M A WOMAN, I'M COMPLETELY RULED BY MY EMOTIONS! I DON'T EVEN CONSIDER THE CONSEQUENCES OF MY ACTIONS! I'M LIKE A RUNAWAY HORSE...
MASTER, I HAVE BROUGHT SILICA FROM THE VILLAGE, AS YOU REQUESTED.

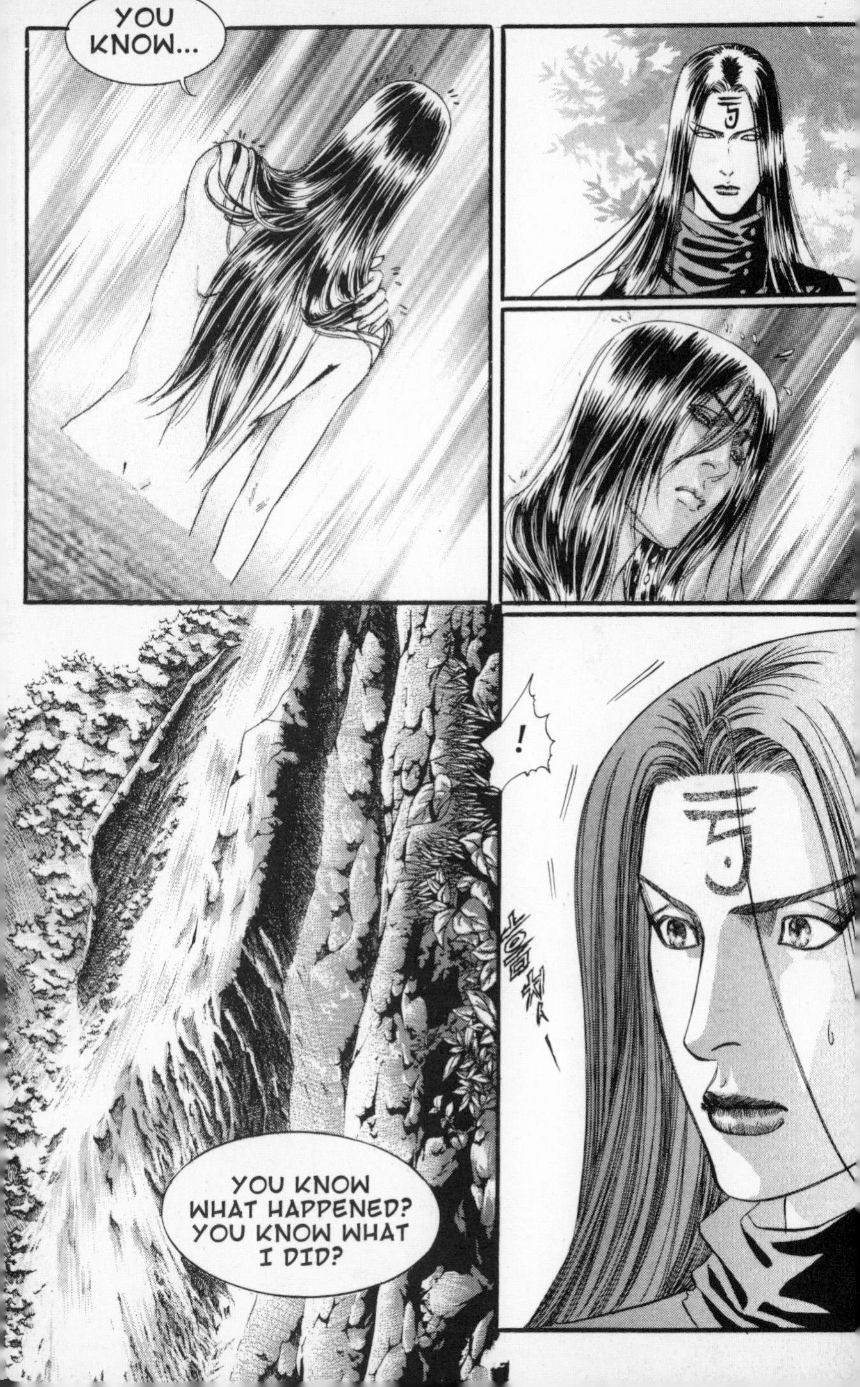
YOU KNOW...
!
YOU KNOW WHAT HAPPENED? YOU KNOW WHAT I DID?

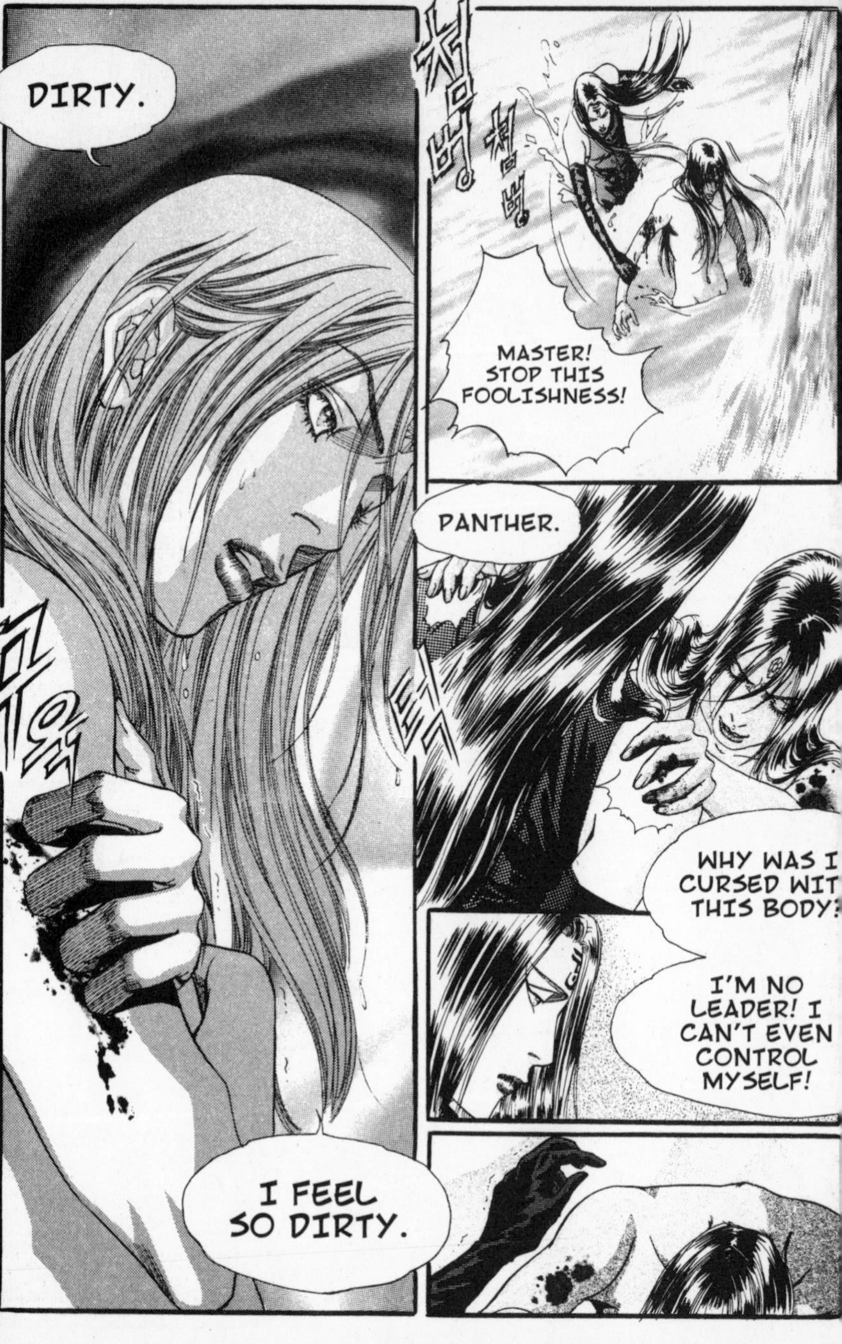
DIRTY.
I FEEL SO DIRTY.
MASTER! STOP THIS FOOLISHNESS!
PANTHER.
WHY WAS I CURSED WIT THIS BODY?
I'M NO LEADER! I CAN'T EVEN CONTROL MYSELF!

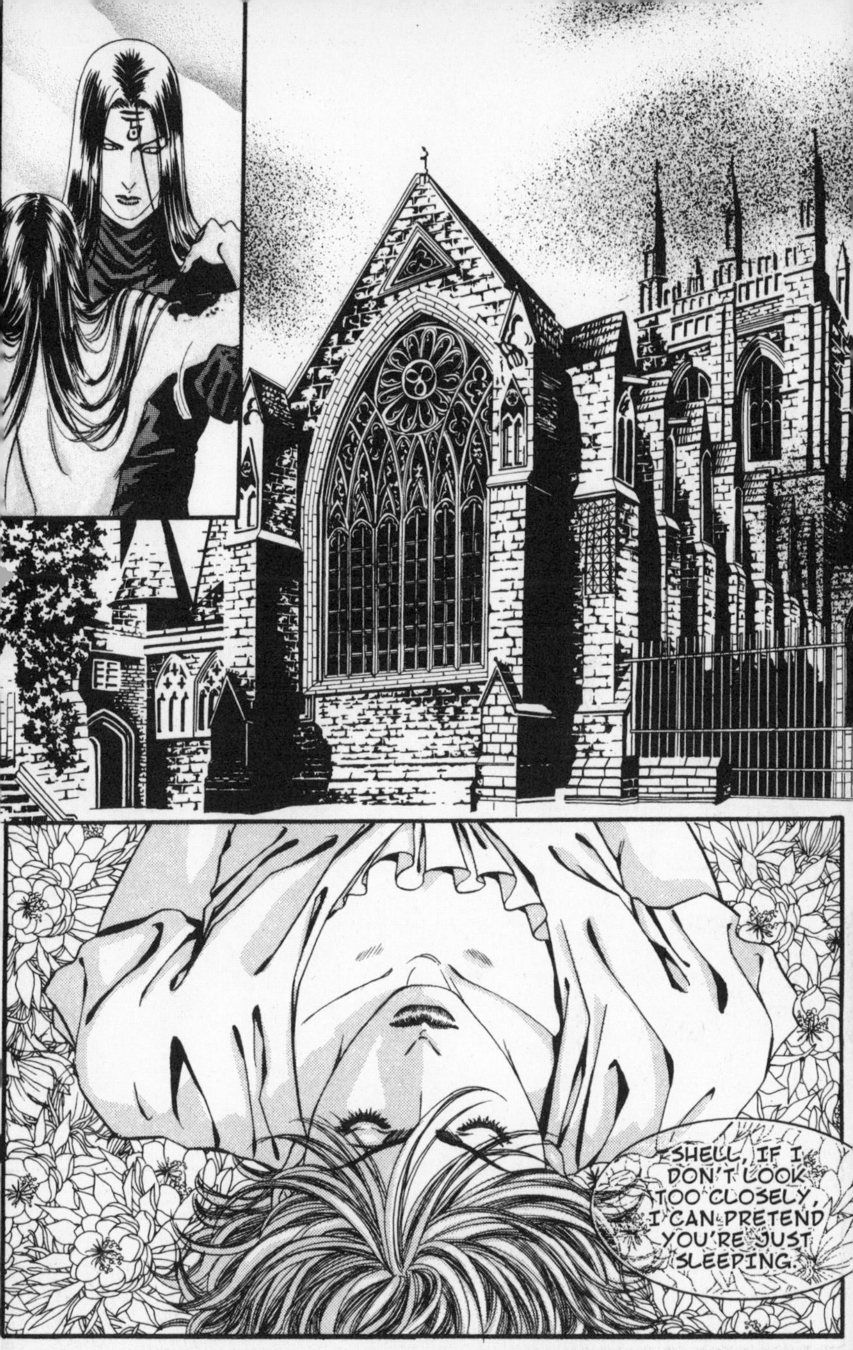
SHELL, IF I DON'T LOOK TOO CLOSELY, I CAN PRETEND YOU'RE JUST SLEEPING.

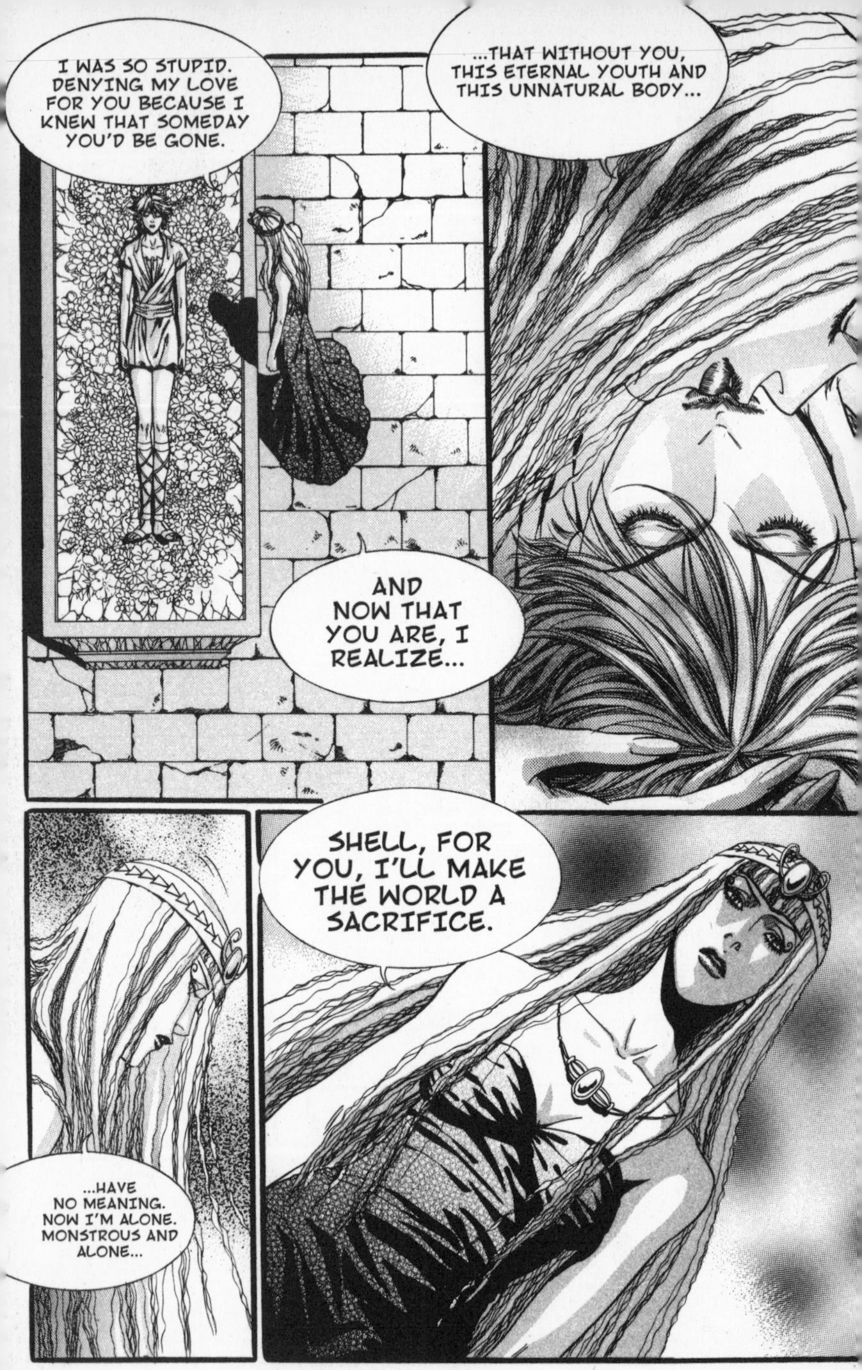
I WAS SO STUPID. DENYING MY LOVE FOR YOU BECAUSE I KNEW THAT SOMEDAY YOU'D BE GONE.
AND NOW THAT YOU ARE, I REALIZE...
...THAT WITHOUT YOU, THIS ETERNAL YOUTH AND THIS UNNATURAL BODY...
...HAVE NO MEANING. NOW I'M ALONE. MONSTROUS AND ALONE...
SHELL, FOR YOU, I'LL MAKE THE WORLD A SACRIFICE.

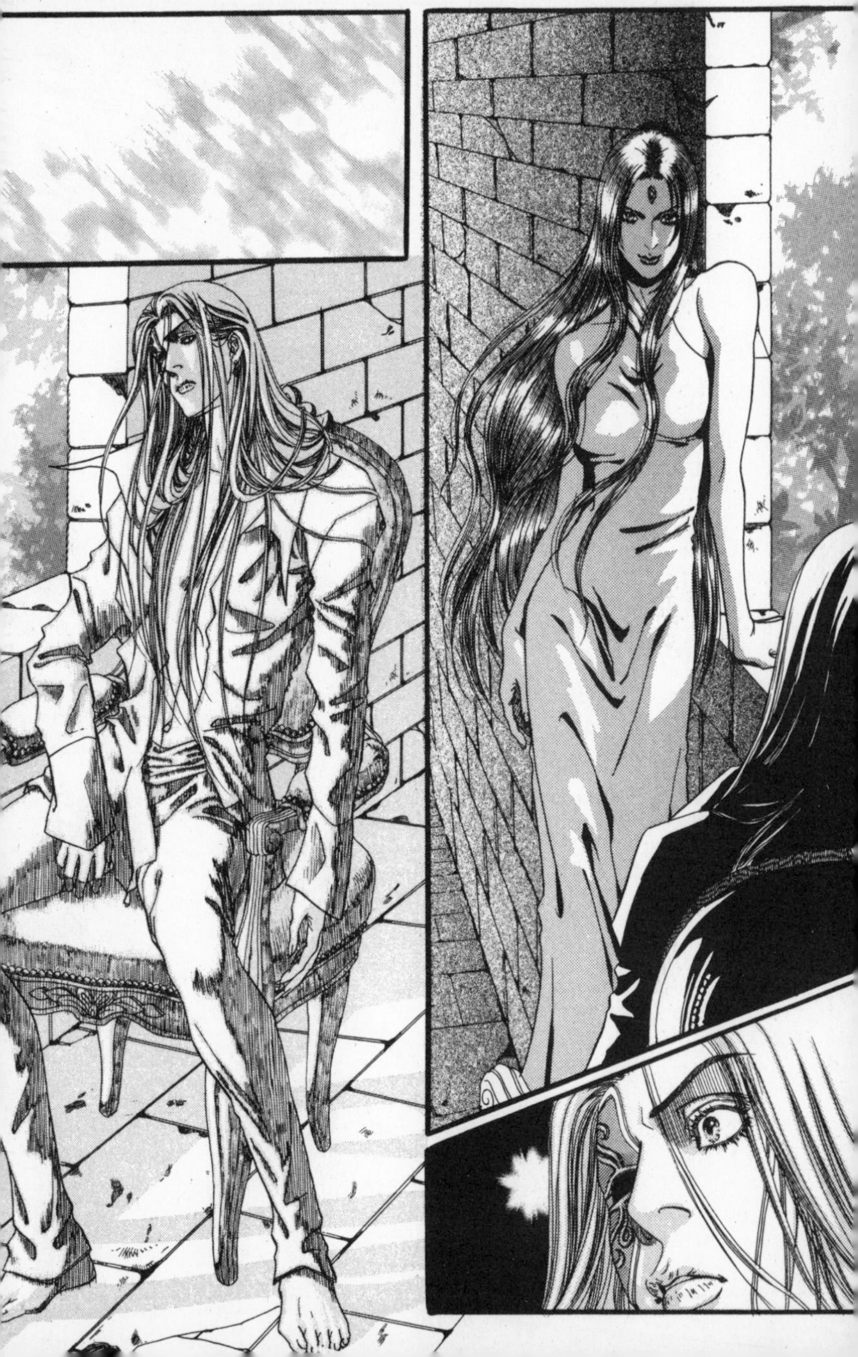

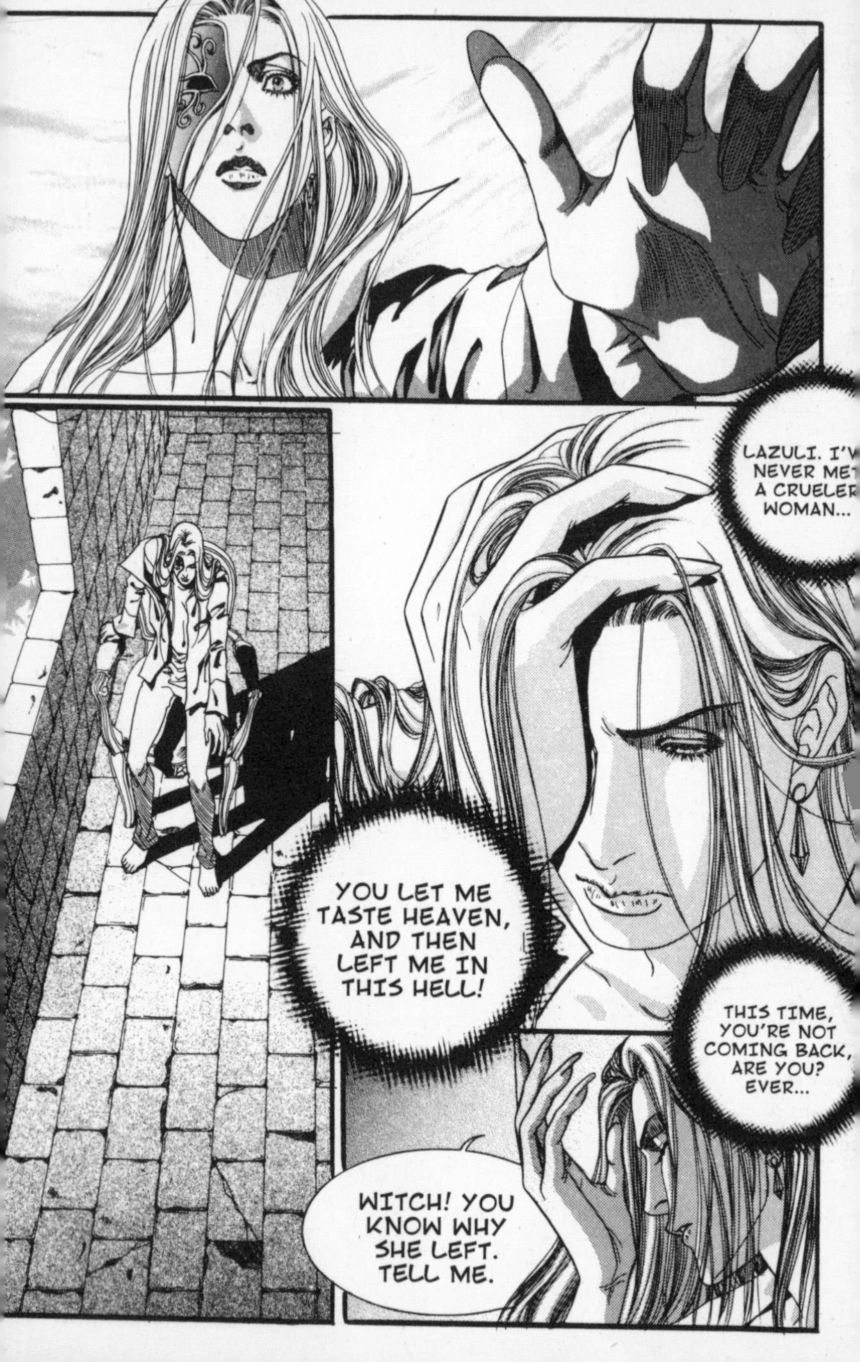
LAZULI. I'V NEVER MET A CRUELER WOMAN...
YOU LET ME TASTE HEAVEN, AND THEN LEFT ME IN THIS HELL!
THIS TIME, YOU'RE NOT COMING BACK, ARE YOU? EVER...
WITCH! YOU KNOW WHY SHE LEFT. TELL ME.

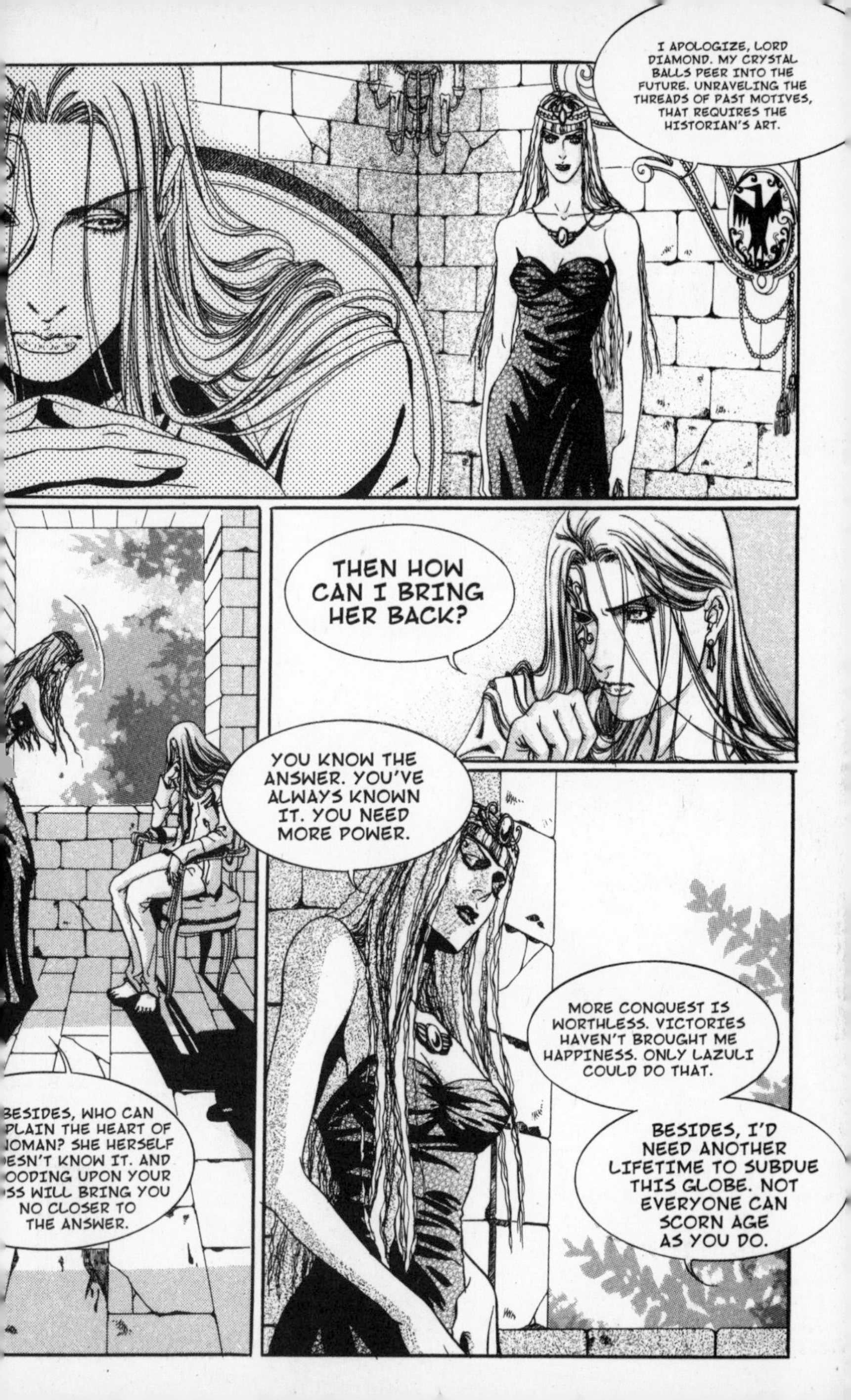
I APOLOGIZE, LORD DIAMOND. MY CRYSTAL BALLS PEER INTO THE FUTURE. UNRAVELING THE THREADS OF PAST MOTIVES, THAT REQUIRES THE HISTORIAN'S ART.
THEN HOW CAN I BRING HER BACK?
YOU KNOW THE ANSWER. YOU'VE ALWAYS KNOWN IT. YOU NEED MORE POWER.
MORE CONQUEST IS WORTHLESS. VICTORIES HAVEN'T BROUGHT ME HAPPINESS. ONLY LAZULI COULD DO THAT.
BESIDES, I'D NEED ANOTHER LIFETIME TO SUBDUE THIS GLOBE. NOT EVERYONE CAN SCORN AGE AS YOU DO.
BESIDES, WHO CAN PLAIN THE HEART OF OMAN? SHE HERSELF ESN'T KNOW IT. AND OODING UPON YOUR SS WILL BRING YOU NO CLOSER TO THE ANSWER.

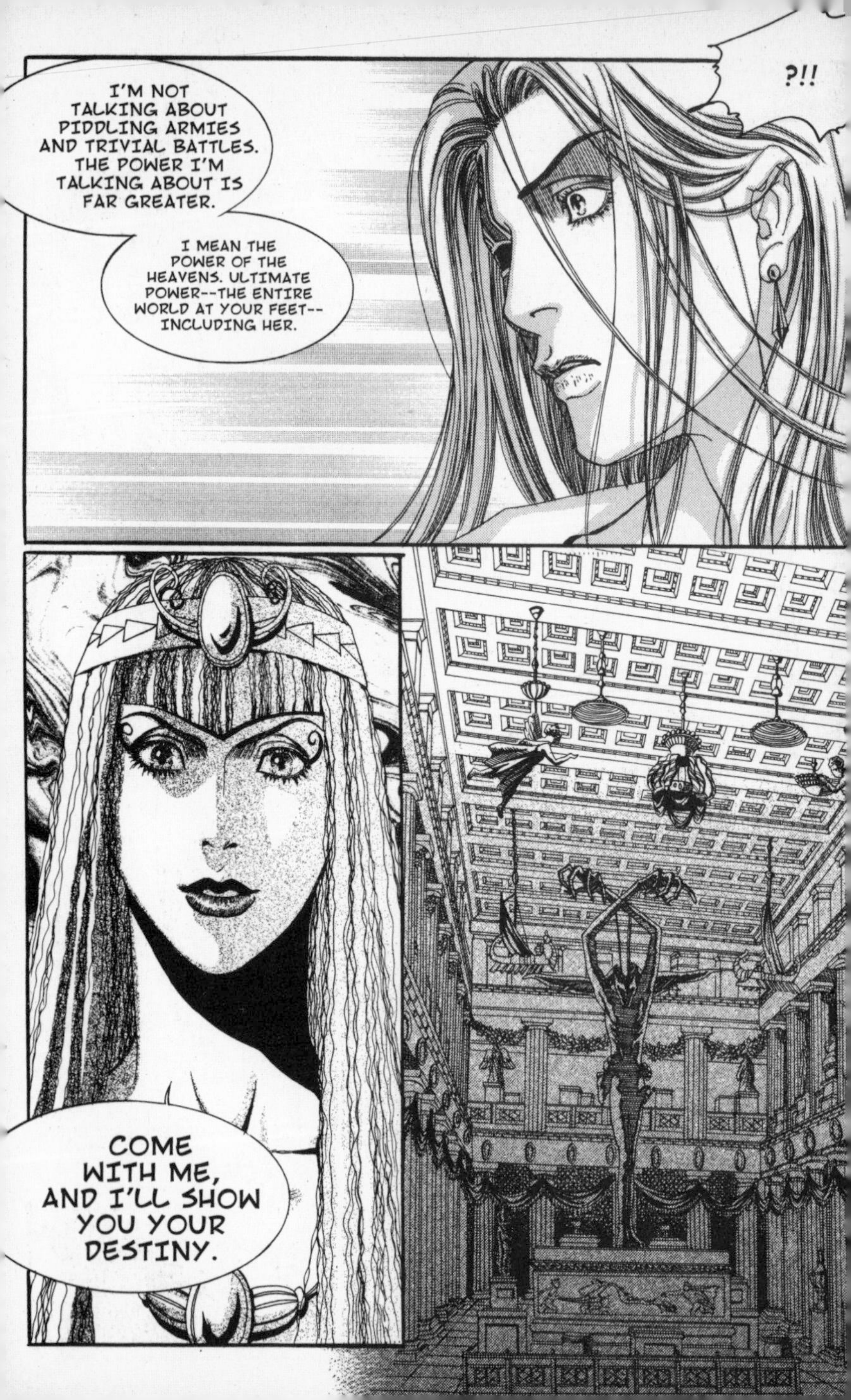
?!!
I'M NOT TALKING ABOUT PIDDLING ARMIES AND TRIVIAL BATTLES. THE POWER I'M TALKING ABOUT IS FAR GREATER.
I MEAN THE POWER OF THE HEAVENS. ULTIMATE POWER--THE ENTIRE WORLD AT YOUR FEET--INCLUDING HER.
COME WITH ME, AND I'LL SHOW YOU YOUR DESTINY.

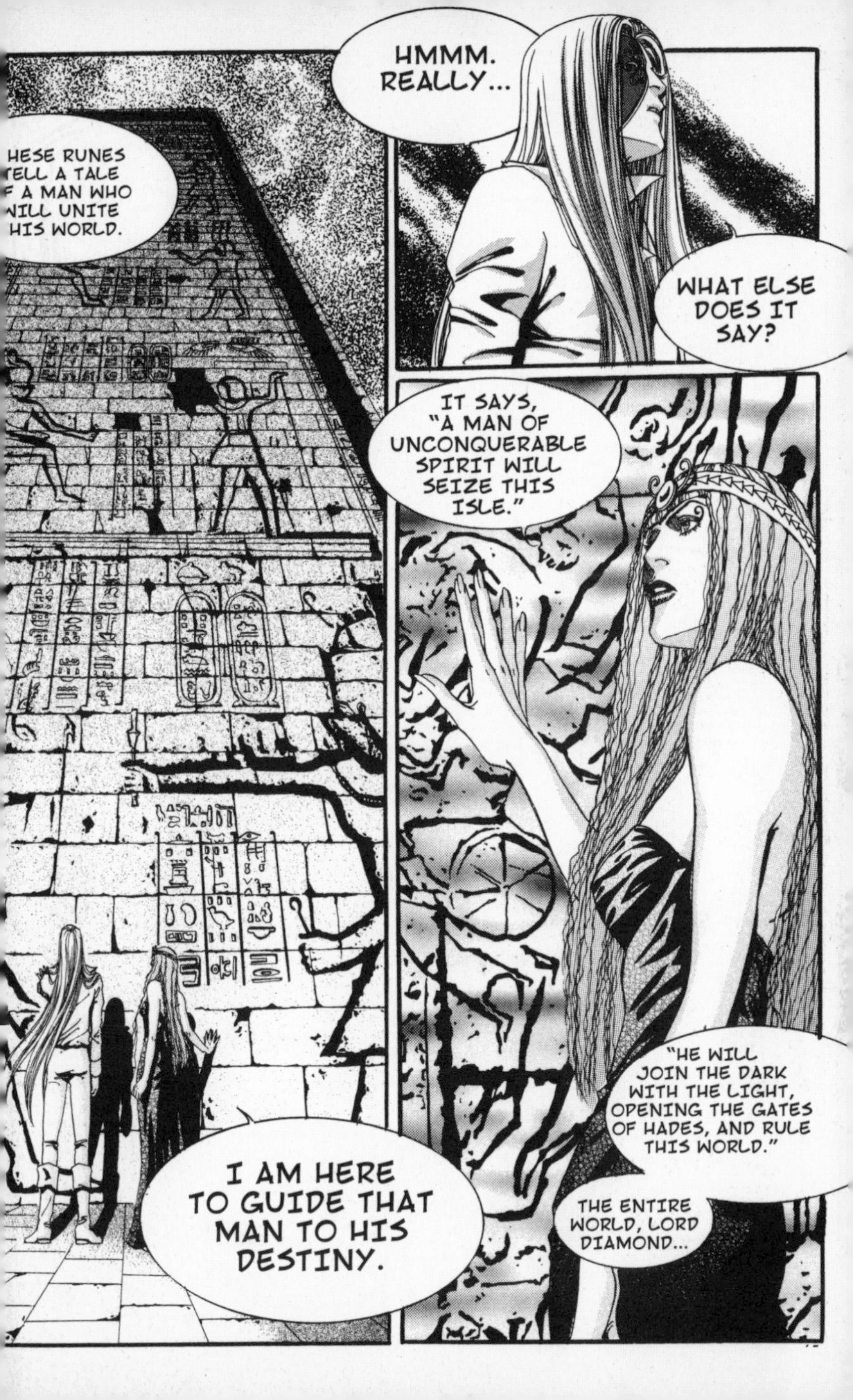
HESE RUNES TELL A TALE F A MAN WHO WILL UNITE HIS WORLD.
HMMM. REALLY...
WHAT ELSE DOES IT SAY?
IT SAYS, "A MAN OF UNCONQUERABLE SPIRIT WILL SEIZE THIS ISLE."
"HE WILL JOIN THE DARK WITH THE LIGHT, OPENING THE GATES OF HADES, AND RULE THIS WORLD."
THE ENTIRE WORLD, LORD DIAMOND...
I AM HERE TO GUIDE THAT MAN TO HIS DESTINY.

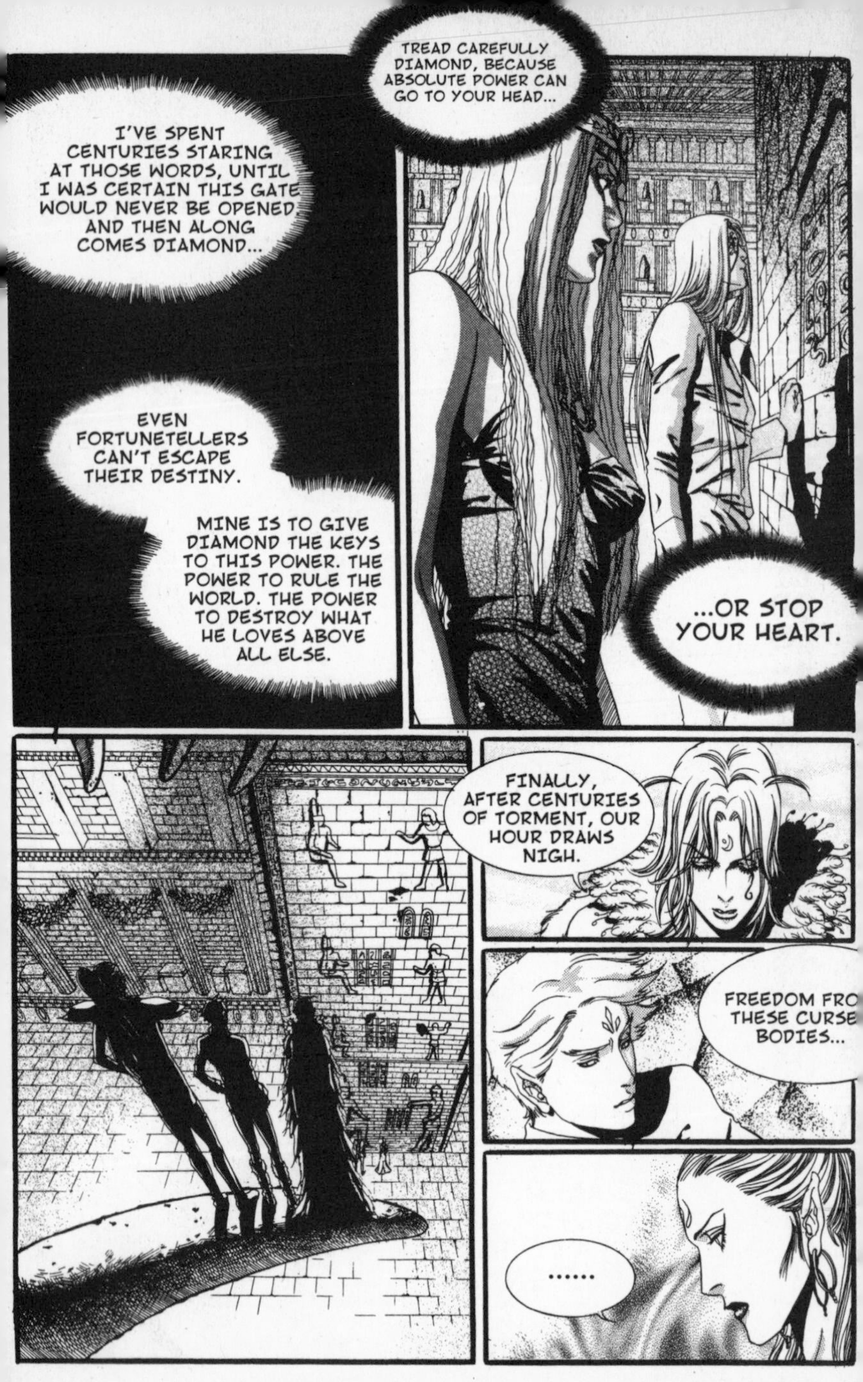
I'VE SPENT CENTURIES STARING AT THOSE WORDS, UNTIL I WAS CERTAIN THIS GATE WOULD NEVER BE OPENED. AND THEN ALONG COMES DIAMOND...
TREAD CAREFULLY DIAMOND, BECAUSE ABSOLUTE POWER CAN GO TO YOUR HEAD...
EVEN FORTUNETELLERS CAN'T ESCAPE THEIR DESTINY.
MINE IS TO GIVE DIAMOND THE KEYS TO THIS POWER. THE POWER TO RULE THE WORLD. THE POWER TO DESTROY WHAT HE LOVES ABOVE ALL ELSE.
...OR STOP YOUR HEART.
FINALLY, AFTER CENTURIES OF TORMENT, OUR HOUR DRAWS NIGH.
FREEDOM FRO THESE CURSE BODIES...
......

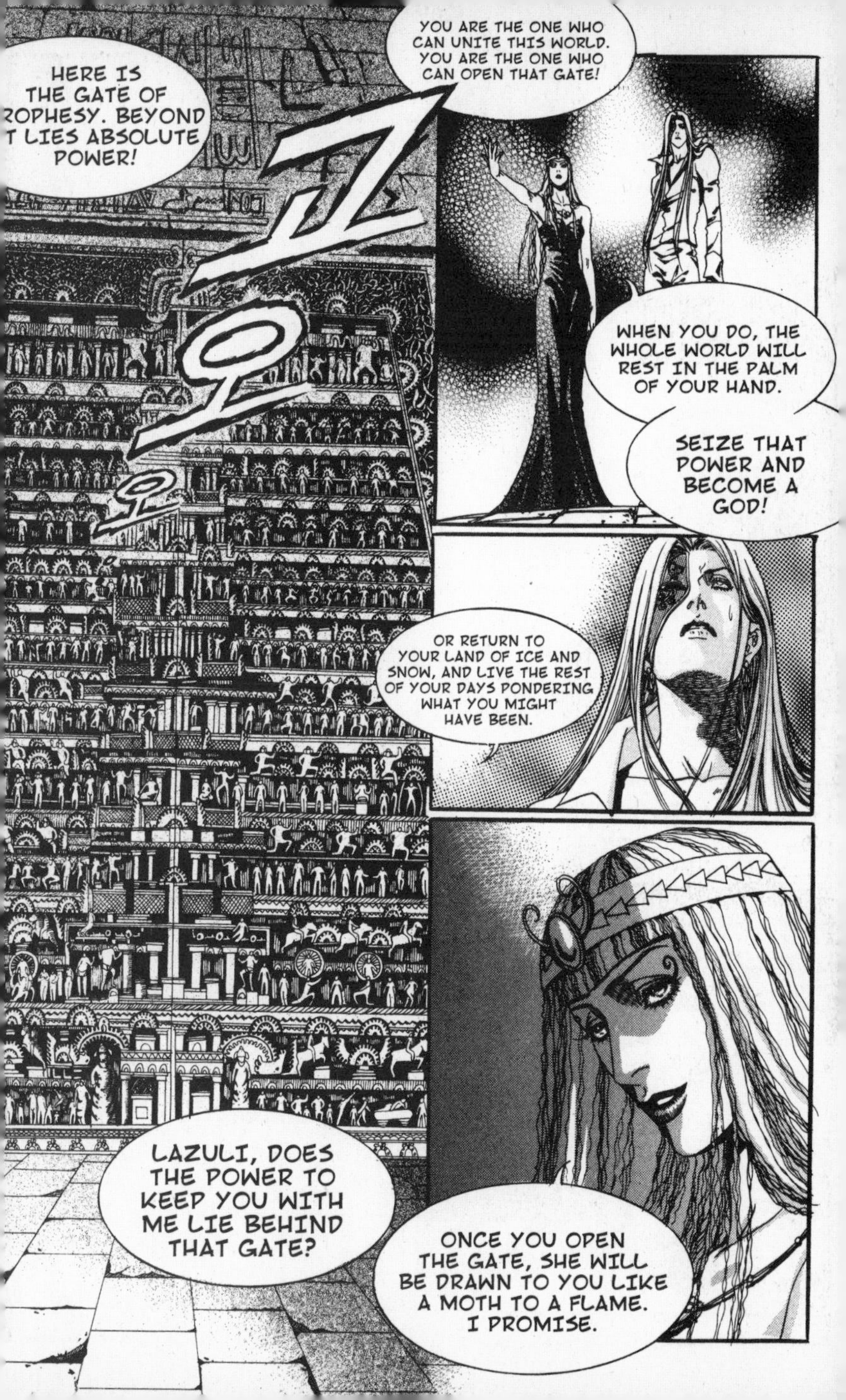
HERE IS THE GATE OF PROPHESY. BEYOND IT LIES ABSOLUTE POWER!
YOU ARE THE ONE WHO CAN UNITE THIS WORLD. YOU ARE THE ONE WHO CAN OPEN THAT GATE!
WHEN YOU DO, THE WHOLE WORLD WILL REST IN THE PALM OF YOUR HAND.
SEIZE THAT POWER AND BECOME A GOD!
OR RETURN TO YOUR LAND OF ICE AND SNOW, AND LIVE THE REST OF YOUR DAYS PONDERING WHAT YOU MIGHT HAVE BEEN.
LAZULI, DOES THE POWER TO KEEP YOU WITH ME LIE BEHIND THAT GATE?
ONCE YOU OPEN THE GATE, SHE WILL BE DRAWN TO YOU LIKE A MOTH TO A FLAME. I PROMISE.

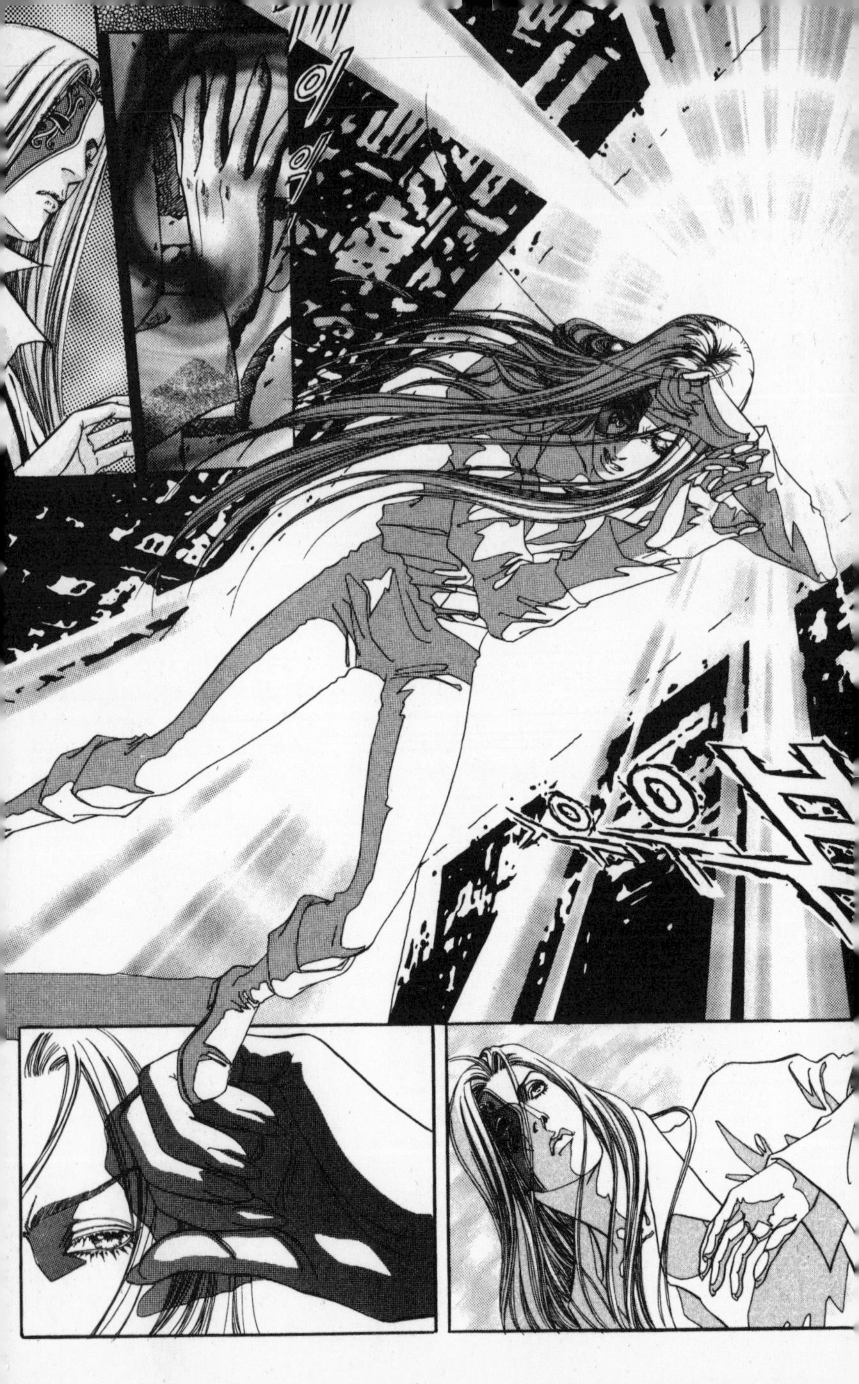

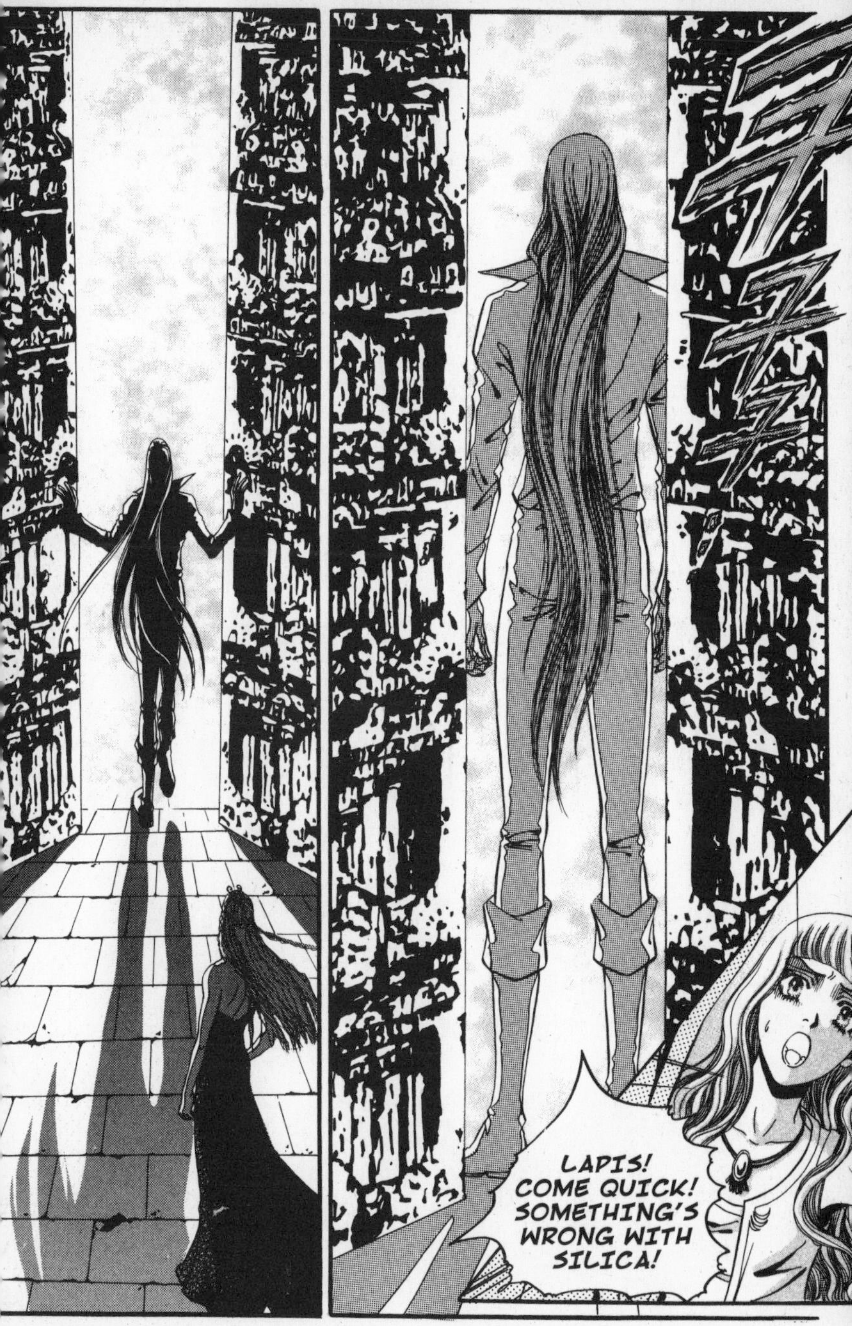
LAPIS! COME QUICK! SOMETHING'S WRONG WITH SILICA!

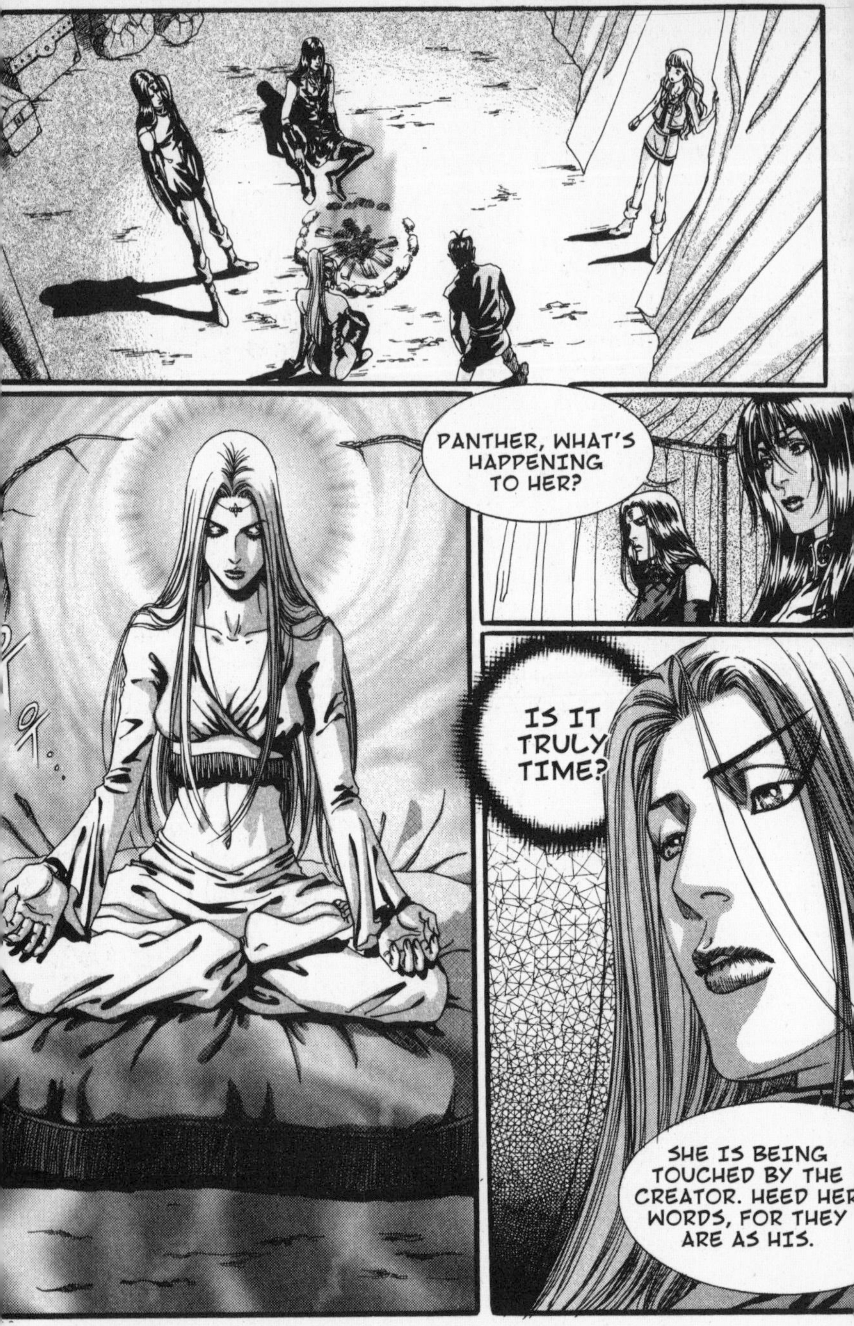
PANTHER, WHAT'S HAPPENING TO HER?
IS IT TRULY TIME?
SHE IS BEING TOUCHED BY THE CREATOR. HEED HER WORDS, FOR THEY ARE AS HIS.

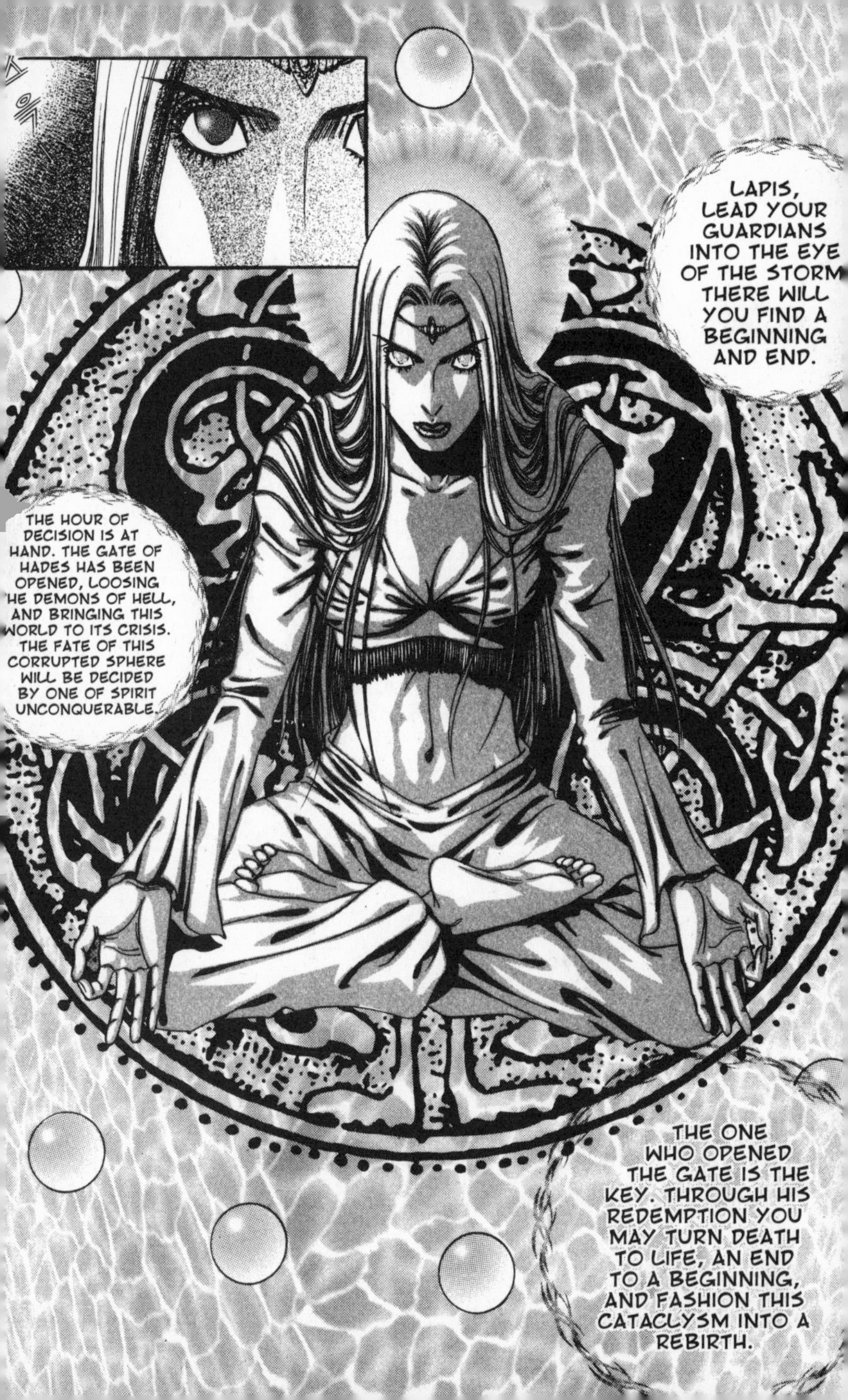

LAPIS, LEAD YOUR GUARDIANS INTO THE EYE OF THE STORM THERE WILL YOU FIND A BEGINNING AND END.
THE HOUR OF DECISION IS AT HAND. THE GATE OF HADES HAS BEEN OPENED, LOOSING HE DEMONS OF HELL, AND BRINGING THIS WORLD TO ITS CRISIS. THE FATE OF THIS CORRUPTED SPHERE WILL BE DECIDED BY ONE OF SPIRIT UNCONQUERABLE.
THE ONE WHO OPENED THE GATE IS THE KEY. THROUGH HIS REDEMPTION YOU MAY TURN DEATH TO LIFE, AN END TO A BEGINNING, AND FASHION THIS CATACLYSM INTO A REBIRTH.

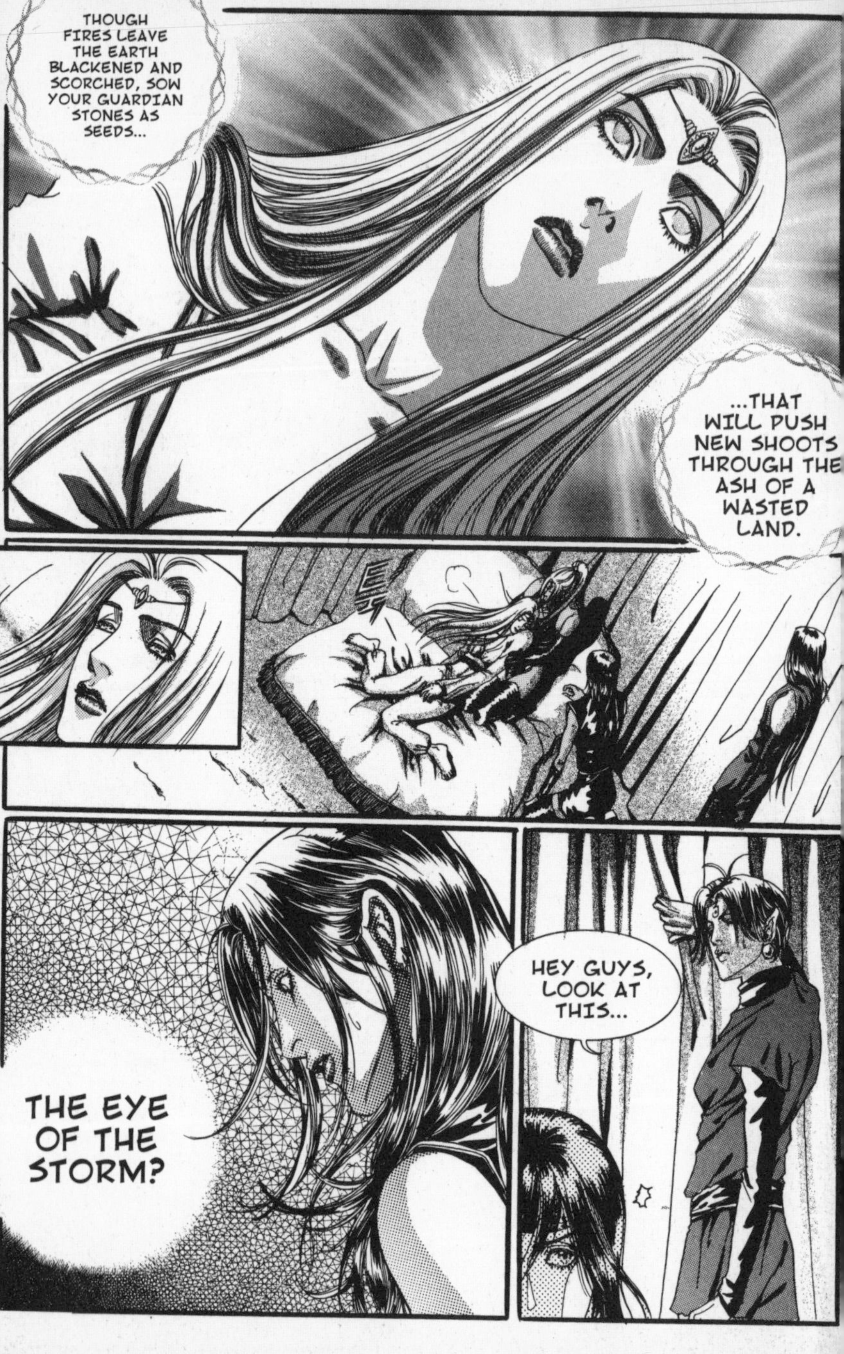
THOUGH FIRES LEAVE THE EARTH BLACKENED AND SCORCHED, SOW YOUR GUARDIAN STONES AS SEEDS...
...THAT WILL PUSH NEW SHOOTS THROUGH THE ASH OF A WASTED LAND.
THE EYE OF THE STORM?
HEY GUYS, LOOK AT THIS...

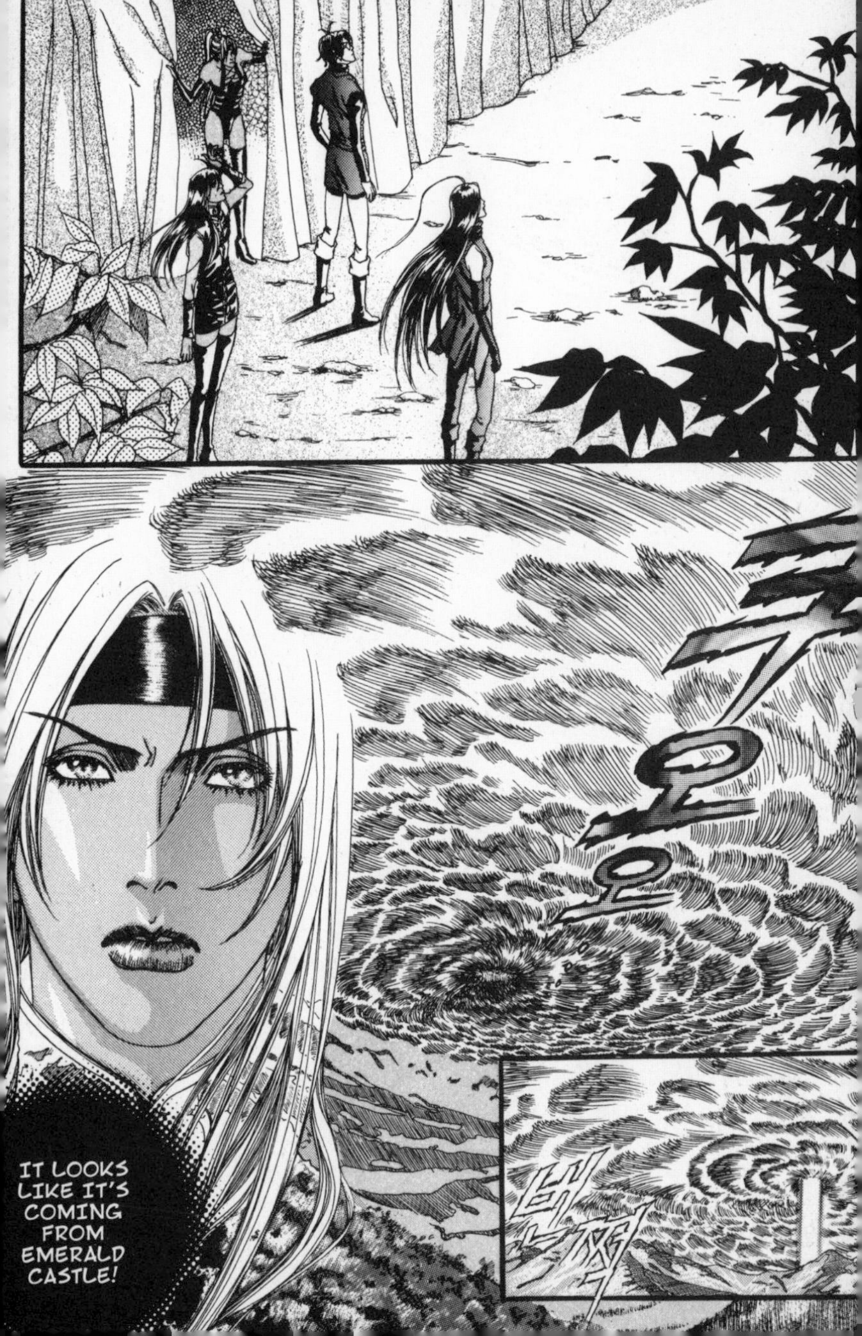
IT LOOKS LIKE IT'S COMING FROM EMERALD CASTLE!

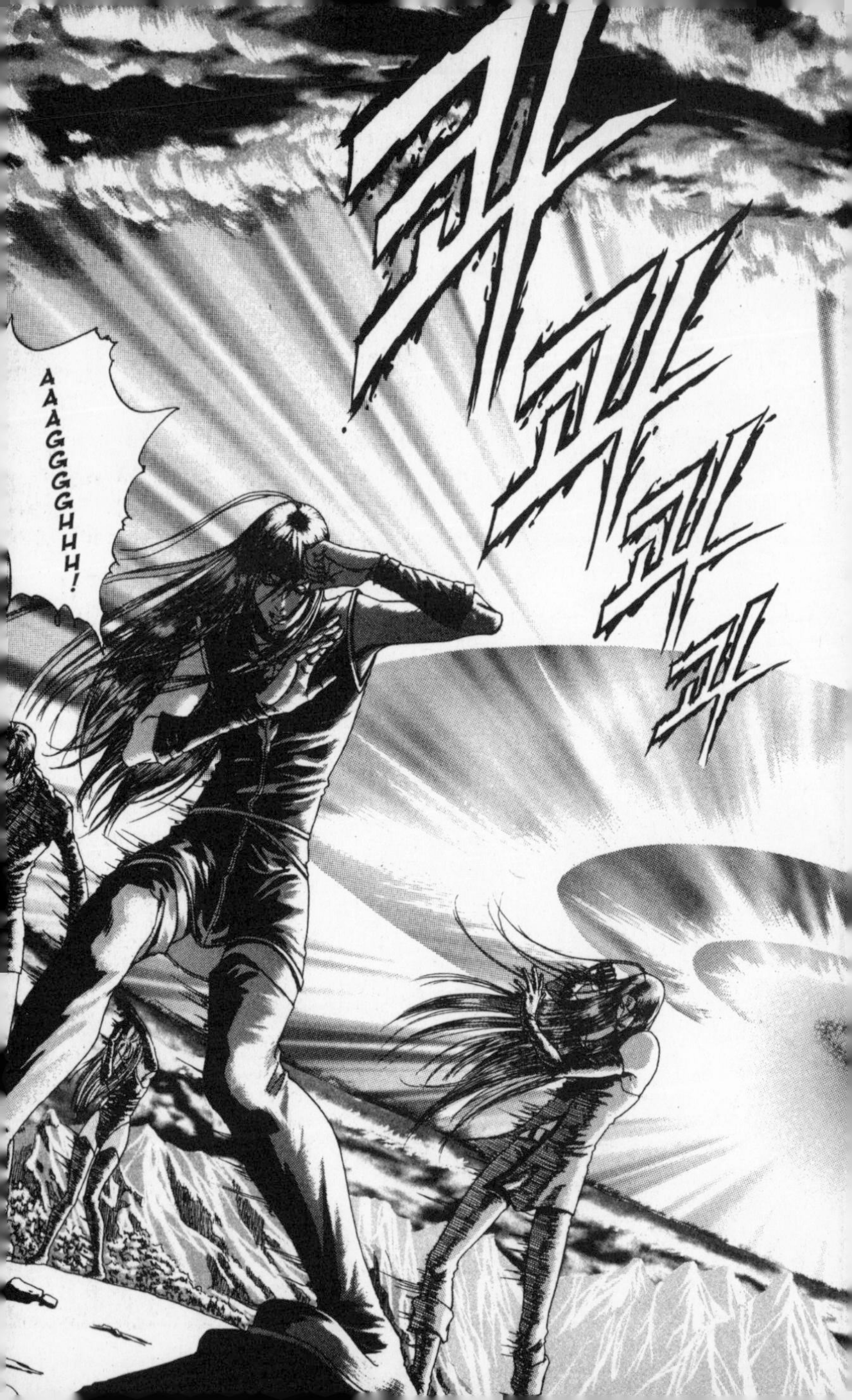
AAAGGGGHHH!

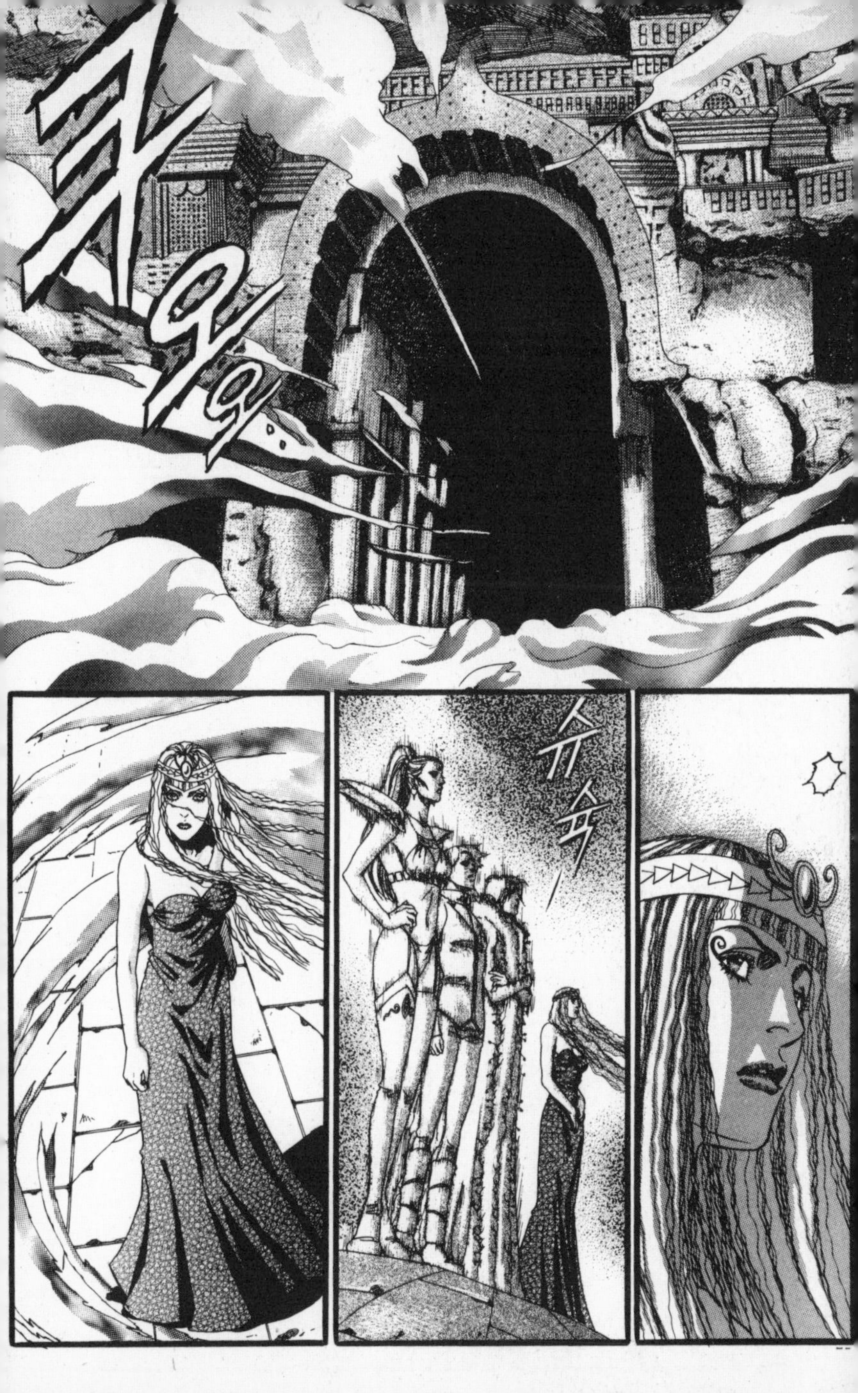

콰우우..
슈슥

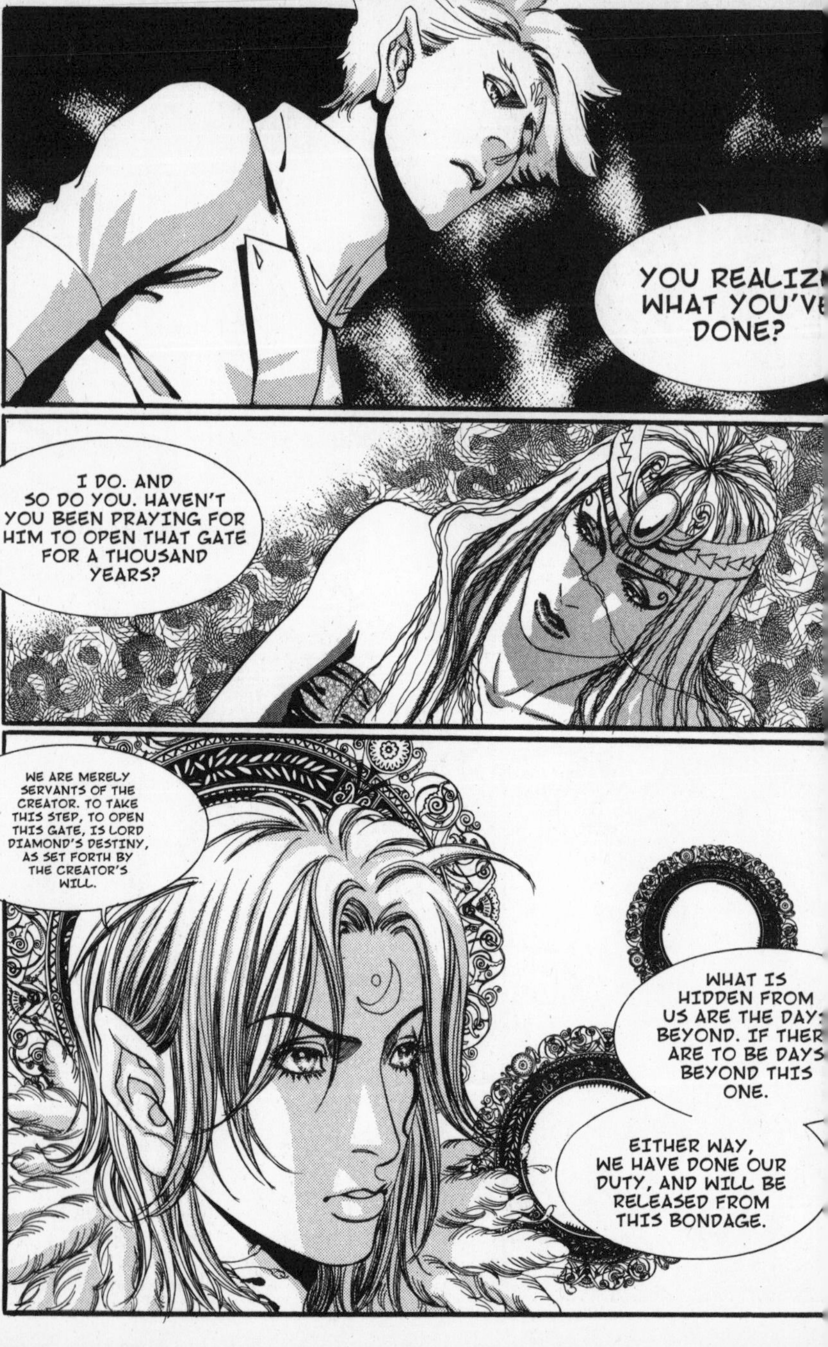
YOU REALIZ WHAT YOU'V DONE?
I DO. AND SO DO YOU. HAVEN'T YOU BEEN PRAYING FOR HIM TO OPEN THAT GATE FOR A THOUSAND YEARS?
WE ARE MERELY SERVANTS OF THE CREATOR. TO TAKE THIS STEP, TO OPEN THIS GATE, IS LORD DIAMOND'S DESTINY, AS SET FORTH BY THE CREATOR'S WILL.
WHAT IS HIDDEN FROM US ARE THE DAY BEYOND. IF THER ARE TO BE DAYS BEYOND THIS ONE.
EITHER WAY, WE HAVE DONE OUR DUTY, AND WILL BE RELEASED FROM THIS BONDAGE.

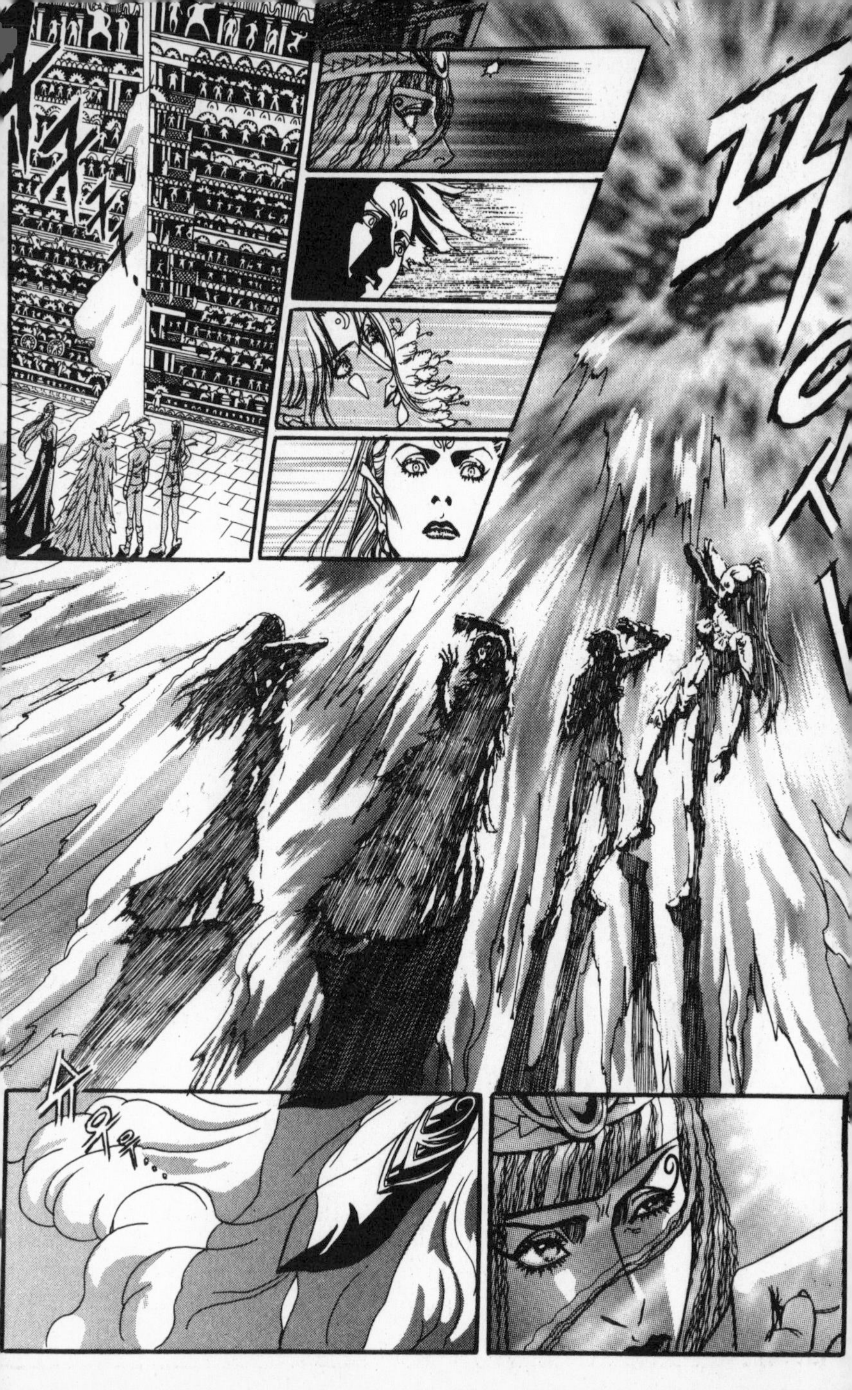
쉬우우...

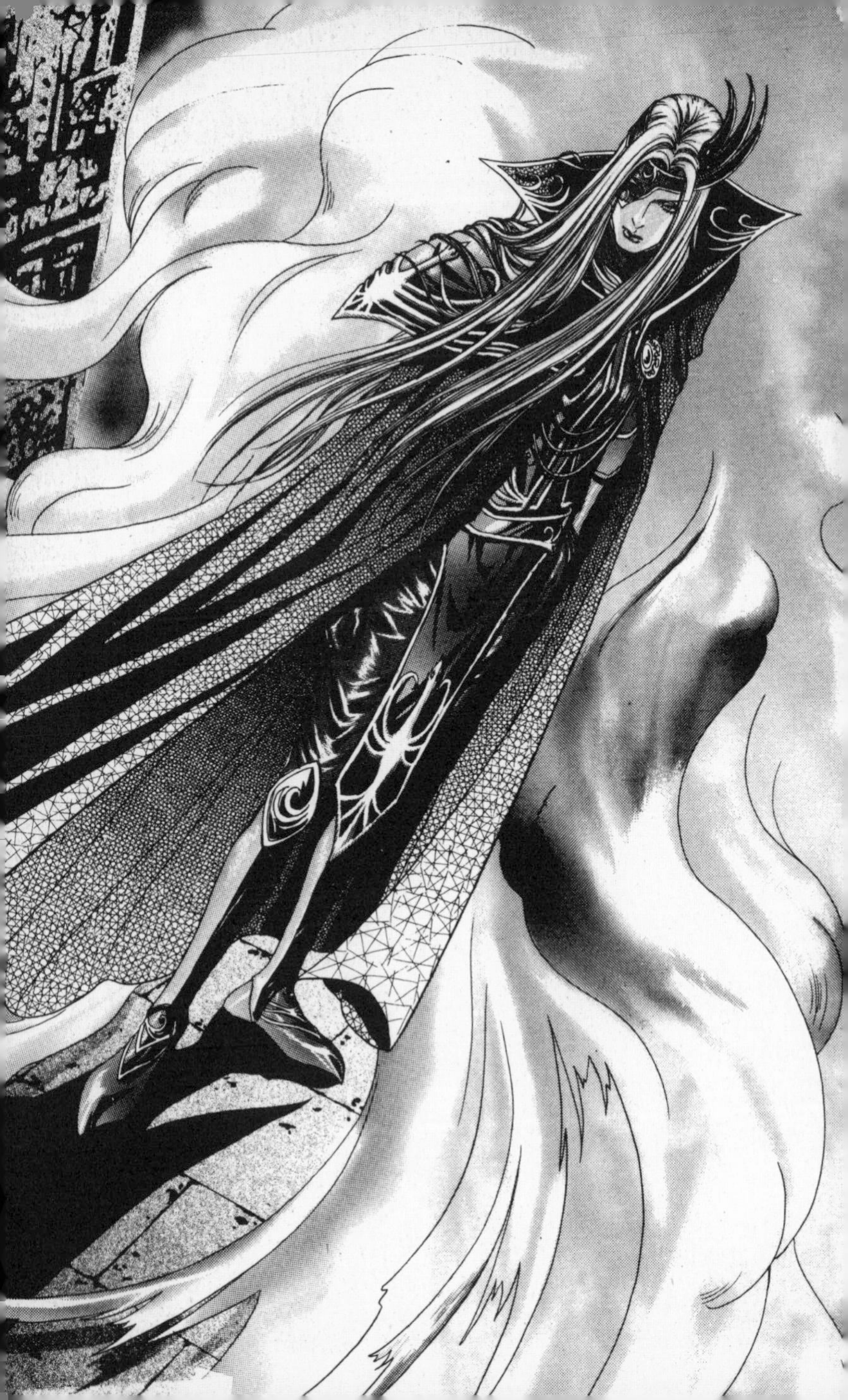

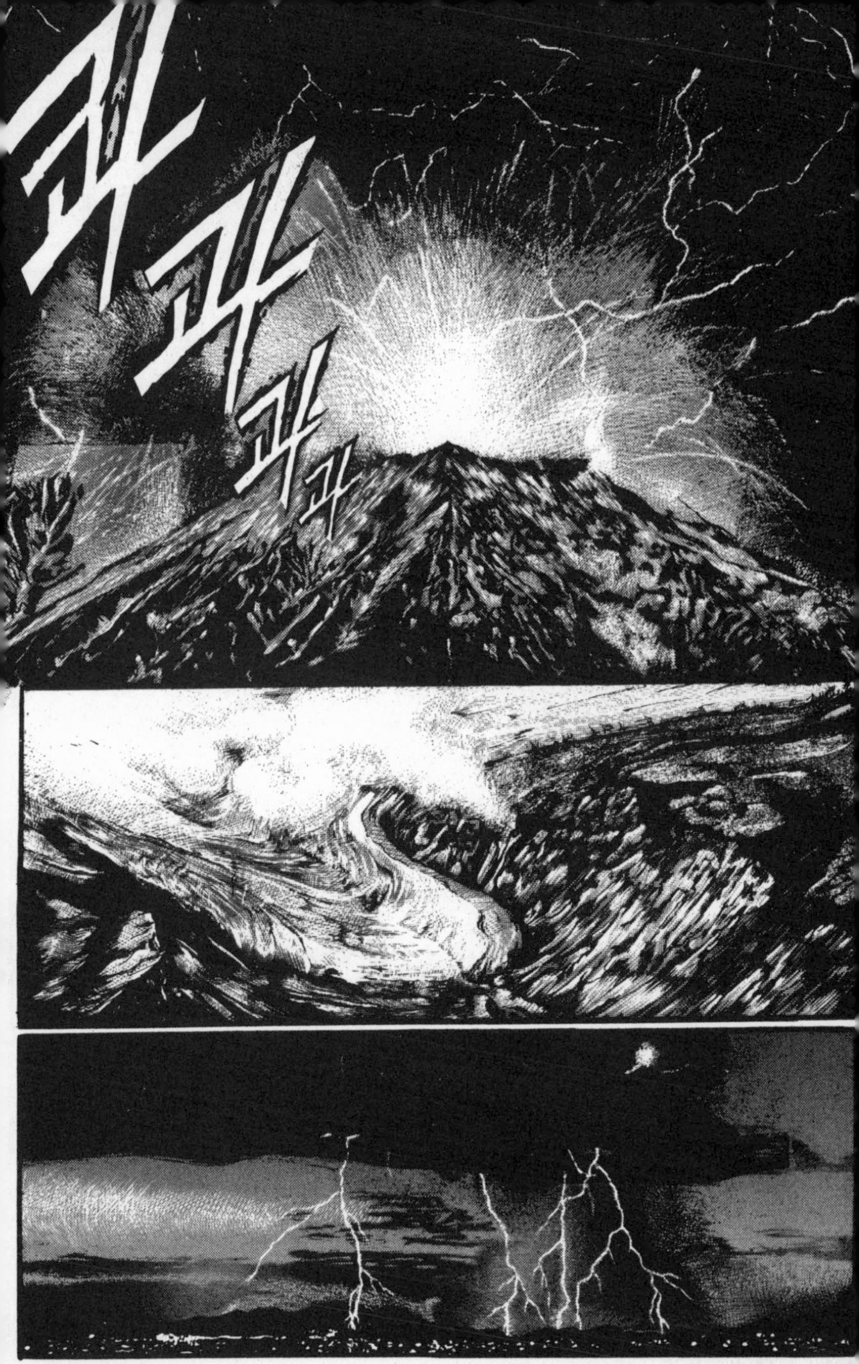
과과과과

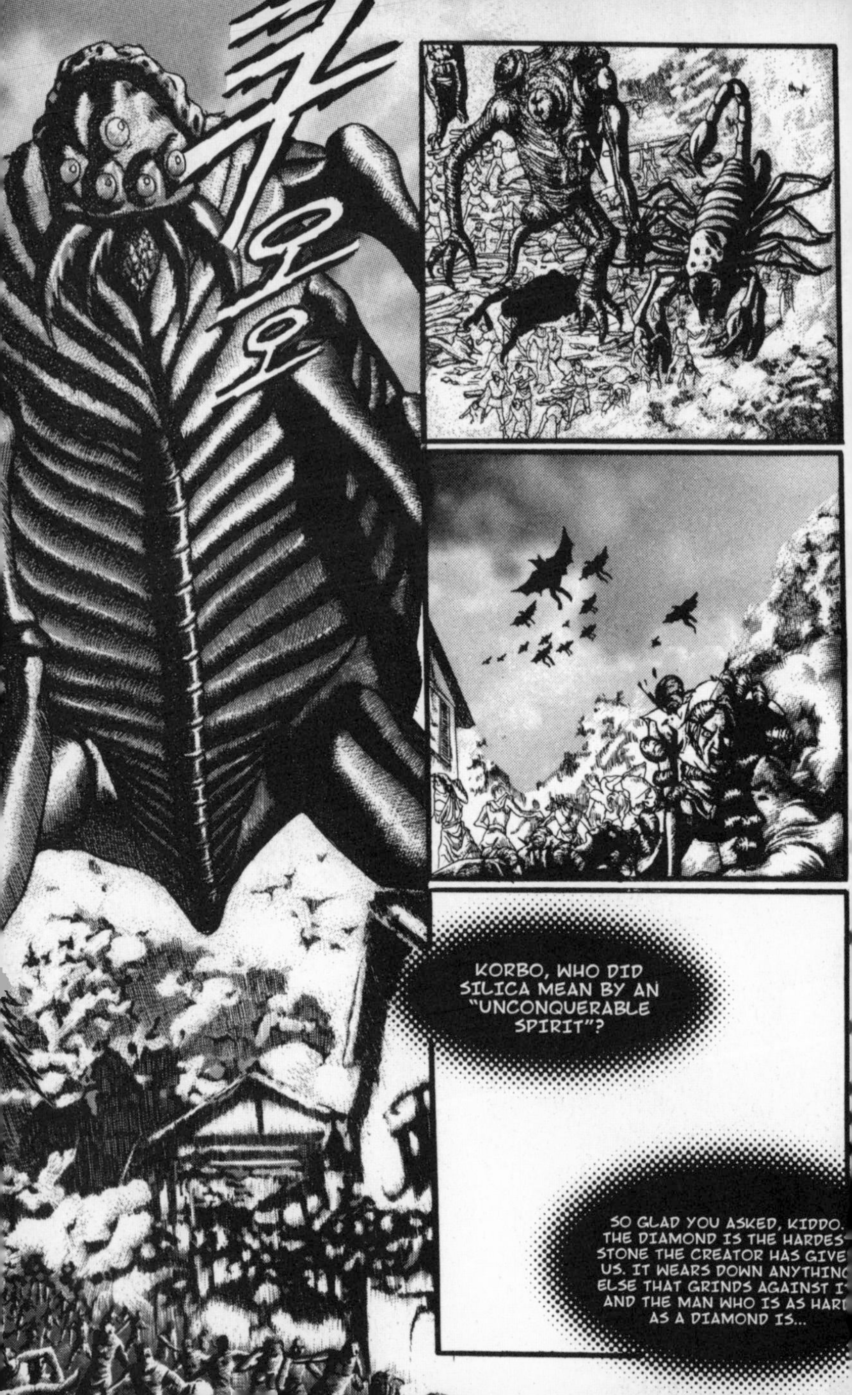
KORBO, WHO DID SILICA MEAN BY AN "UNCONQUERABLE SPIRIT"?
SO GLAD YOU ASKED, KIDDO. THE DIAMOND IS THE HARDES STONE THE CREATOR HAS GIVE US. IT WEARS DOWN ANYTHING ELSE THAT GRINDS AGAINST I AND THE MAN WHO IS AS HARI AS A DIAMOND IS...

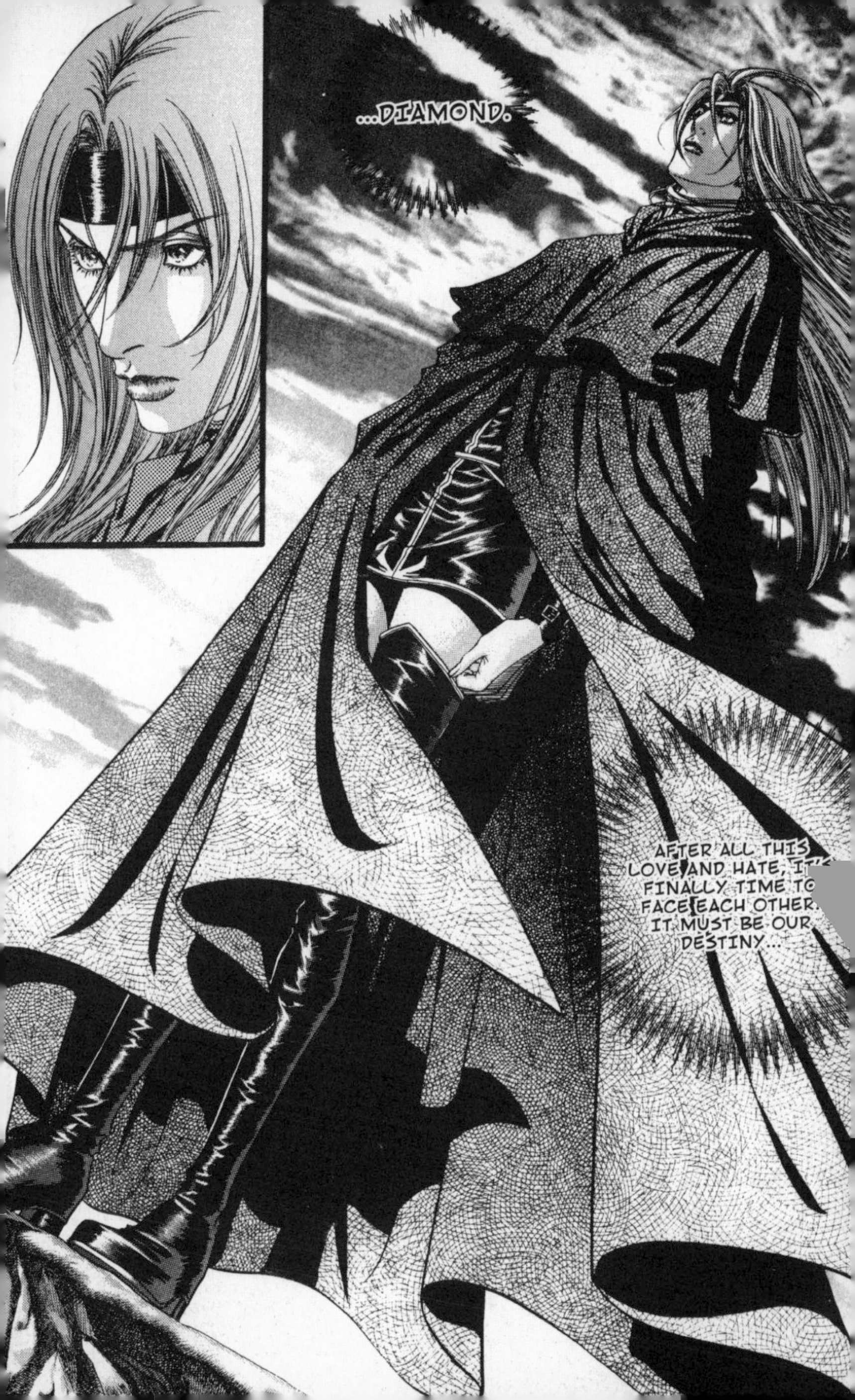
...DIAMOND.
AFTER ALL THIS LOVE AND HATE, IT FINALLY TIME TO FACE EACH OTHER. IT MUST BE OUR DESTINY...

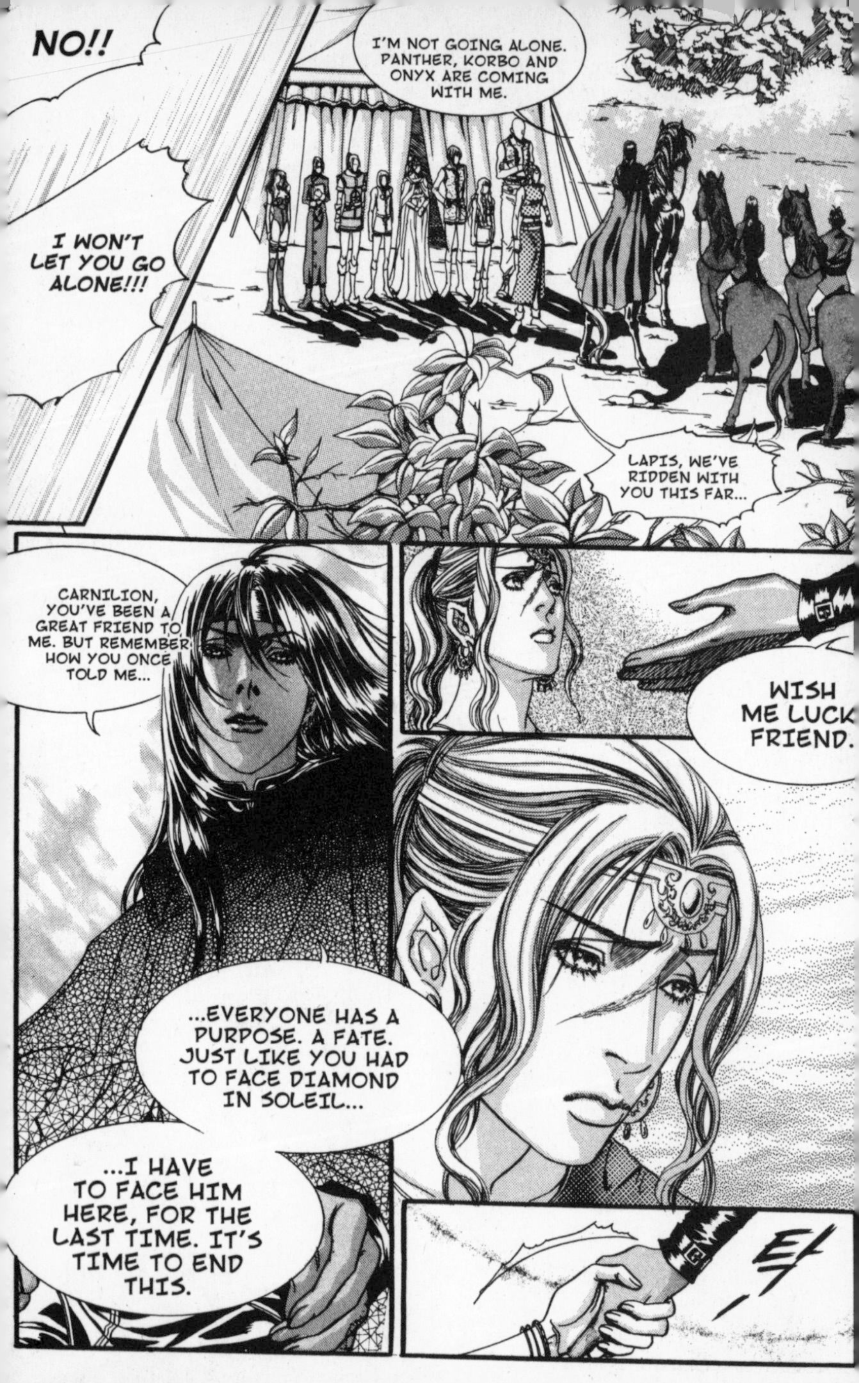
NO!!
I'M NOT GOING ALONE. PANTHER, KORBO AND ONYX ARE COMING WITH ME.
I WON'T LET YOU GO ALONE!!!
LAPIS, WE'VE RIDDEN WITH YOU THIS FAR...
CARNILION, YOU'VE BEEN A GREAT FRIEND TO ME. BUT REMEMBER HOW YOU ONCE TOLD ME...
WISH ME LUCK FRIEND.
...EVERYONE HAS A PURPOSE. A FATE. JUST LIKE YOU HAD TO FACE DIAMOND IN SOLEIL...
...I HAVE TO FACE HIM HERE, FOR THE LAST TIME. IT'S TIME TO END THIS.

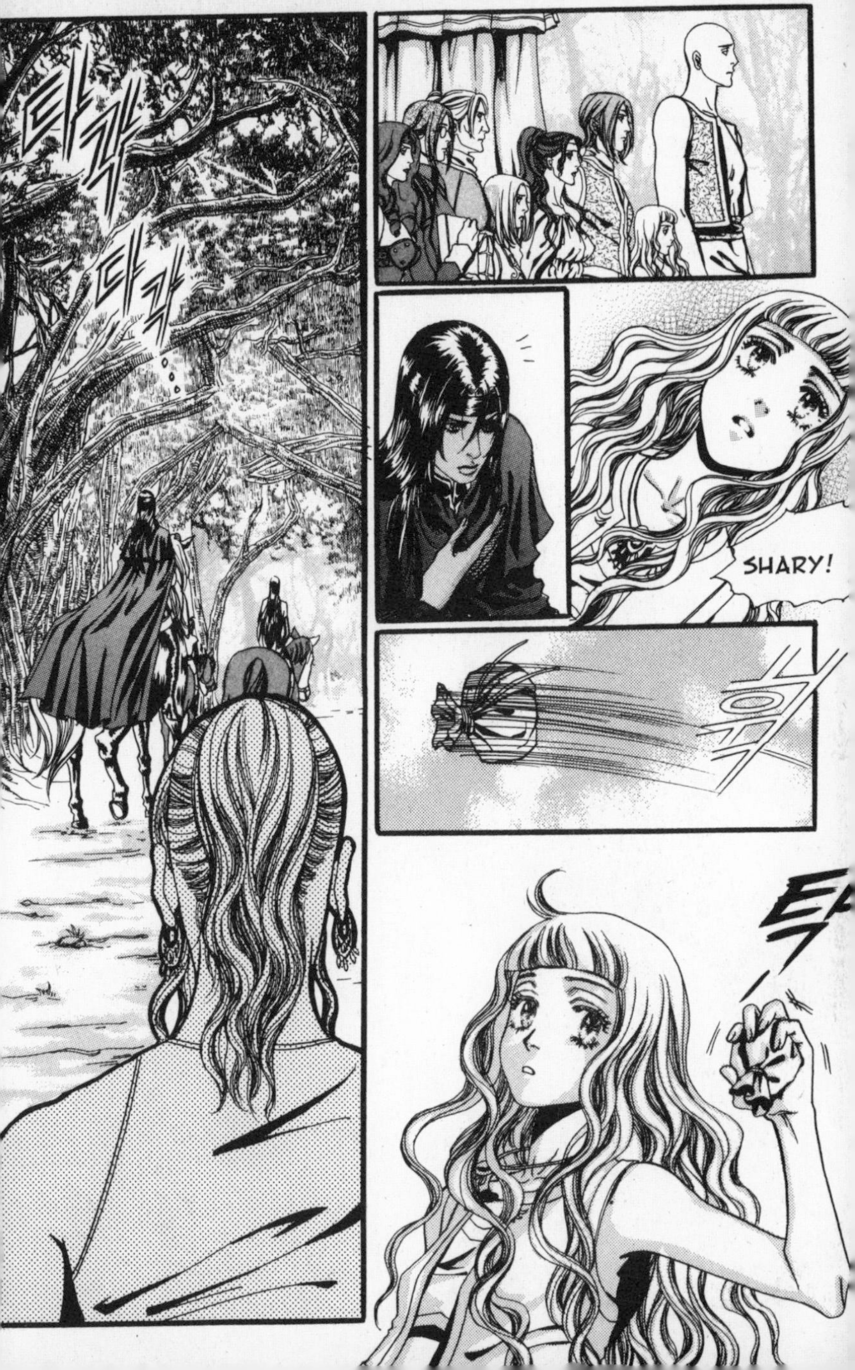
SHARY!

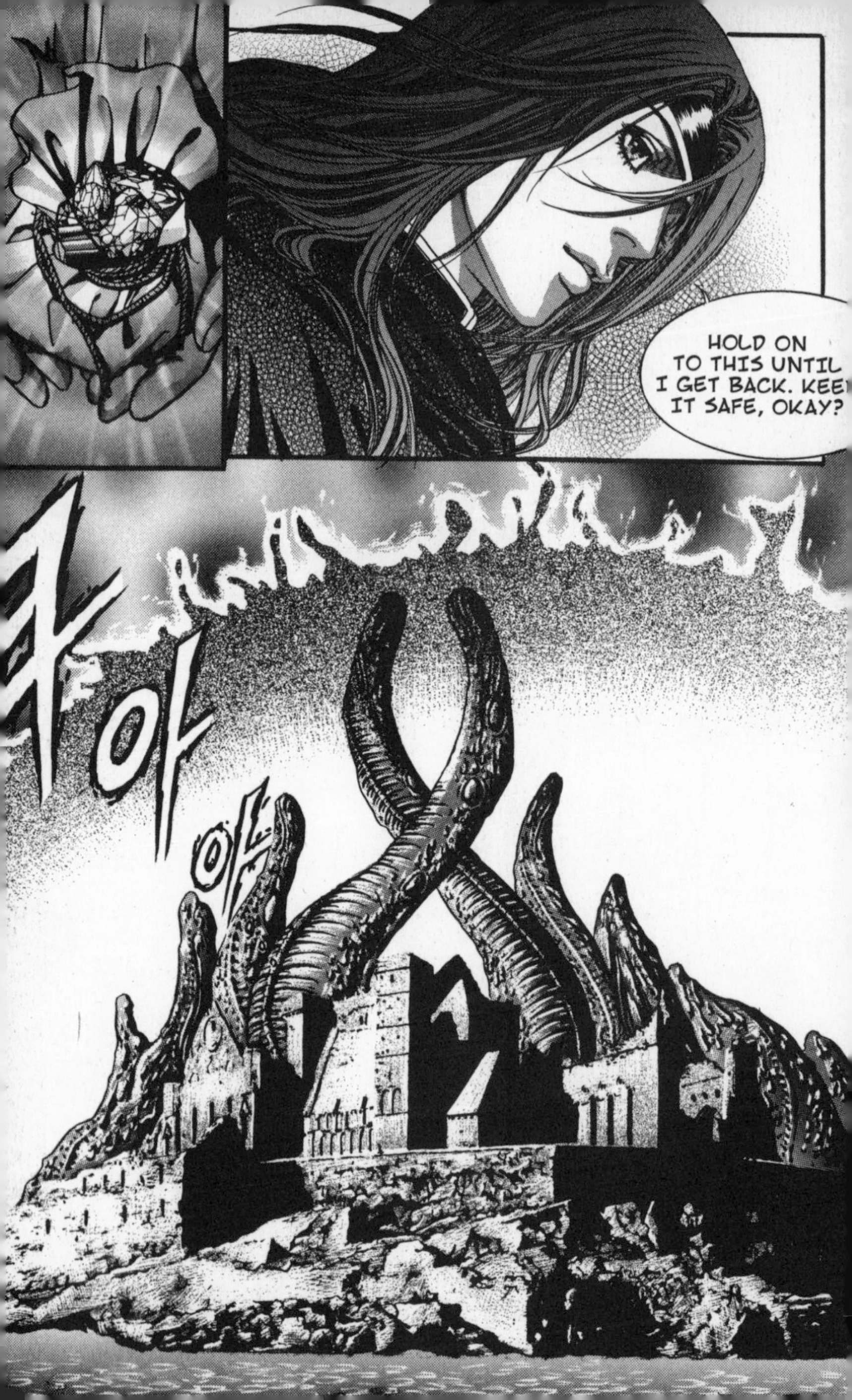
HOLD ON TO THIS UNTIL I GET BACK. KEE IT SAFE, OKAY?

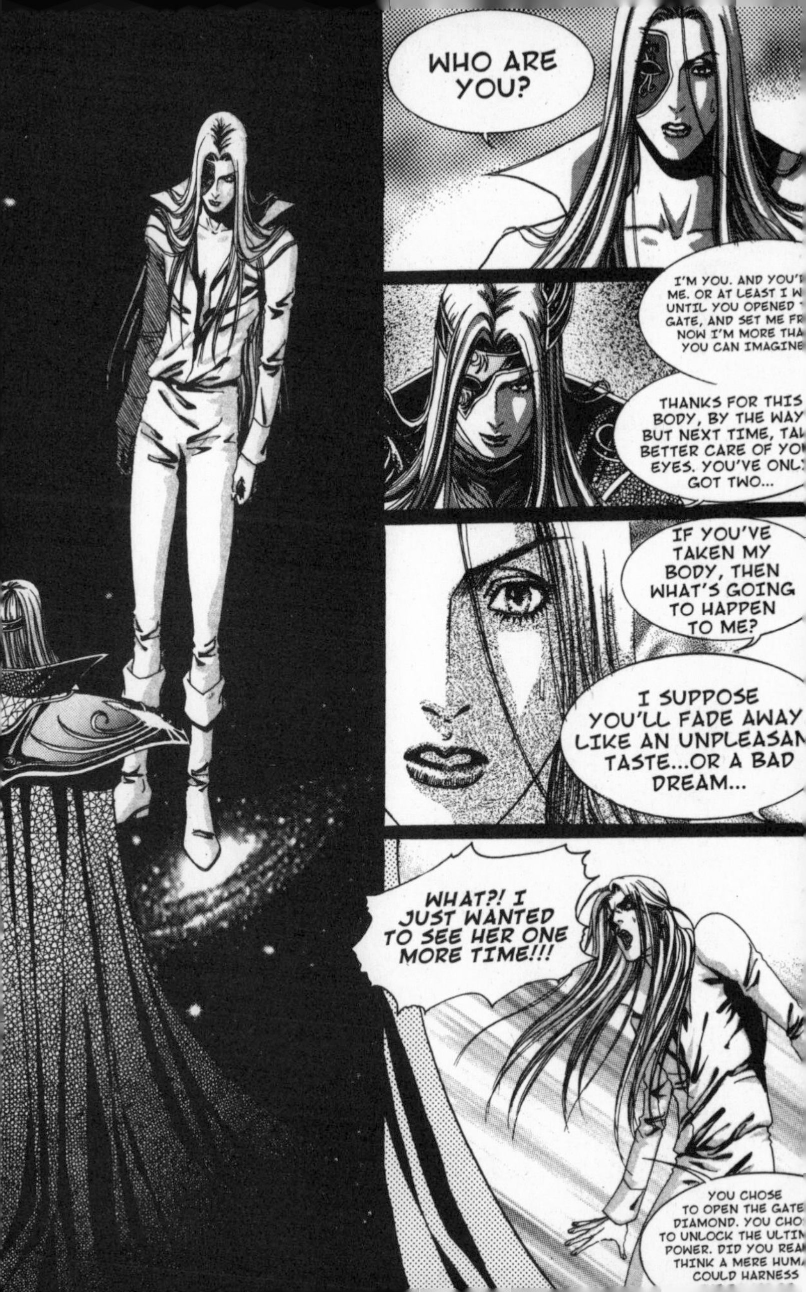
WHO ARE YOU?
I'M YOU. AND YOU'R ME. OR AT LEAST I W UNTIL YOU OPENED T GATE, AND SET ME FR NOW I'M MORE THA YOU CAN IMAGINE
THANKS FOR THIS BODY, BY THE WAY BUT NEXT TIME, TAK BETTER CARE OF YO EYES. YOU'VE ONL GOT TWO...
IF YOU'VE TAKEN MY BODY, THEN WHAT'S GOING TO HAPPEN TO ME?
I SUPPOSE YOU'LL FADE AWAY LIKE AN UNPLEASAN TASTE...OR A BAD DREAM...
WHAT?! I JUST WANTED TO SEE HER ONE MORE TIME!!!
YOU CHOSE TO OPEN THE GATE DIAMOND. YOU CHOS TO UNLOCK THE ULTIM POWER. DID YOU REA THINK A MERE HUMA COULD HARNESS

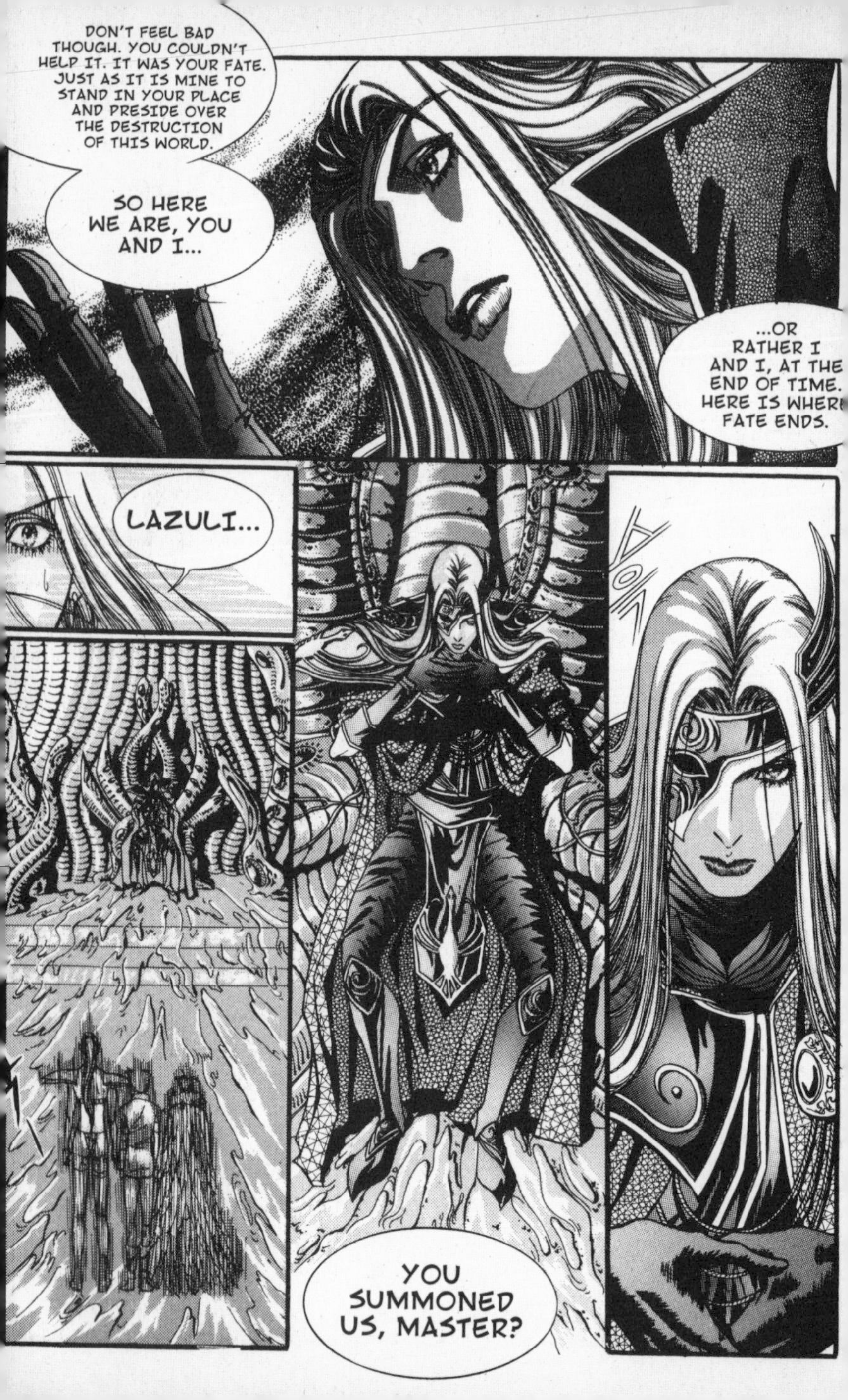
DON'T FEEL BAD THOUGH. YOU COULDN'T HELP IT. IT WAS YOUR FATE. JUST AS IT IS MINE TO STAND IN YOUR PLACE AND PRESIDE OVER THE DESTRUCTION OF THIS WORLD.
SO HERE WE ARE, YOU AND I...
...OR RATHER I AND I, AT THE END OF TIME. HERE IS WHERE FATE ENDS.
LAZULI...
VOOA
YOU SUMMONED US, MASTER?

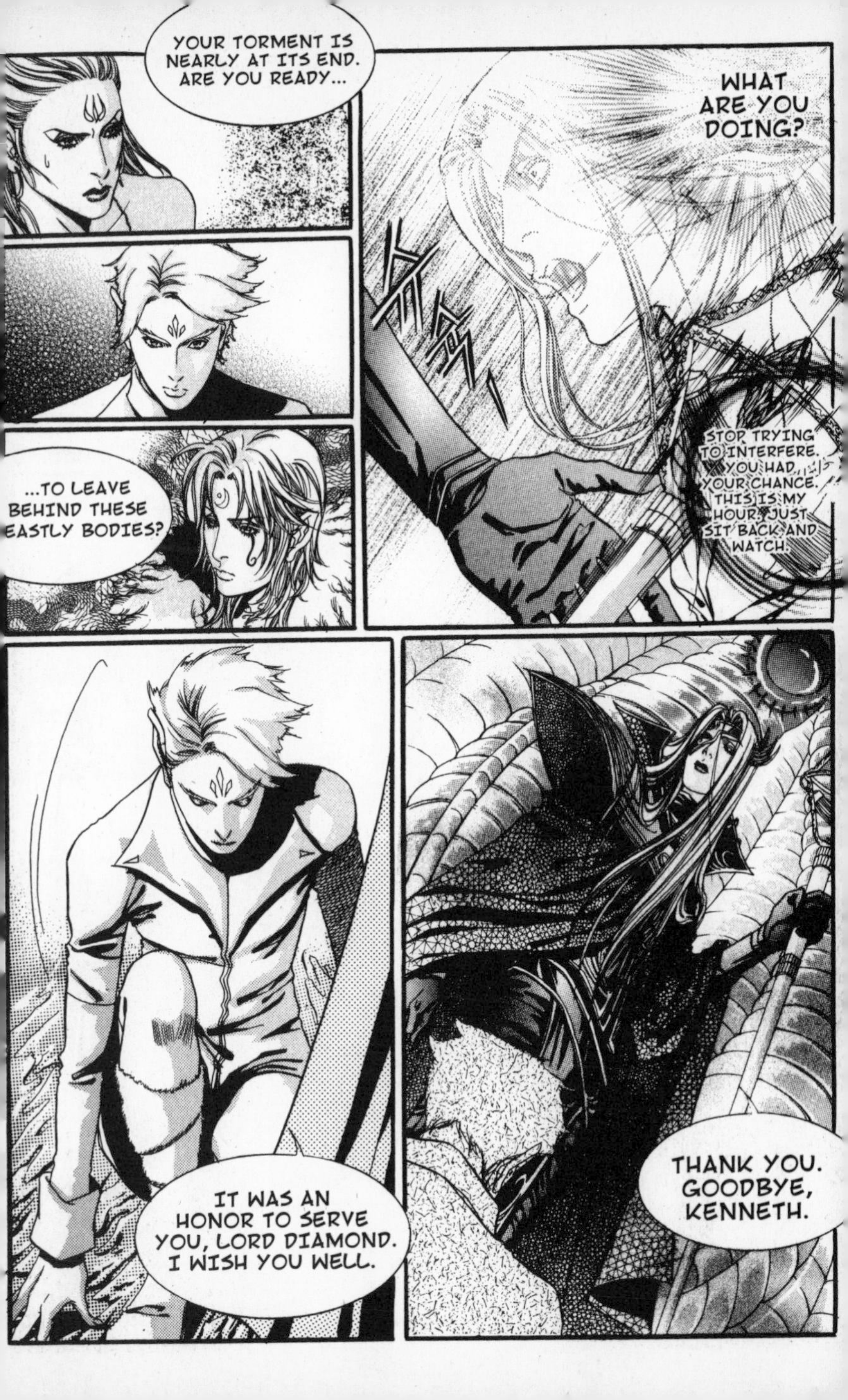
YOUR TORMENT IS NEARLY AT ITS END. ARE YOU READY...
WHAT ARE YOU DOING?
...TO LEAVE BEHIND THESE EASTLY BODIES?
STOP TRYING TO INTERFERE. YOU HAD YOUR CHANCE. THIS IS MY HOUR. JUST SIT BACK AND WATCH.
IT WAS AN HONOR TO SERVE YOU, LORD DIAMOND. I WISH YOU WELL.
THANK YOU. GOODBYE, KENNETH.

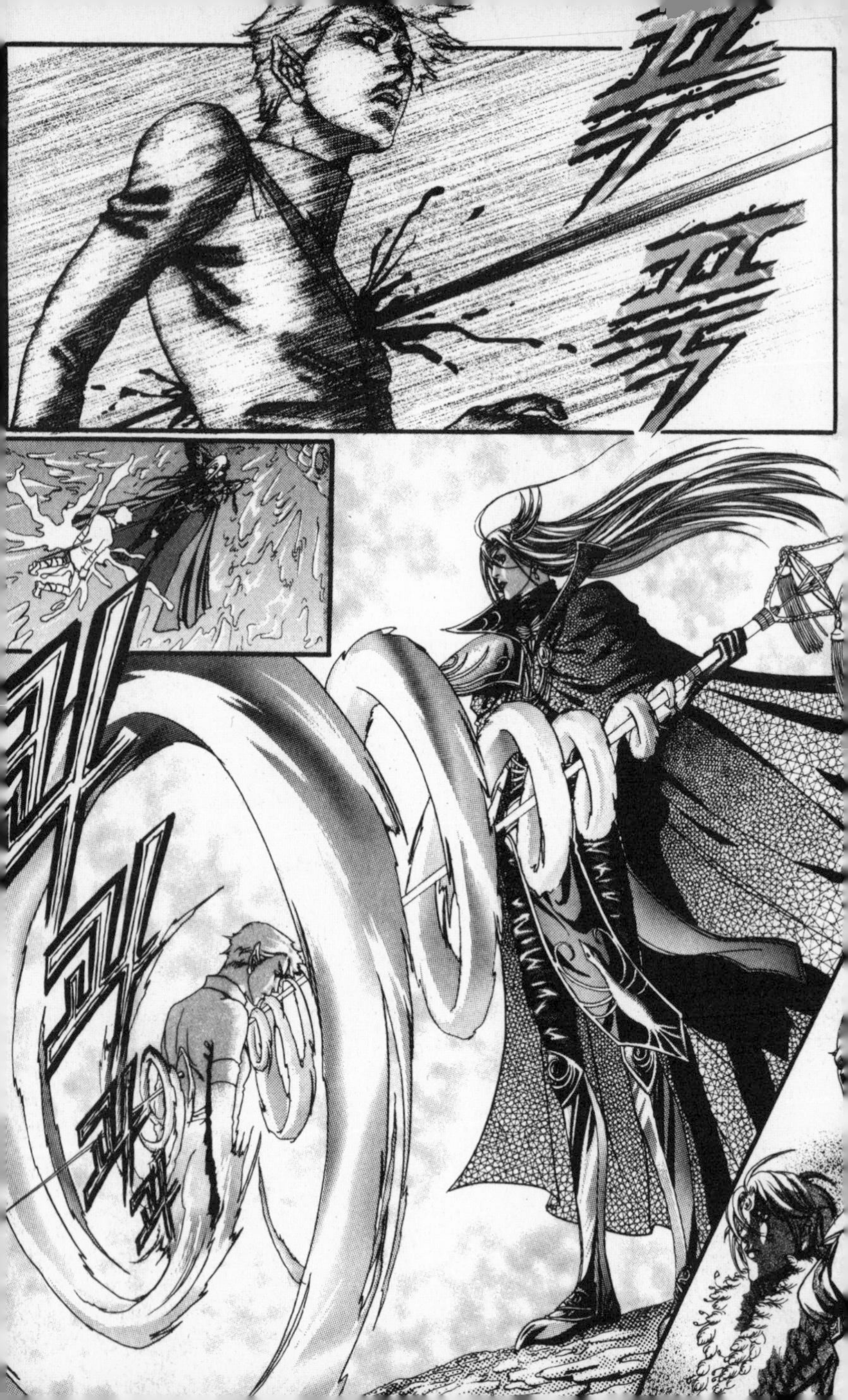

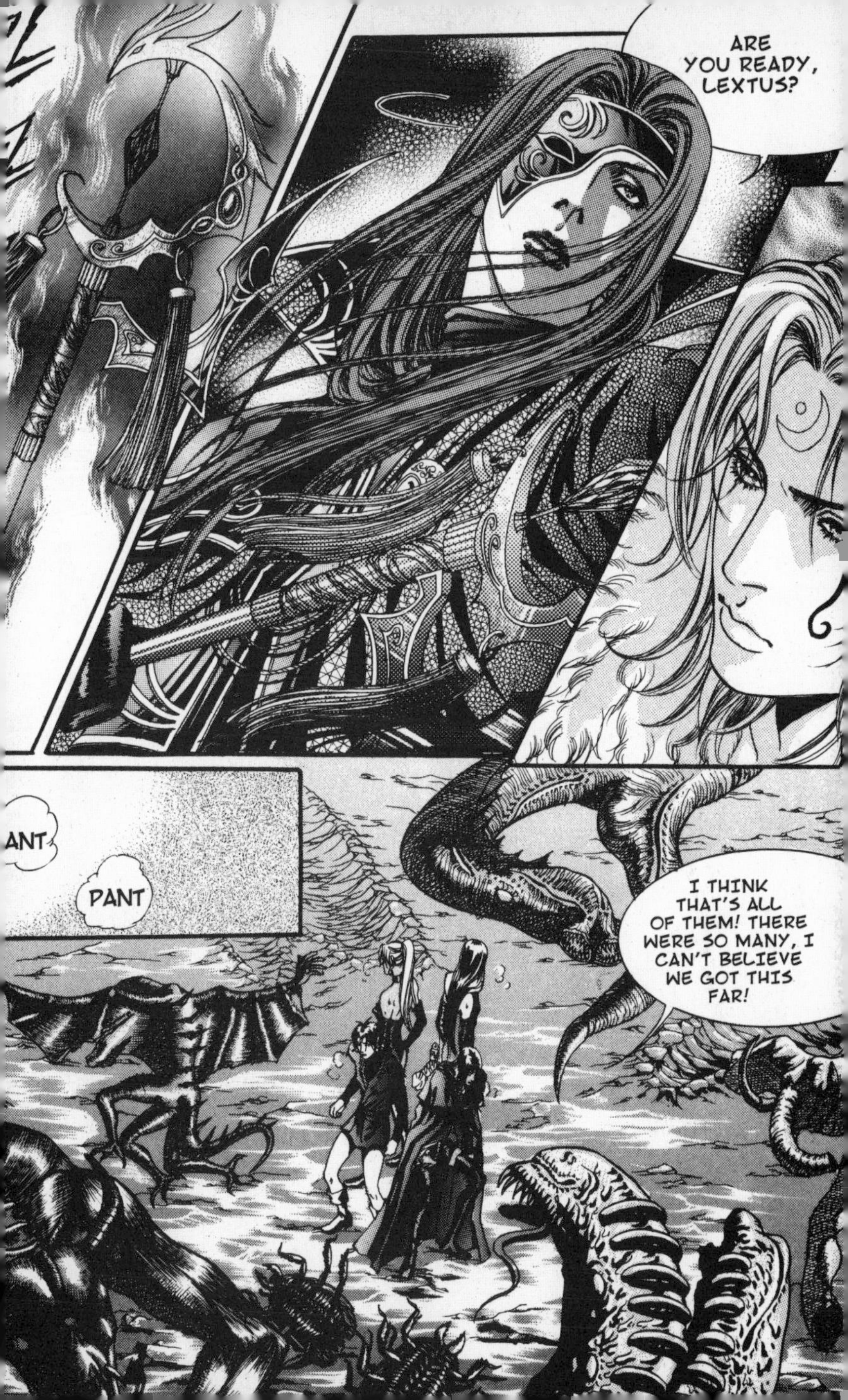
ARE YOU READY, LEXTUS?
I THINK THAT'S ALL OF THEM! THERE WERE SO MANY, I CAN'T BELIEVE WE GOT THIS FAR!
ANT
PANT

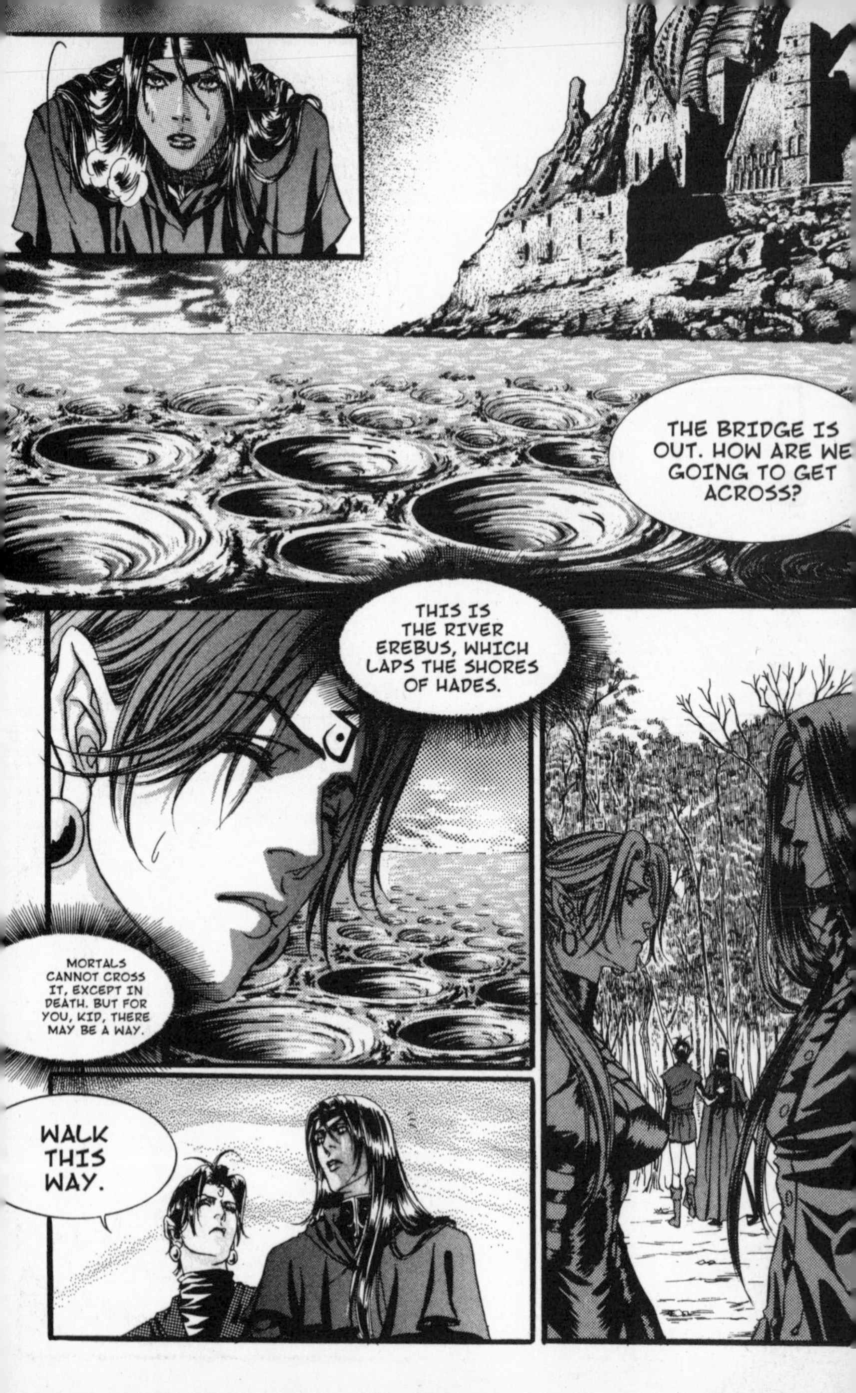
THE BRIDGE IS OUT. HOW ARE WE GOING TO GET ACROSS?
THIS IS THE RIVER EREBUS, WHICH LAPS THE SHORES OF HADES.
MORTALS CANNOT CROSS IT, EXCEPT IN DEATH. BUT FOR YOU, KID, THERE MAY BE A WAY.
WALK THIS WAY.

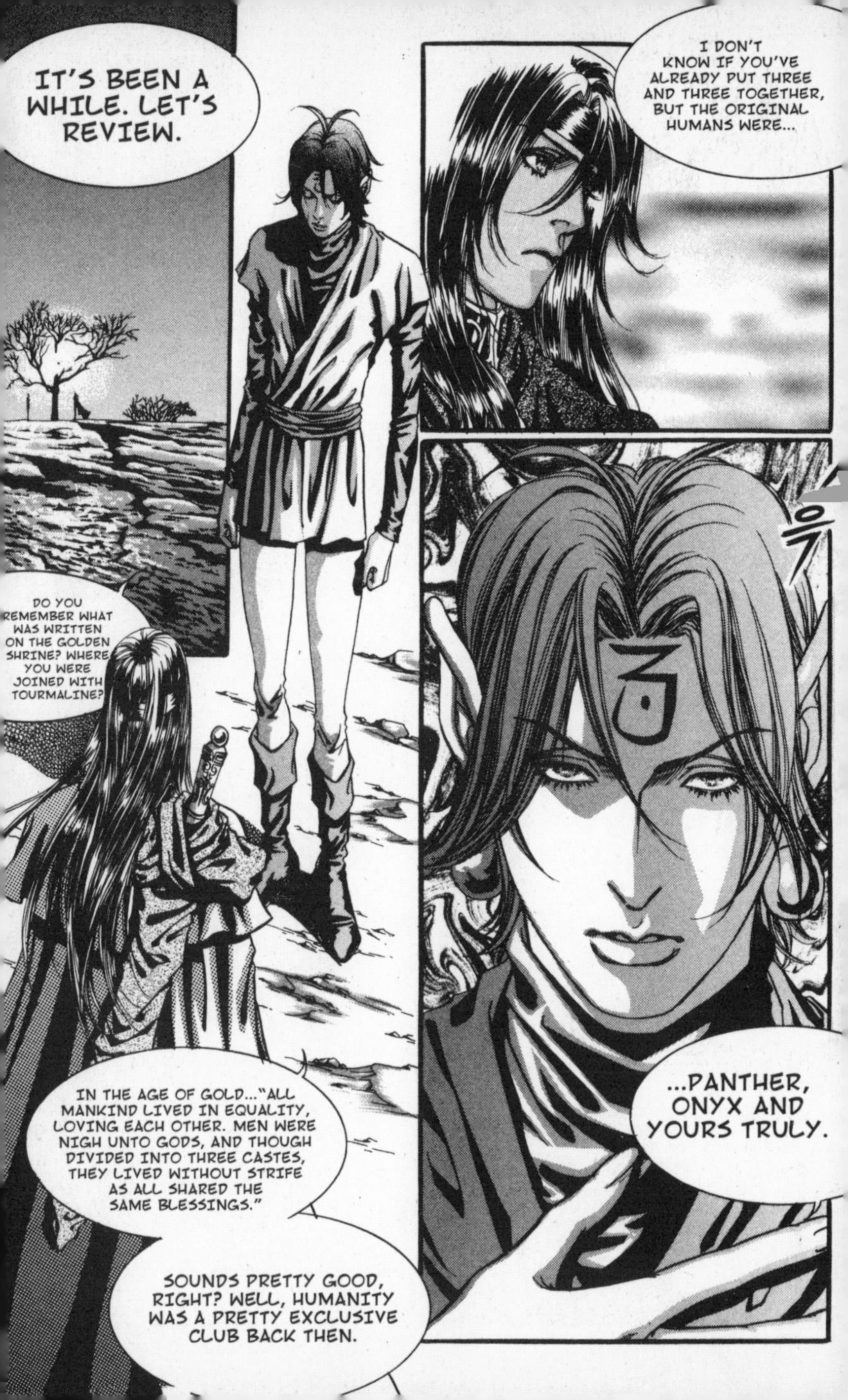
IT'S BEEN A WHILE. LET'S REVIEW.
DO YOU REMEMBER WHAT WAS WRITTEN ON THE GOLDEN SHRINE? WHERE YOU WERE JOINED WITH TOURMALINE?
IN THE AGE OF GOLD..."ALL MANKIND LIVED IN EQUALITY, LOVING EACH OTHER. MEN WERE NIGH UNTO GODS, AND THOUGH DIVIDED INTO THREE CASTES, THEY LIVED WITHOUT STRIFE AS ALL SHARED THE SAME BLESSINGS."
SOUNDS PRETTY GOOD, RIGHT? WELL, HUMANITY WAS A PRETTY EXCLUSIVE CLUB BACK THEN.
I DON'T KNOW IF YOU'VE ALREADY PUT THREE AND THREE TOGETHER, BUT THE ORIGINAL HUMANS WERE...
...PANTHER, ONYX AND YOURS TRULY.

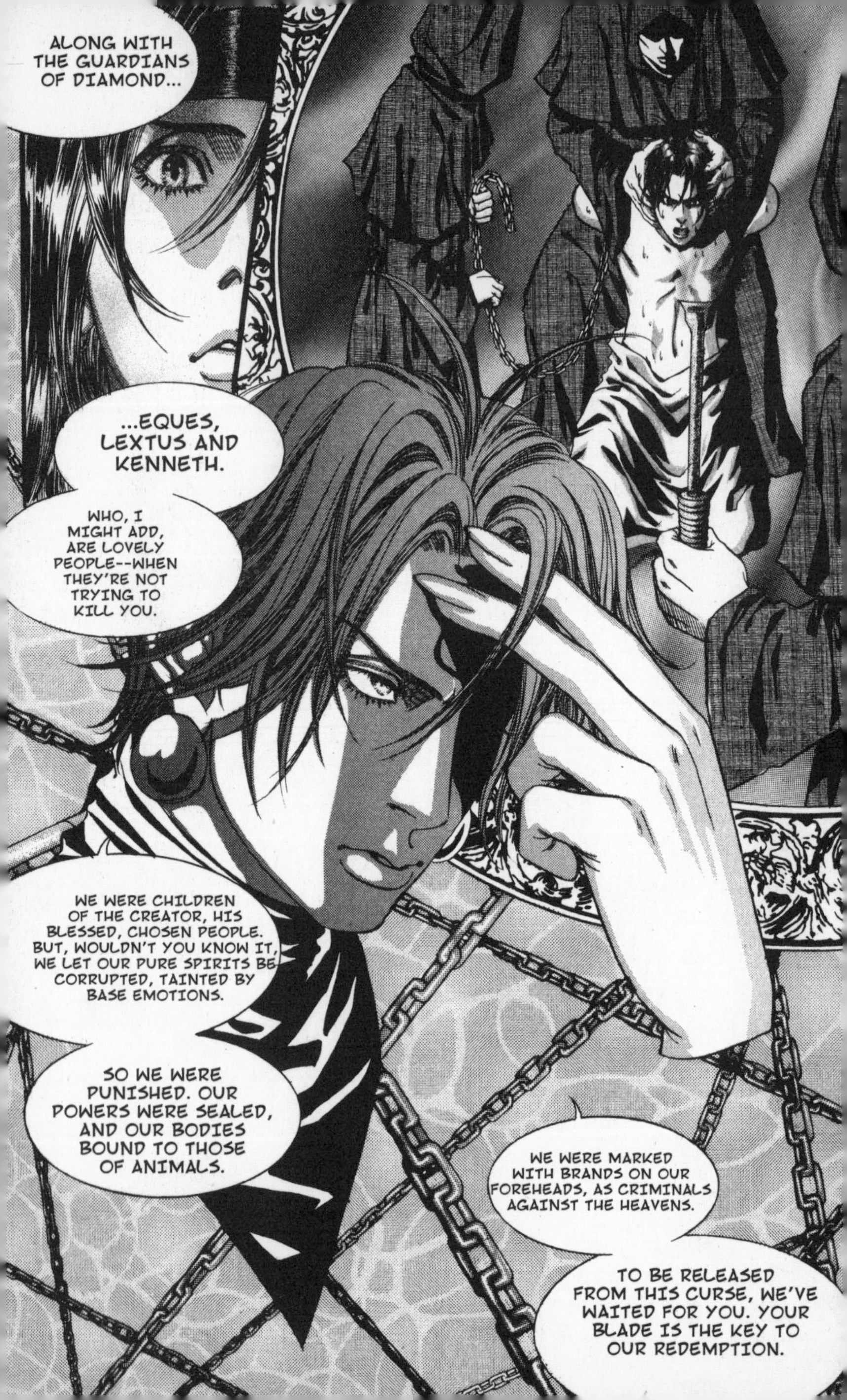
ALONG WITH THE GUARDIANS OF DIAMOND...
...EQUES, LEXTUS AND KENNETH.
WHO, I MIGHT ADD, ARE LOVELY PEOPLE--WHEN THEY'RE NOT TRYING TO KILL YOU.
WE WERE CHILDREN OF THE CREATOR, HIS BLESSED, CHOSEN PEOPLE. BUT, WOULDN'T YOU KNOW IT, WE LET OUR PURE SPIRITS BE CORRUPTED, TAINTED BY BASE EMOTIONS.
SO WE WERE PUNISHED. OUR POWERS WERE SEALED, AND OUR BODIES BOUND TO THOSE OF ANIMALS.
WE WERE MARKED WITH BRANDS ON OUR FOREHEADS, AS CRIMINALS AGAINST THE HEAVENS.
TO BE RELEASED FROM THIS CURSE, WE'VE WAITED FOR YOU. YOUR BLADE IS THE KEY TO OUR REDEMPTION.

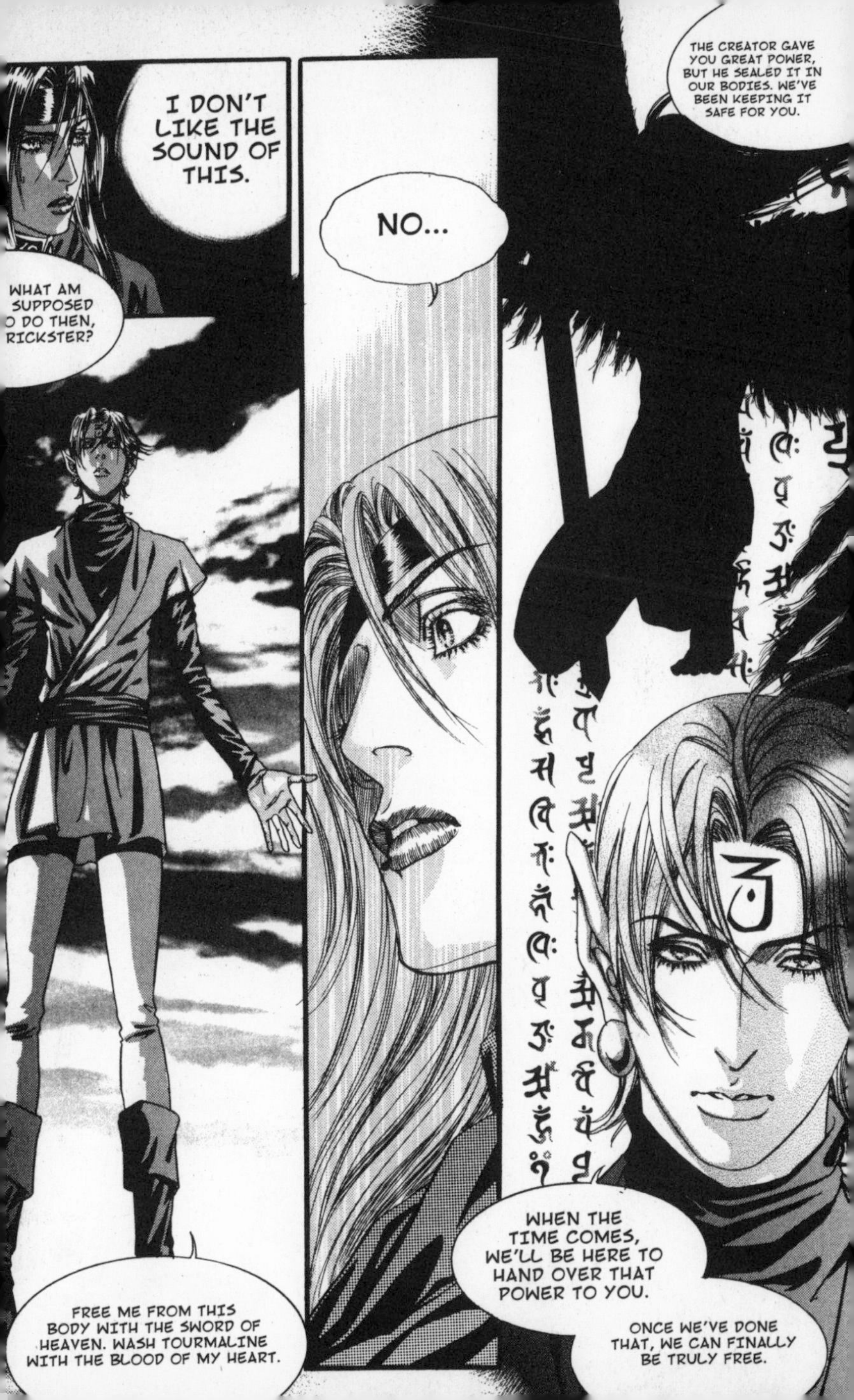
I DON'T LIKE THE SOUND OF THIS.
WHAT AM SUPPOSED O DO THEN, RICKSTER?
NO...
THE CREATOR GAVE YOU GREAT POWER, BUT HE SEALED IT IN OUR BODIES. WE'VE BEEN KEEPING IT SAFE FOR YOU.
FREE ME FROM THIS BODY WITH THE SWORD OF HEAVEN. WASH TOURMALINE WITH THE BLOOD OF MY HEART.
WHEN THE TIME COMES, WE'LL BE HERE TO HAND OVER THAT POWER TO YOU.
ONCE WE'VE DONE THAT, WE CAN FINALLY BE TRULY FREE.

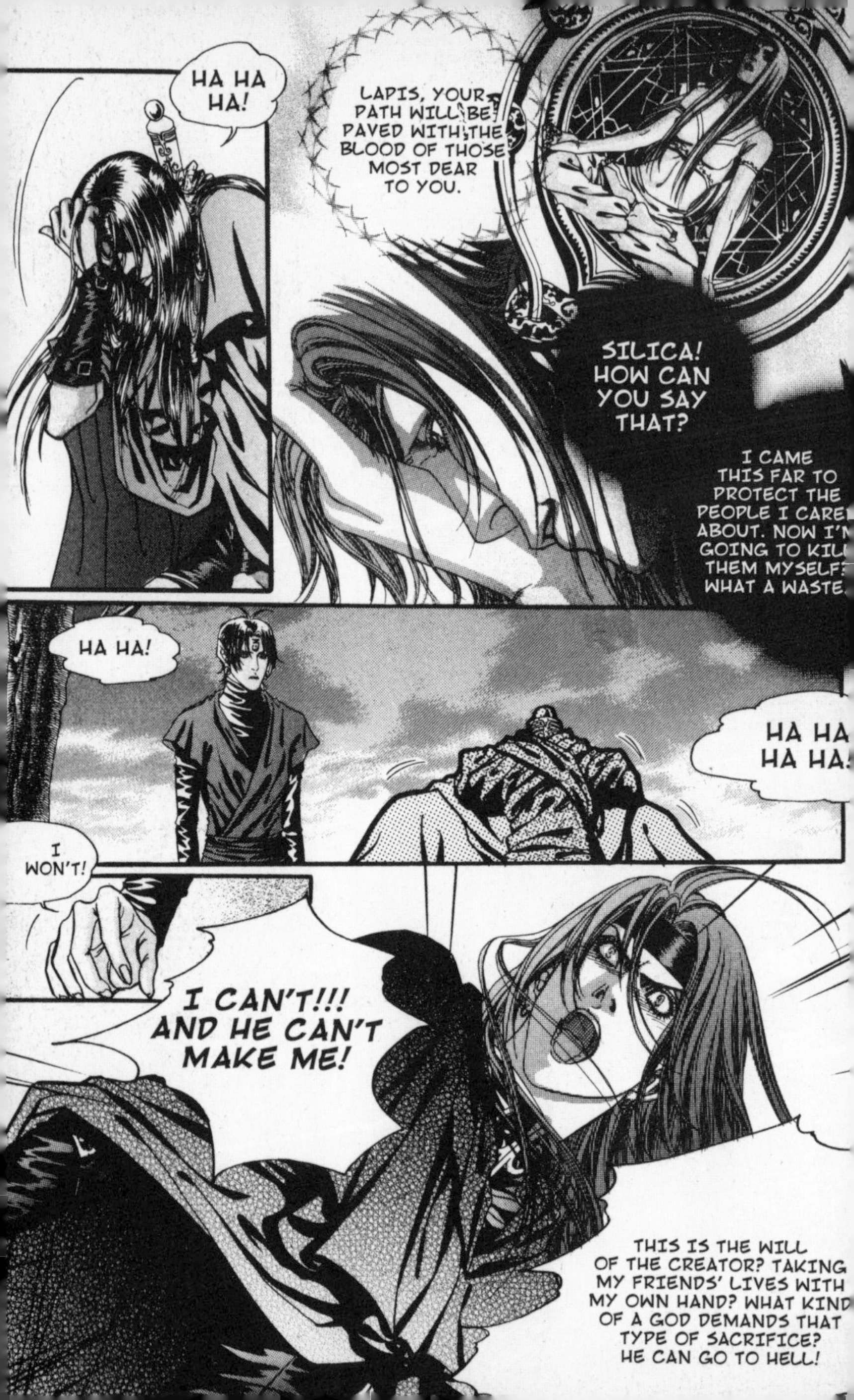
HA HA HA!
LAPIS, YOUR PATH WILL BE PAVED WITH THE BLOOD OF THOSE MOST DEAR TO YOU.
SILICA! HOW CAN YOU SAY THAT?
I CAME THIS FAR TO PROTECT THE PEOPLE I CARE ABOUT. NOW I'M GOING TO KILL THEM MYSELF? WHAT A WASTE.
HA HA!
HA HA HA HA!
I WON'T!
I CAN'T!!! AND HE CAN'T MAKE ME!
THIS IS THE WILL OF THE CREATOR? TAKING MY FRIENDS' LIVES WITH MY OWN HAND? WHAT KIND OF A GOD DEMANDS THAT TYPE OF SACRIFICE? HE CAN GO TO HELL!

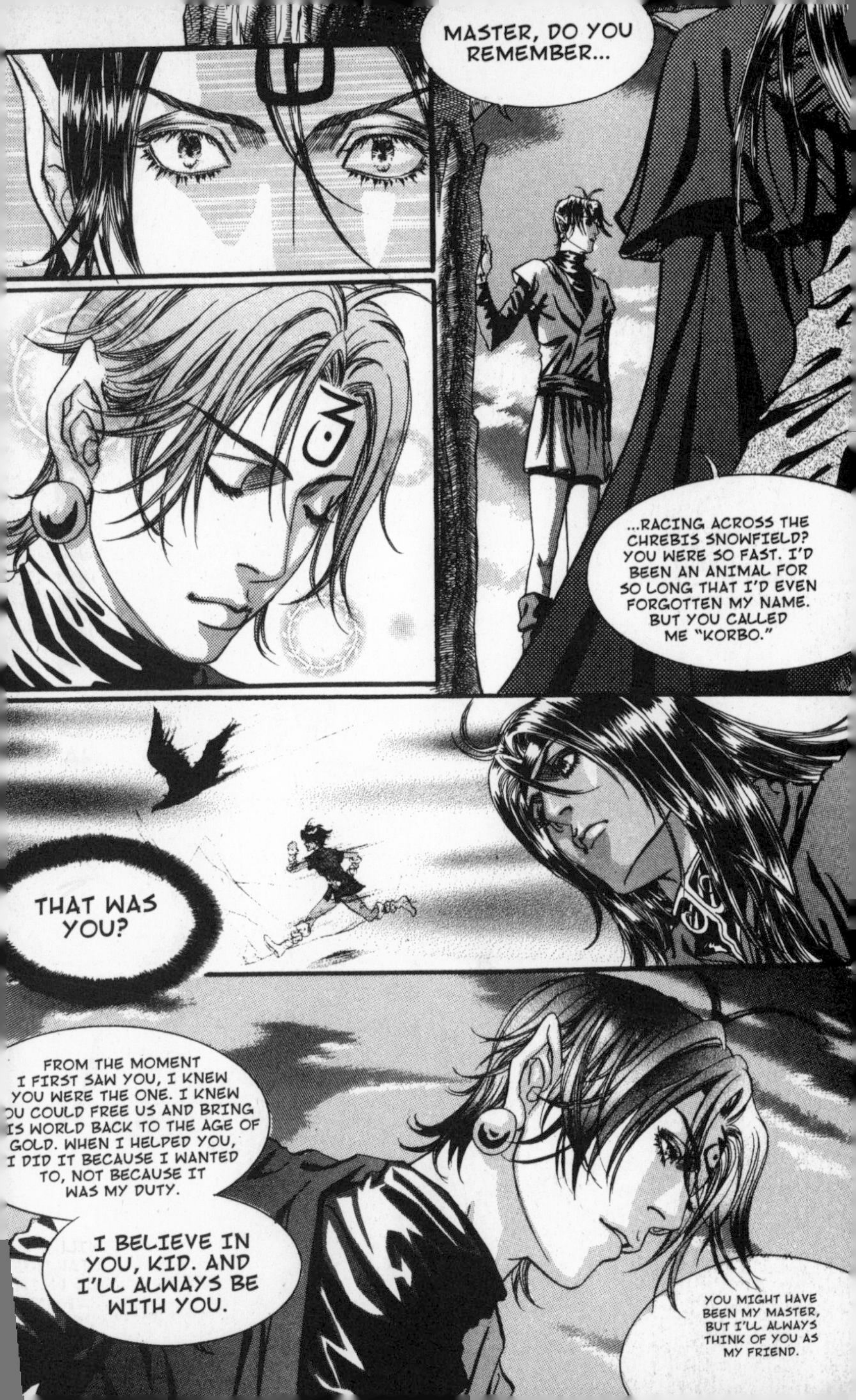
MASTER, DO YOU REMEMBER...
...RACING ACROSS THE CHREBIS SNOWFIELD? YOU WERE SO FAST. I'D BEEN AN ANIMAL FOR SO LONG THAT I'D EVEN FORGOTTEN MY NAME. BUT YOU CALLED ME "KORBO."
THAT WAS YOU?
FROM THE MOMENT I FIRST SAW YOU, I KNEW YOU WERE THE ONE. I KNEW OU COULD FREE US AND BRING IS WORLD BACK TO THE AGE OF GOLD. WHEN I HELPED YOU, I DID IT BECAUSE I WANTED TO, NOT BECAUSE IT WAS MY DUTY.
YOU MIGHT HAVE BEEN MY MASTER, BUT I'LL ALWAYS THINK OF YOU AS MY FRIEND.
I BELIEVE IN YOU, KID. AND I'LL ALWAYS BE WITH YOU.

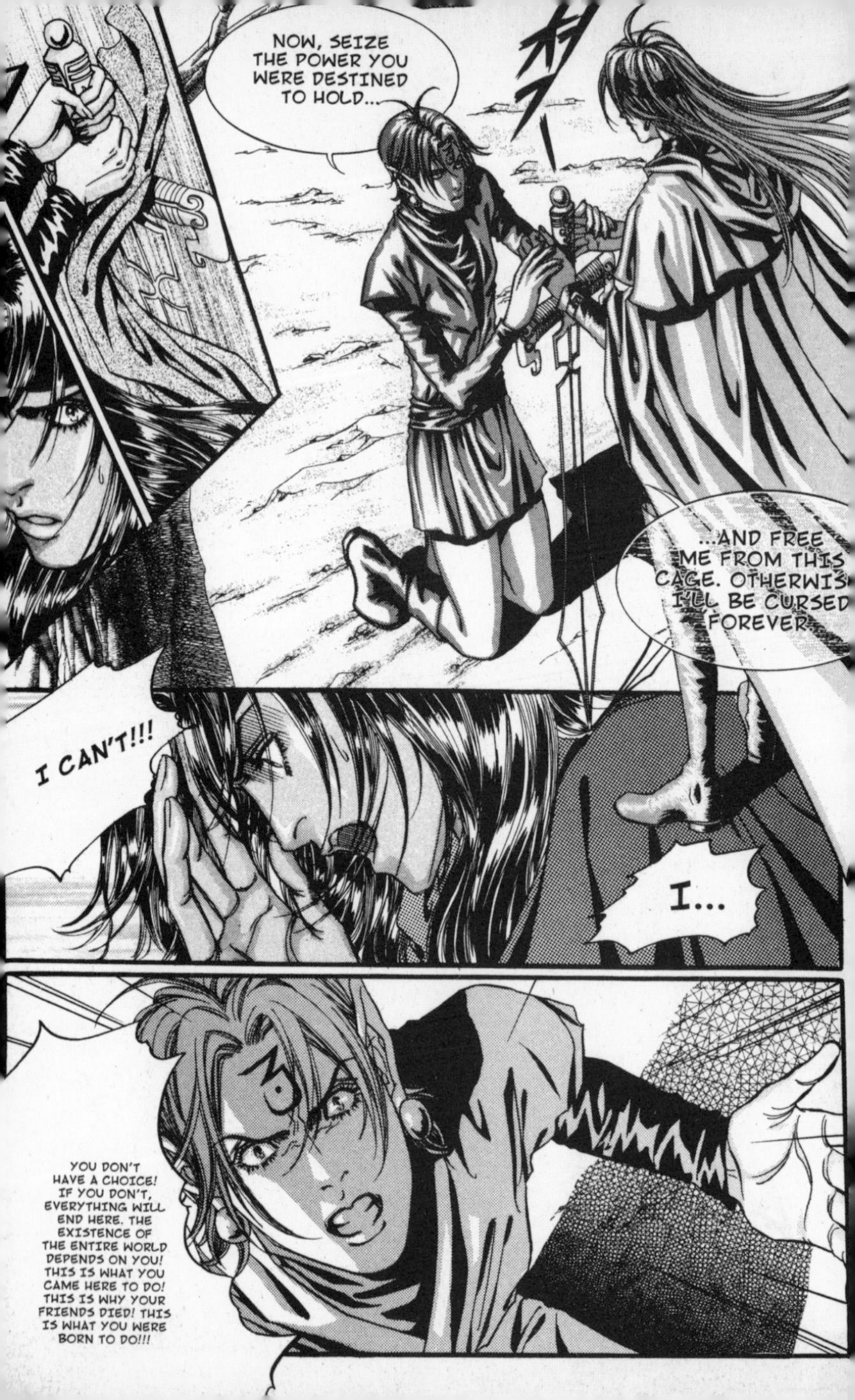

NOW, SEIZE THE POWER YOU WERE DESTINED TO HOLD...
...AND FREE ME FROM THIS CAGE. OTHERWIS I'LL BE CURSED FOREVER
I CAN'T!!!
I...
YOU DON'T HAVE A CHOICE! IF YOU DON'T, EVERYTHING WILL END HERE. THE EXISTENCE OF THE ENTIRE WORLD DEPENDS ON YOU! THIS IS WHAT YOU CAME HERE TO DO! THIS IS WHY YOUR FRIENDS DIED! THIS IS WHAT YOU WERE BORN TO DO!!!

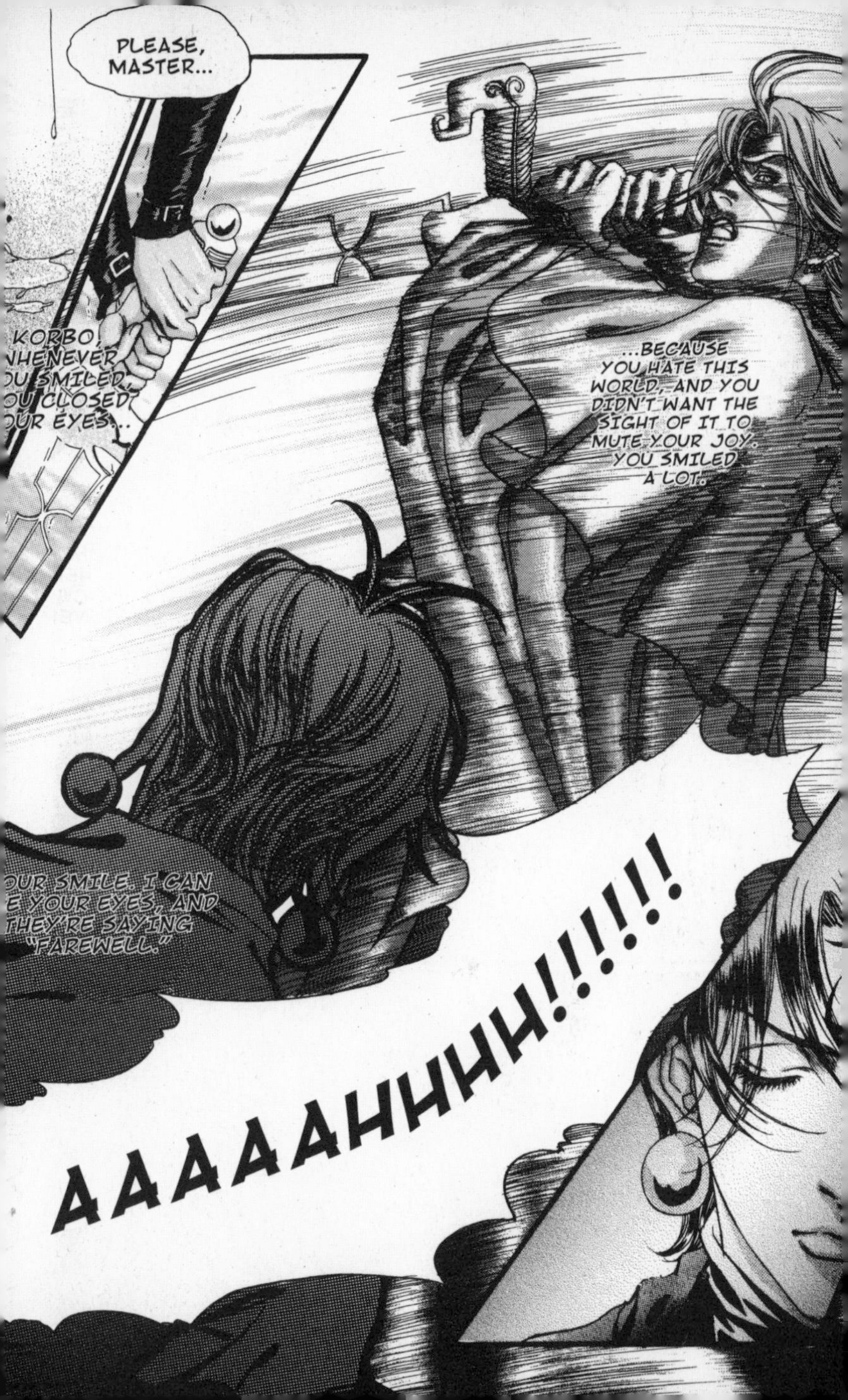
PLEASE, MASTER...
KORBO, WHENEVER OU SMILED, OU CLOSED OUR EYES...
...BECAUSE YOU HATE THIS WORLD, AND YOU DIDN'T WANT THE SIGHT OF IT TO MUTE YOUR JOY. YOU SMILED A LOT.
OUR SMILE. I CAN E YOUR EYES, AND HEY'RE SAYING "FAREWELL."
AAAAAHHHH!!!!!!

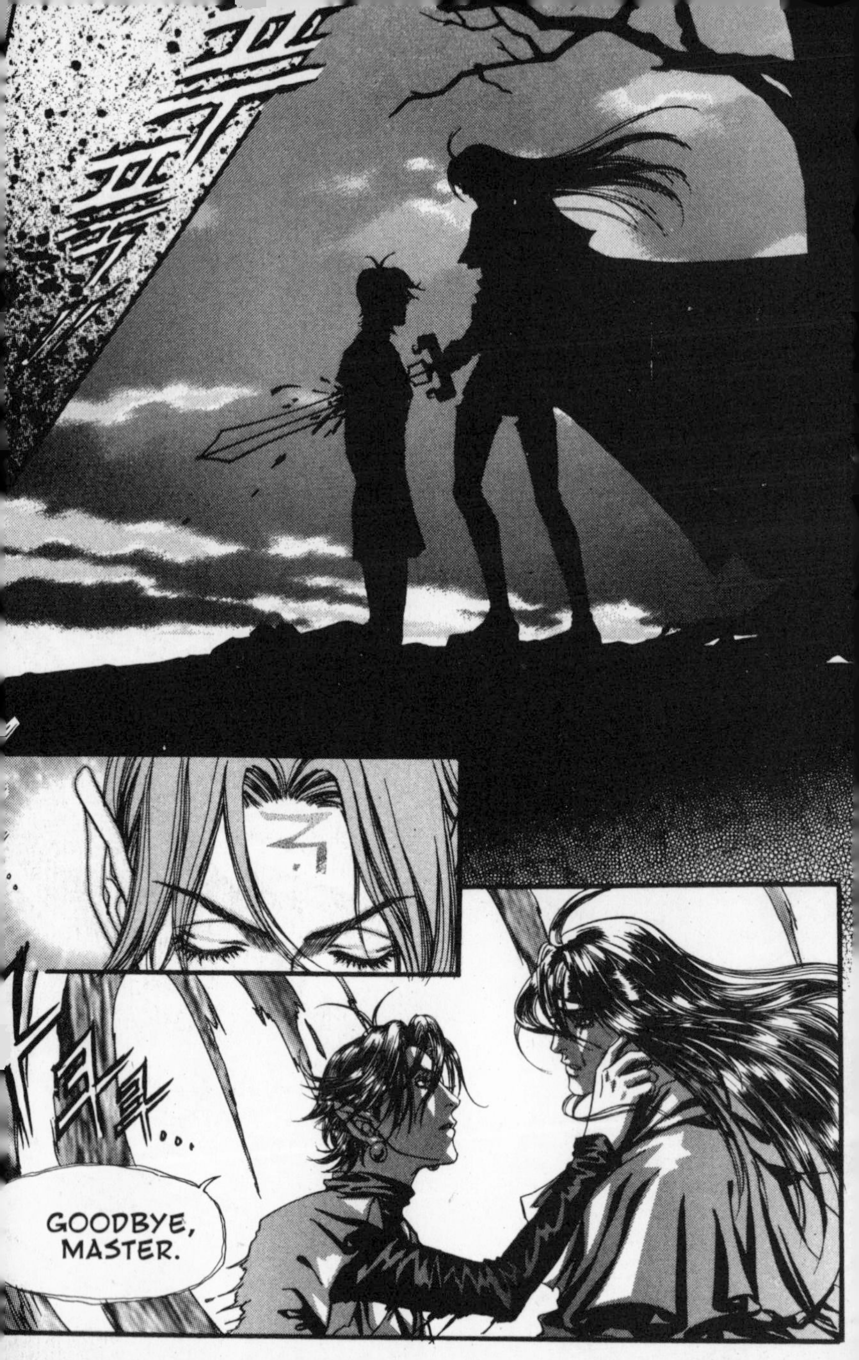
GOODBYE, MASTER.

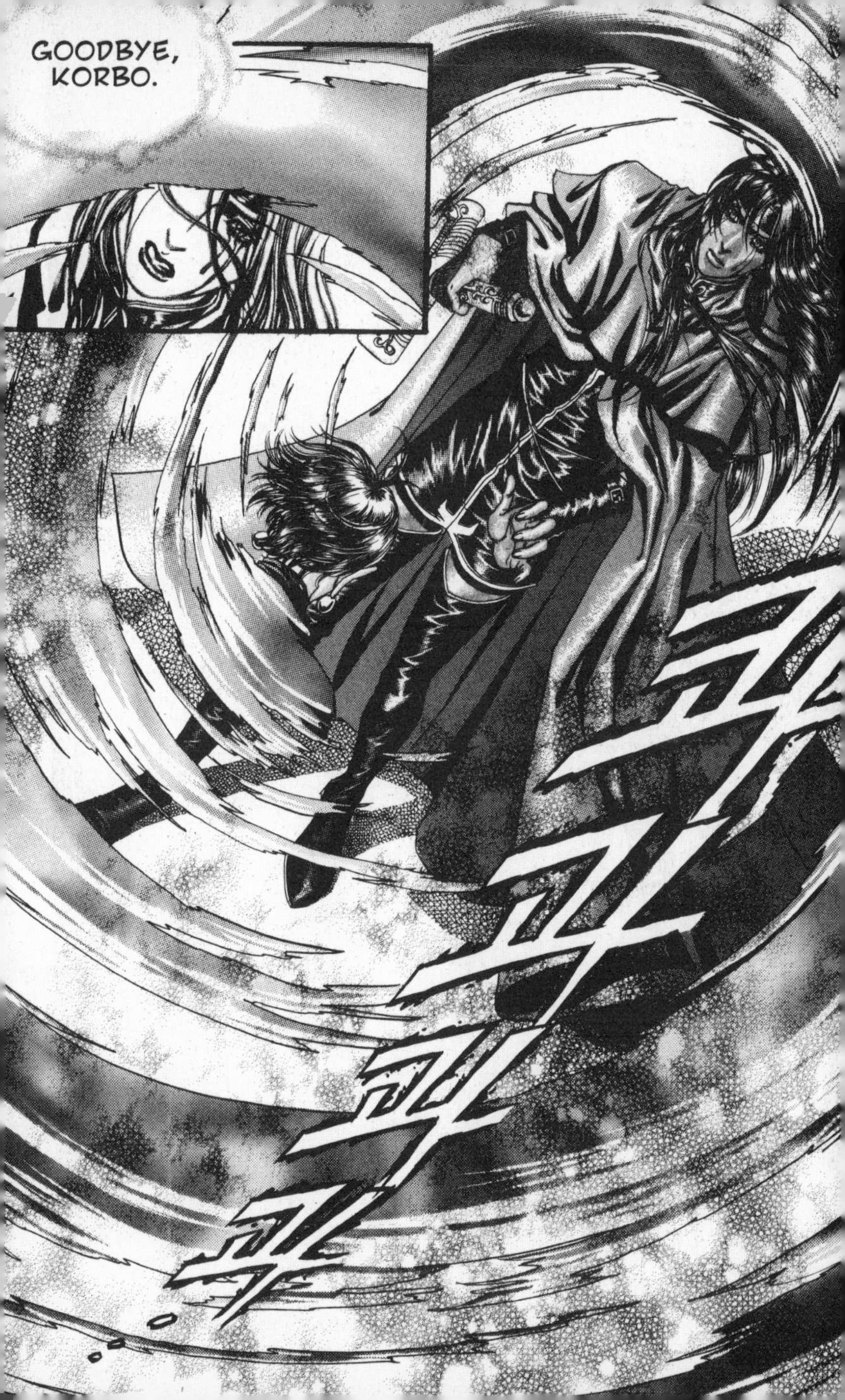
GOODBYE, KORBO.

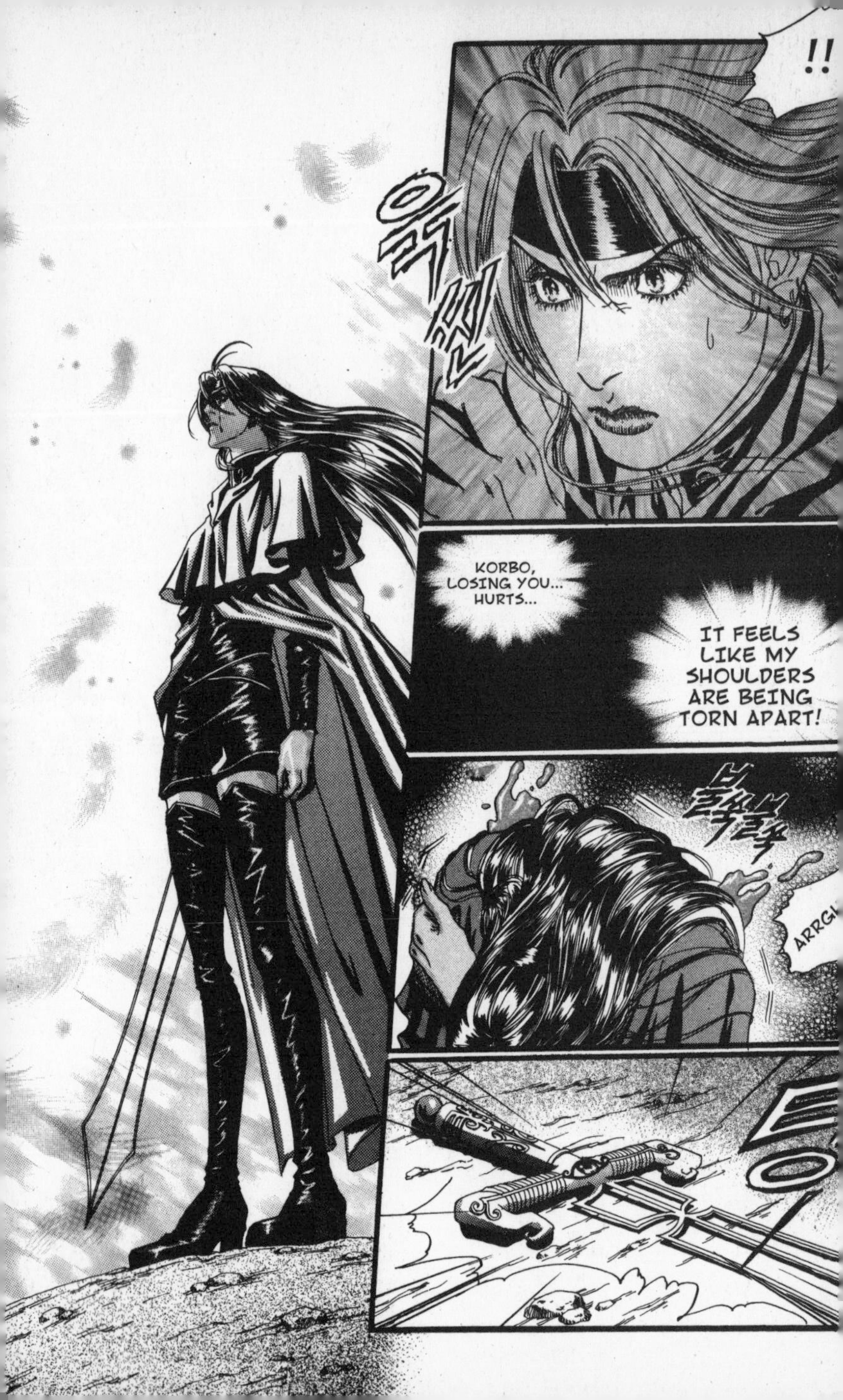
!!
KORBO, LOSING YOU... HURTS...
IT FEELS LIKE MY SHOULDERS ARE BEING TORN APART!

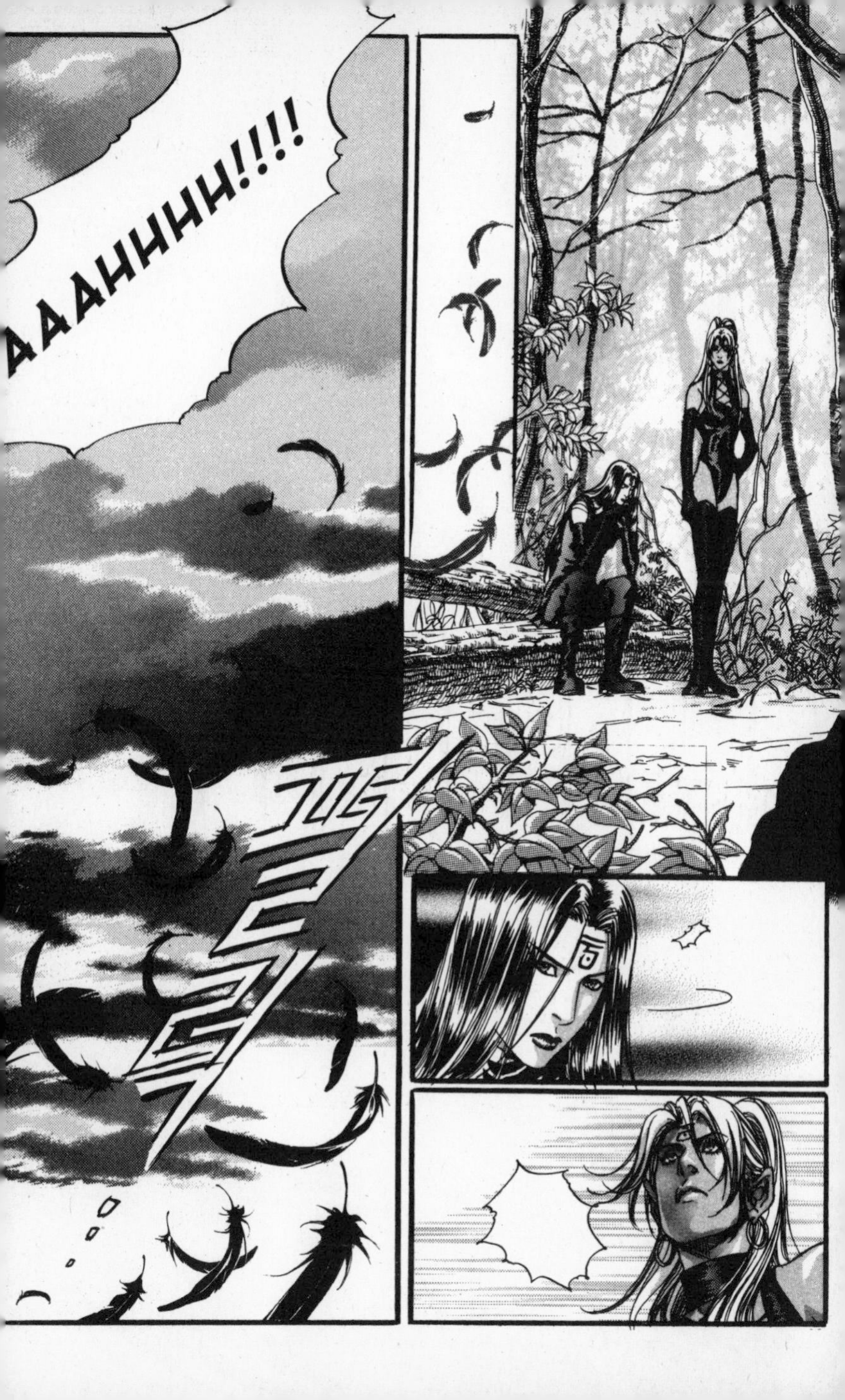
AAAHHHH!!!!

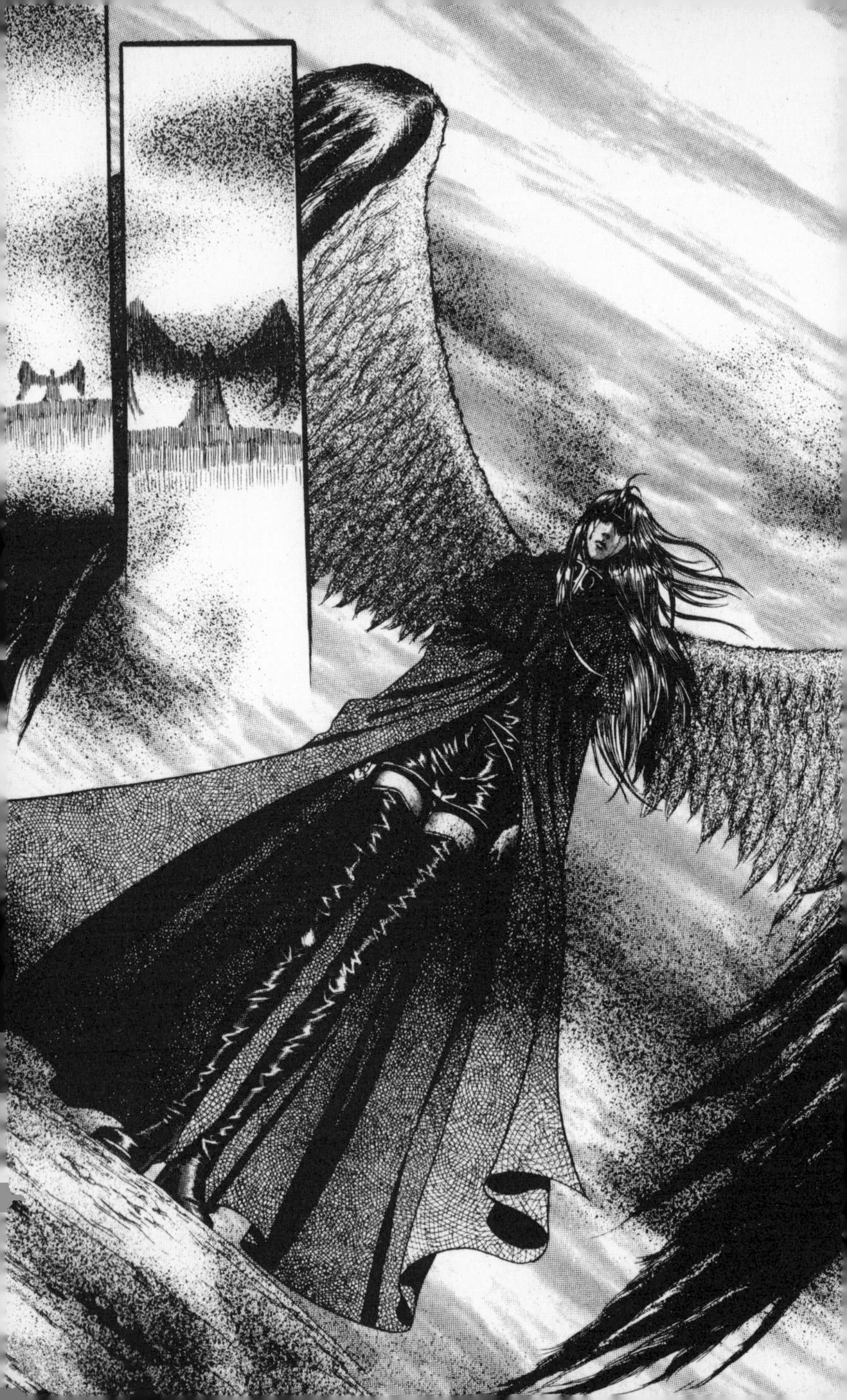

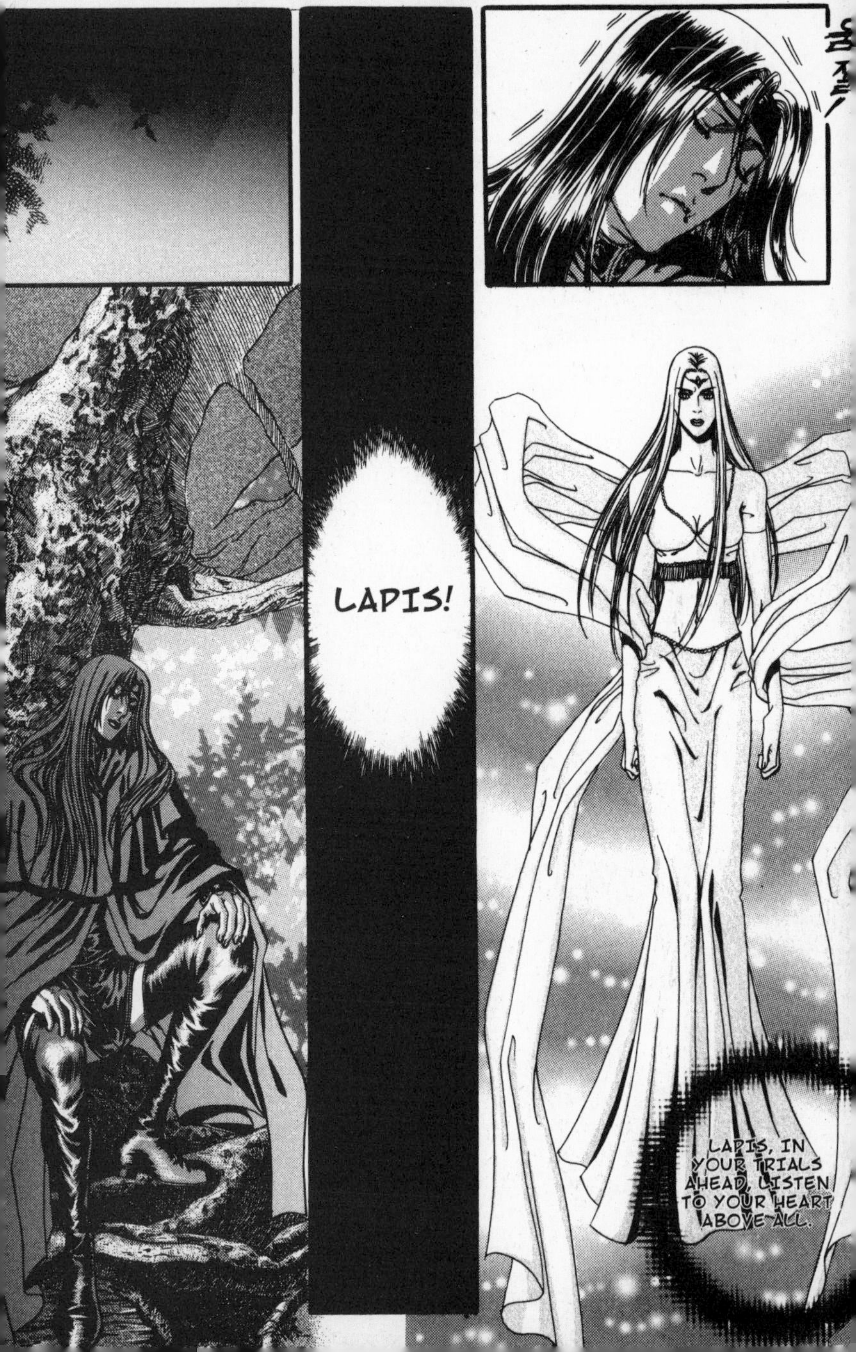
LAPIS!
LAPIS, IN YOUR TRIALS AHEAD, LISTEN TO YOUR HEART ABOVE ALL.

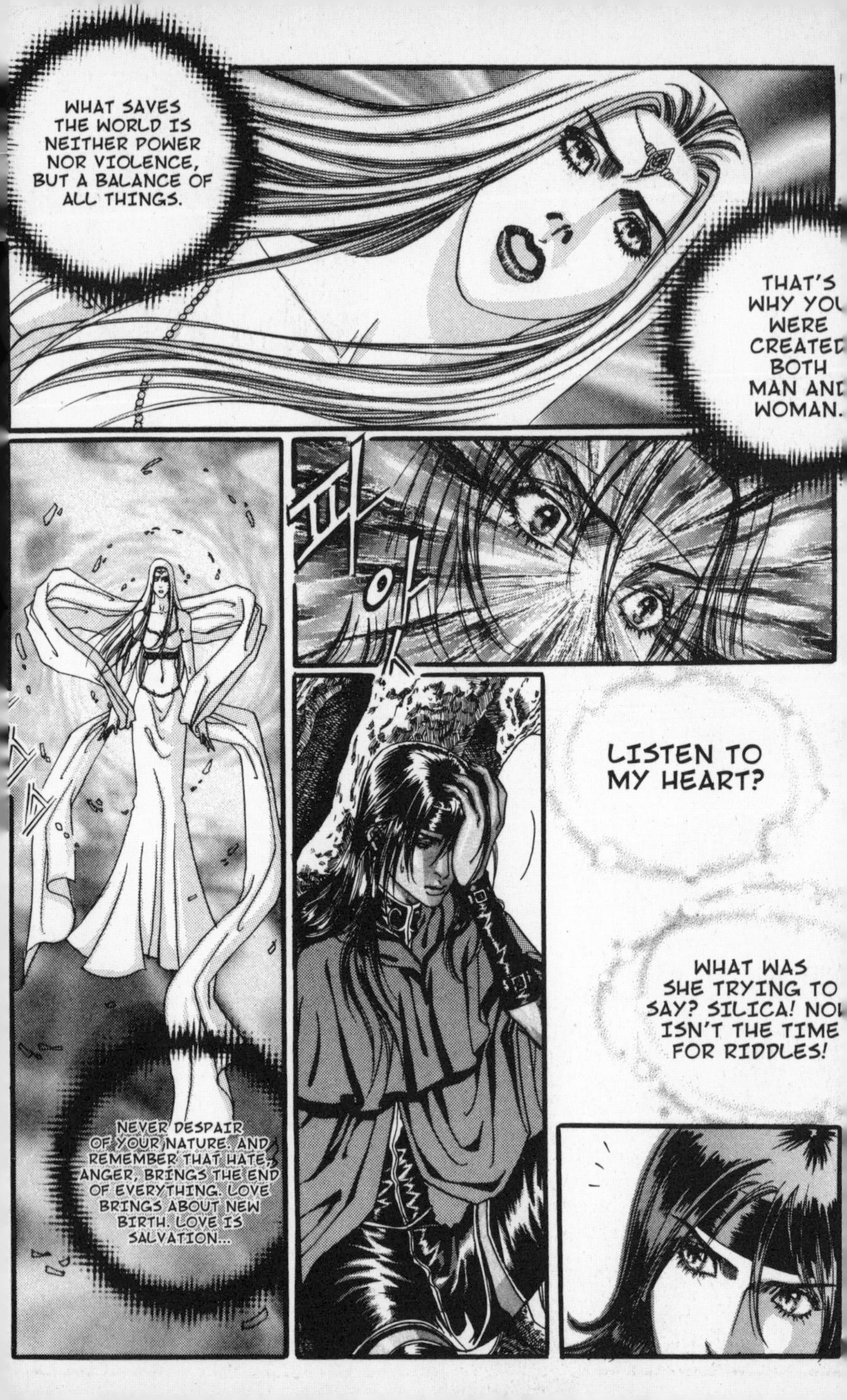
WHAT SAVES THE WORLD IS NEITHER POWER NOR VIOLENCE, BUT A BALANCE OF ALL THINGS.
THAT'S WHY YOU WERE CREATED BOTH MAN AND WOMAN.
NEVER DESPAIR OF YOUR NATURE. AND REMEMBER THAT HATE, ANGER, BRINGS THE END OF EVERYTHING. LOVE BRINGS ABOUT NEW BIRTH. LOVE IS SALVATION...
LISTEN TO MY HEART?
WHAT WAS SHE TRYING TO SAY? SILICA! NOW ISN'T THE TIME FOR RIDDLES!

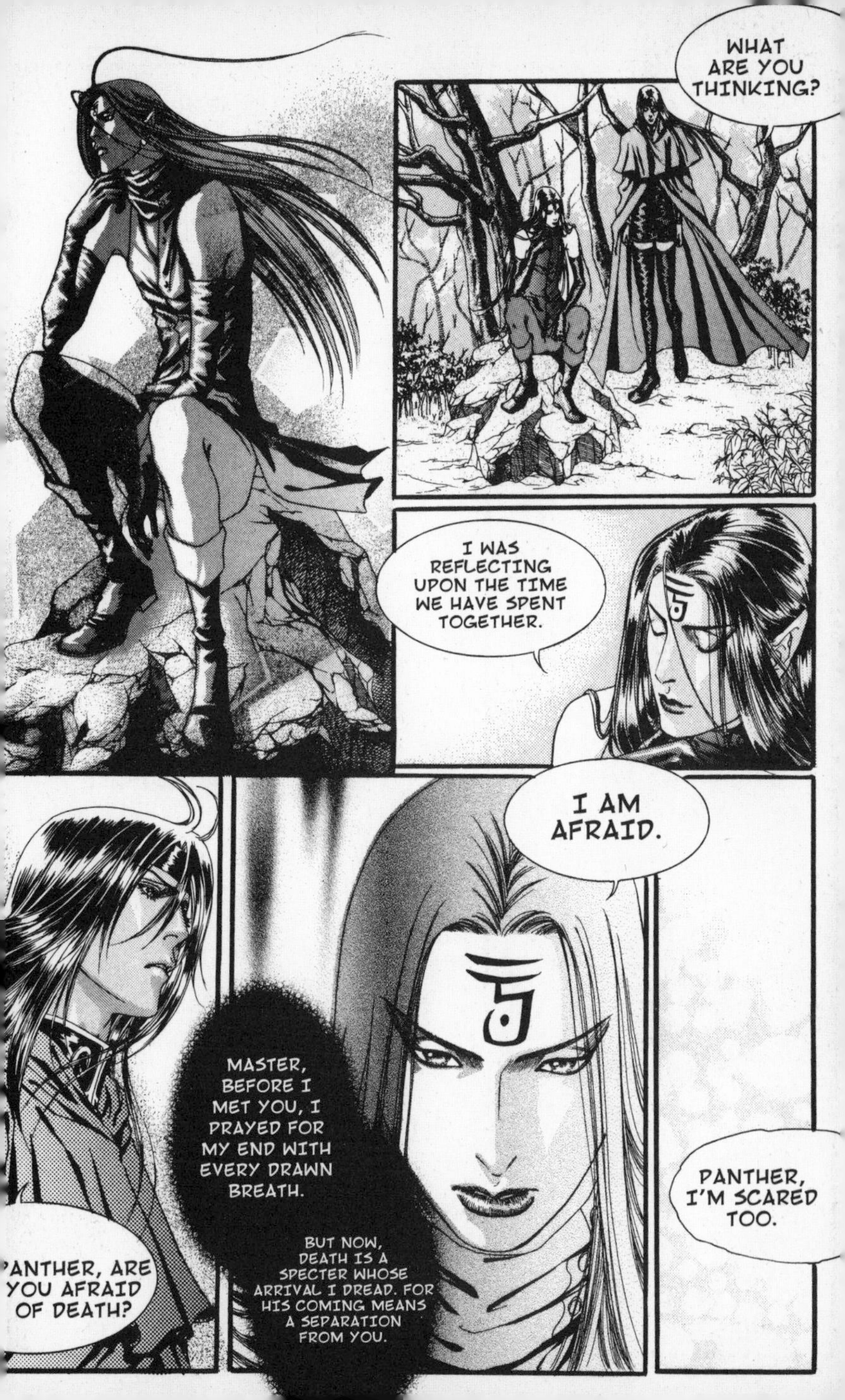
WHAT ARE YOU THINKING?
I WAS REFLECTING UPON THE TIME WE HAVE SPENT TOGETHER.
I AM AFRAID.
PANTHER, I'M SCARED TOO.
MASTER, BEFORE I MET YOU, I PRAYED FOR MY END WITH EVERY DRAWN BREATH.
BUT NOW, DEATH IS A SPECTER WHOSE ARRIVAL I DREAD. FOR HIS COMING MEANS A SEPARATION FROM YOU.
PANTHER, ARE YOU AFRAID OF DEATH?

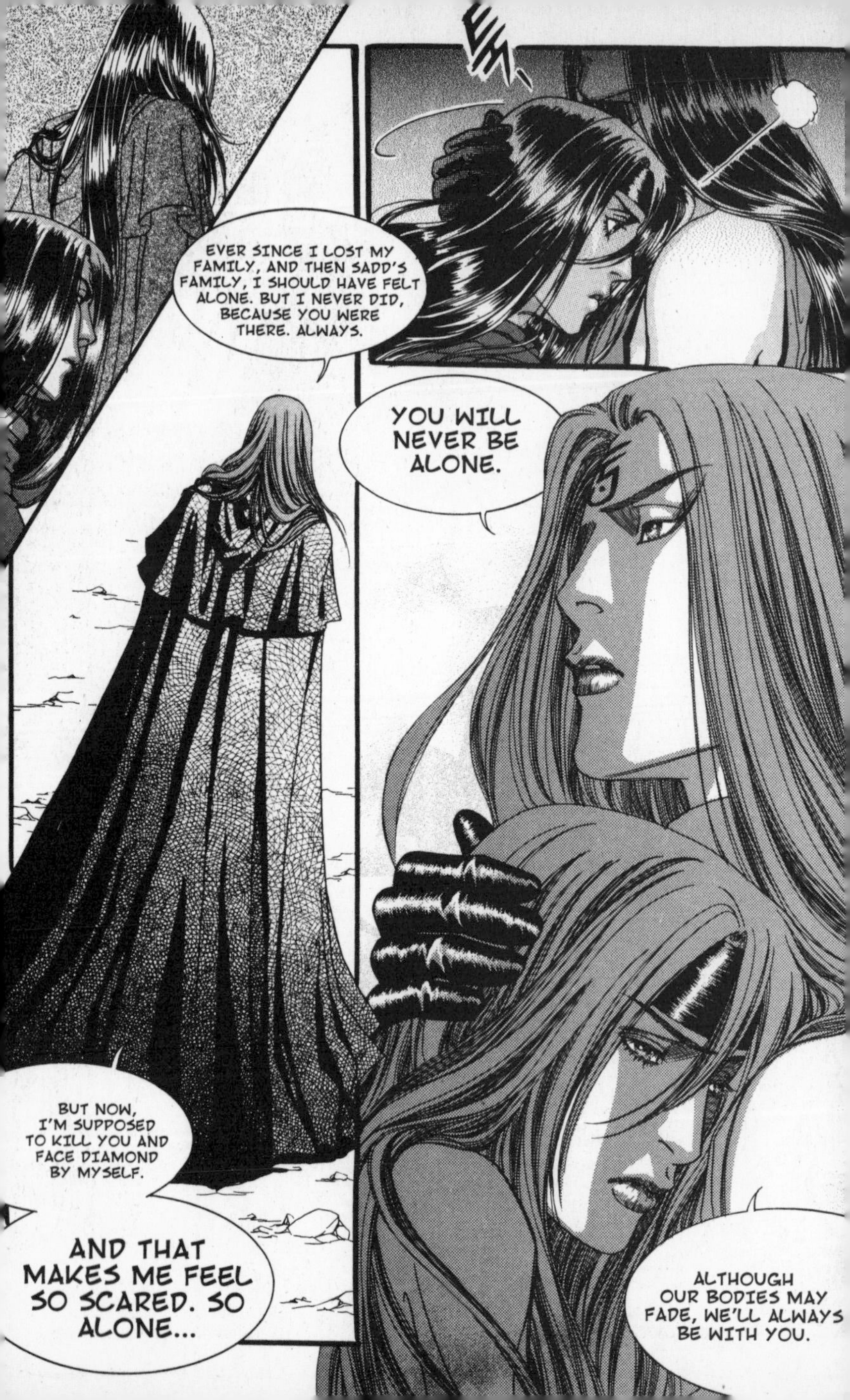
EVER SINCE I LOST MY FAMILY, AND THEN SADD'S FAMILY, I SHOULD HAVE FELT ALONE. BUT I NEVER DID, BECAUSE YOU WERE THERE. ALWAYS.
YOU WILL NEVER BE ALONE.
BUT NOW, I'M SUPPOSED TO KILL YOU AND FACE DIAMOND BY MYSELF.
AND THAT MAKES ME FEEL SO SCARED. SO ALONE...
ALTHOUGH OUR BODIES MAY FADE, WE'LL ALWAYS BE WITH YOU.

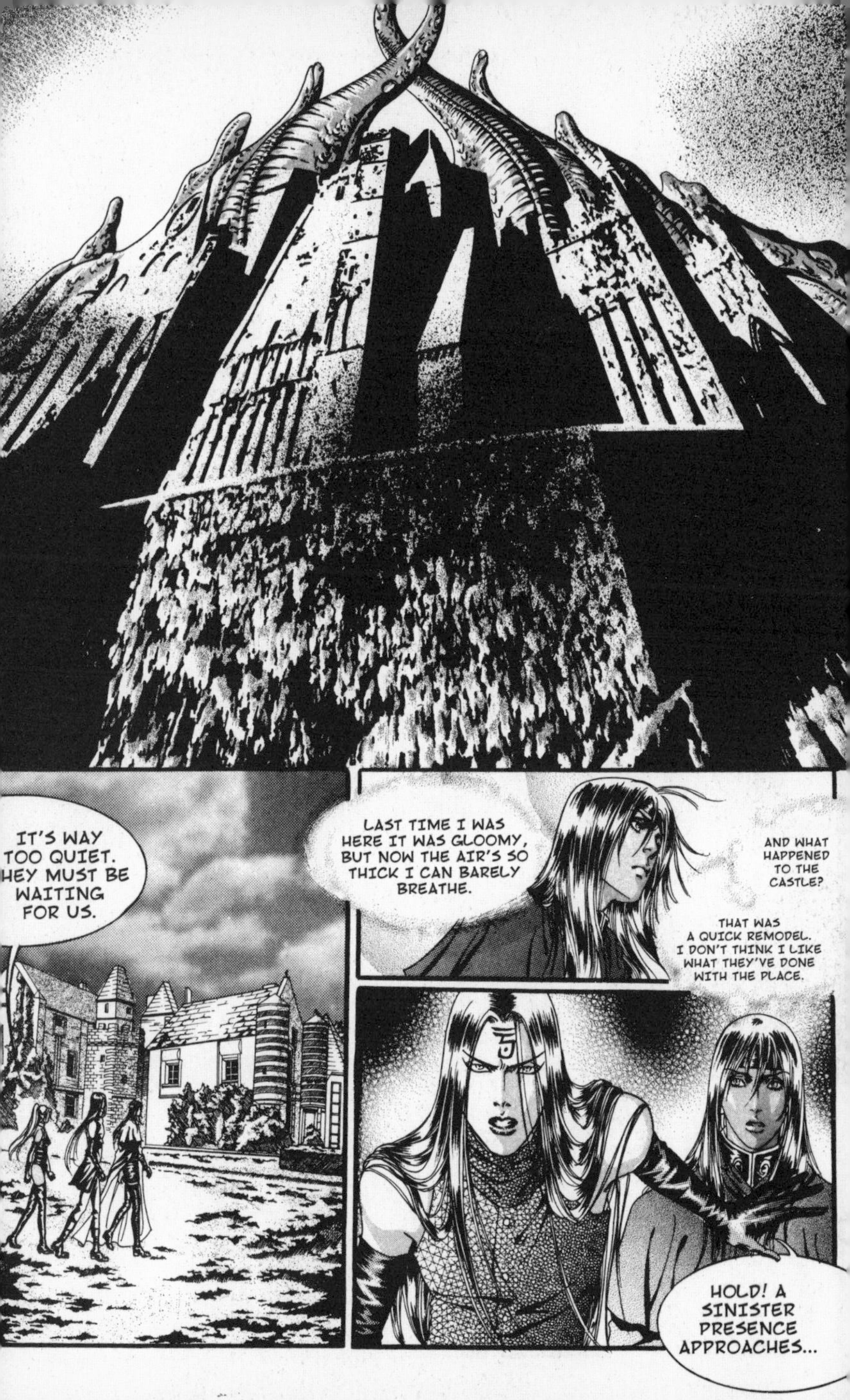
IT'S WAY TOO QUIET. HEY MUST BE WAITING FOR US.
LAST TIME I WAS HERE IT WAS GLOOMY, BUT NOW THE AIR'S SO THICK I CAN BARELY BREATHE.
AND WHAT HAPPENED TO THE CASTLE?
THAT WAS A QUICK REMODEL. I DON'T THINK I LIKE WHAT THEY'VE DONE WITH THE PLACE.
HOLD! A SINISTER PRESENCE APPROACHES...

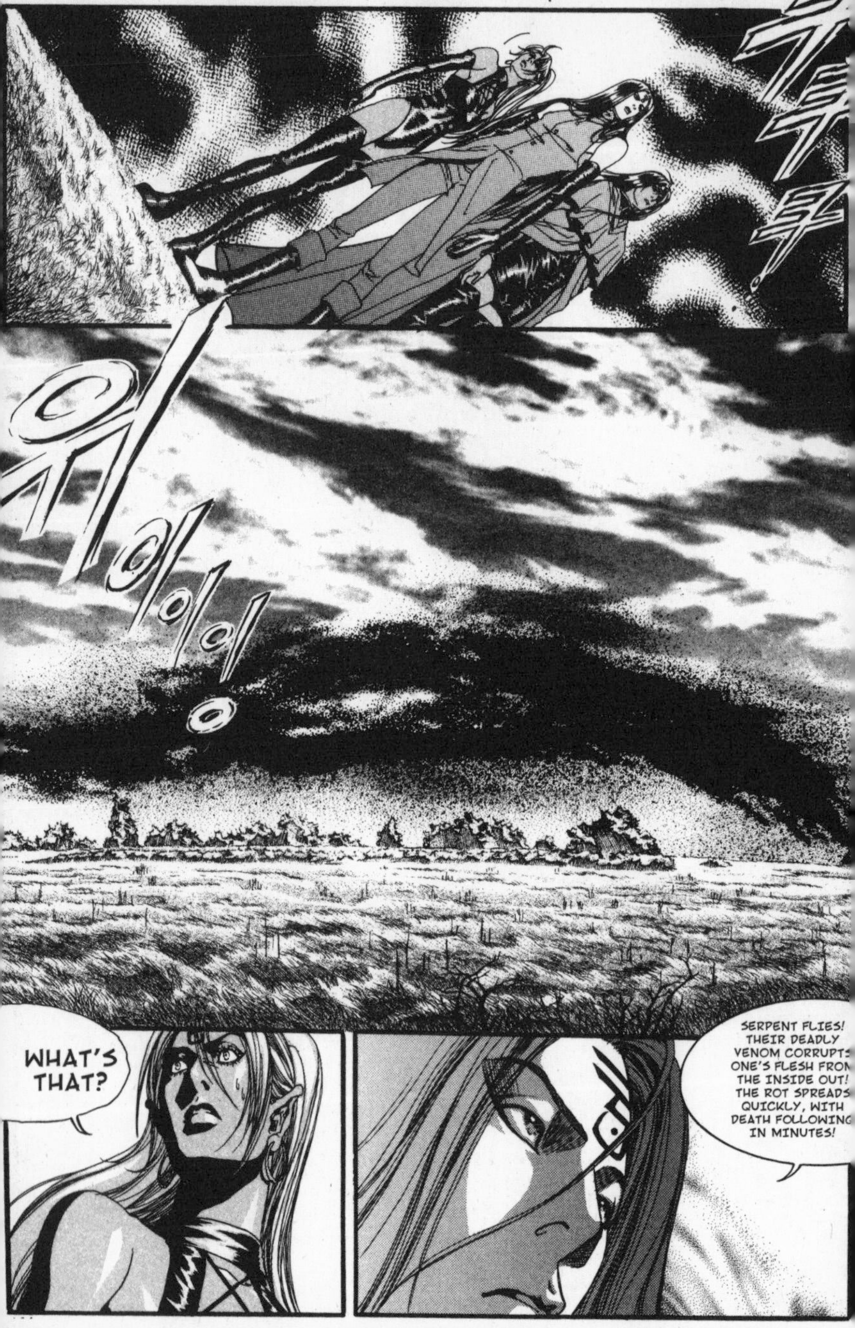
WHAT'S THAT?
SERPENT FLIES! THEIR DEADLY VENOM CORRUPTS ONE'S FLESH FROM THE INSIDE OUT! THE ROT SPREADS QUICKLY, WITH DEATH FOLLOWING IN MINUTES!

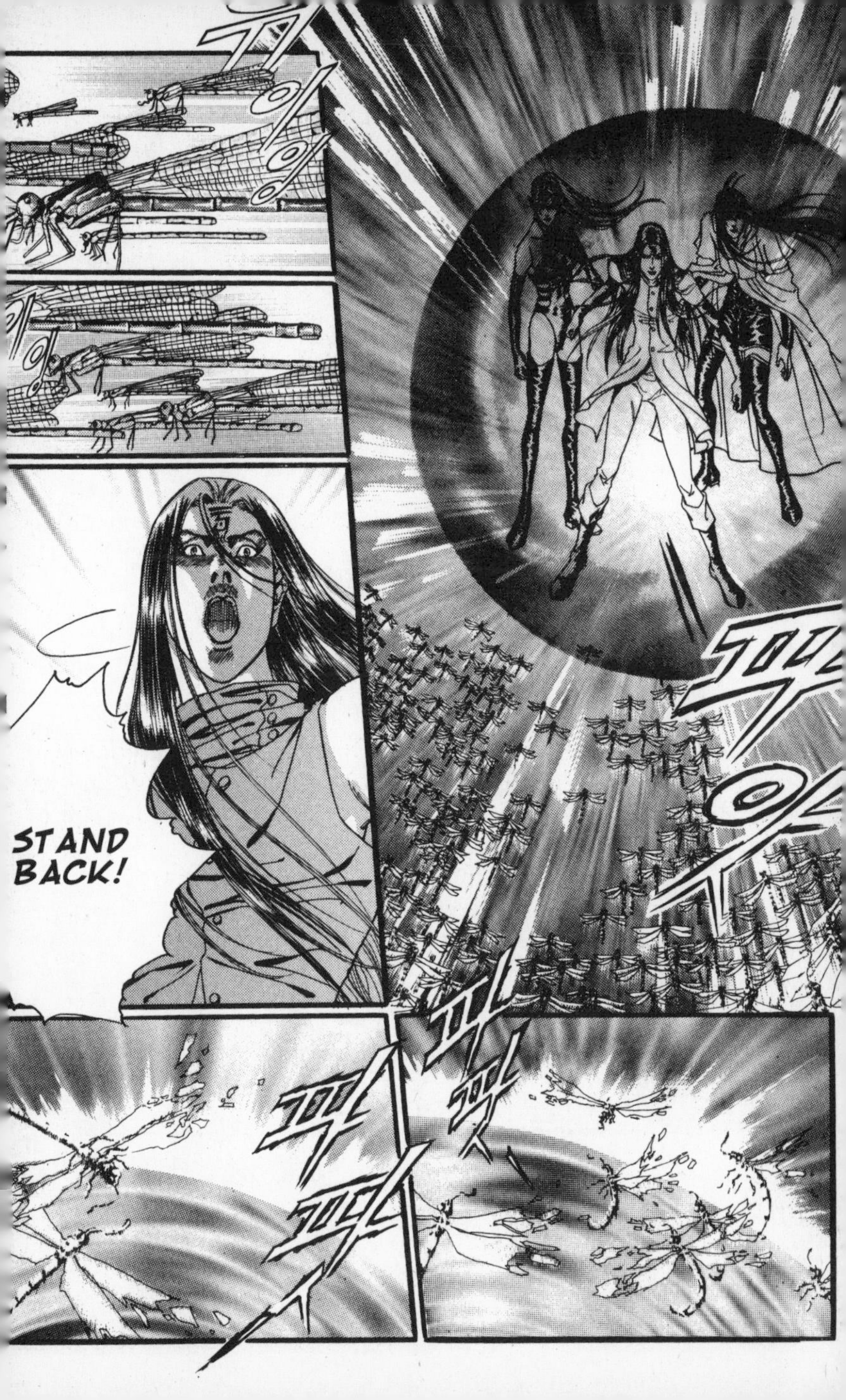
STAND BACK!

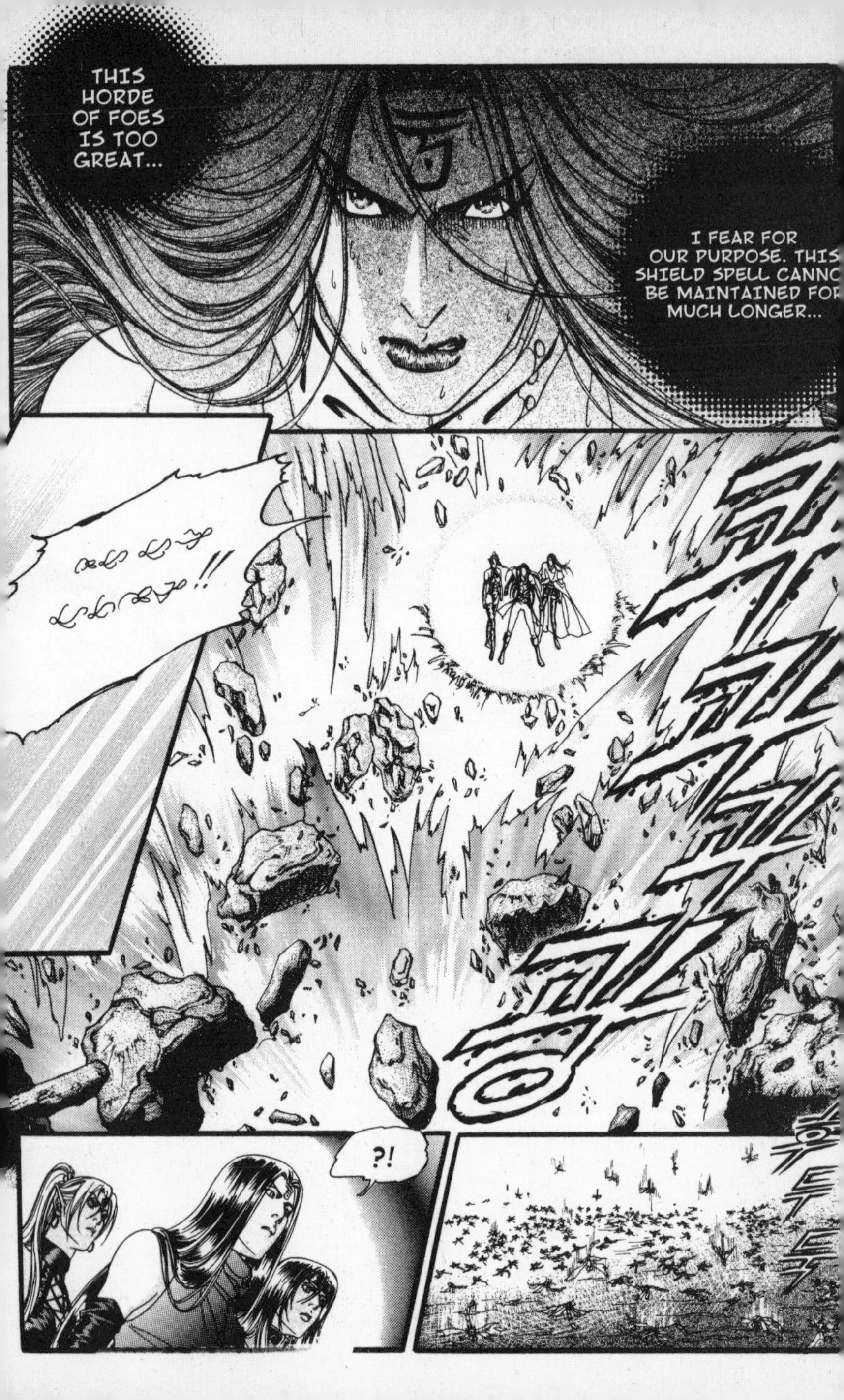
THIS HORDE OF FOES IS TOO GREAT...
I FEAR FOR OUR PURPOSE. THIS SHIELD SPELL CANNO BE MAINTAINED FOR MUCH LONGER...
?!

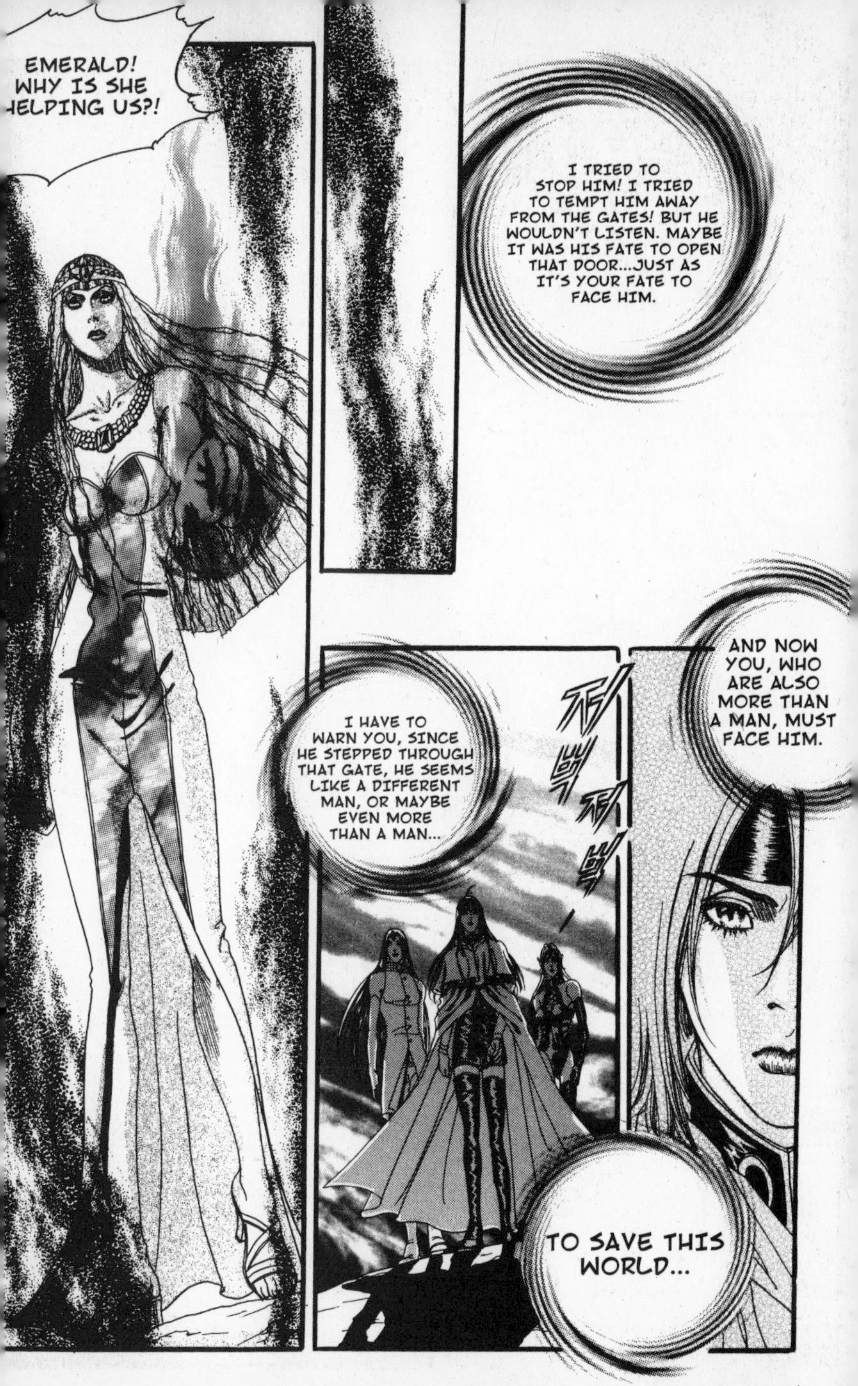
EMERALD! WHY IS SHE HELPING US?!
I TRIED TO STOP HIM! I TRIED TO TEMPT HIM AWAY FROM THE GATES! BUT HE WOULDN'T LISTEN. MAYBE IT WAS HIS FATE TO OPEN THAT DOOR...JUST AS IT'S YOUR FATE TO FACE HIM.
I HAVE TO WARN YOU, SINCE HE STEPPED THROUGH THAT GATE, HE SEEMS LIKE A DIFFERENT MAN, OR MAYBE EVEN MORE THAN A MAN...
AND NOW YOU, WHO ARE ALSO MORE THAN A MAN, MUST FACE HIM.
TO SAVE THIS WORLD...

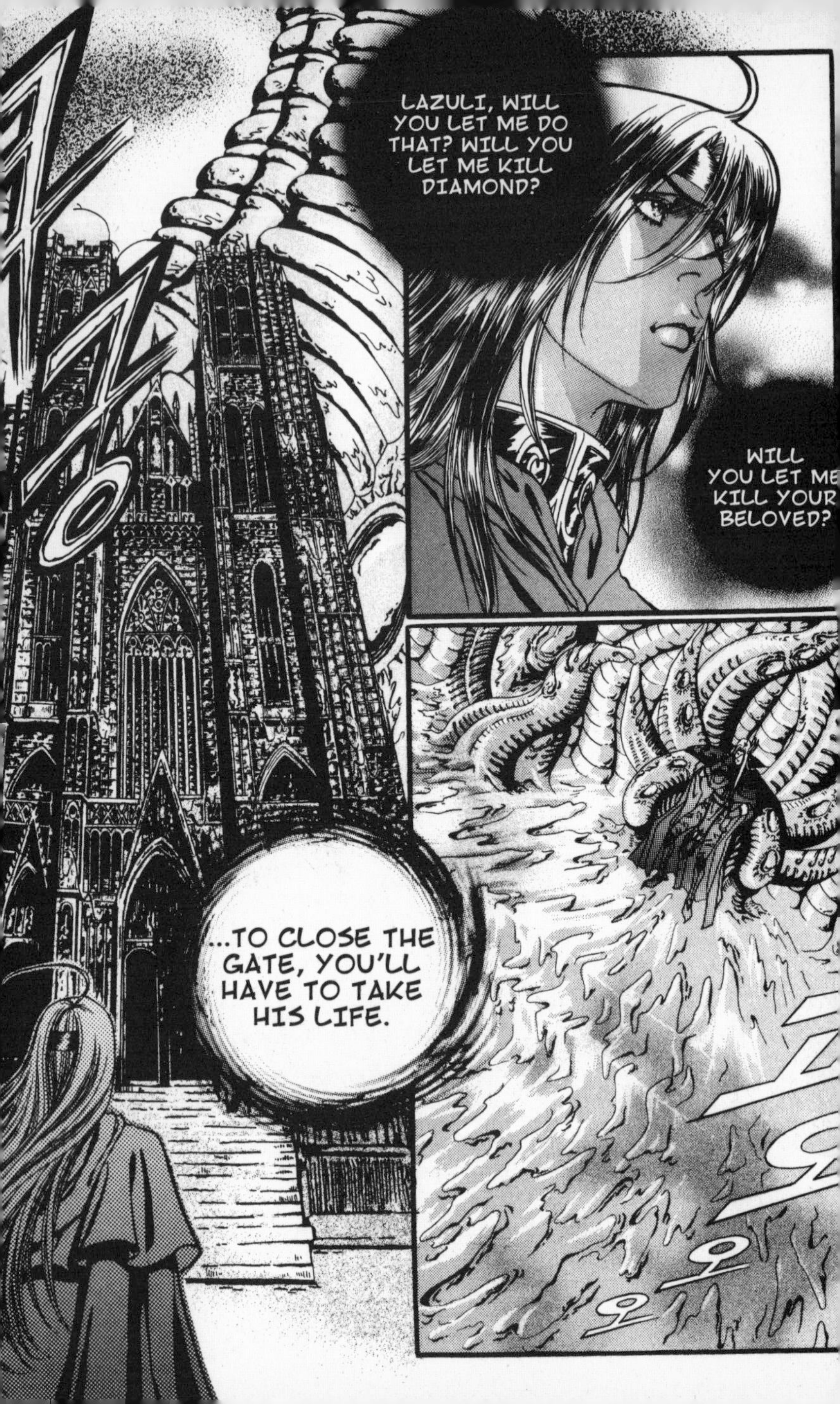
...TO CLOSE THE GATE, YOU'LL HAVE TO TAKE HIS LIFE.
LAZULI, WILL YOU LET ME DO THAT? WILL YOU LET ME KILL DIAMOND?
WILL YOU LET ME KILL YOUR BELOVED?

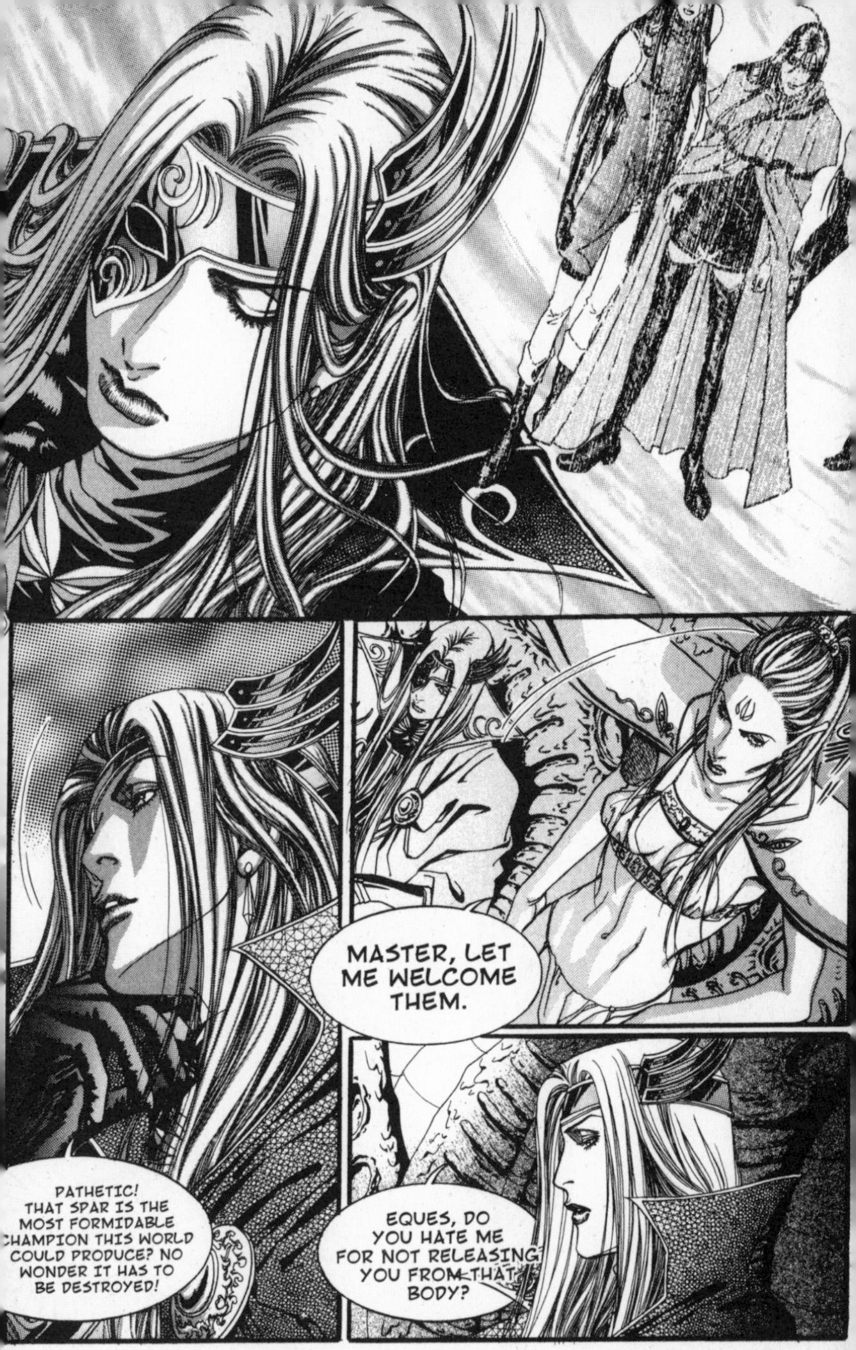
MASTER, LET ME WELCOME THEM.
PATHETIC! THAT SPAR IS THE MOST FORMIDABLE CHAMPION THIS WORLD COULD PRODUCE? NO WONDER IT HAS TO BE DESTROYED!
EQUES, DO YOU HATE ME FOR NOT RELEASING YOU FROM THAT BODY?

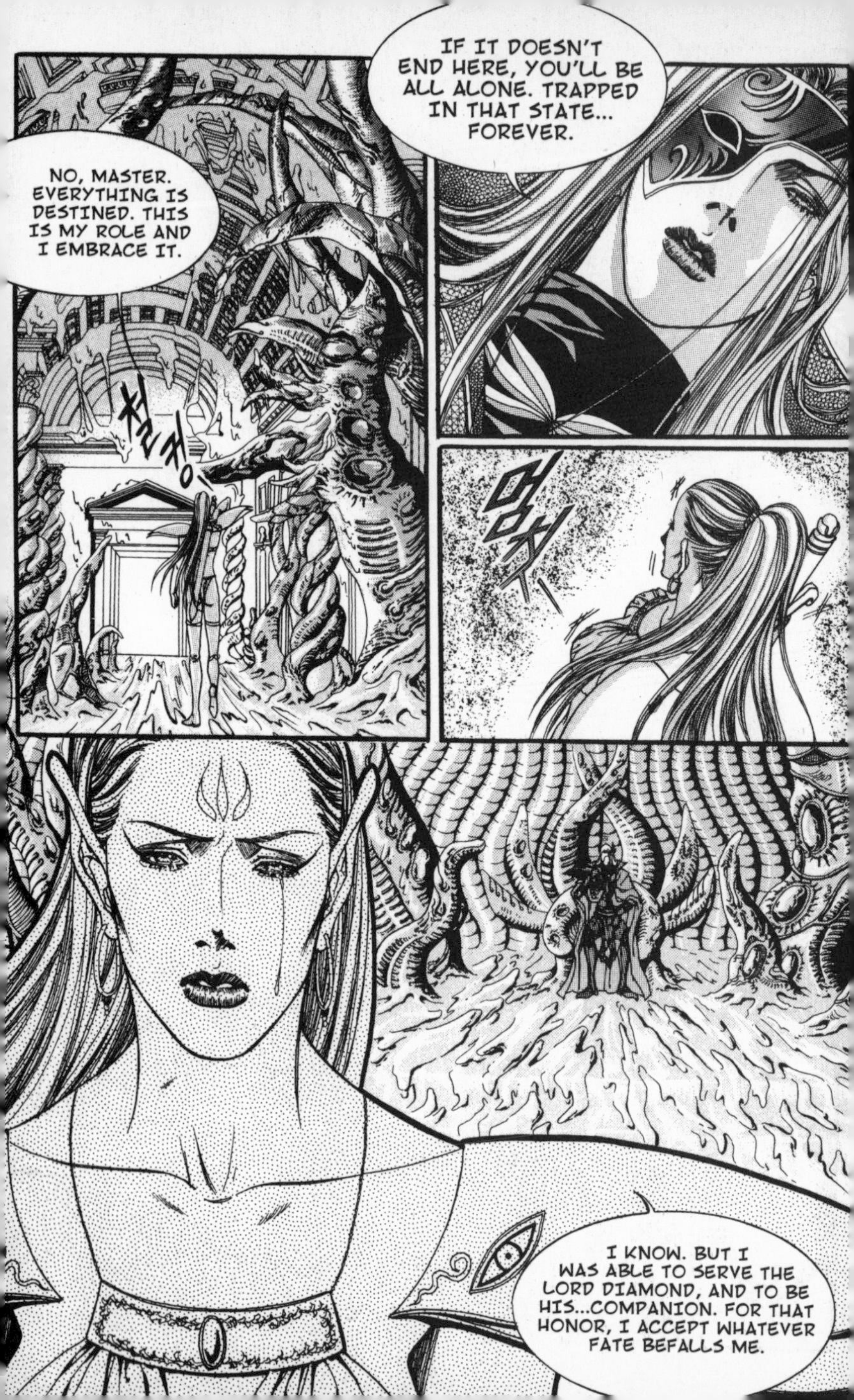
NO, MASTER. EVERYTHING IS DESTINED. THIS IS MY ROLE AND I EMBRACE IT.
IF IT DOESN'T END HERE, YOU'LL BE ALL ALONE. TRAPPED IN THAT STATE... FOREVER.
I KNOW. BUT I WAS ABLE TO SERVE THE LORD DIAMOND, AND TO BE HIS...COMPANION. FOR THAT HONOR, I ACCEPT WHATEVER FATE BEFALLS ME.

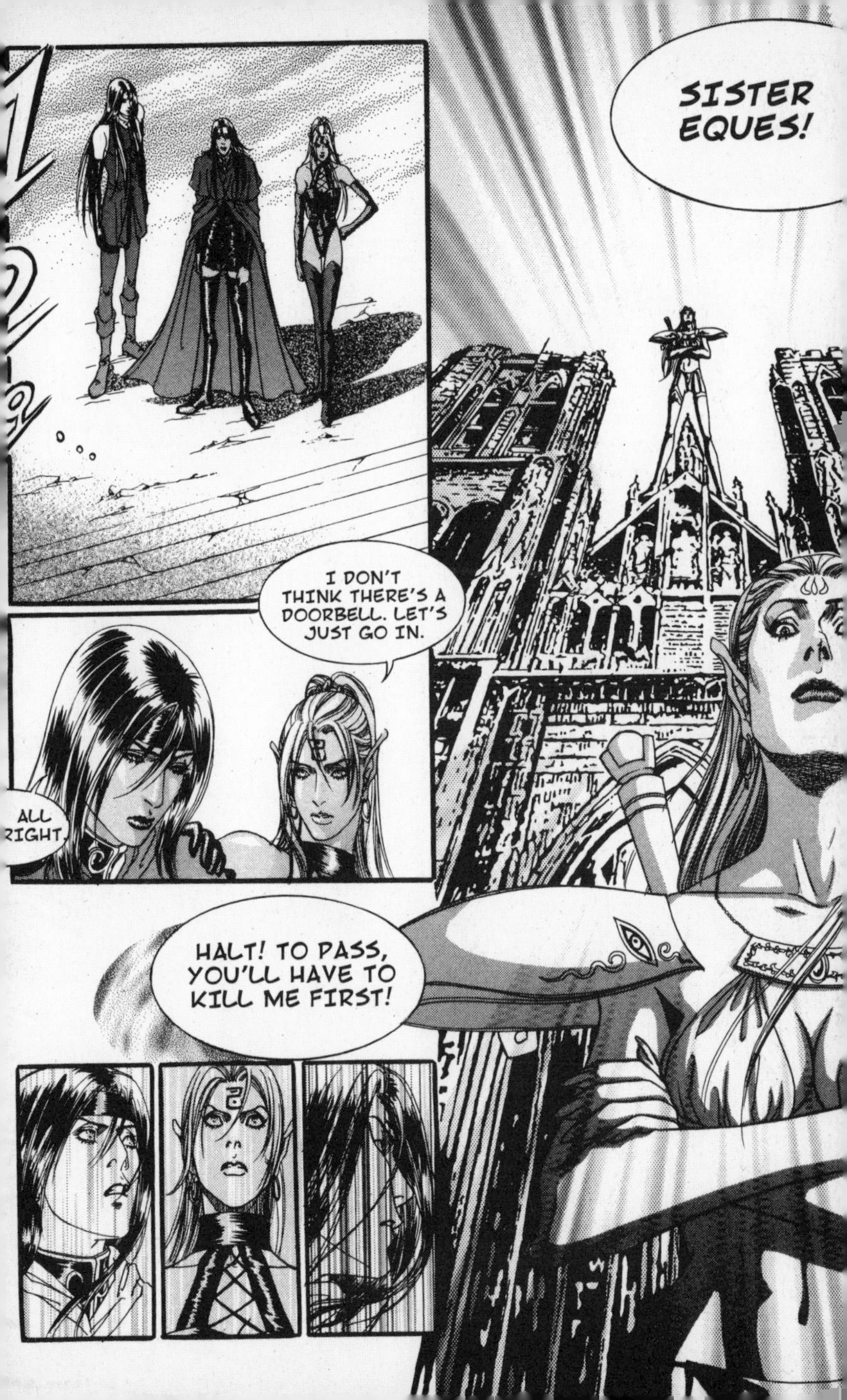
SISTER EQUES!
I DON'T THINK THERE'S A DOORBELL. LET'S JUST GO IN.
ALL RIGHT.
HALT! TO PASS, YOU'LL HAVE TO KILL ME FIRST!

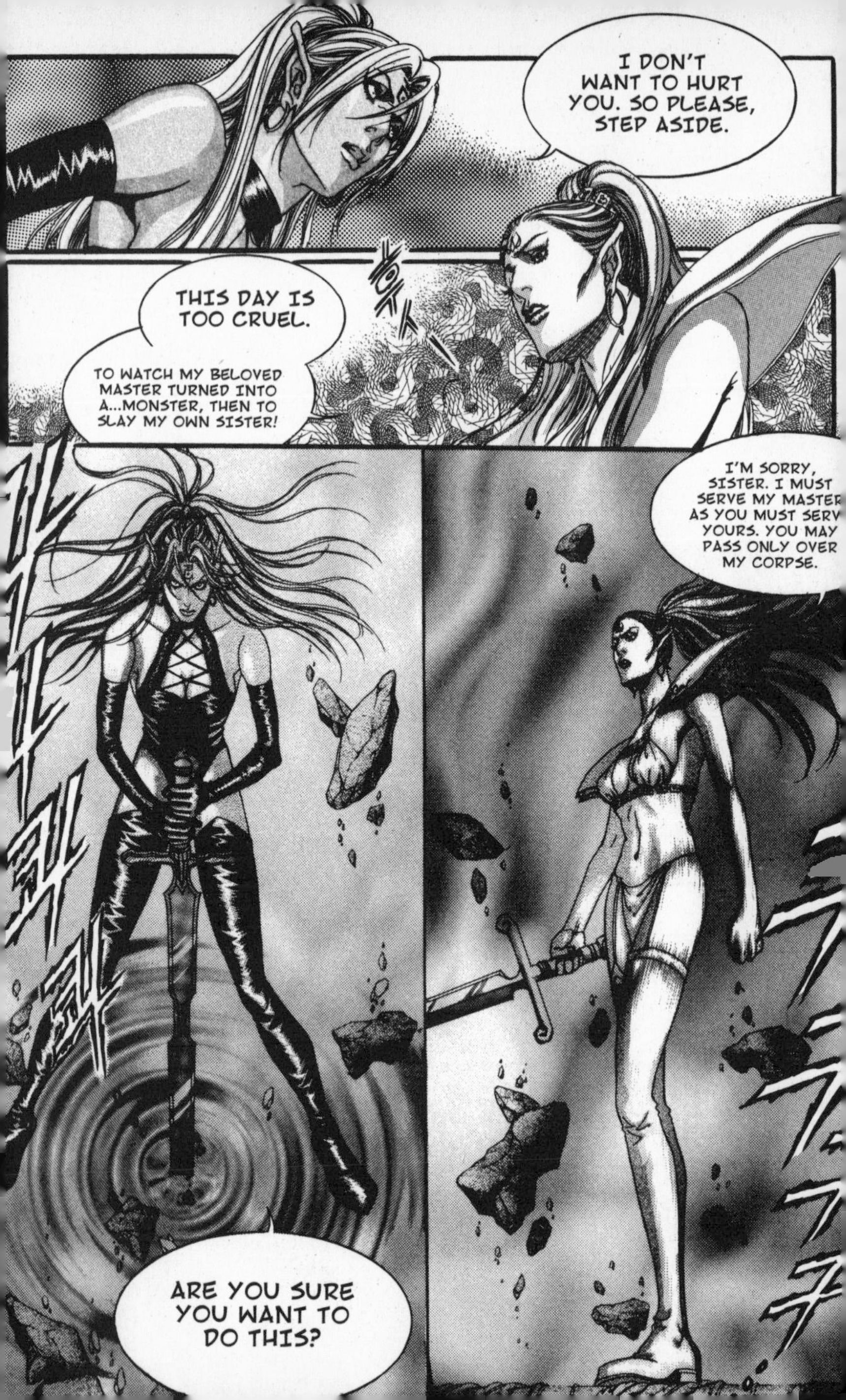
I DON'T WANT TO HURT YOU. SO PLEASE, STEP ASIDE.
THIS DAY IS TOO CRUEL.
TO WATCH MY BELOVED MASTER TURNED INTO A...MONSTER, THEN TO SLAY MY OWN SISTER!
I'M SORRY, SISTER. I MUST SERVE MY MASTER AS YOU MUST SERV YOURS. YOU MAY PASS ONLY OVER MY CORPSE.
ARE YOU SURE YOU WANT TO DO THIS?

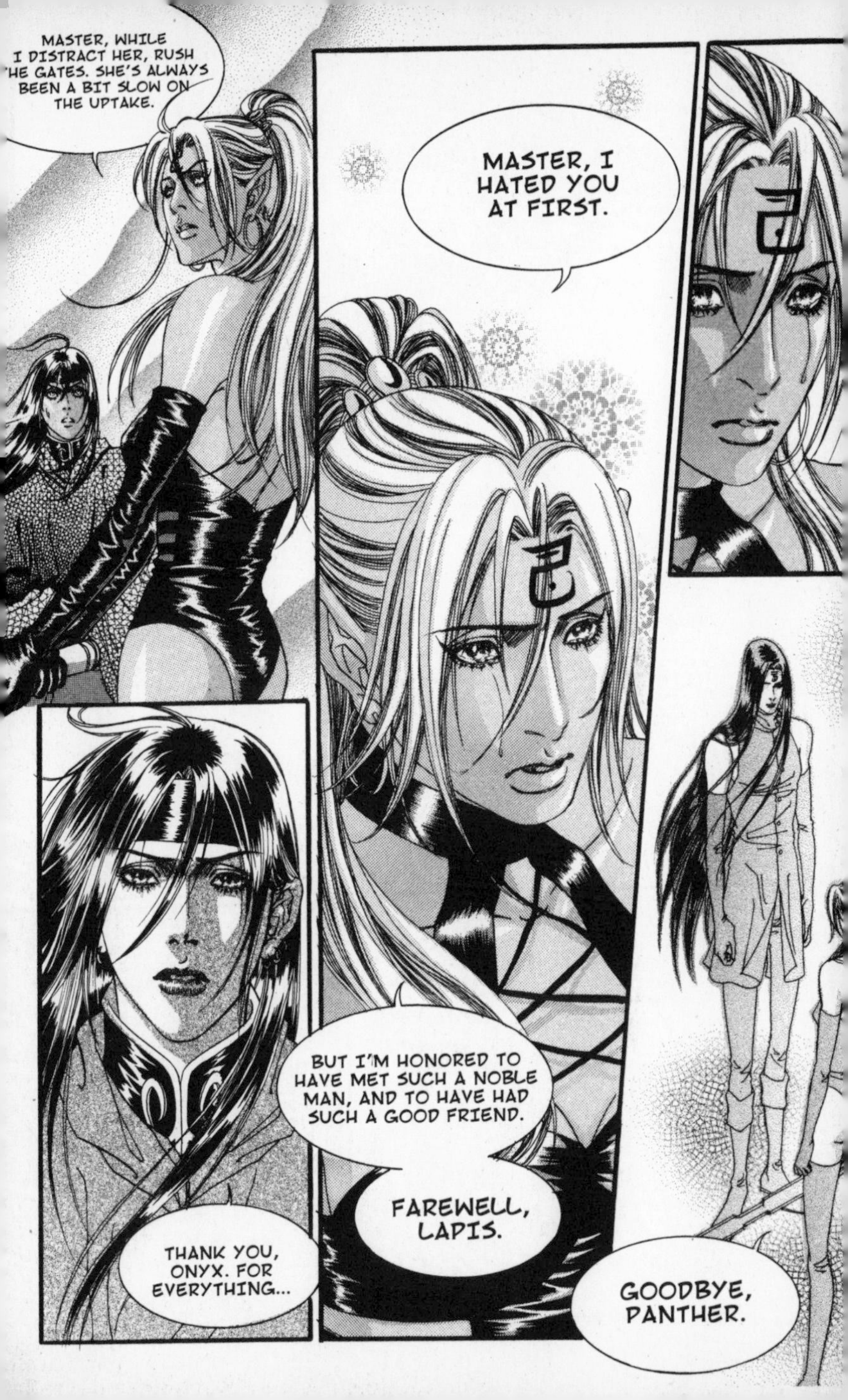
MASTER, WHILE I DISTRACT HER, RUSH THE GATES. SHE'S ALWAYS BEEN A BIT SLOW ON THE UPTAKE.
MASTER, I HATED YOU AT FIRST.
BUT I'M HONORED TO HAVE MET SUCH A NOBLE MAN, AND TO HAVE HAD SUCH A GOOD FRIEND.
FAREWELL, LAPIS.
THANK YOU, ONYX. FOR EVERYTHING...
GOODBYE, PANTHER.

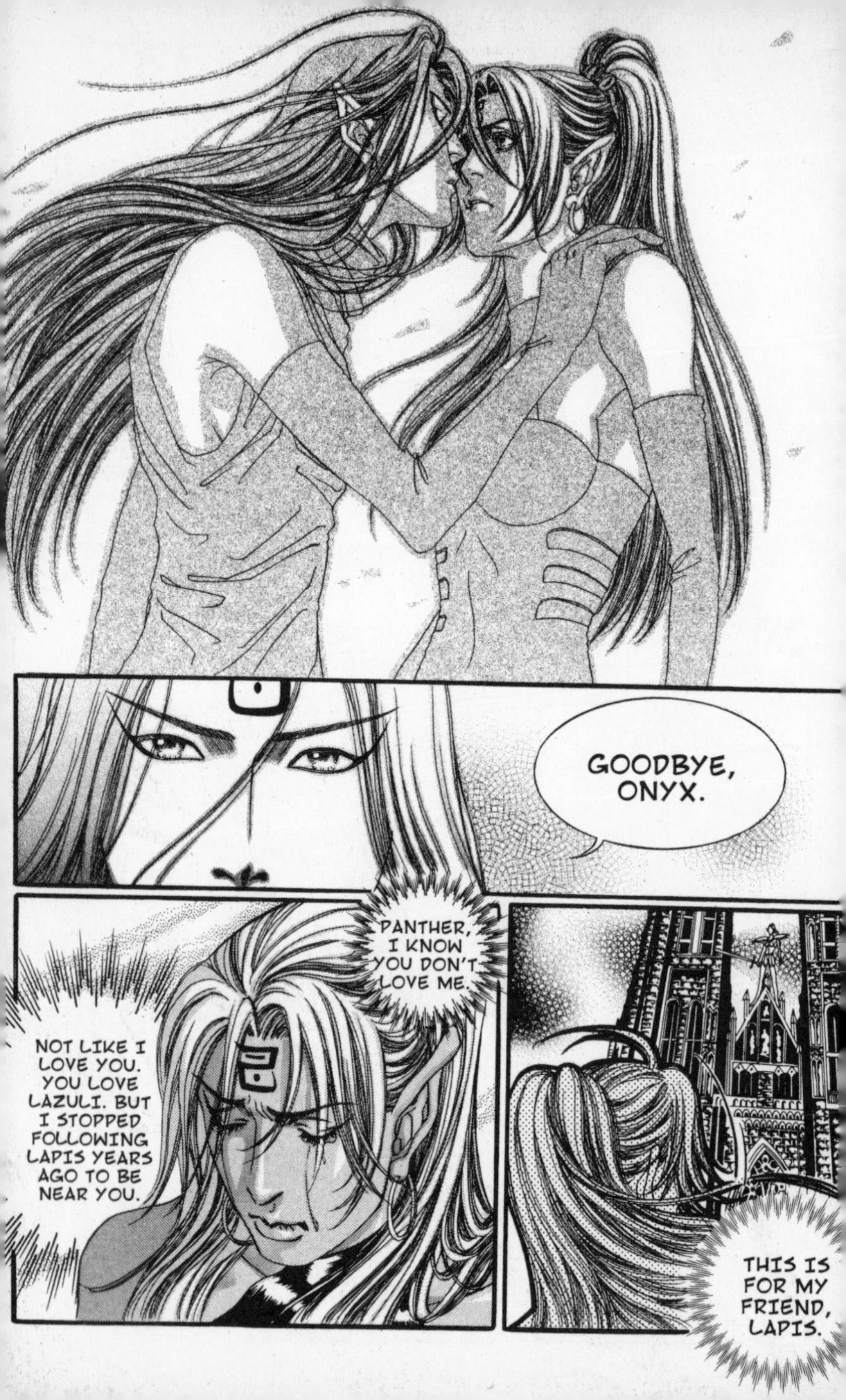
GOODBYE, ONYX.
PANTHER, I KNOW YOU DON'T LOVE ME.
NOT LIKE I LOVE YOU. YOU LOVE LAZULI. BUT I STOPPED FOLLOWING LAPIS YEARS AGO TO BE NEAR YOU.
THIS IS FOR MY FRIEND, LAPIS.

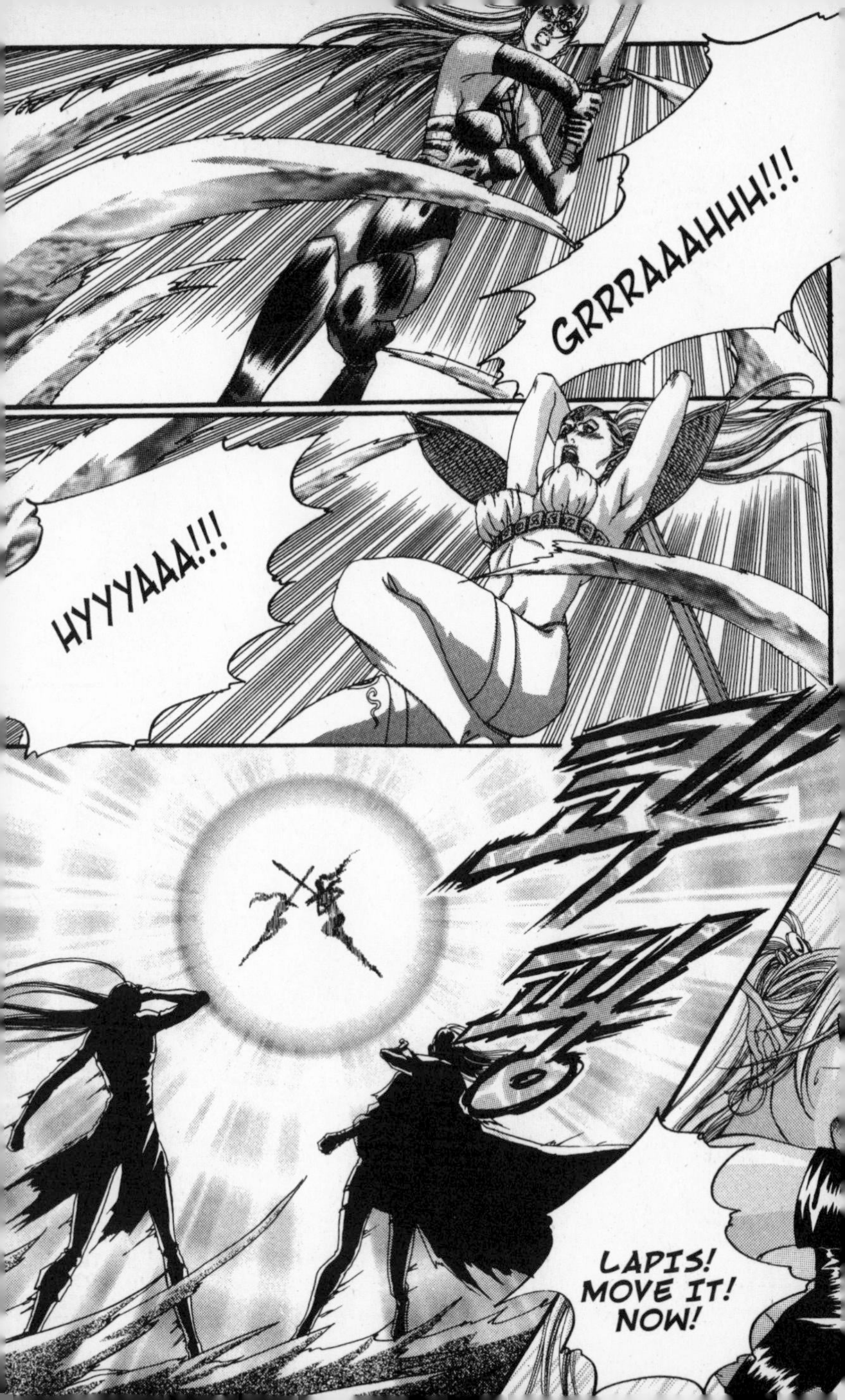
GRRRAAAHHH!!!
HYYYAAA!!!
LAPIS! MOVE IT! NOW!

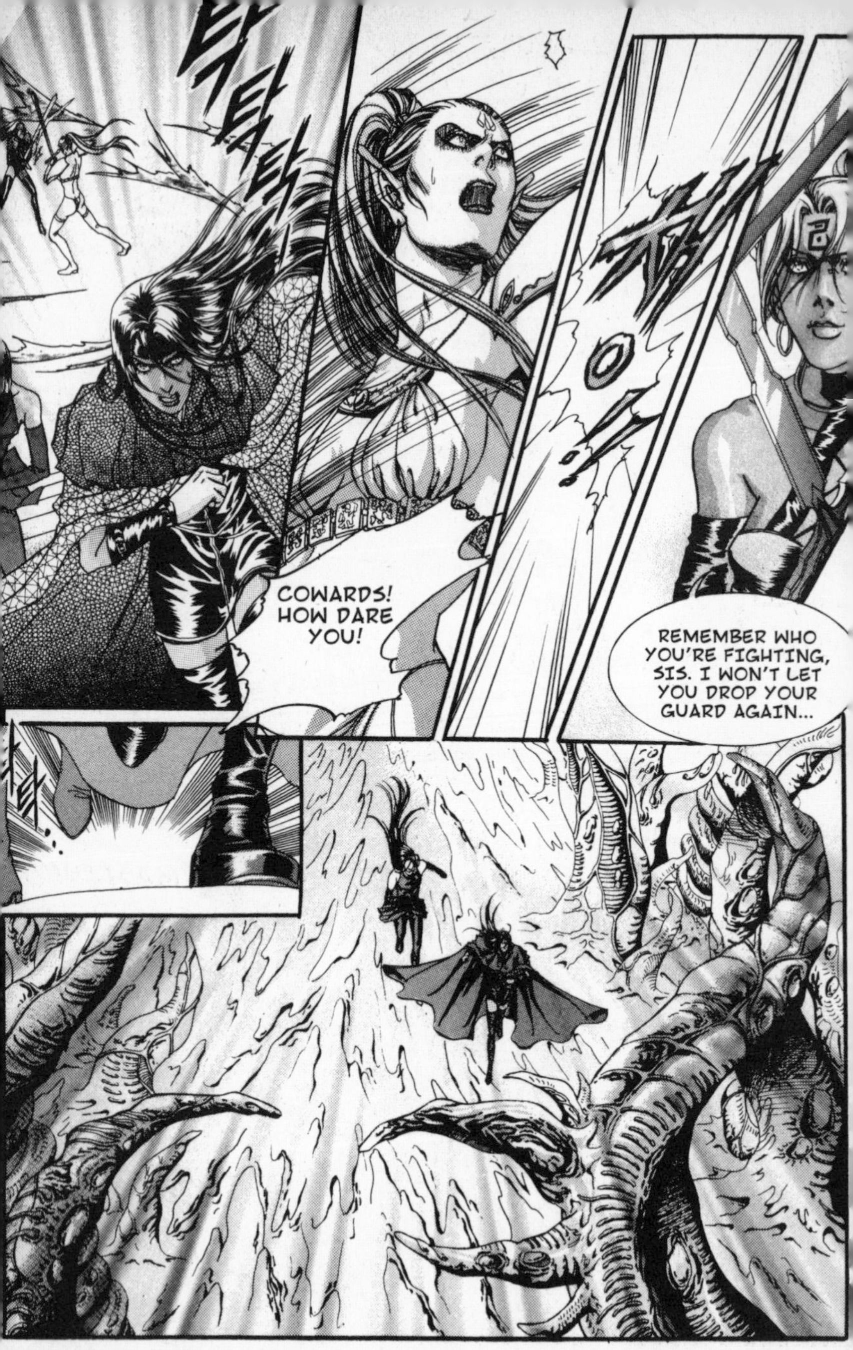
COWARDS! HOW DARE YOU!
REMEMBER WHO YOU'RE FIGHTING, SIS. I WON'T LET YOU DROP YOUR GUARD AGAIN...

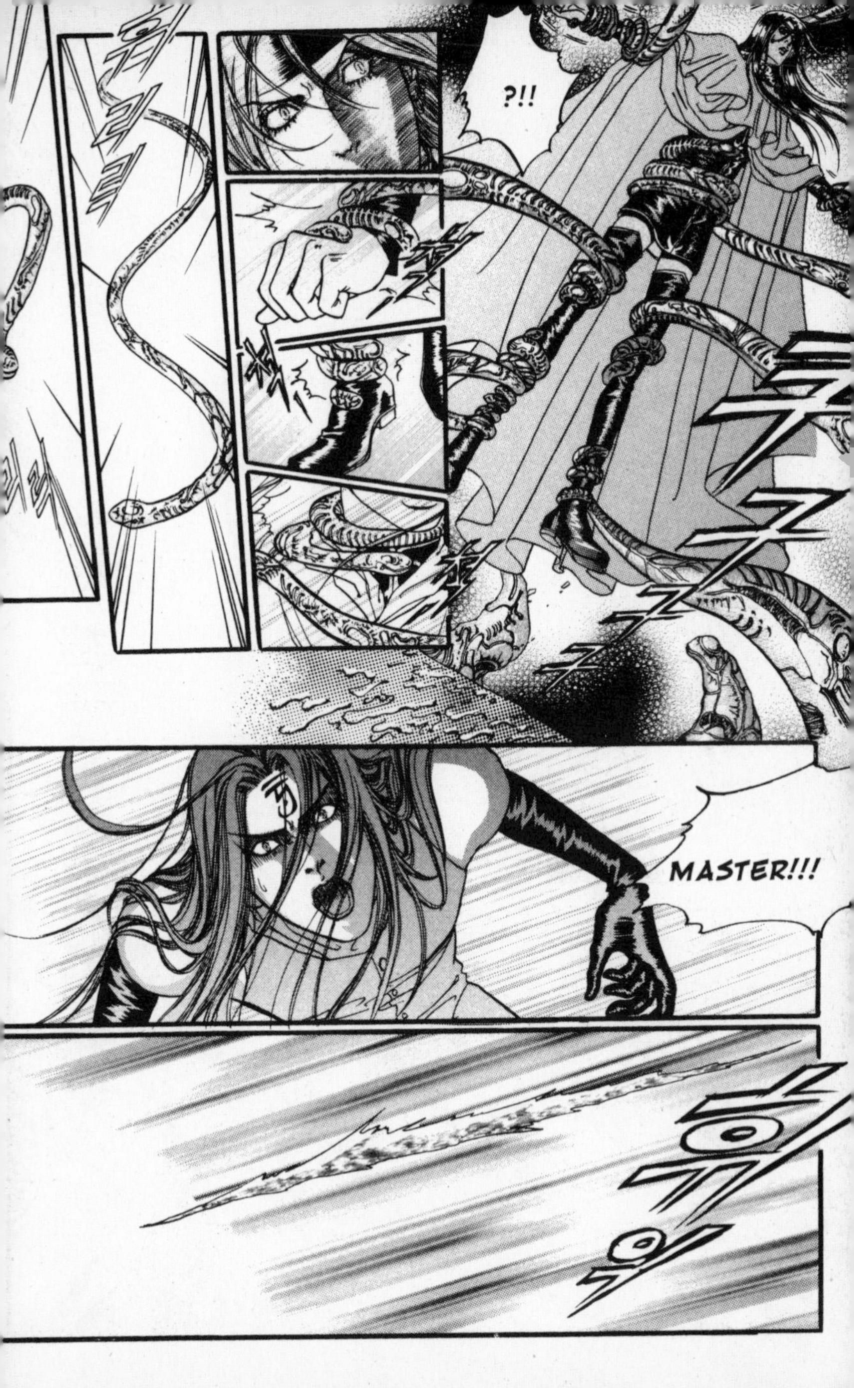
?!!
MASTER!!!

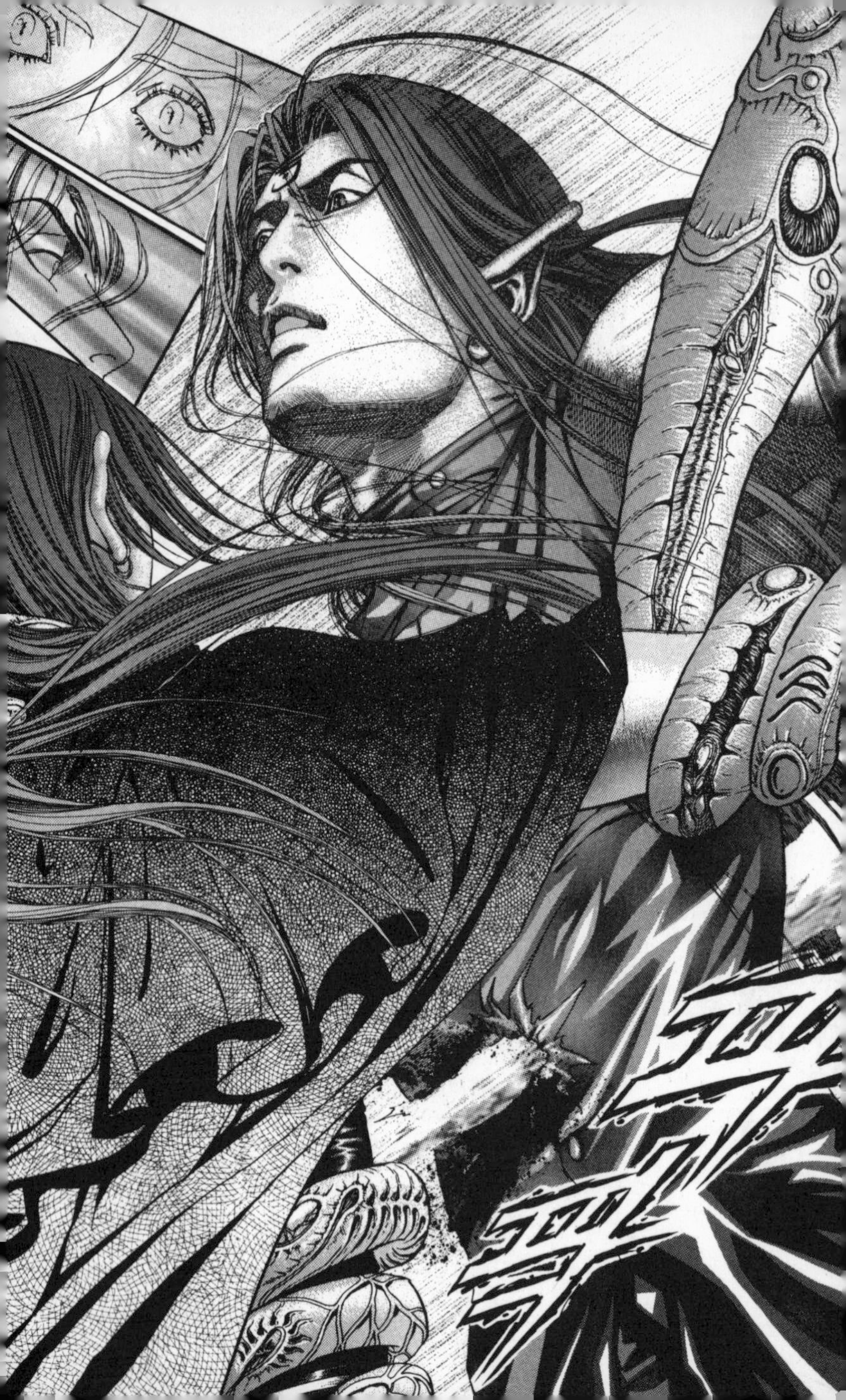

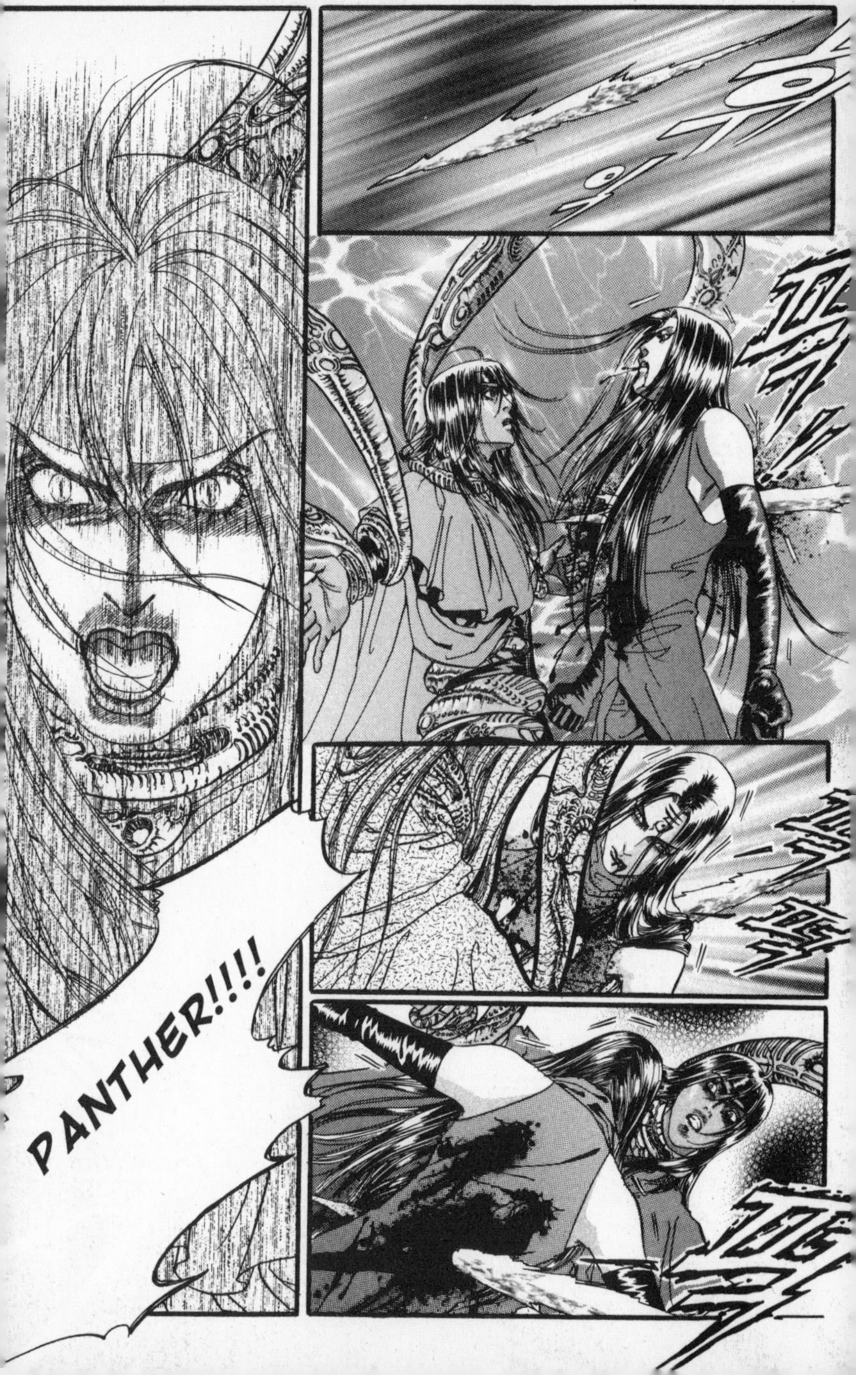
PANTHER!!!!

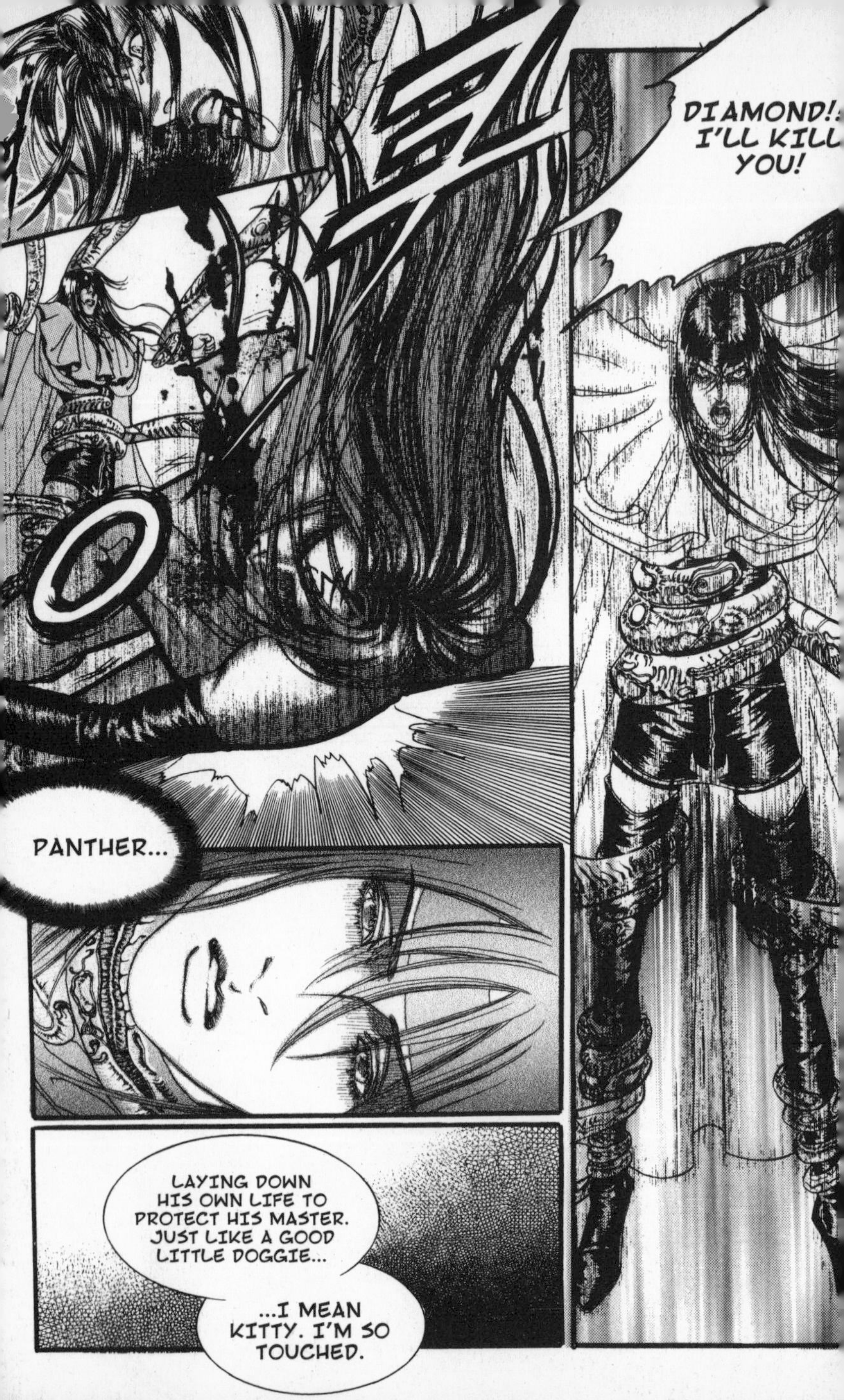
DIAMOND!!
I'LL KILL YOU!
PANTHER...
LAYING DOWN HIS OWN LIFE TO PROTECT HIS MASTER. JUST LIKE A GOOD LITTLE DOGGIE...
...I MEAN KITTY. I'M SO TOUCHED.

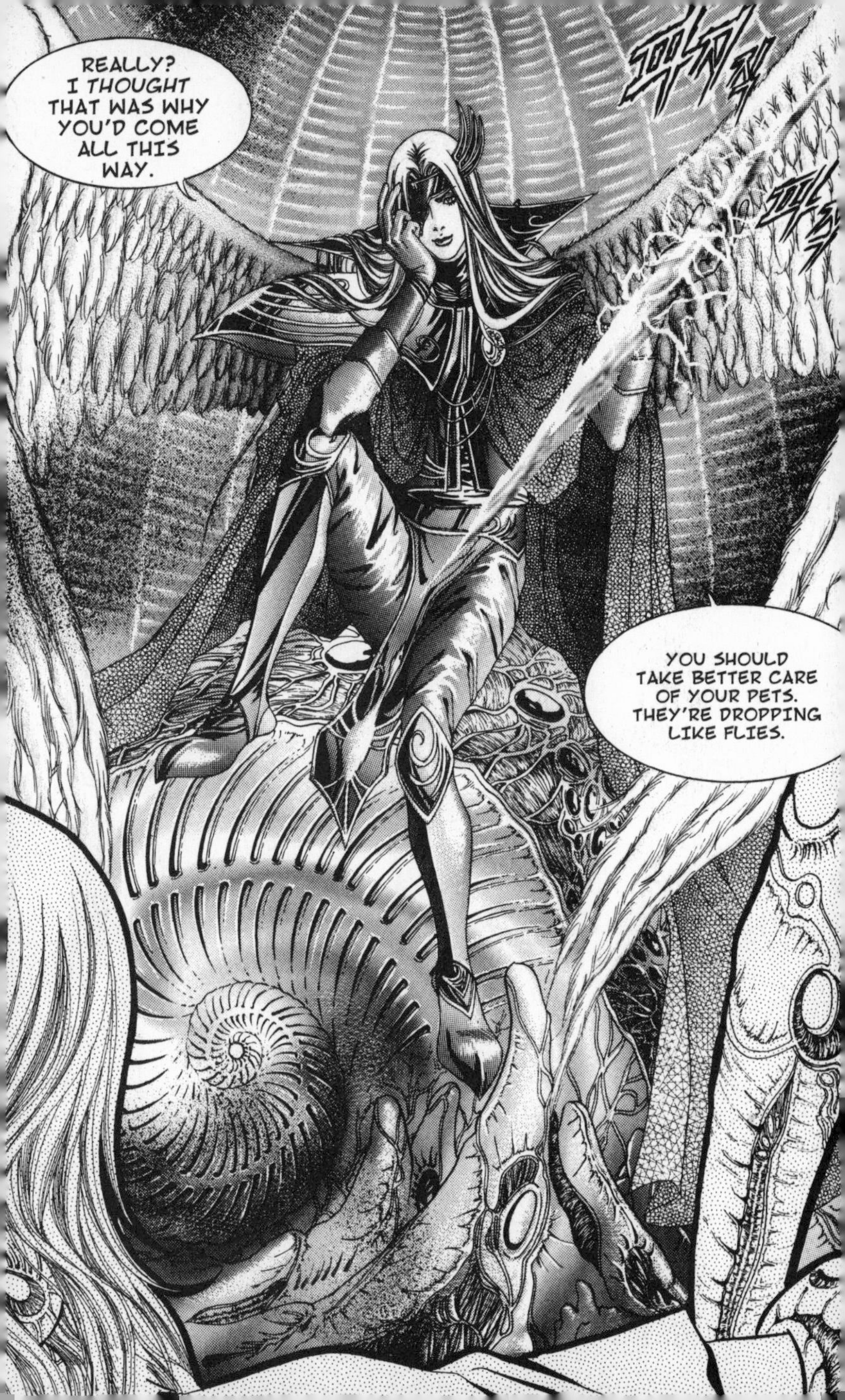
REALLY? I THOUGHT THAT WAS WHY YOU'D COME ALL THIS WAY.
YOU SHOULD TAKE BETTER CARE OF YOUR PETS. THEY'RE DROPPING LIKE FLIES.

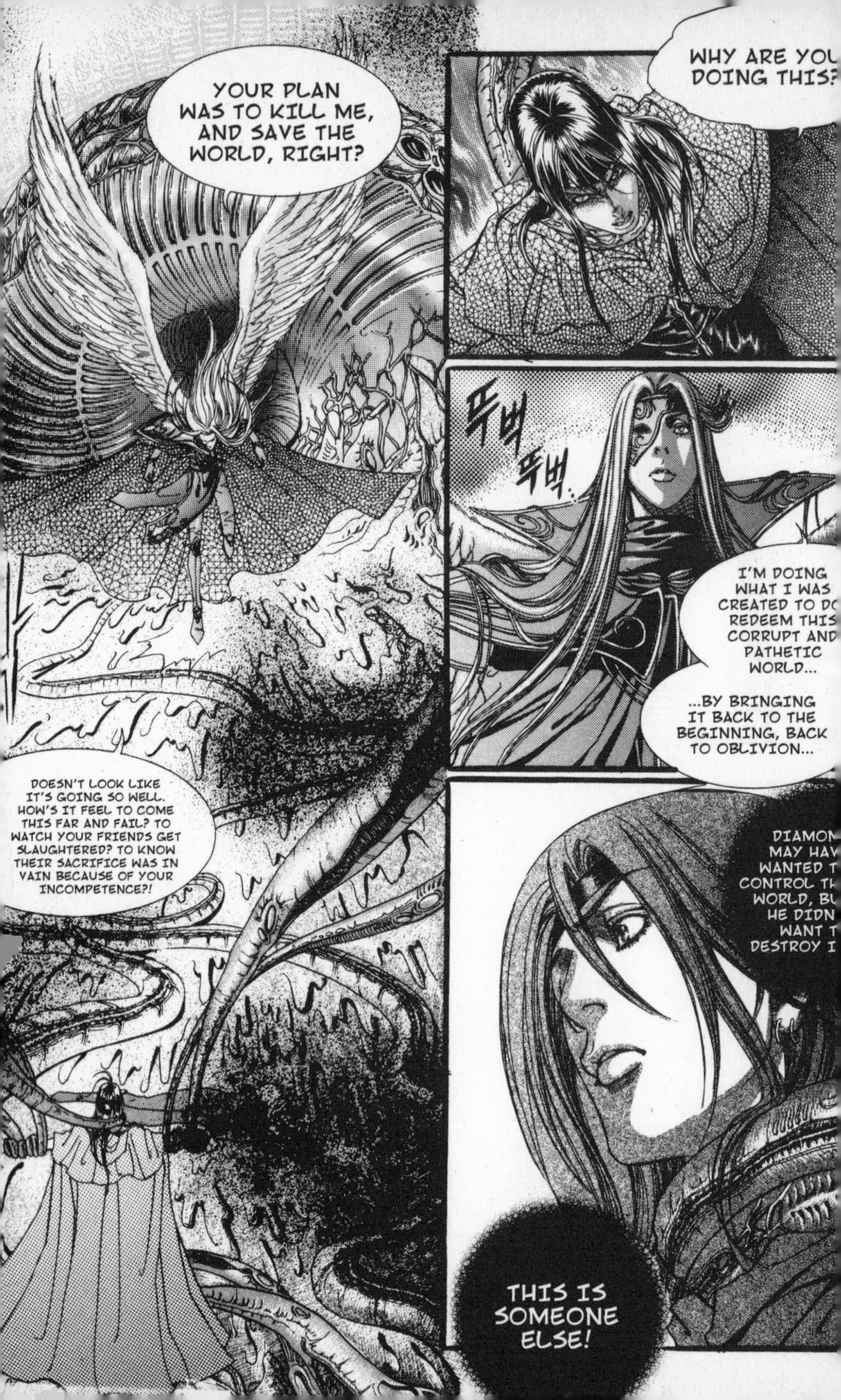
YOUR PLAN WAS TO KILL ME, AND SAVE THE WORLD, RIGHT?
WHY ARE YOU DOING THIS?
뚜벅 뚜벅...
I'M DOING WHAT I WAS CREATED TO DO REDEEM THIS CORRUPT AND PATHETIC WORLD...
...BY BRINGING IT BACK TO THE BEGINNING, BACK TO OBLIVION...
DOESN'T LOOK LIKE IT'S GOING SO WELL. HOW'S IT FEEL TO COME THIS FAR AND FAIL? TO WATCH YOUR FRIENDS GET SLAUGHTERED? TO KNOW THEIR SACRIFICE WAS IN VAIN BECAUSE OF YOUR INCOMPETENCE?!
DIAMON MAY HAV WANTED T CONTROL TH WORLD, BU HE DIDN WANT T DESTROY I
THIS IS SOMEONE ELSE!

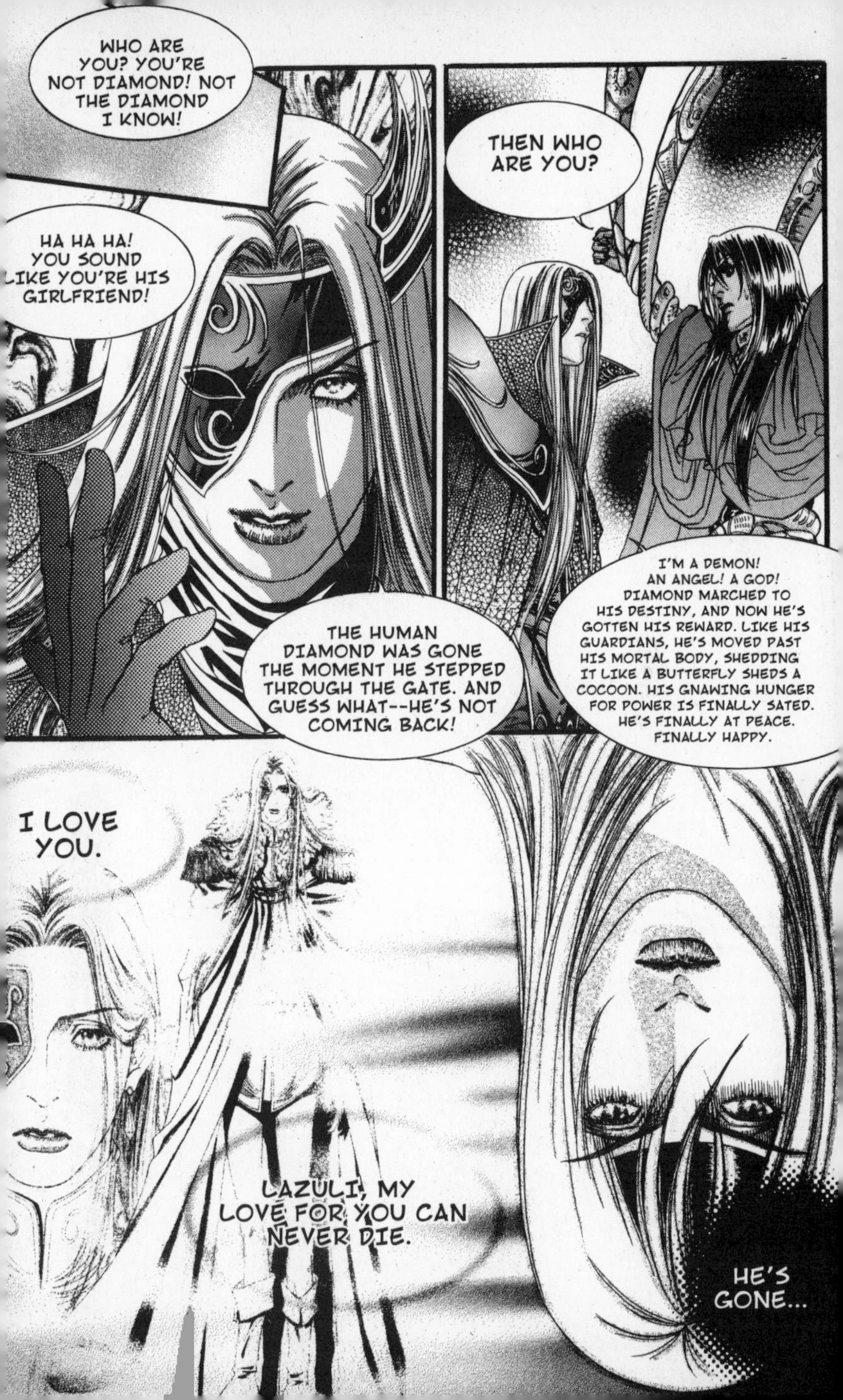
WHO ARE YOU? YOU'RE NOT DIAMOND! NOT THE DIAMOND I KNOW!
HA HA HA! YOU SOUND LIKE YOU'RE HIS GIRLFRIEND!
THEN WHO ARE YOU?
THE HUMAN DIAMOND WAS GONE THE MOMENT HE STEPPED THROUGH THE GATE. AND GUESS WHAT--HE'S NOT COMING BACK!
I'M A DEMON! AN ANGEL! A GOD! DIAMOND MARCHED TO HIS DESTINY, AND NOW HE'S GOTTEN HIS REWARD. LIKE HIS GUARDIANS, HE'S MOVED PAST HIS MORTAL BODY, SHEDDING IT LIKE A BUTTERFLY SHEDS A COCOON. HIS GNAWING HUNGER FOR POWER IS FINALLY SATED. HE'S FINALLY AT PEACE. FINALLY HAPPY.
I LOVE YOU.
LAZULI, MY LOVE FOR YOU CAN NEVER DIE.
HE'S GONE...

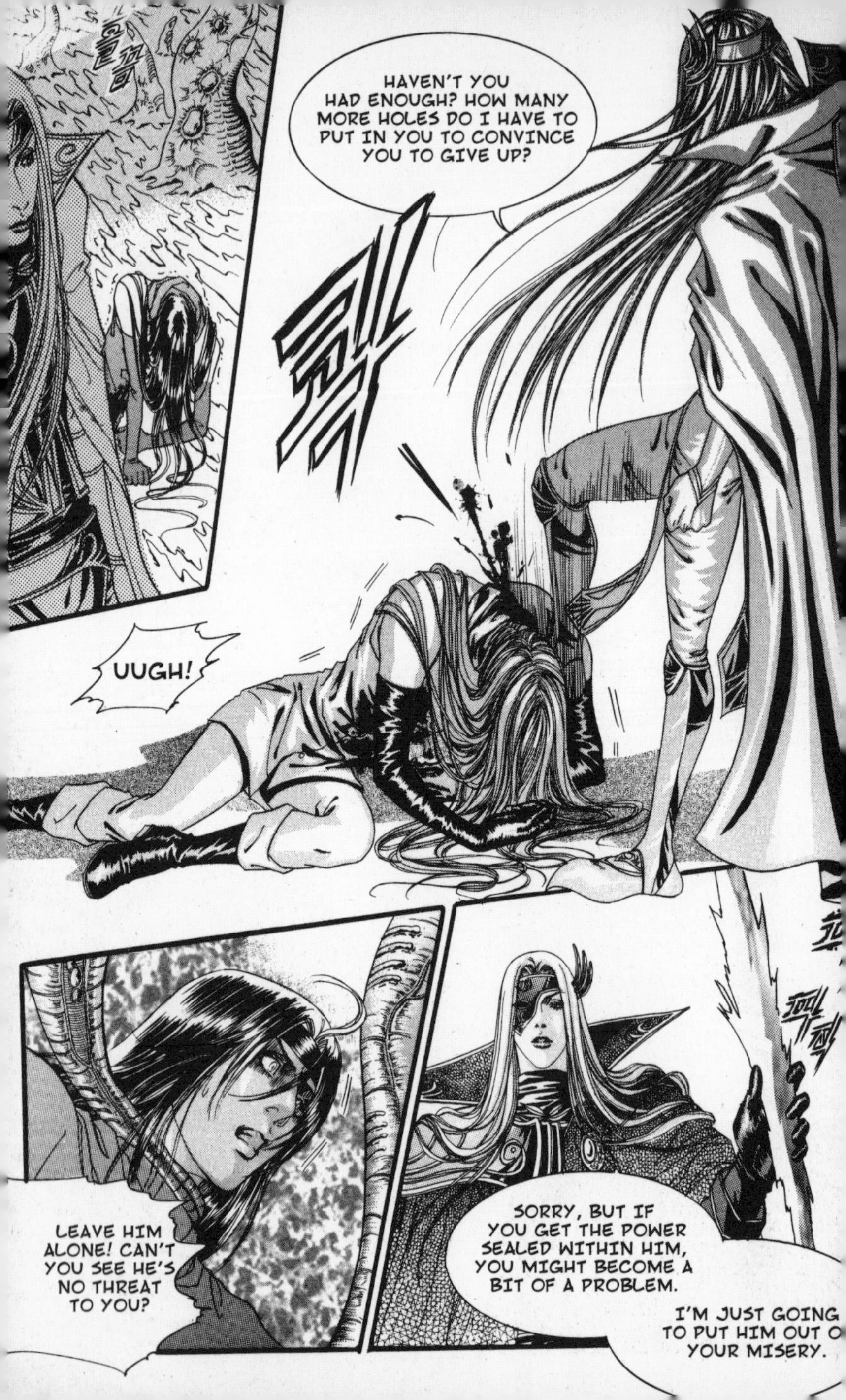
HAVEN'T YOU HAD ENOUGH? HOW MANY MORE HOLES DO I HAVE TO PUT IN YOU TO CONVINCE YOU TO GIVE UP?
UUGH!
SORRY, BUT IF YOU GET THE POWER SEALED WITHIN HIM, YOU MIGHT BECOME A BIT OF A PROBLEM.
I'M JUST GOING TO PUT HIM OUT O YOUR MISERY.
LEAVE HIM ALONE! CAN'T YOU SEE HE'S NO THREAT TO YOU?

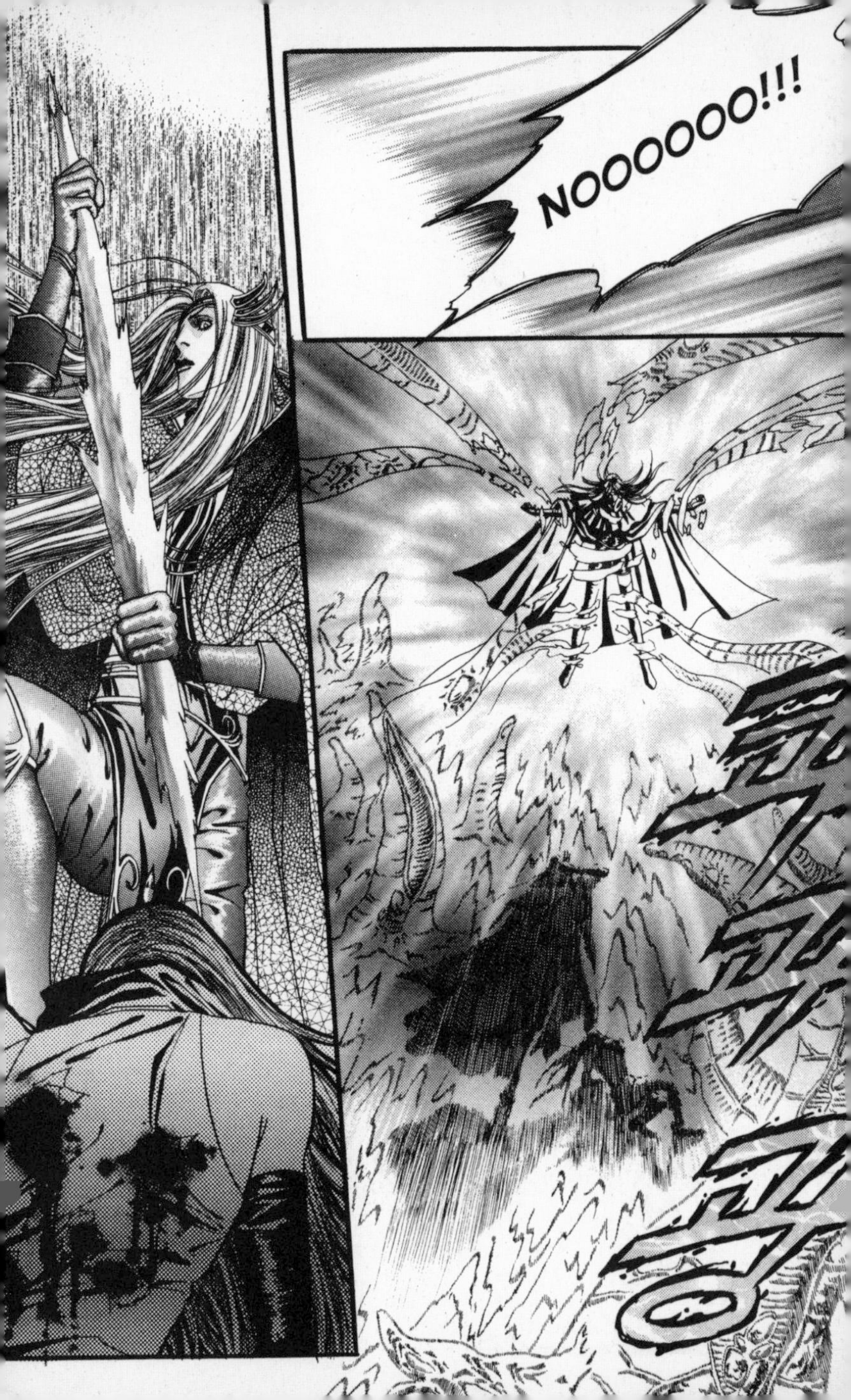
NOOOOOO!!!

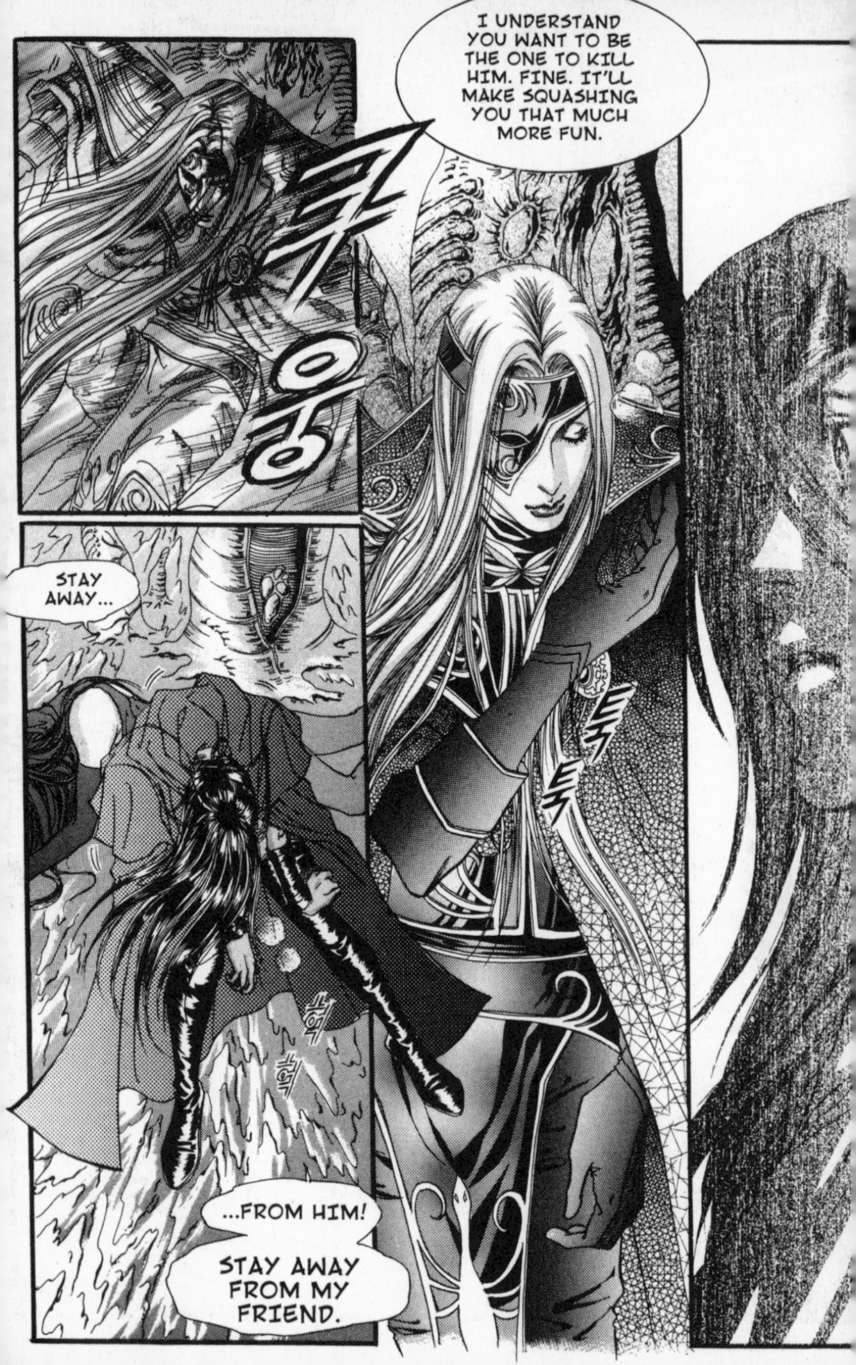
I UNDERSTAND YOU WANT TO BE THE ONE TO KILL HIM. FINE. IT'LL MAKE SQUASHING YOU THAT MUCH MORE FUN.
STAY AWAY...
...FROM HIM!
STAY AWAY FROM MY FRIEND.

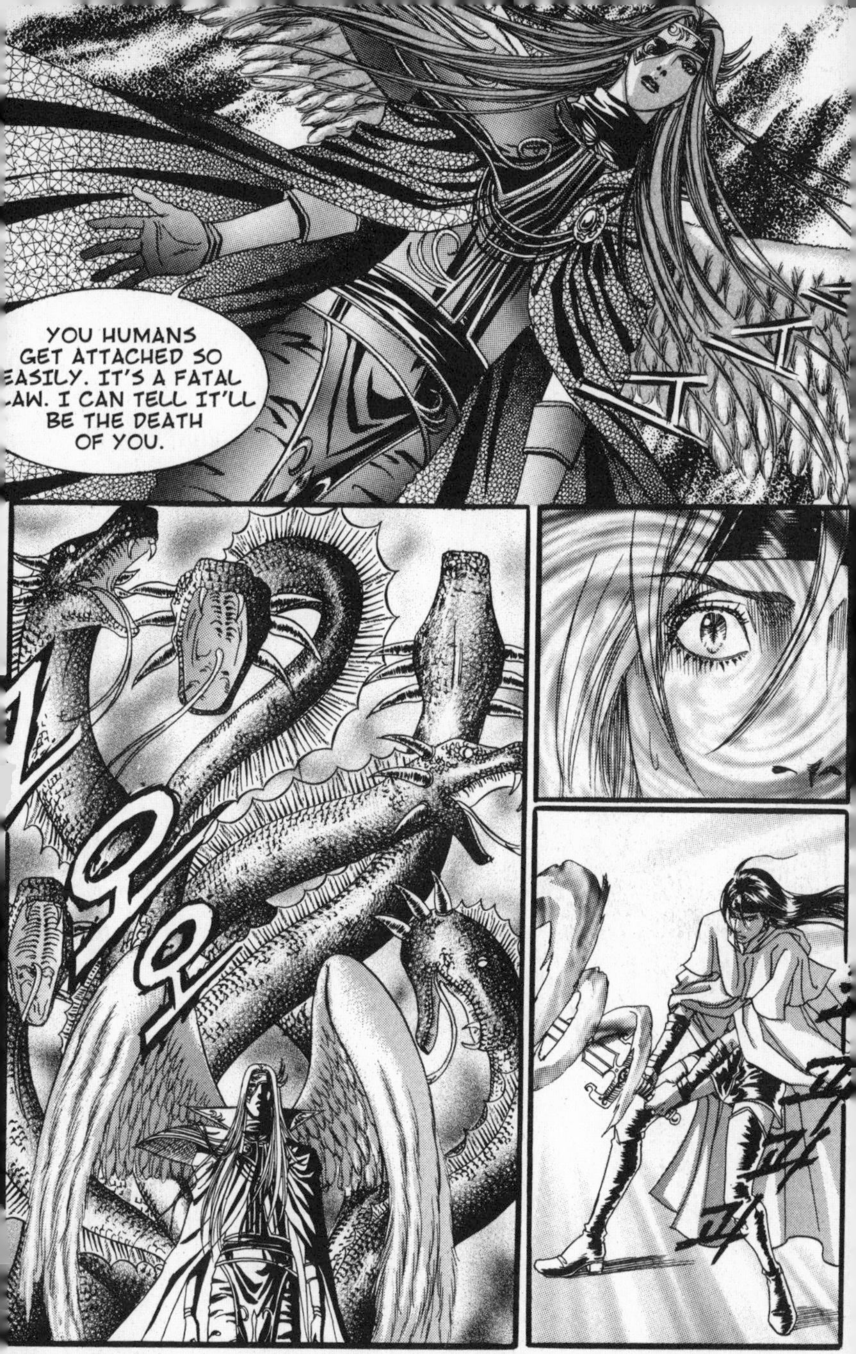
YOU HUMANS GET ATTACHED SO EASILY. IT'S A FATAL LAW. I CAN TELL IT'LL BE THE DEATH OF YOU.

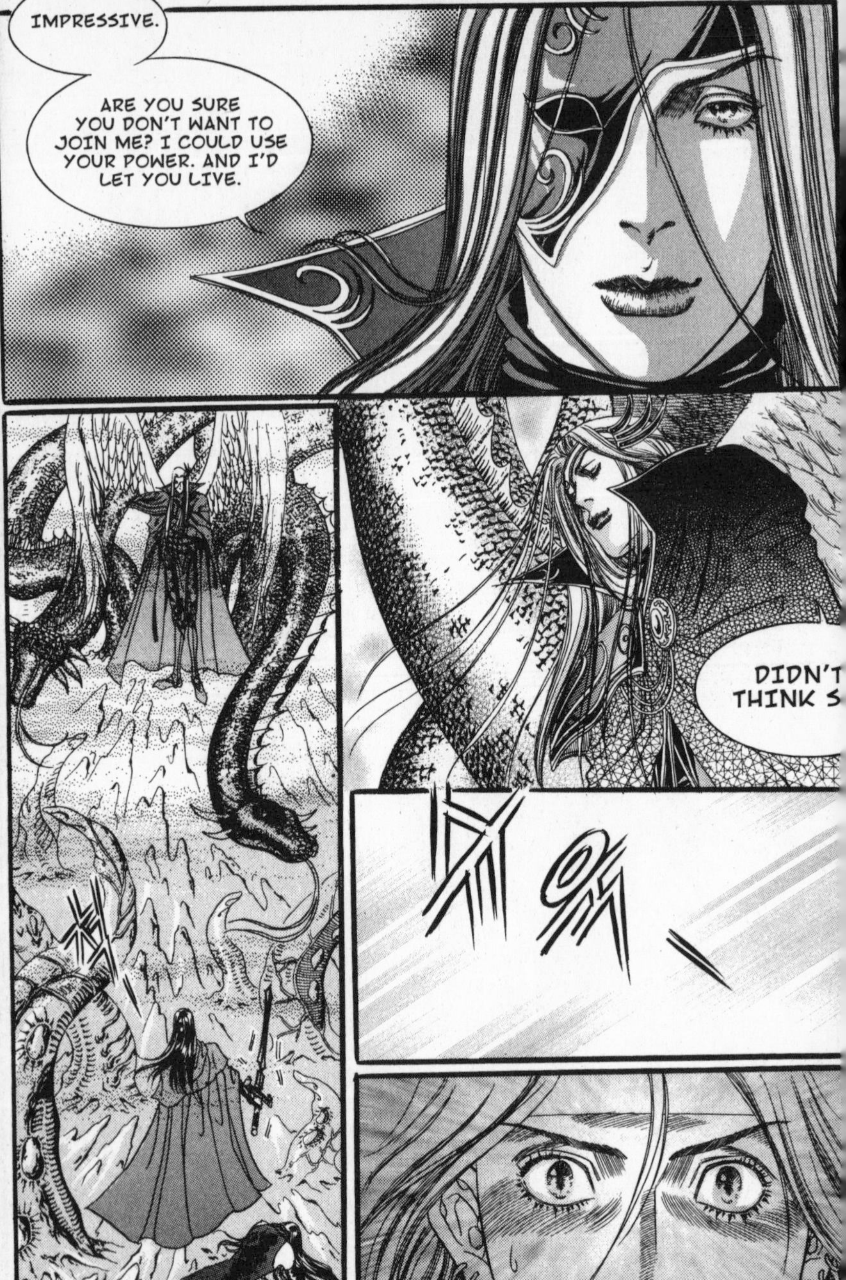
IMPRESSIVE.
ARE YOU SURE YOU DON'T WANT TO JOIN ME? I COULD USE YOUR POWER. AND I'D LET YOU LIVE.
DIDN'T THINK S

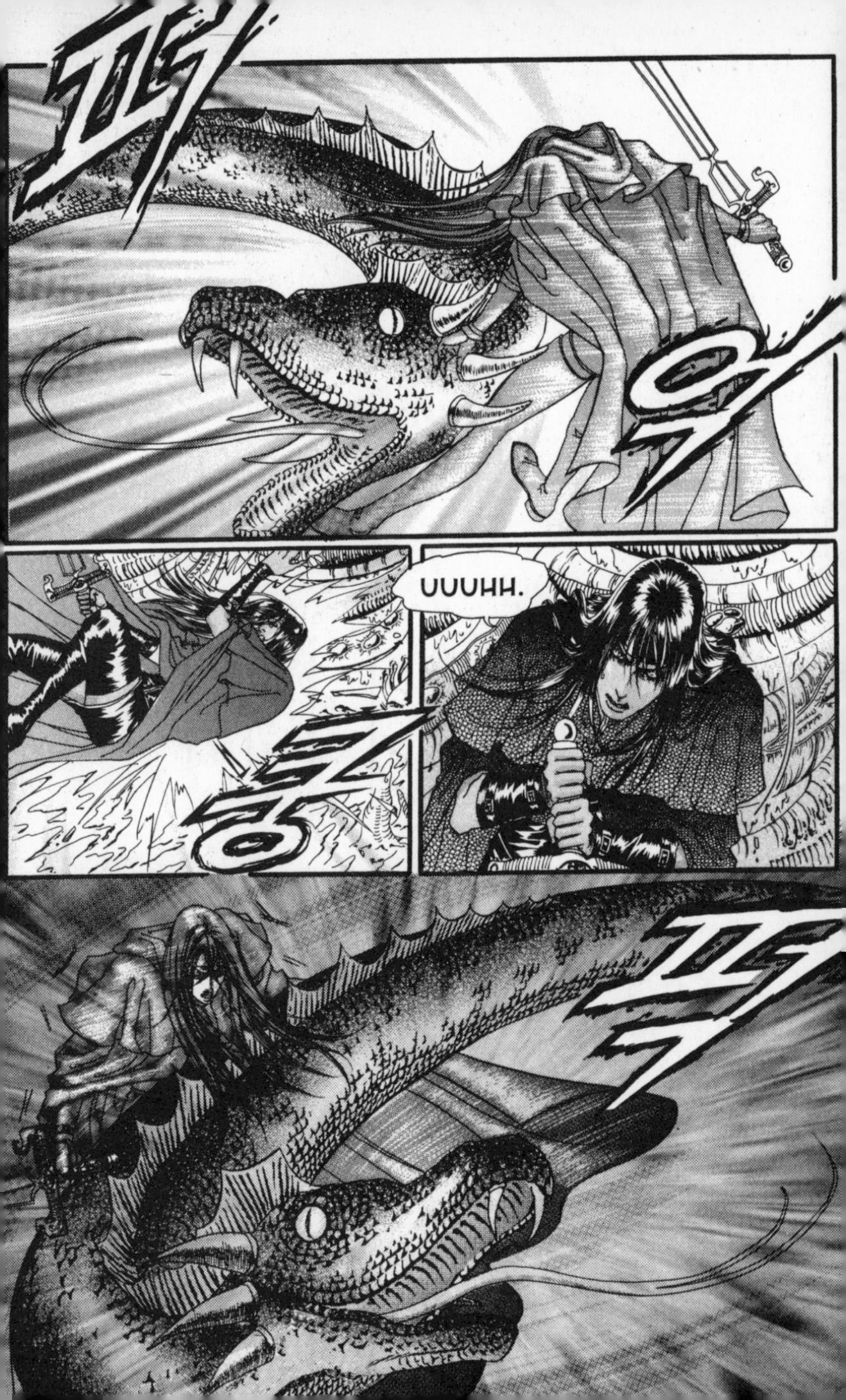
UUUHH.

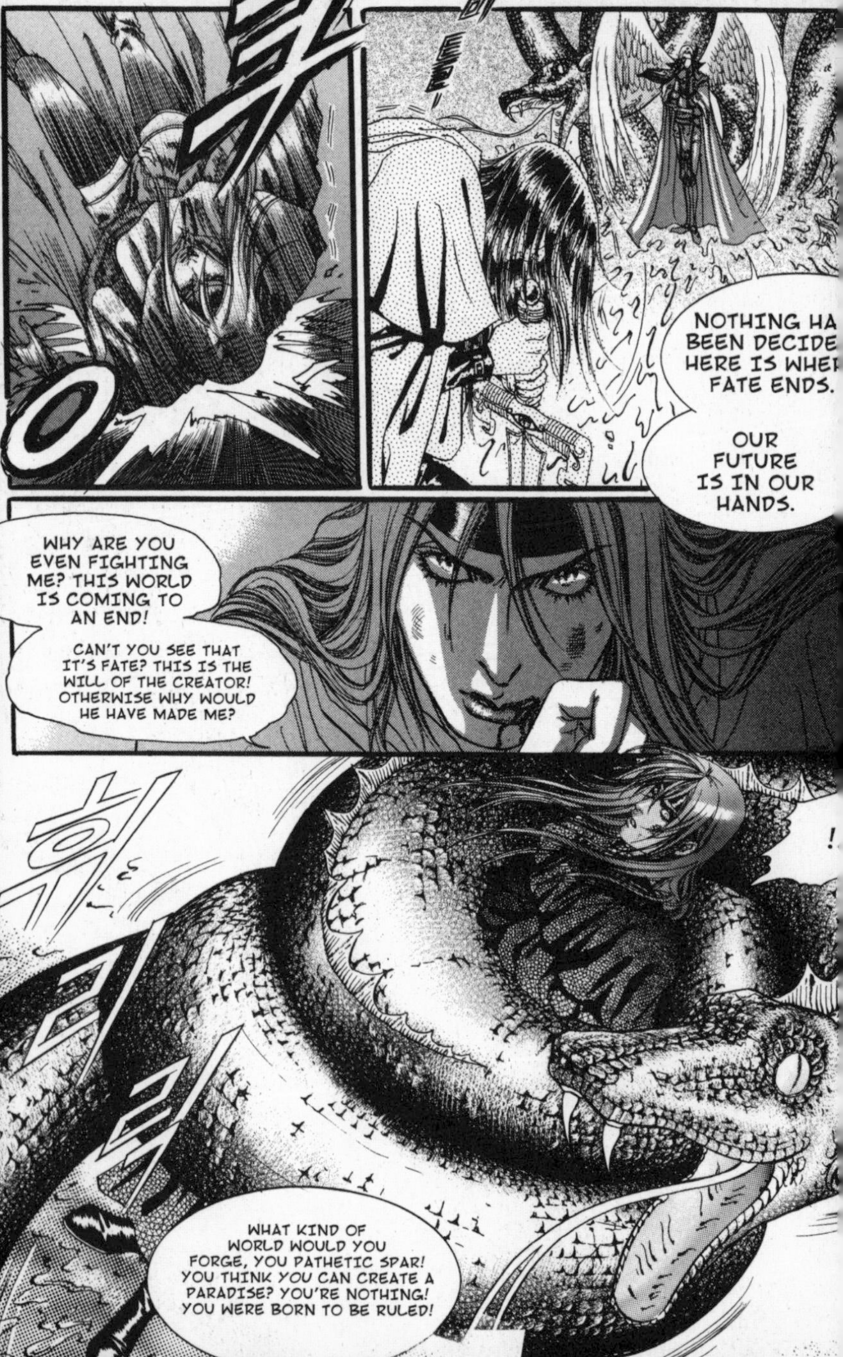
NOTHING HA BEEN DECIDE HERE IS WHEI FATE ENDS.
OUR FUTURE IS IN OUR HANDS.
WHY ARE YOU EVEN FIGHTING ME? THIS WORLD IS COMING TO AN END!
CAN'T YOU SEE THAT IT'S FATE? THIS IS THE WILL OF THE CREATOR! OTHERWISE WHY WOULD HE HAVE MADE ME?
!
WHAT KIND OF WORLD WOULD YOU FORGE, YOU PATHETIC SPAR! YOU THINK YOU CAN CREATE A PARADISE? YOU'RE NOTHING! YOU WERE BORN TO BE RULED!

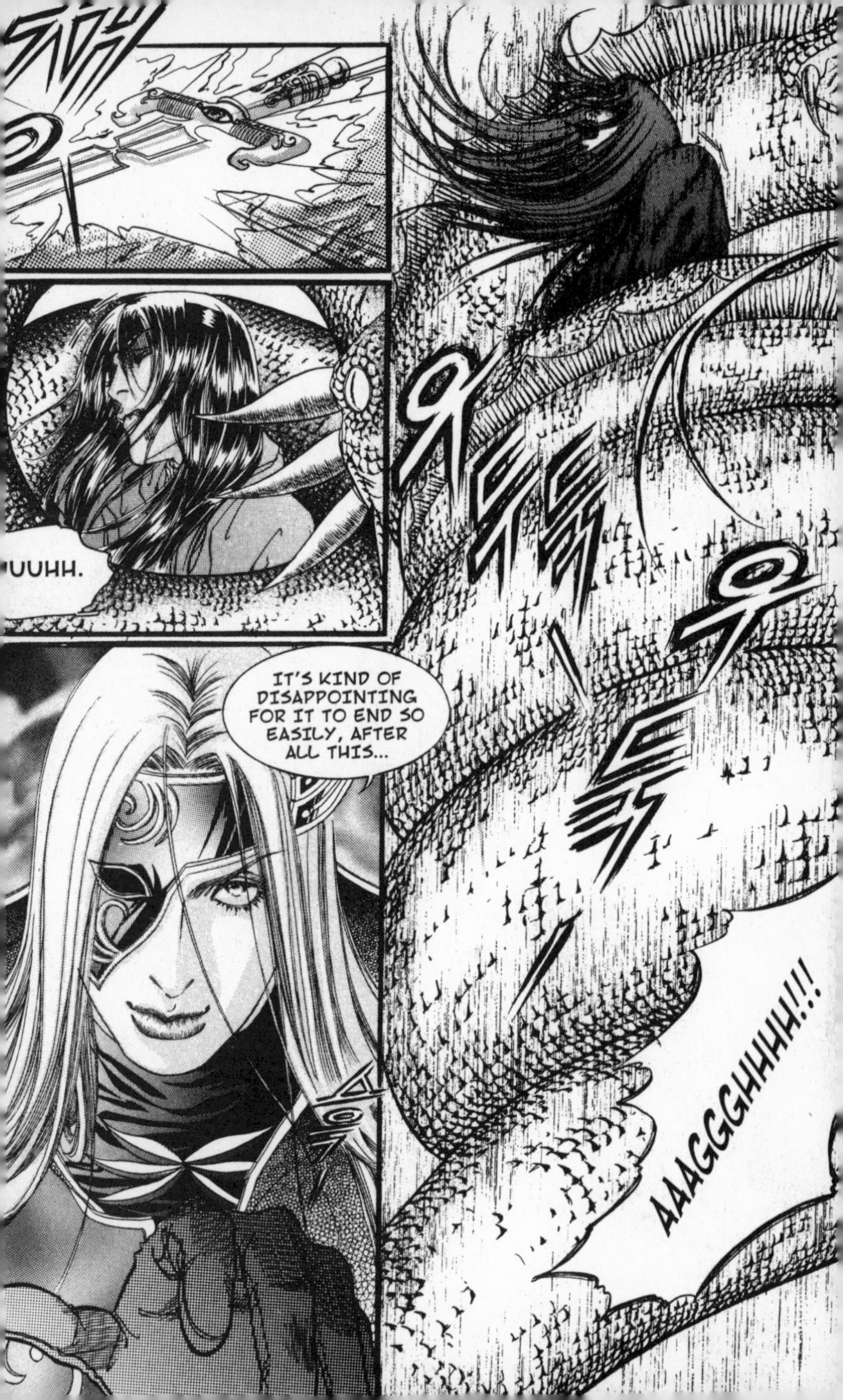
UUHH.
IT'S KIND OF DISAPPOINTING FOR IT TO END SO EASILY, AFTER ALL THIS...
AAAGGGHHHH!!!

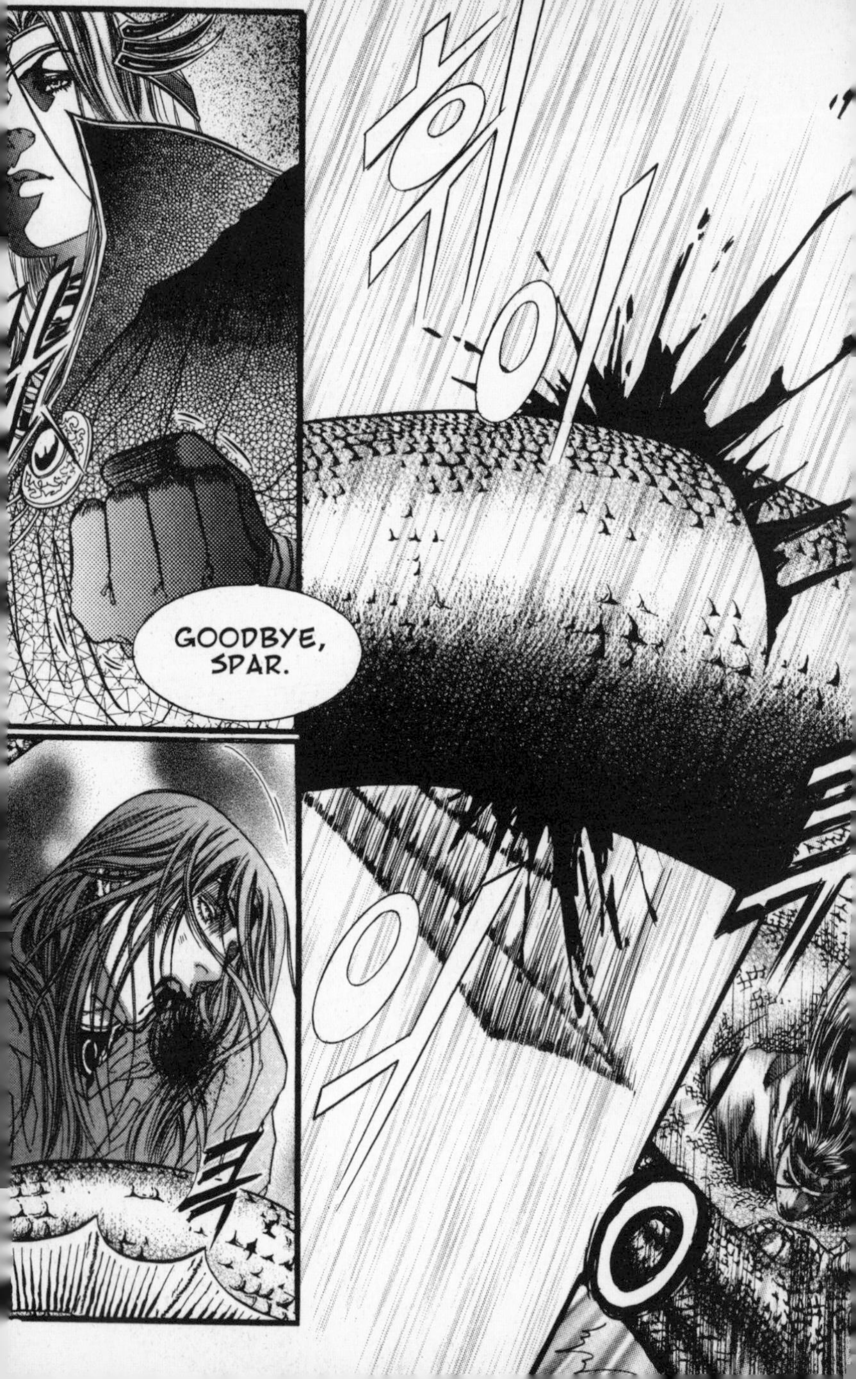
GOODBYE, SPAR.

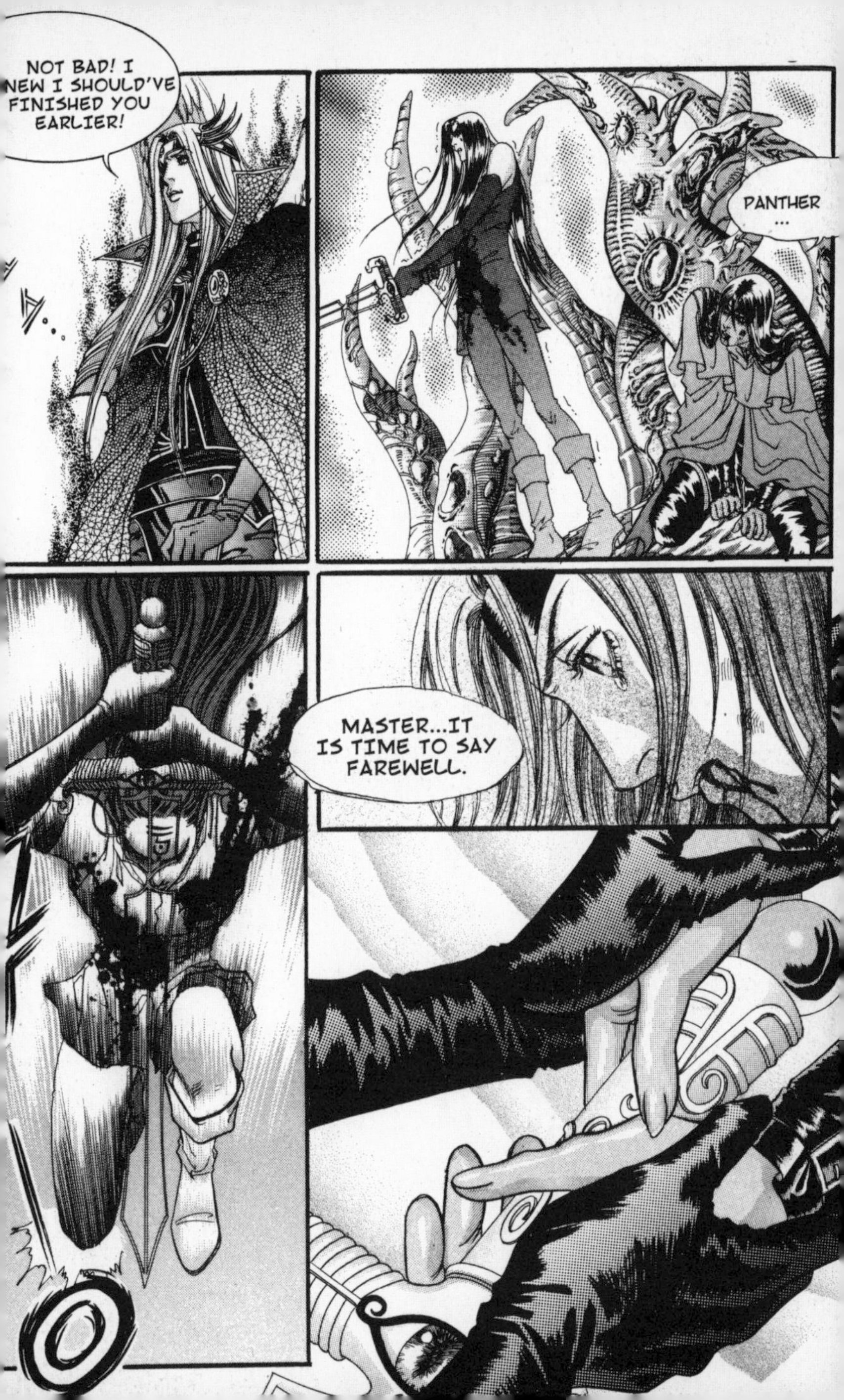
NOT BAD! I NEW I SHOULD'VE FINISHED YOU EARLIER!
PANTHER ...
MASTER...IT IS TIME TO SAY FAREWELL.

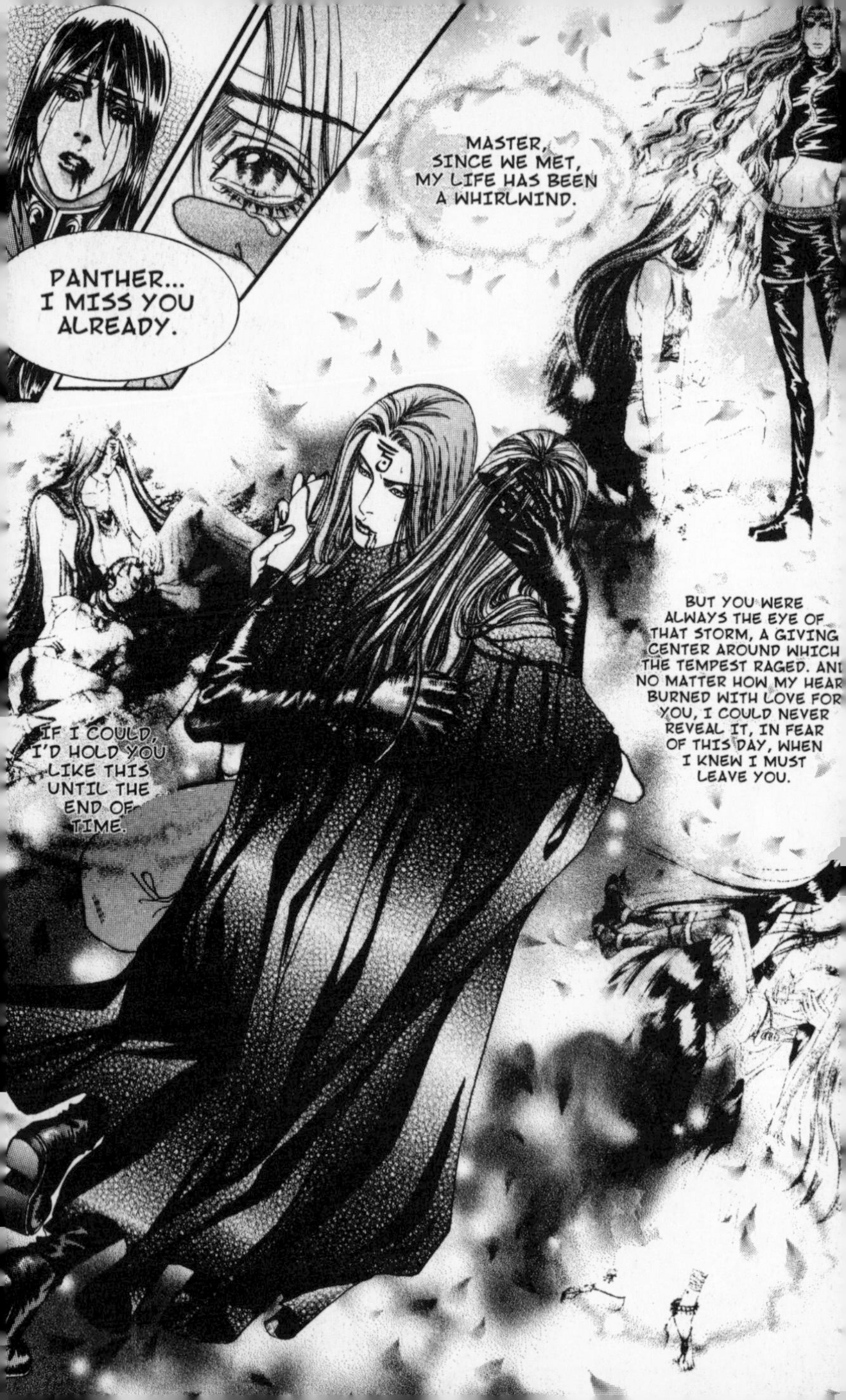
PANTHER... I MISS YOU ALREADY.
MASTER, SINCE WE MET, MY LIFE HAS BEEN A WHIRLWIND.
BUT YOU WERE ALWAYS THE EYE OF THAT STORM, A GIVING CENTER AROUND WHICH THE TEMPEST RAGED. AN
NO MATTER HOW MY HEAR BURNED WITH LOVE FOR YOU, I COULD NEVER REVEAL IT, IN FEAR OF THIS DAY, WHEN I KNEW I MUST LEAVE YOU.
IF I COULD, I'D HOLD YOU LIKE THIS UNTIL THE END OF TIME.

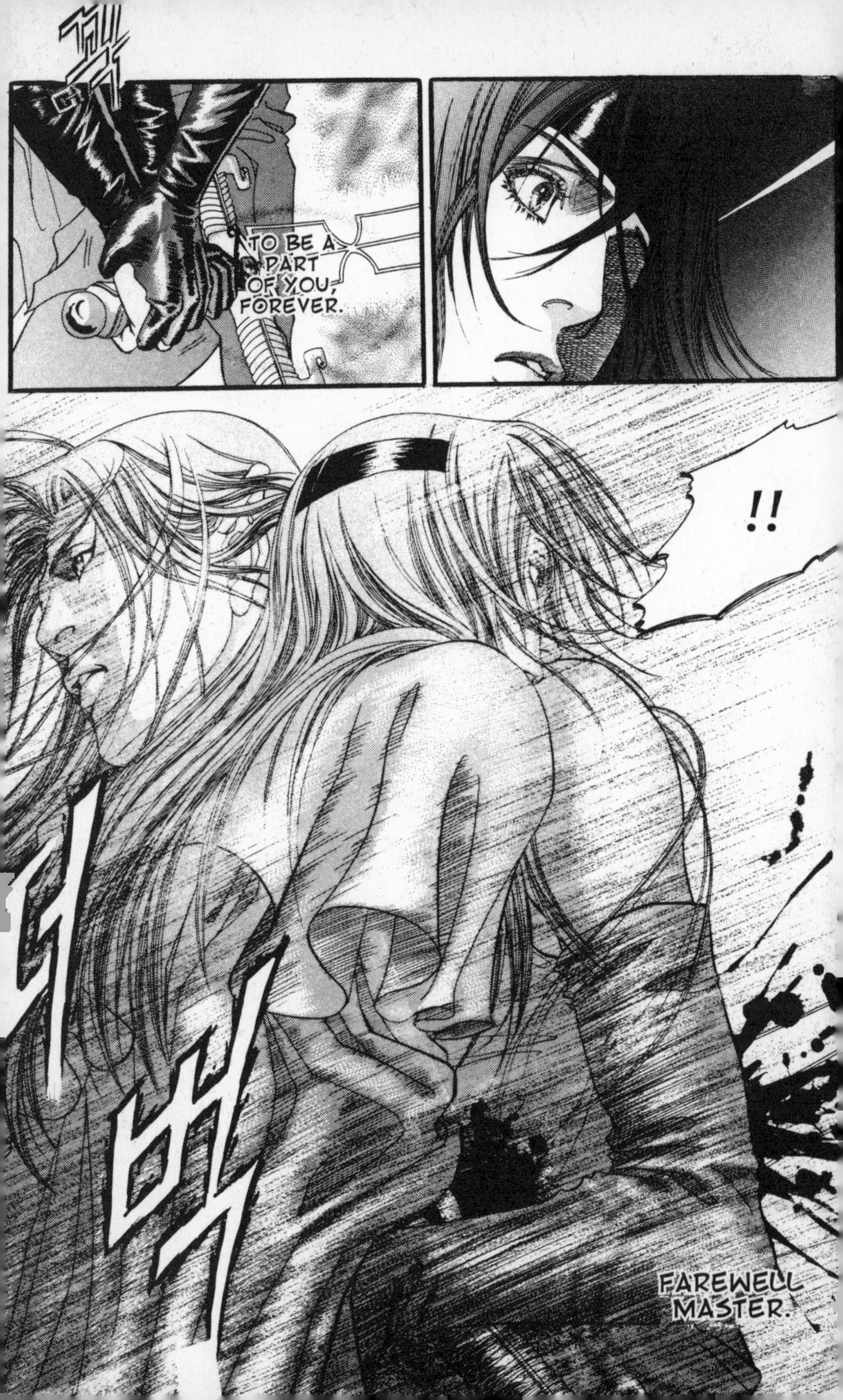

TO BE A PART OF YOU, FOREVER.
!!
FAREWELL MASTER.

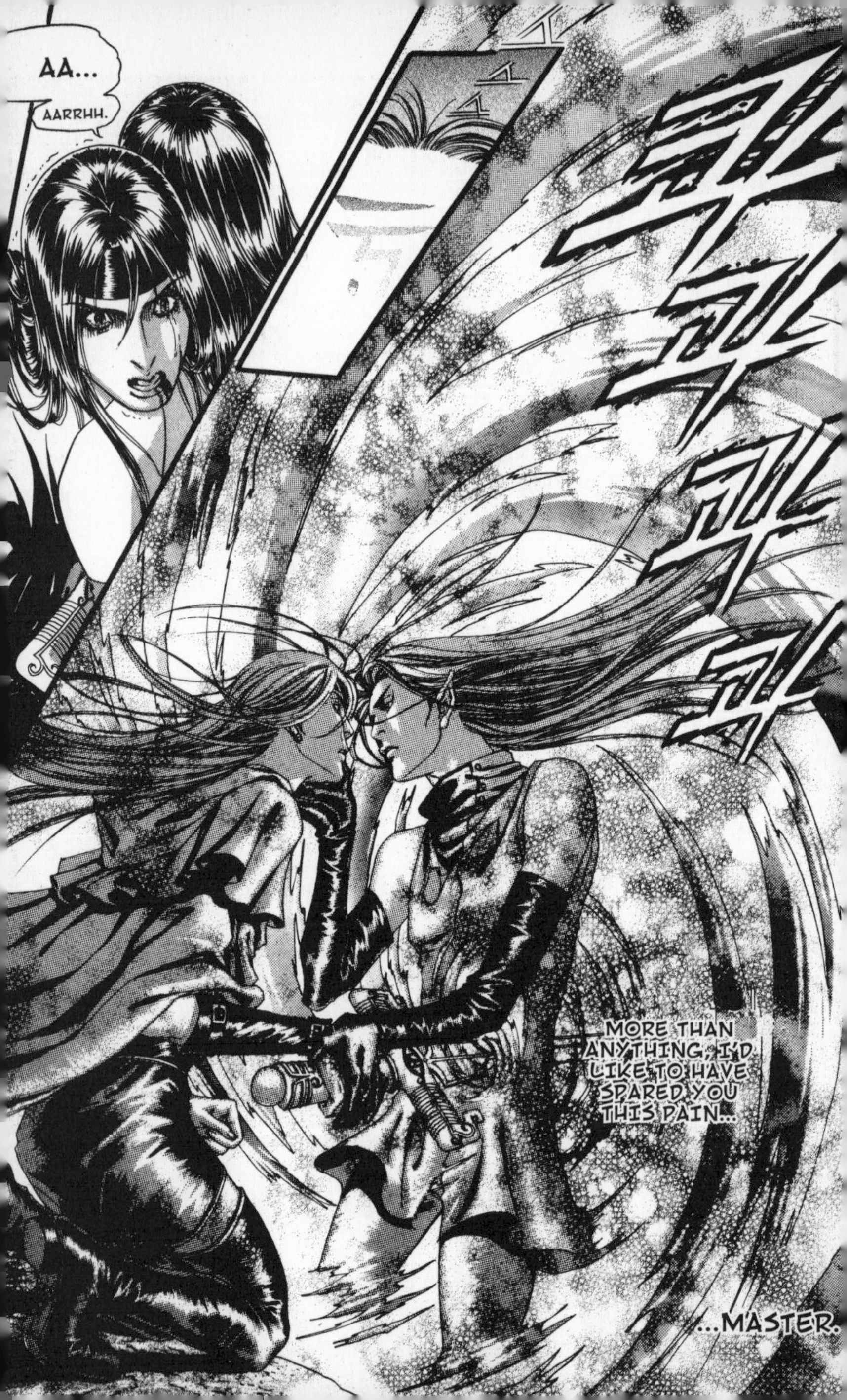

AA...
AARRHH.
MORE THAN ANYTHING, I'D LIKE TO HAVE SPARED YOU THIS PAIN...
...MASTER.

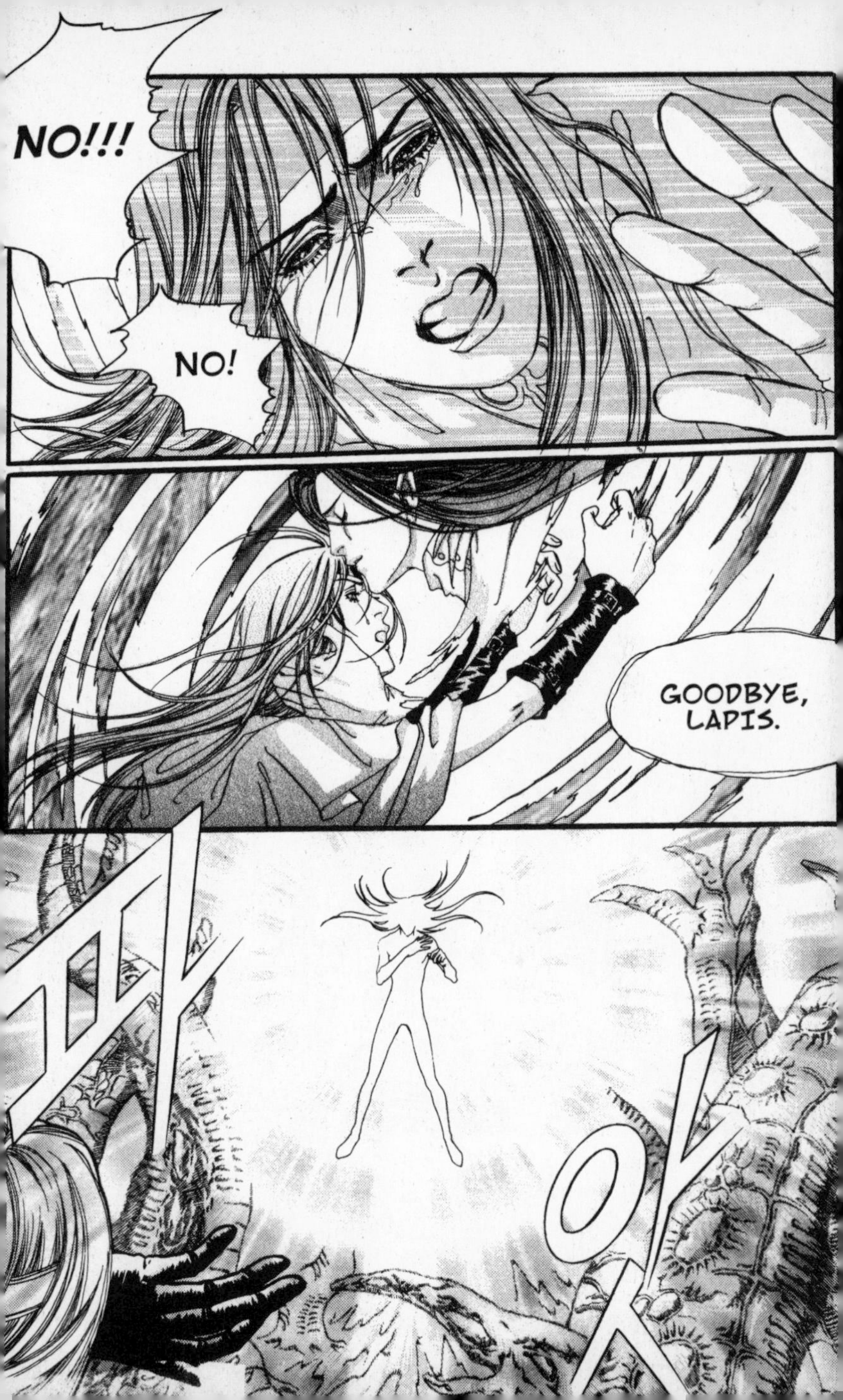
NO!!!
NO!
GOODBYE, LAPIS.

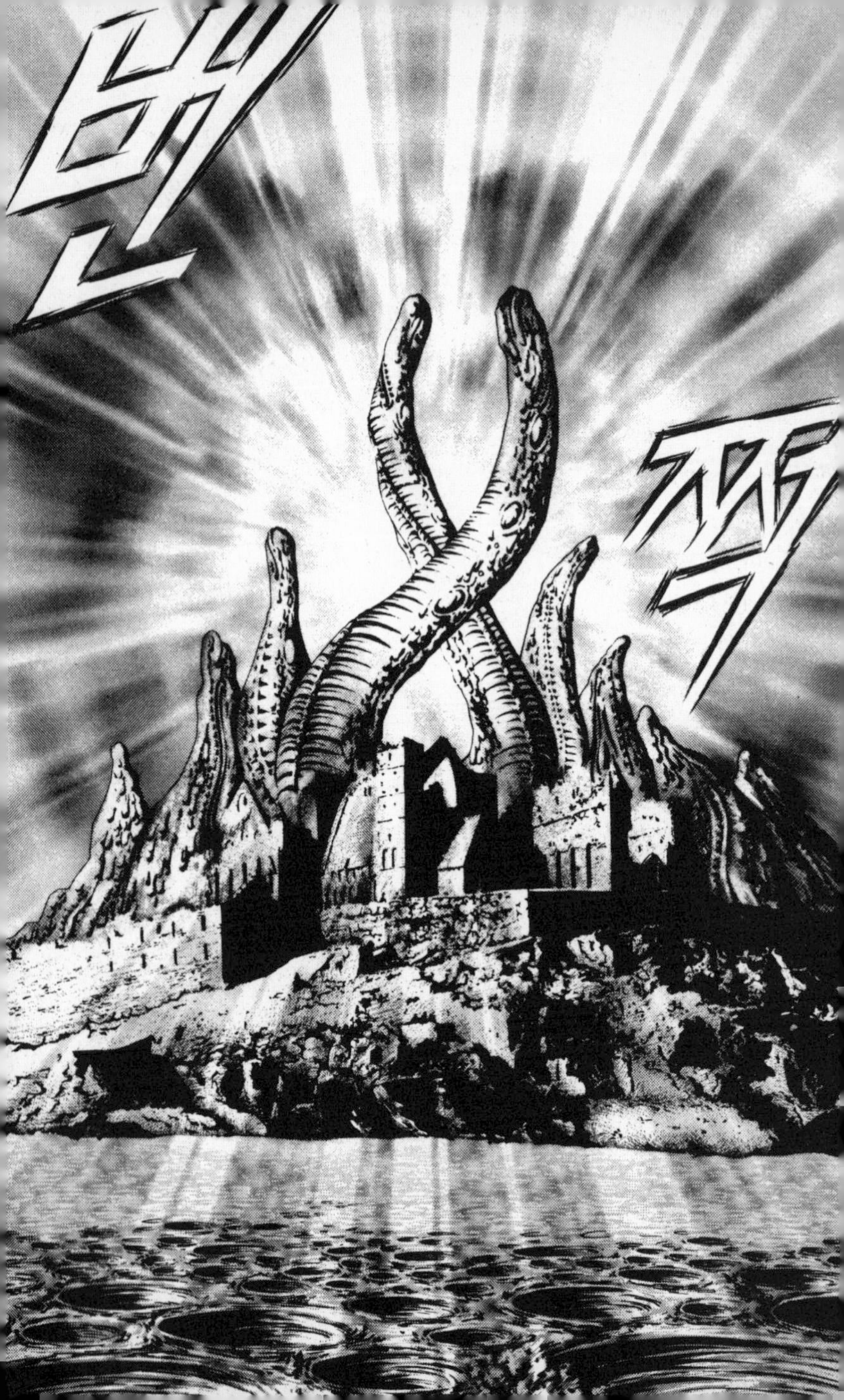

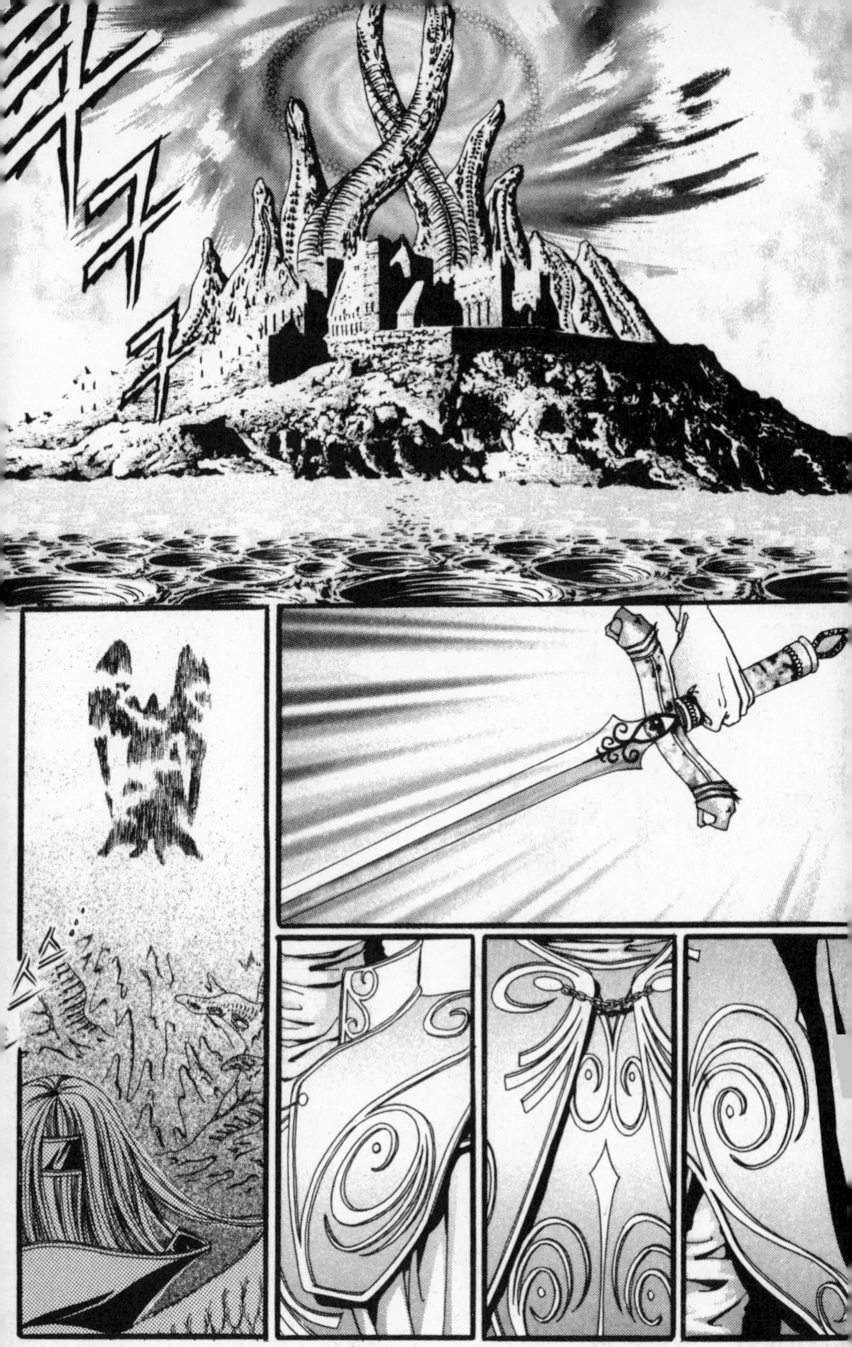

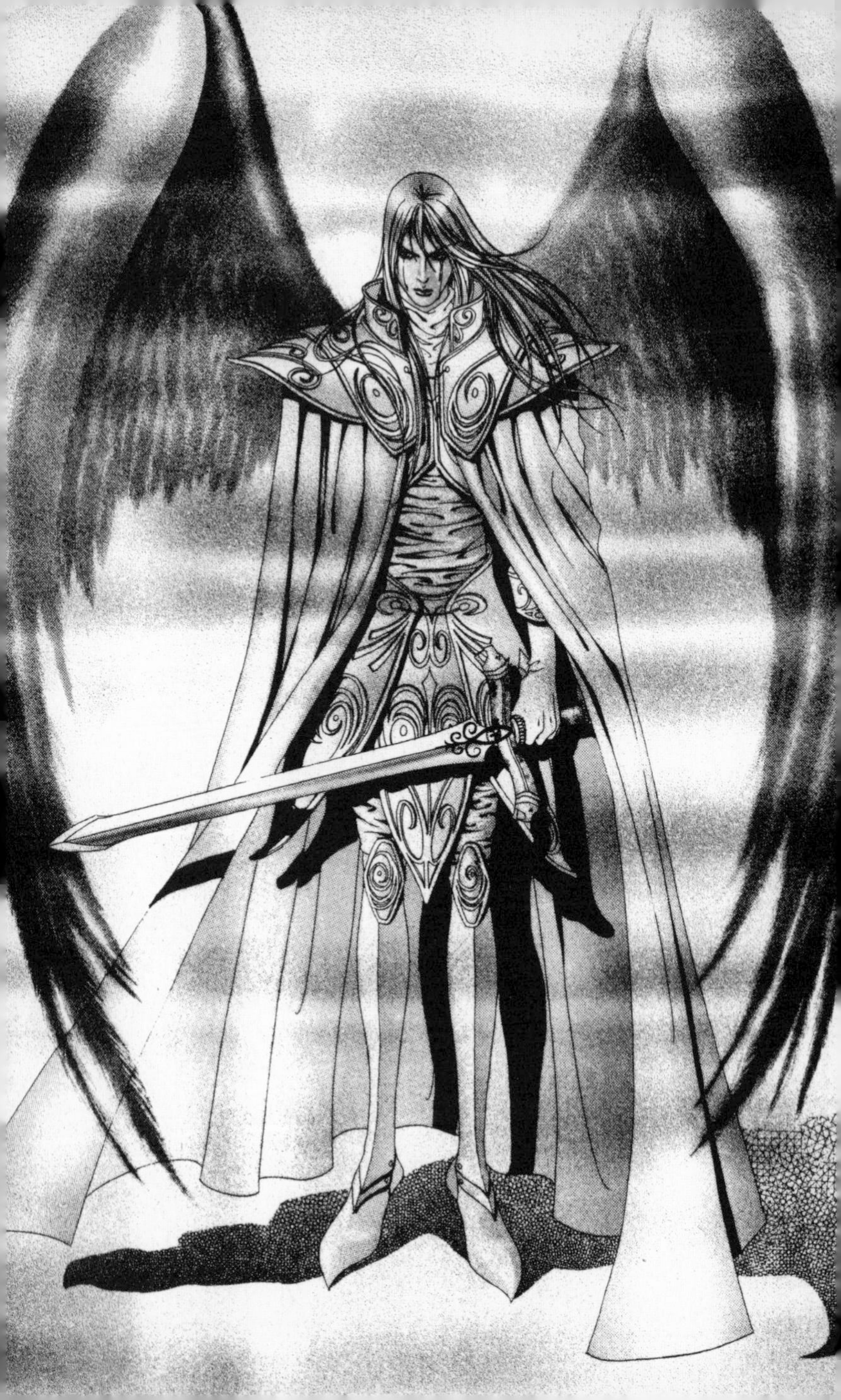

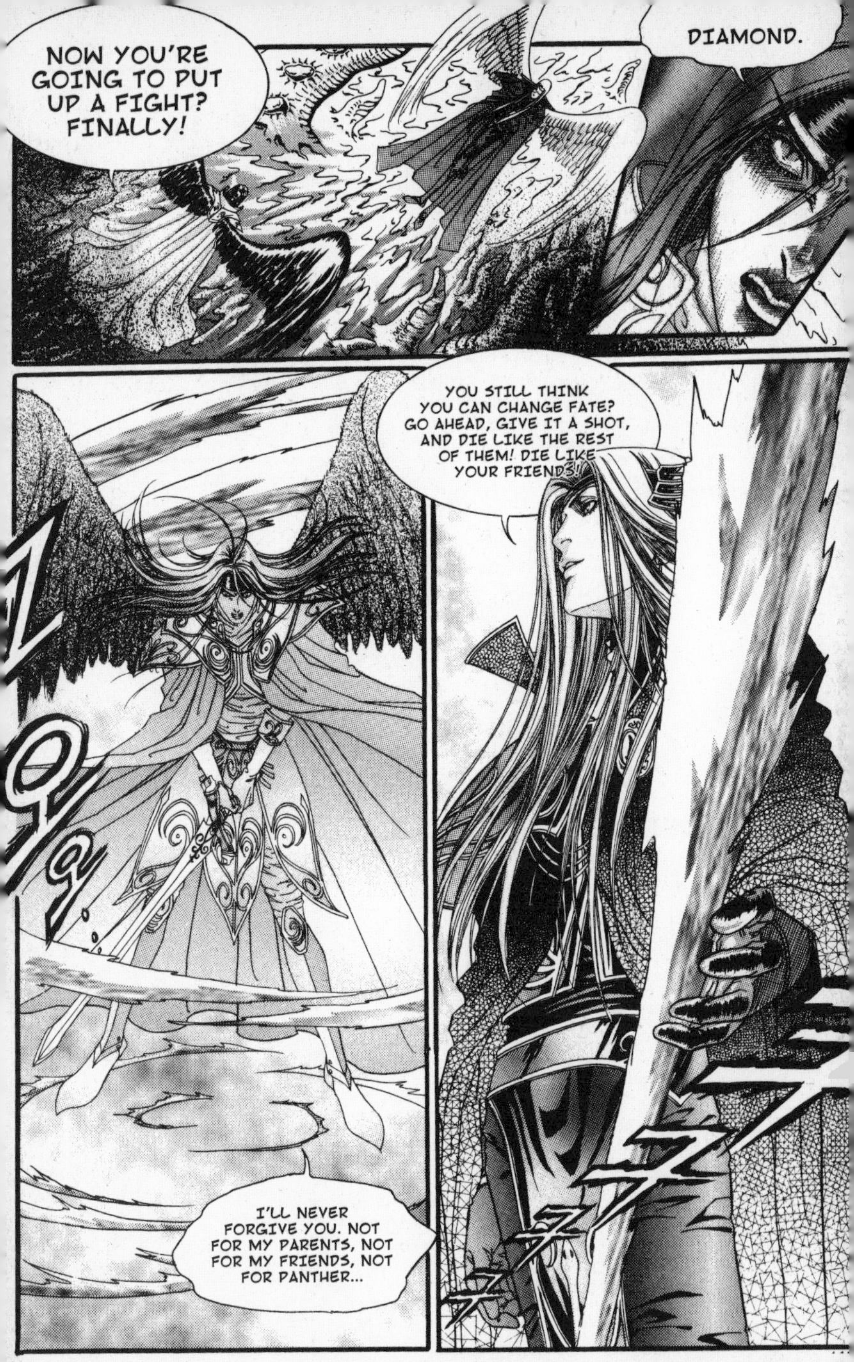
NOW YOU'RE GOING TO PUT UP A FIGHT? FINALLY!
DIAMOND.
YOU STILL THINK YOU CAN CHANGE FATE? GO AHEAD, GIVE IT A SHOT, AND DIE LIKE THE REST OF THEM! DIE LIKE YOUR FRIENDS!
I'LL NEVER FORGIVE YOU. NOT FOR MY PARENTS, NOT FOR MY FRIENDS, NOT FOR PANTHER...

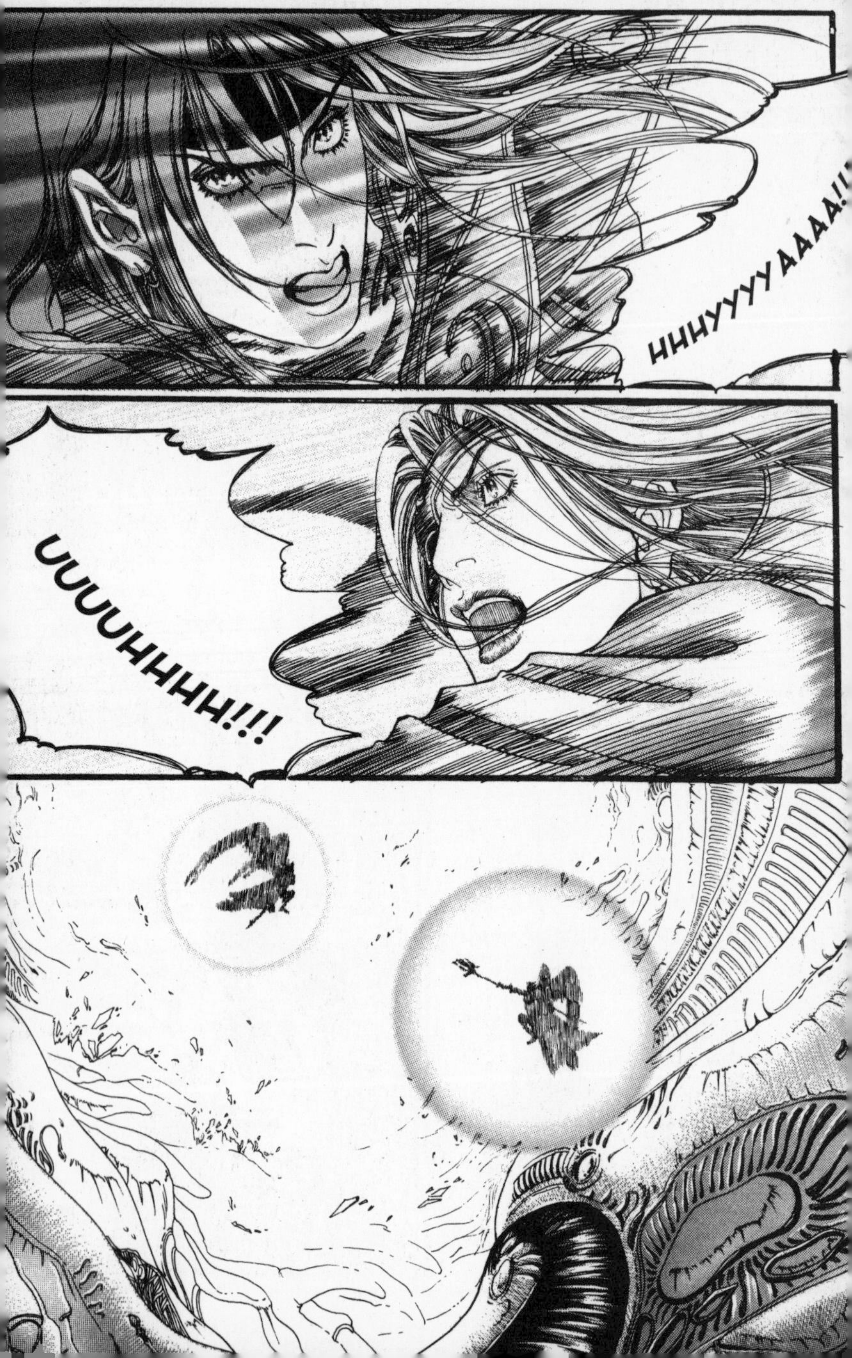
HHHYYYYAAAA!!!
UUUUHHHHH!!!

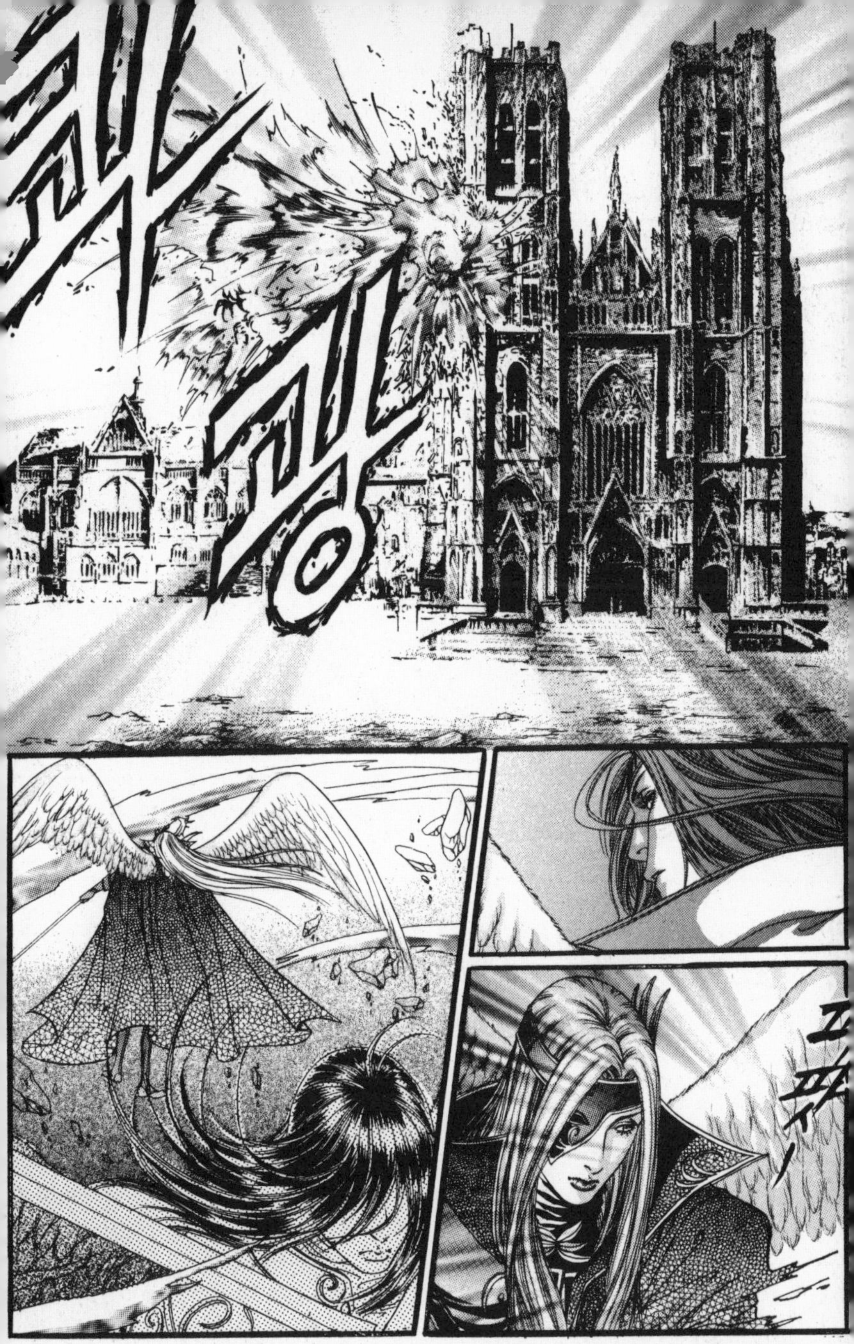
콰가캉

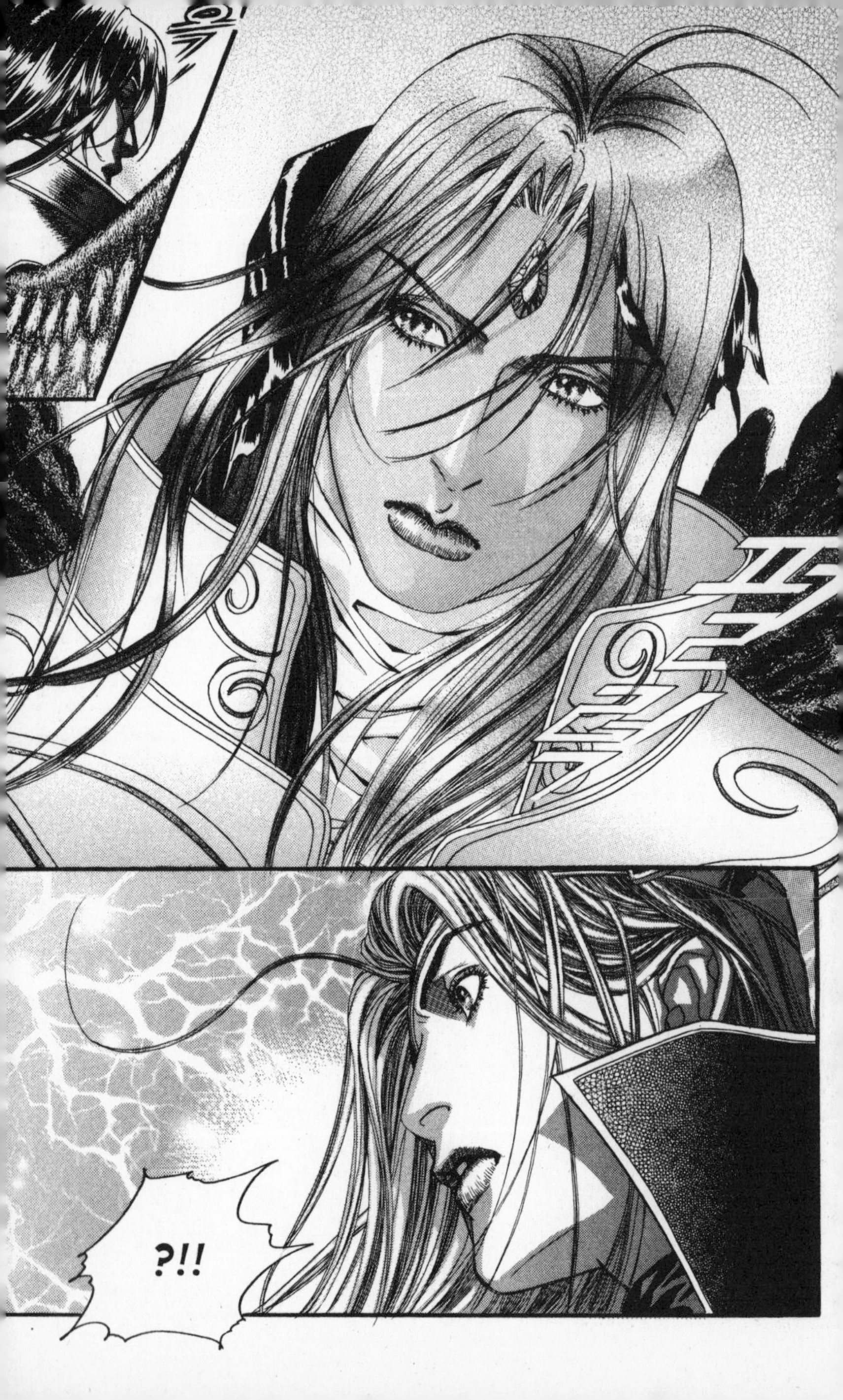
?!!

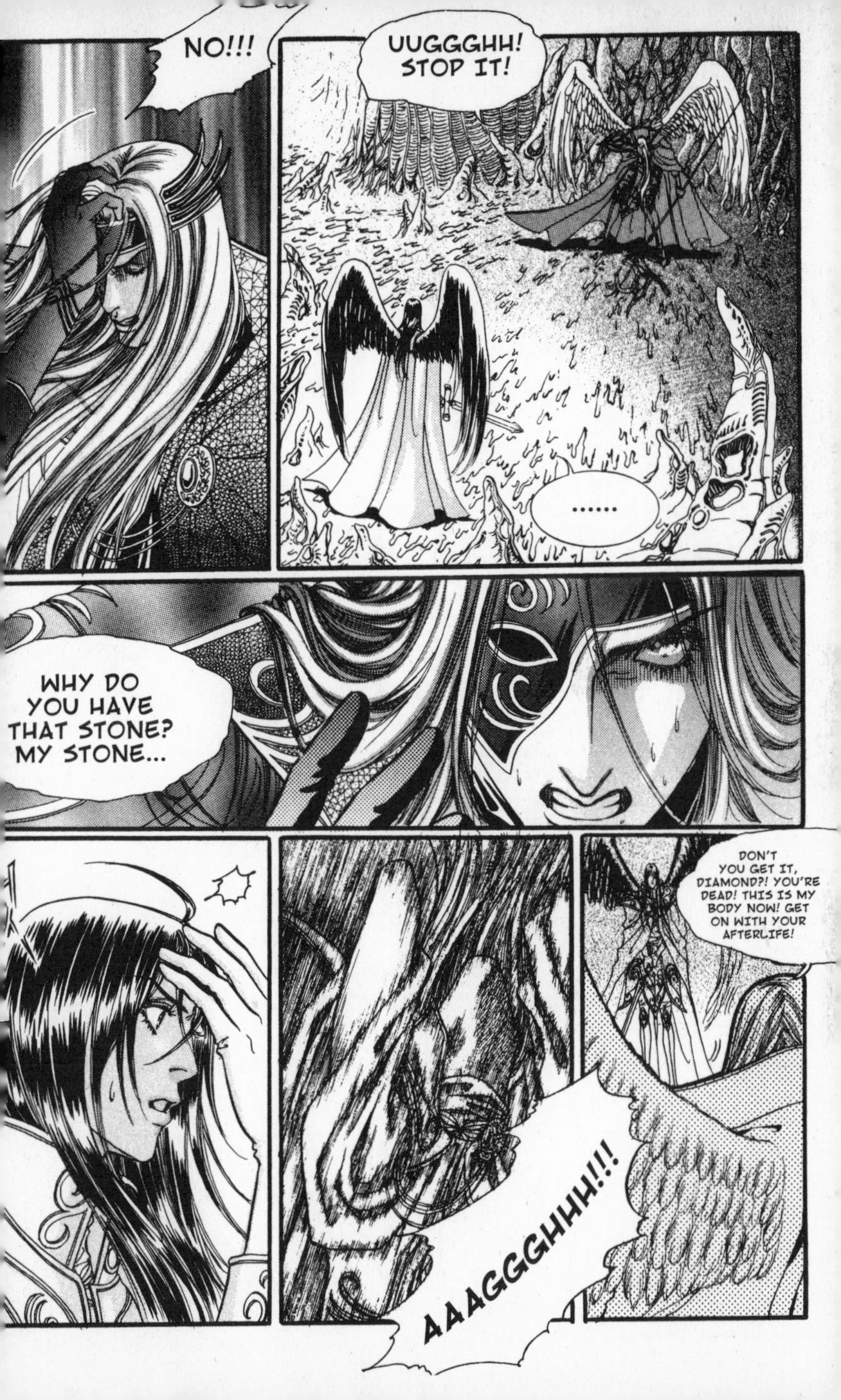
NO!!!
UUGGGHH! STOP IT!
......
WHY DO YOU HAVE THAT STONE? MY STONE...
DON'T YOU GET IT, DIAMOND?! YOU'RE DEAD! THIS IS MY BODY NOW! GET ON WITH YOUR AFTERLIFE!
AAAGGGHHH!!!

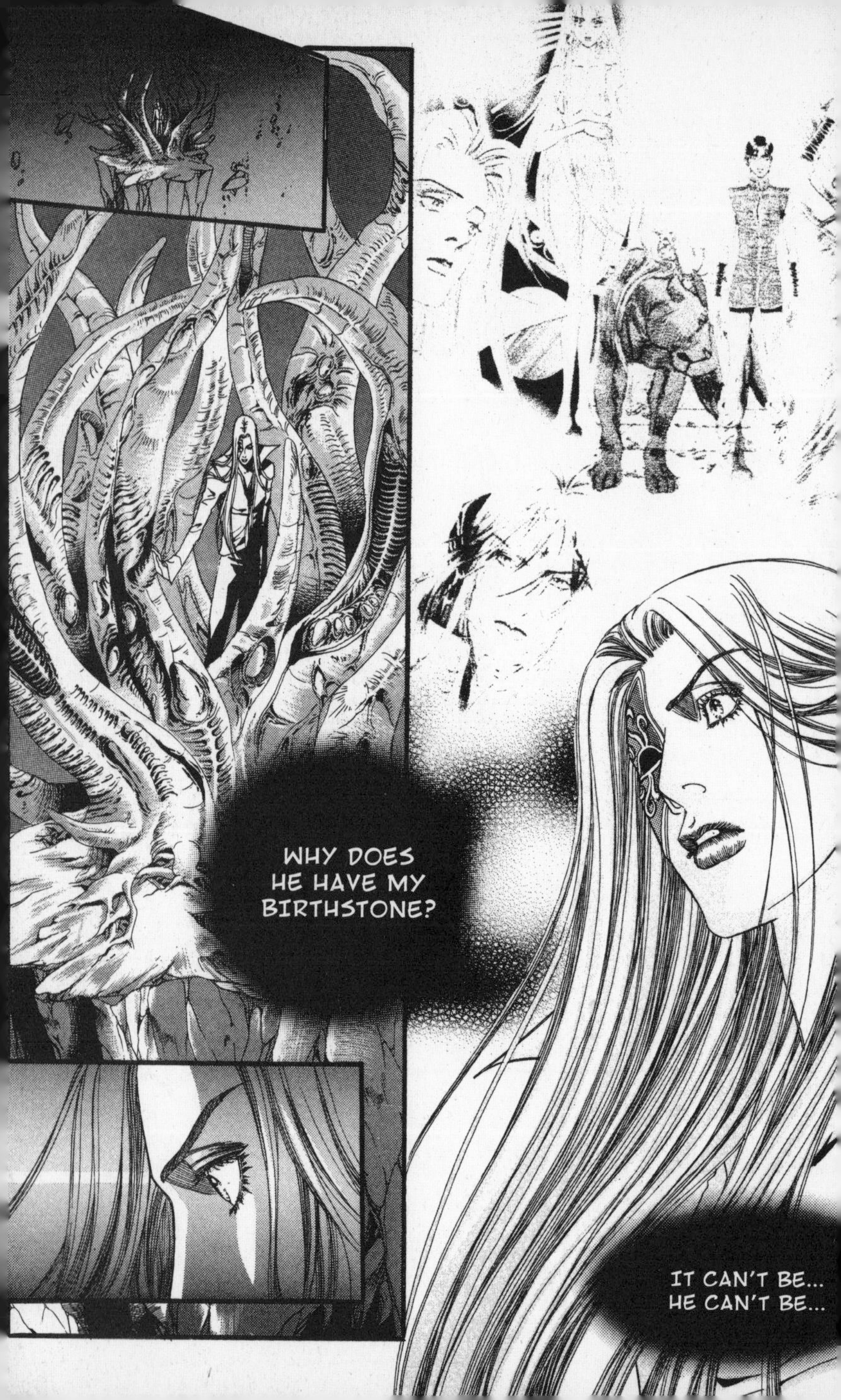
WHY DOES
HE HAVE MY
BIRTHSTONE?
IT CAN'T BE...
HE CAN'T BE...

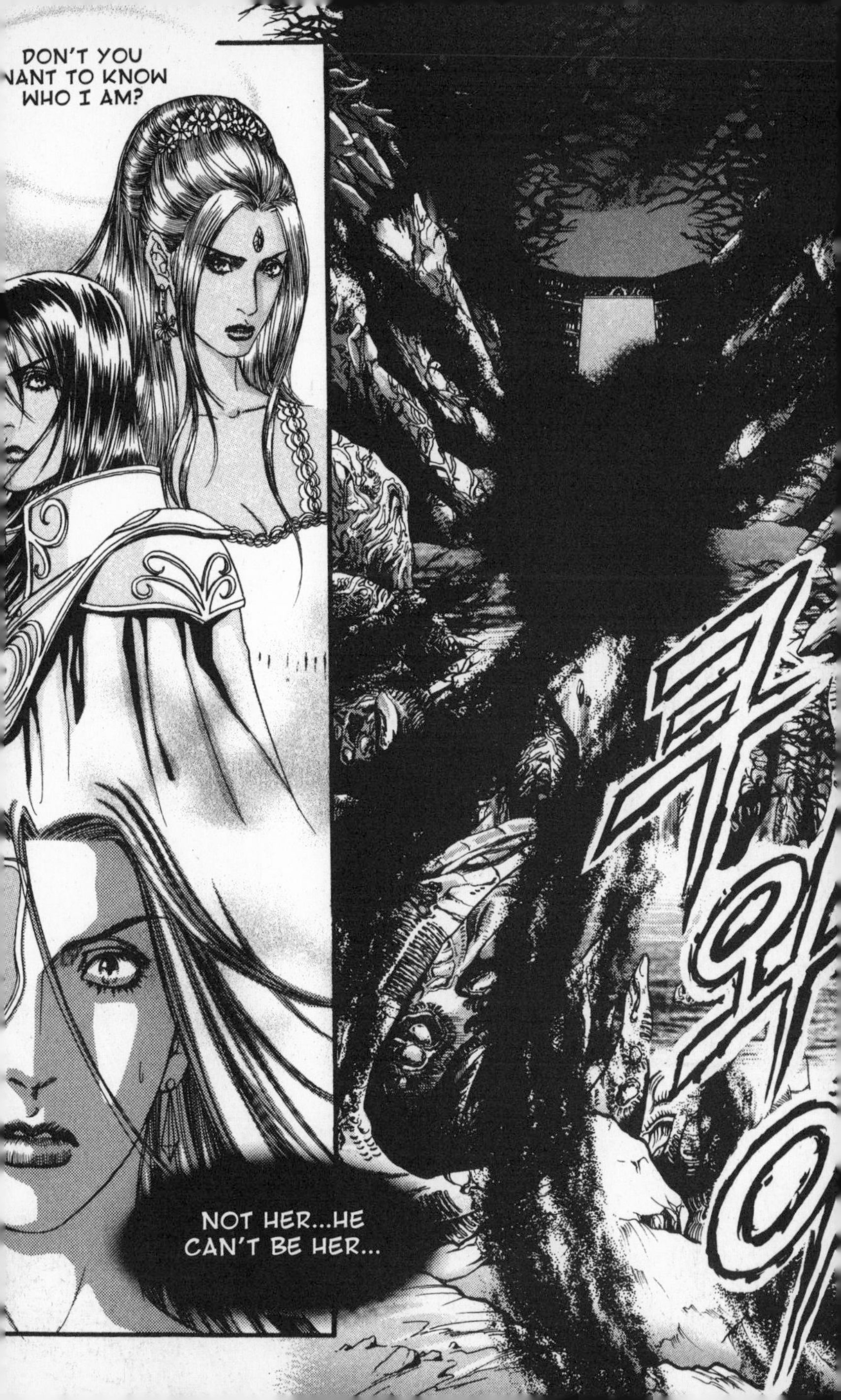

DON'T YOU WANT TO KNOW WHO I AM?
NOT HER...HE CAN'T BE HER...

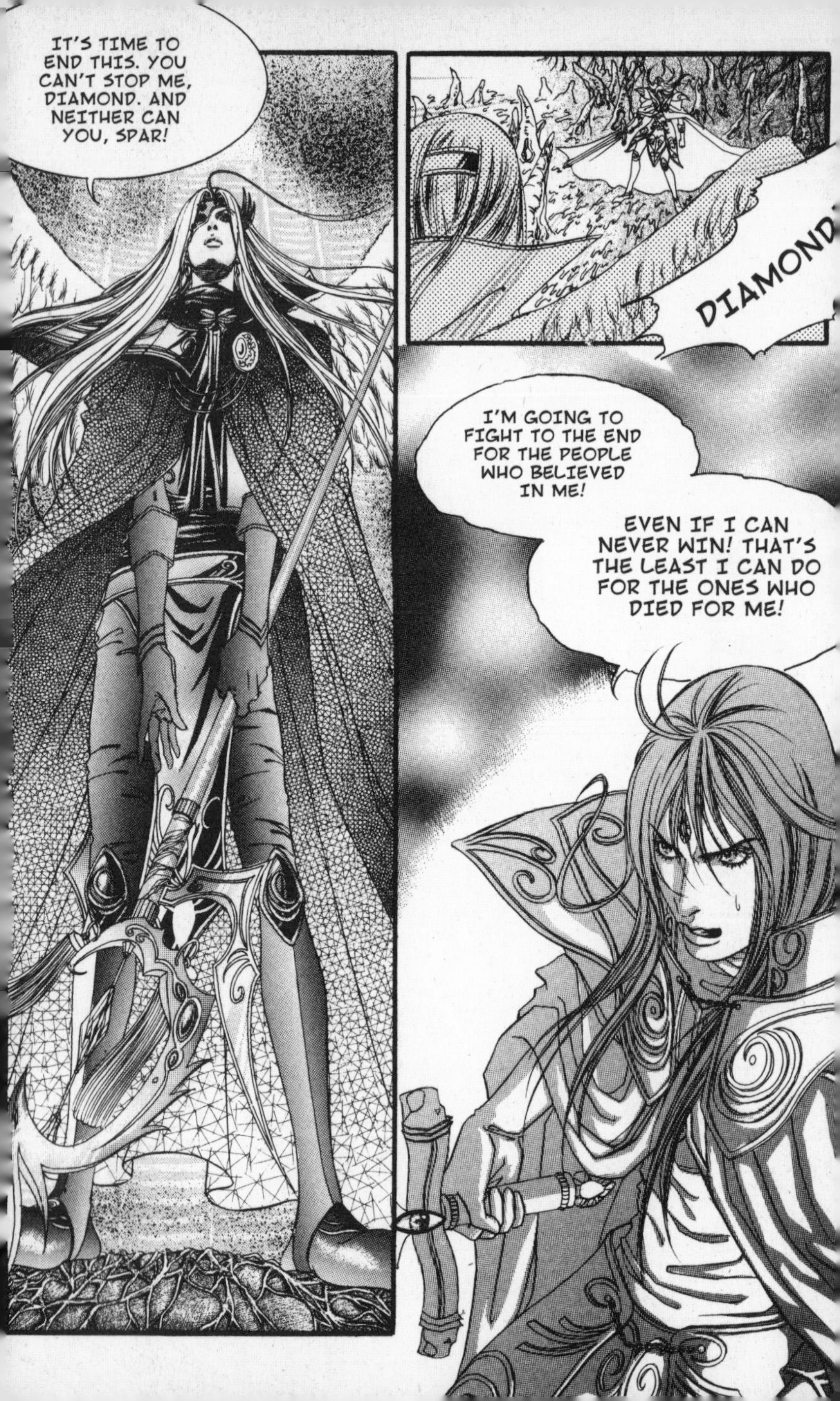
IT'S TIME TO END THIS. YOU CAN'T STOP ME, DIAMOND. AND NEITHER CAN YOU, SPAR!
DIAMOND!
I'M GOING TO FIGHT TO THE END FOR THE PEOPLE WHO BELIEVED IN ME!
EVEN IF I CAN NEVER WIN! THAT'S THE LEAST I CAN DO FOR THE ONES WHO DIED FOR ME!

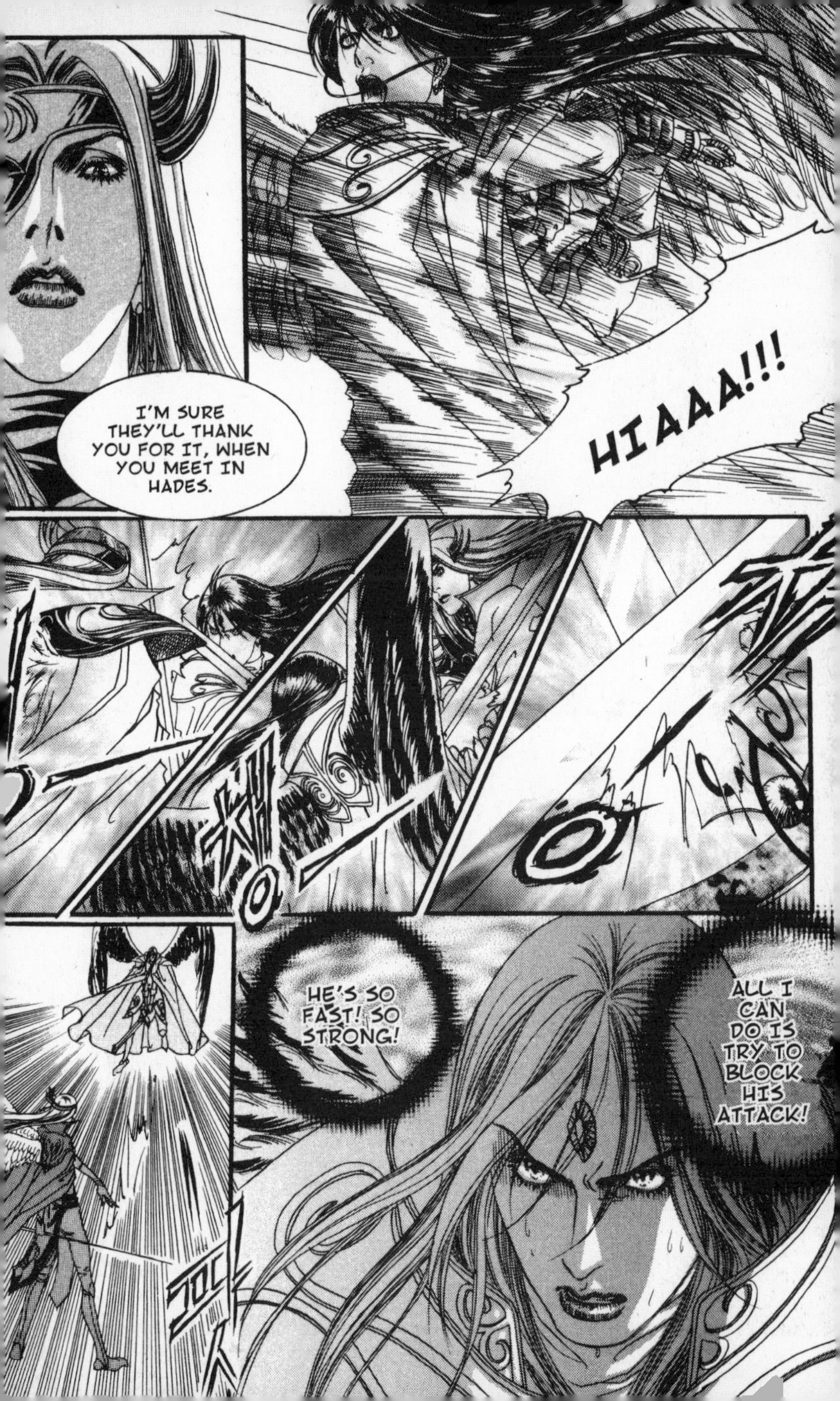
HIAAA!!!
I'M SURE THEY'LL THANK YOU FOR IT, WHEN YOU MEET IN HADES.
ALL I CAN DO IS TRY TO BLOCK HIS ATTACK!
HE'S SO FAST! SO STRONG!

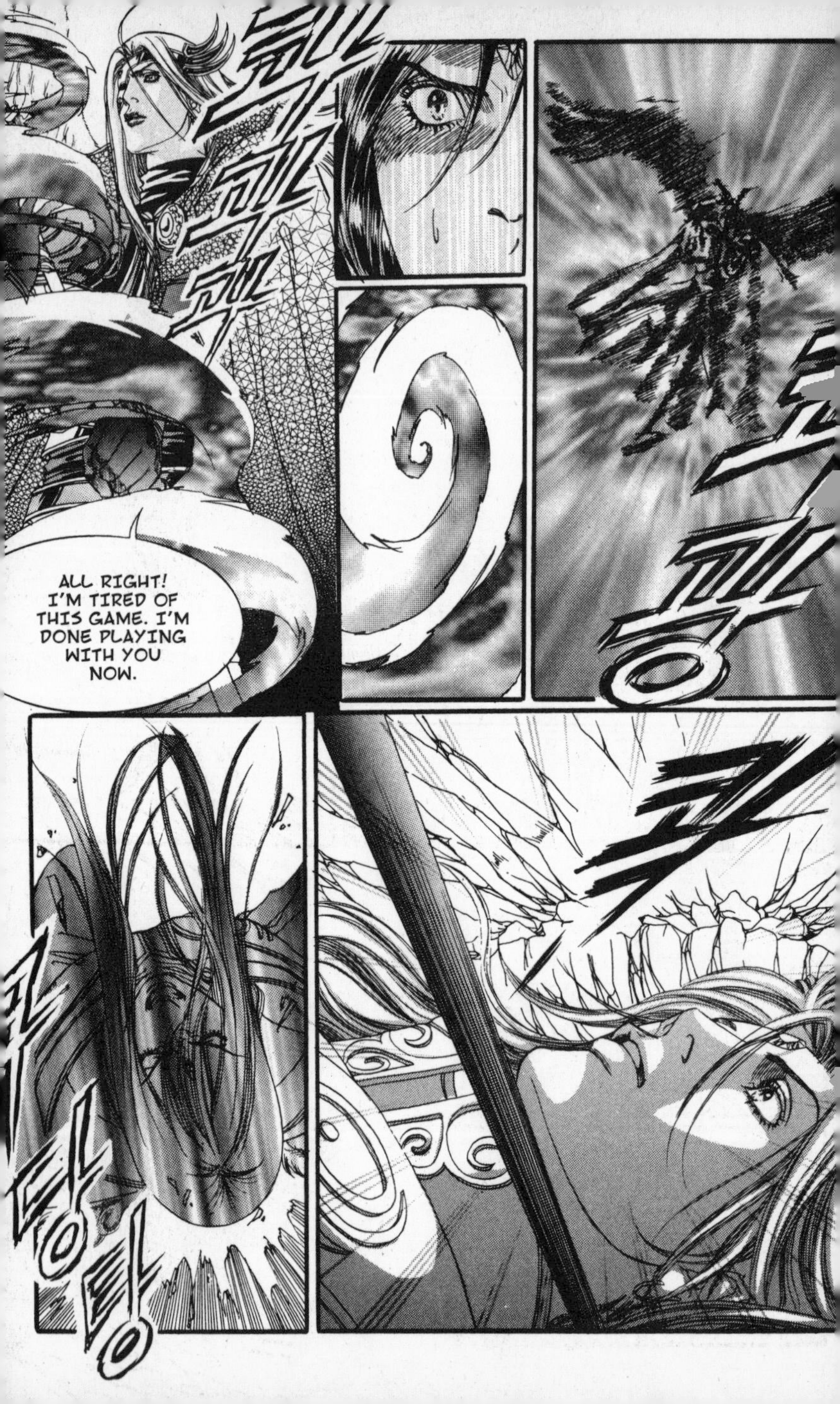
ALL RIGHT! I'M TIRED OF THIS GAME. I'M DONE PLAYING WITH YOU NOW.

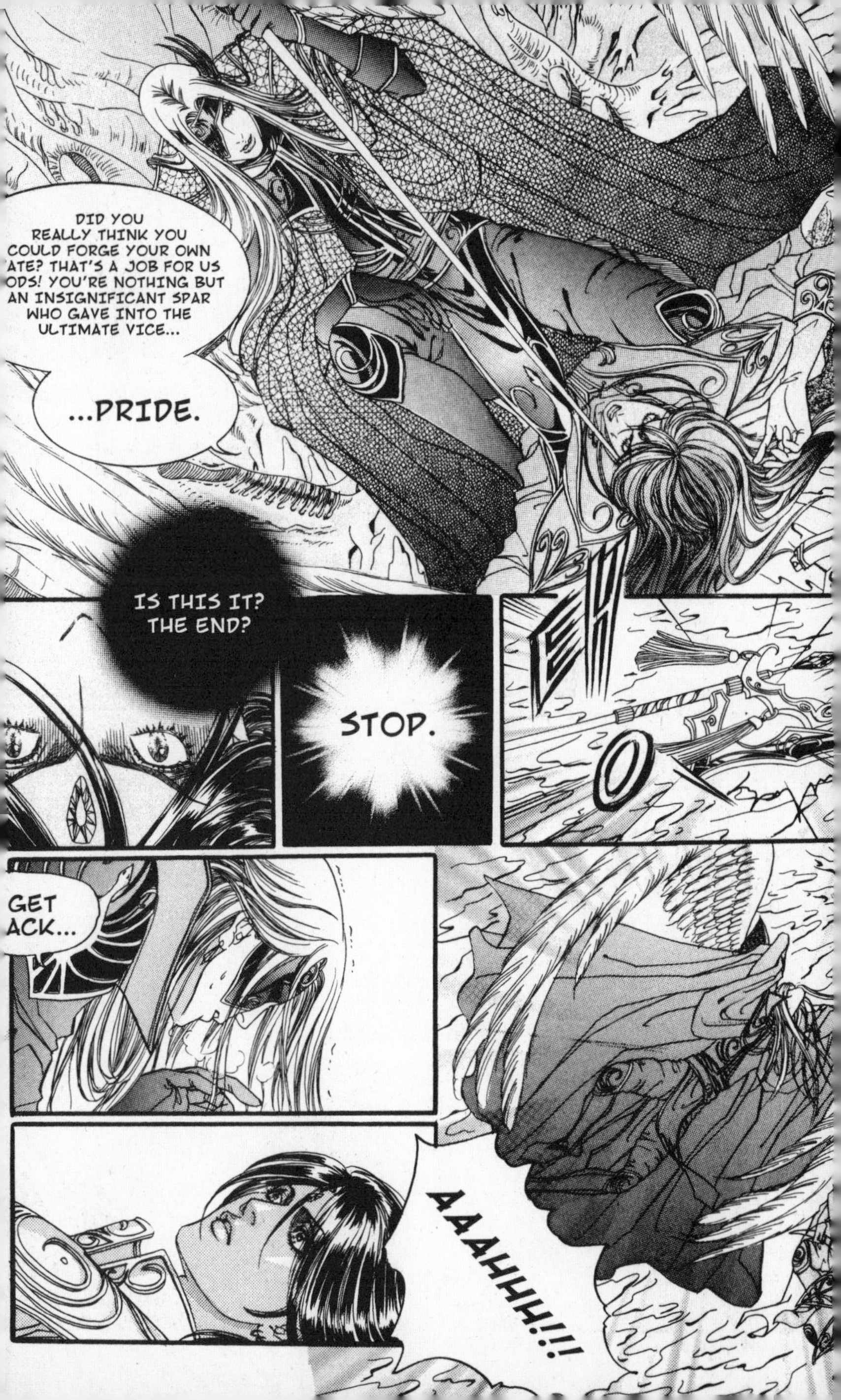
DID YOU REALLY THINK YOU COULD FORGE YOUR OWN ATE? THAT'S A JOB FOR US ODS! YOU'RE NOTHING BUT AN INSIGNIFICANT SPAR WHO GAVE INTO THE ULTIMATE VICE...
...PRIDE.
IS THIS IT? THE END?
STOP.
GET ACK...
AAAHHH!!!

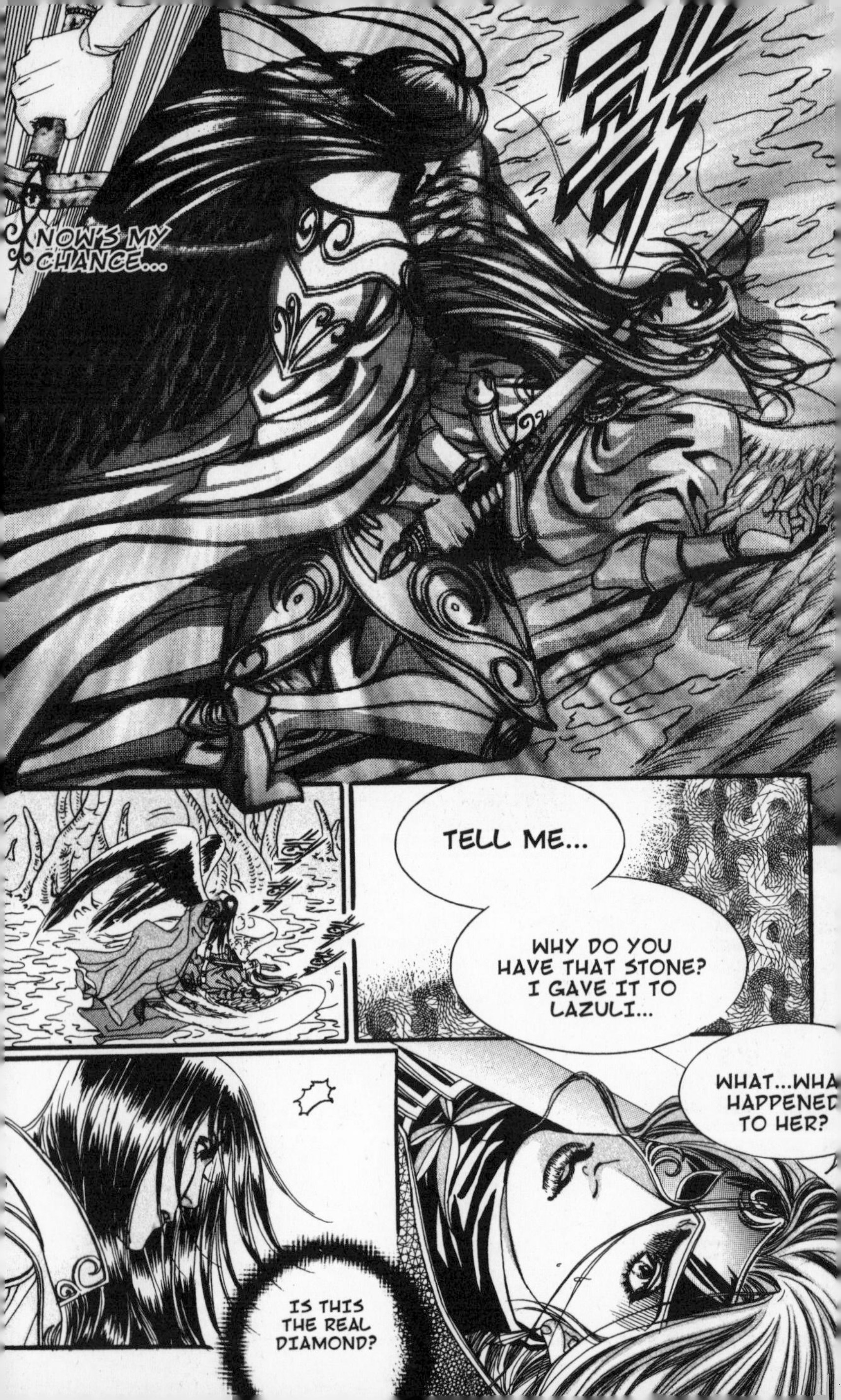
NOW'S MY CHANCE...
TELL ME...
WHY DO YOU HAVE THAT STONE? I GAVE IT TO LAZULI...
WHAT...WHA HAPPENED TO HER?
IS THIS THE REAL DIAMOND?

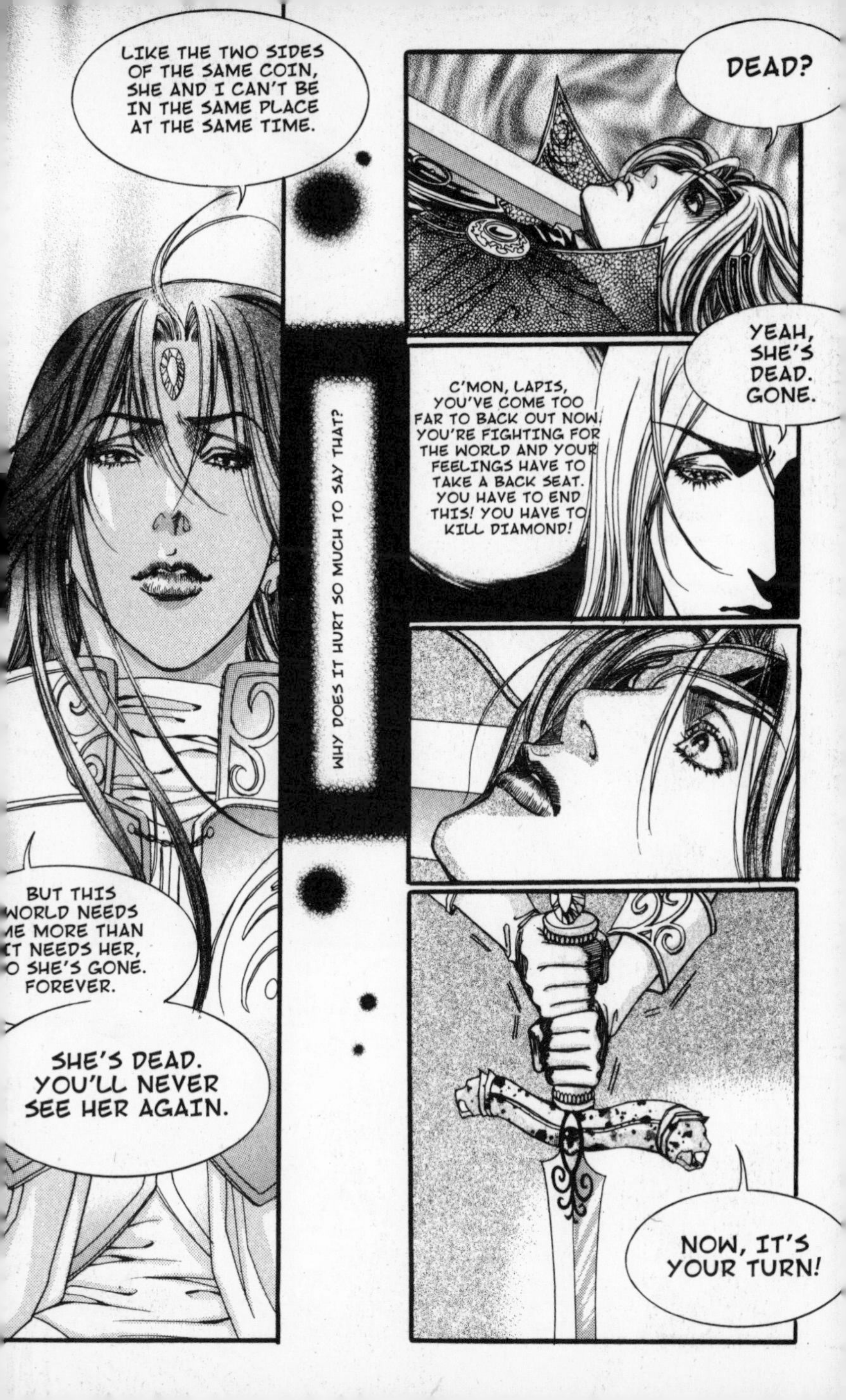
LIKE THE TWO SIDES OF THE SAME COIN, SHE AND I CAN'T BE IN THE SAME PLACE AT THE SAME TIME.
BUT THIS WORLD NEEDS ME MORE THAN IT NEEDS HER, SO SHE'S GONE. FOREVER.
SHE'S DEAD. YOU'LL NEVER SEE HER AGAIN.
DEAD?
YEAH, SHE'S DEAD. GONE.
C'MON, LAPIS, YOU'VE COME TOO FAR TO BACK OUT NOW. YOU'RE FIGHTING FOR THE WORLD AND YOUR FEELINGS HAVE TO TAKE A BACK SEAT. YOU HAVE TO END THIS! YOU HAVE TO KILL DIAMOND!
WHY DOES IT HURT SO MUCH TO SAY THAT?
NOW, IT'S YOUR TURN!

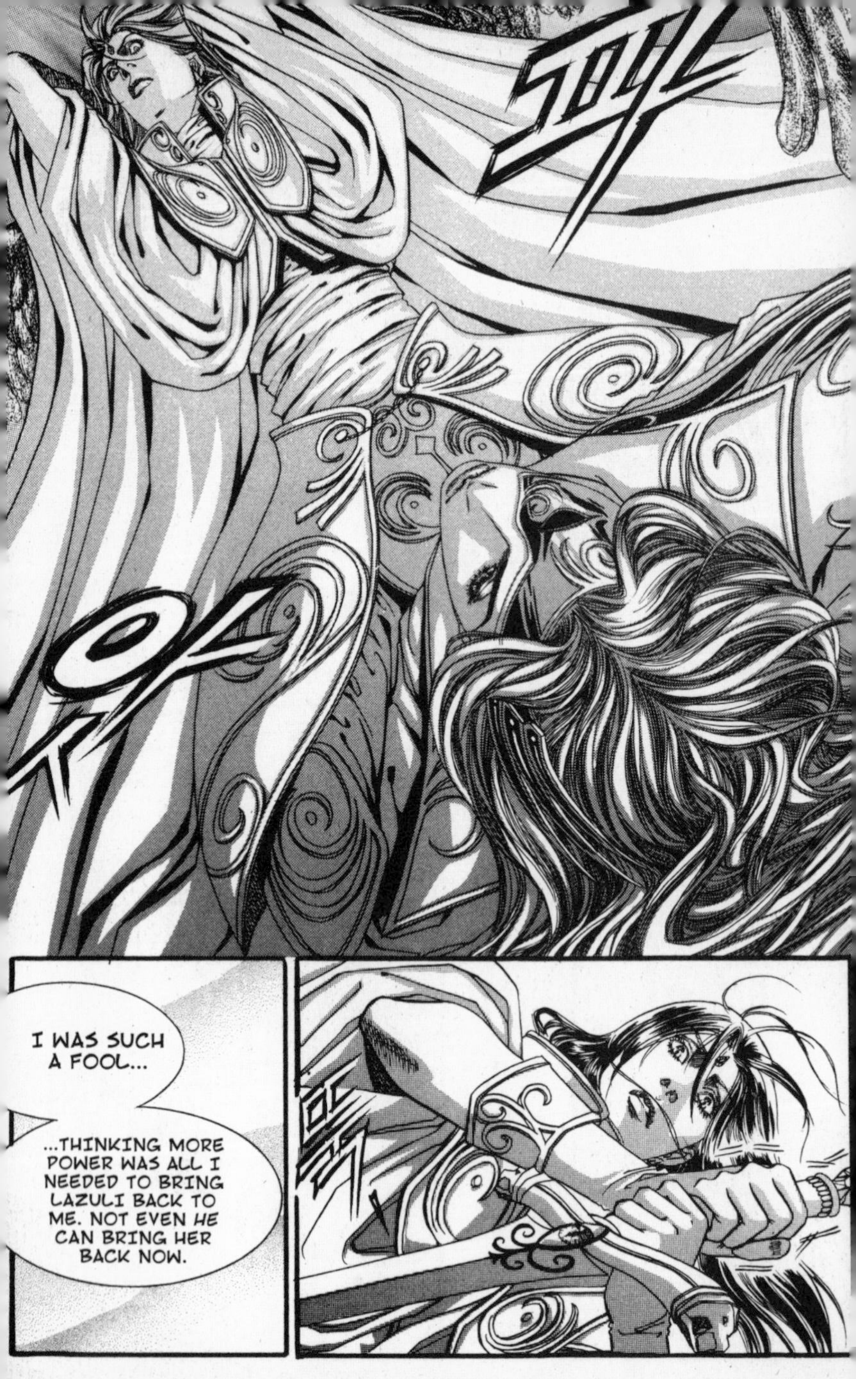
I WAS SUCH A FOOL...
...THINKING MORE POWER WAS ALL I NEEDED TO BRING LAZULI BACK TO ME. NOT EVEN HE CAN BRING HER BACK NOW.

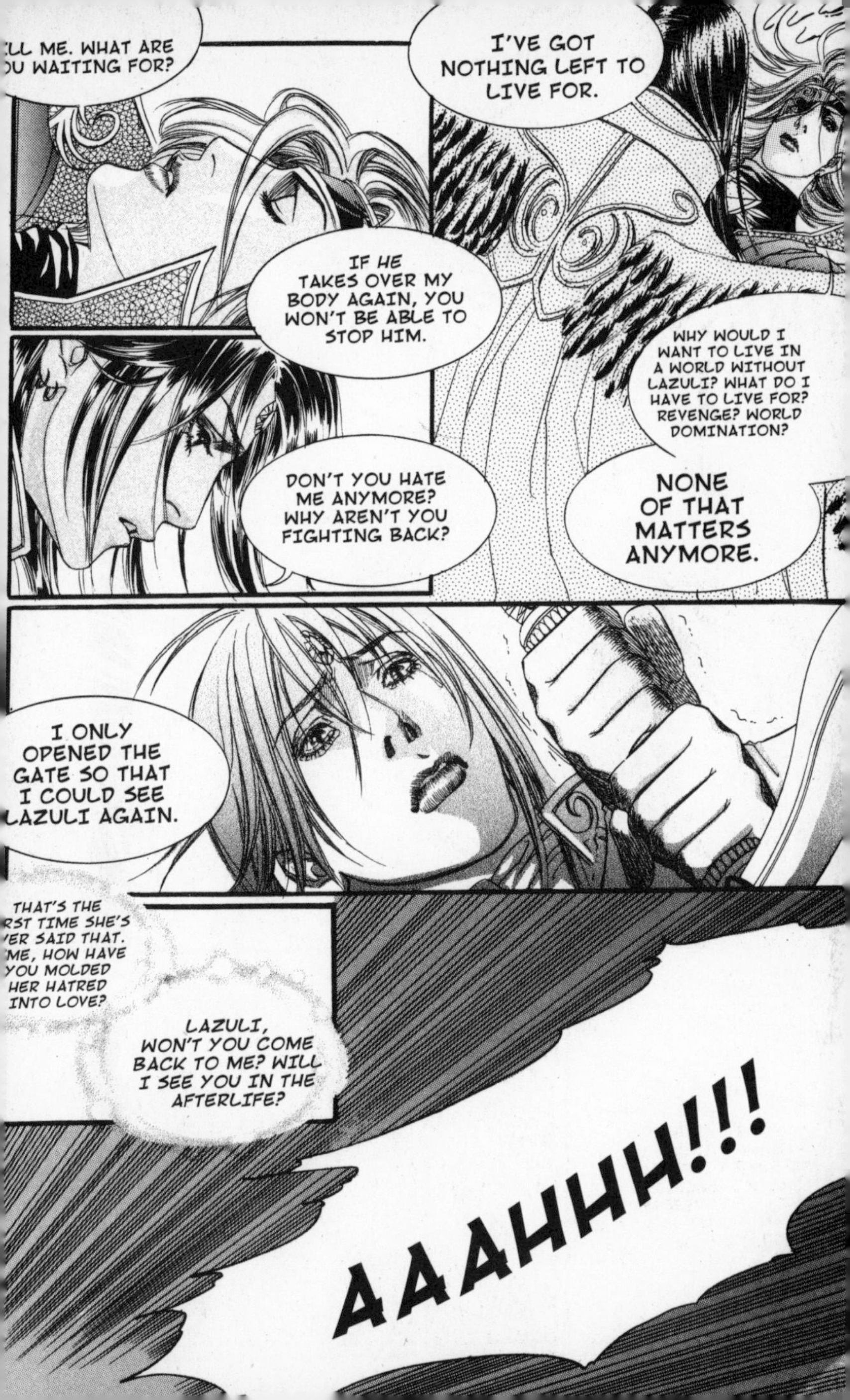
LL ME. WHAT ARE
OU WAITING FOR?
I'VE GOT NOTHING LEFT TO LIVE FOR.
IF HE TAKES OVER MY BODY AGAIN, YOU WON'T BE ABLE TO STOP HIM.
WHY WOULD I WANT TO LIVE IN A WORLD WITHOUT LAZULI? WHAT DO I HAVE TO LIVE FOR? REVENGE? WORLD DOMINATION?
DON'T YOU HATE ME ANYMORE? WHY AREN'T YOU FIGHTING BACK?
NONE OF THAT MATTERS ANYMORE.
I ONLY OPENED THE GATE SO THAT I COULD SEE LAZULI AGAIN.
THAT'S THE
RST TIME SHE'S
VER SAID THAT.
ME, HOW HAVE
YOU MOLDED
HER HATRED
INTO LOVE?
LAZULI, WON'T YOU COME BACK TO ME? WILL I SEE YOU IN THE AFTERLIFE?
AAAHHH!!!

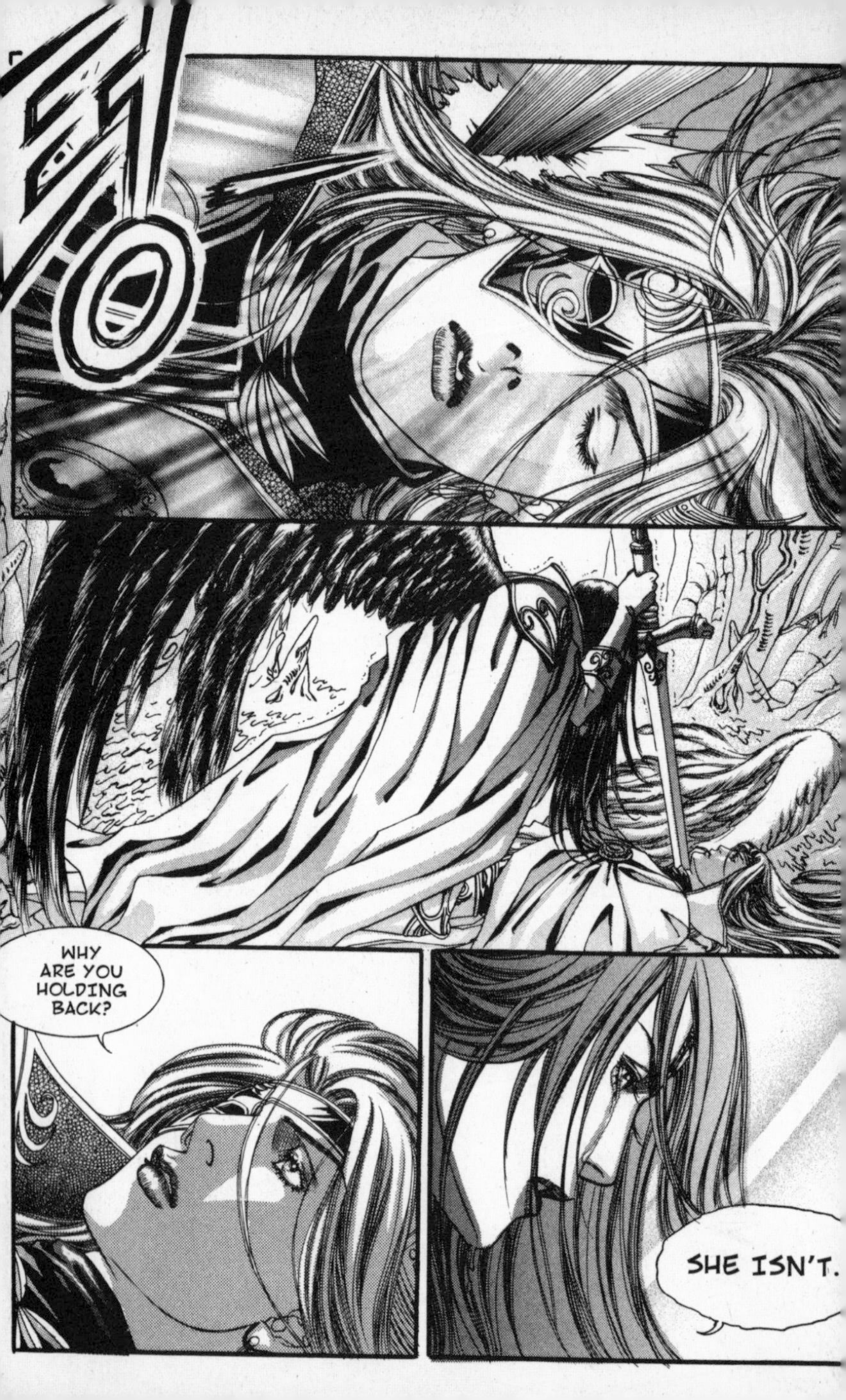
WHY ARE YOU HOLDING BACK?
SHE ISN'T.

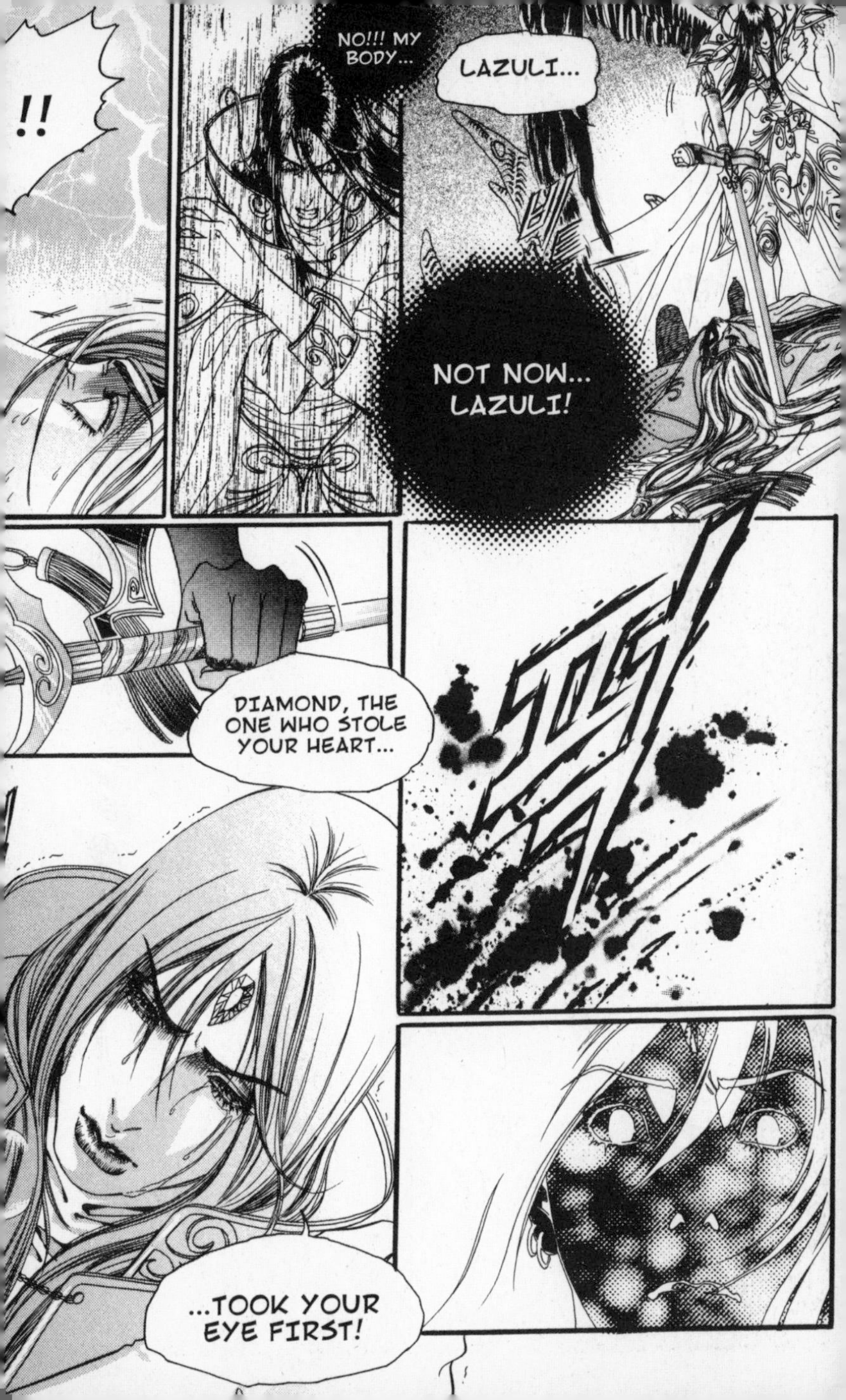

!!
NO!!! MY BODY...
LAZULI...
NOT NOW... LAZULI!
DIAMOND, THE ONE WHO STOLE YOUR HEART...
...TOOK YOUR EYE FIRST!

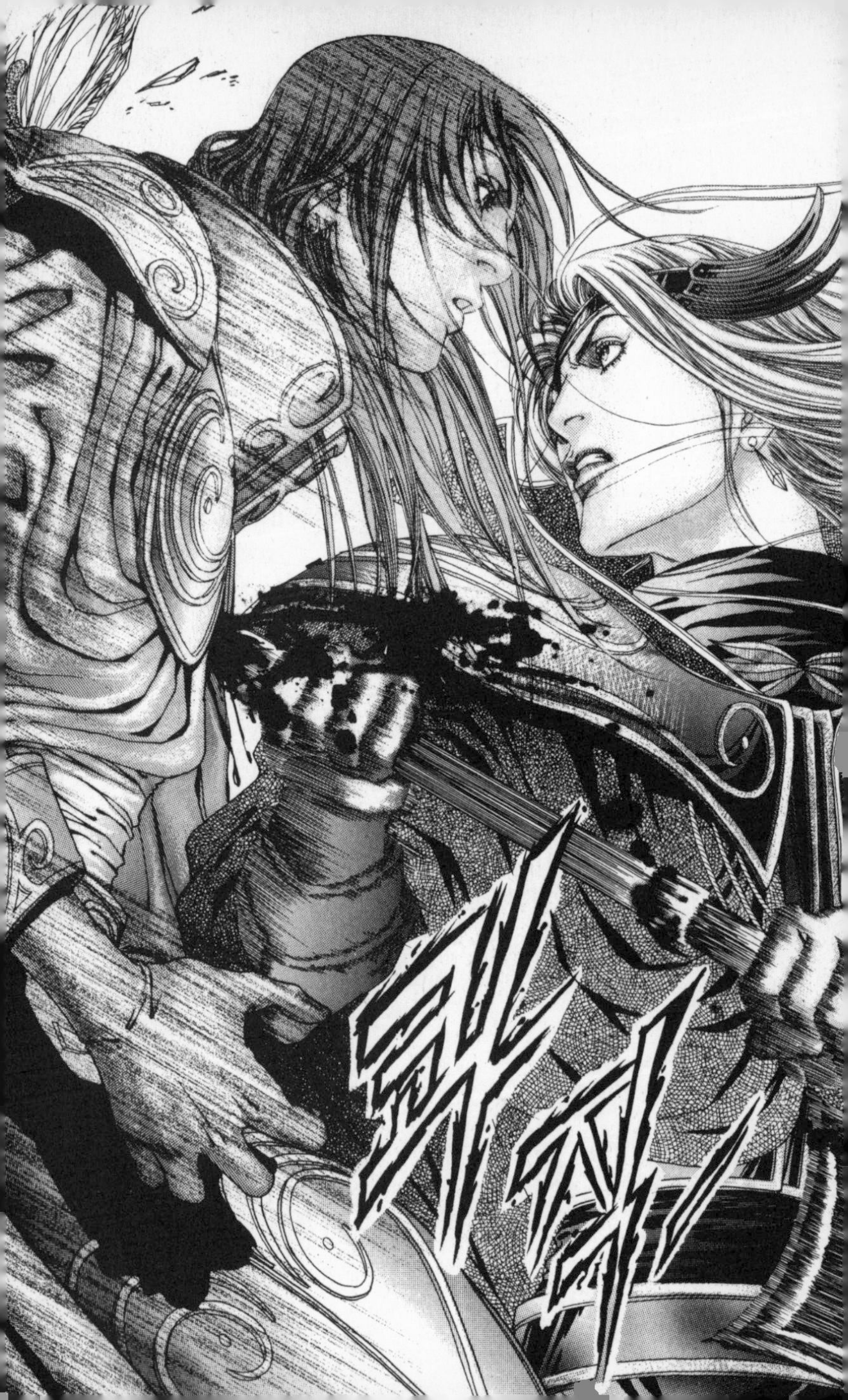

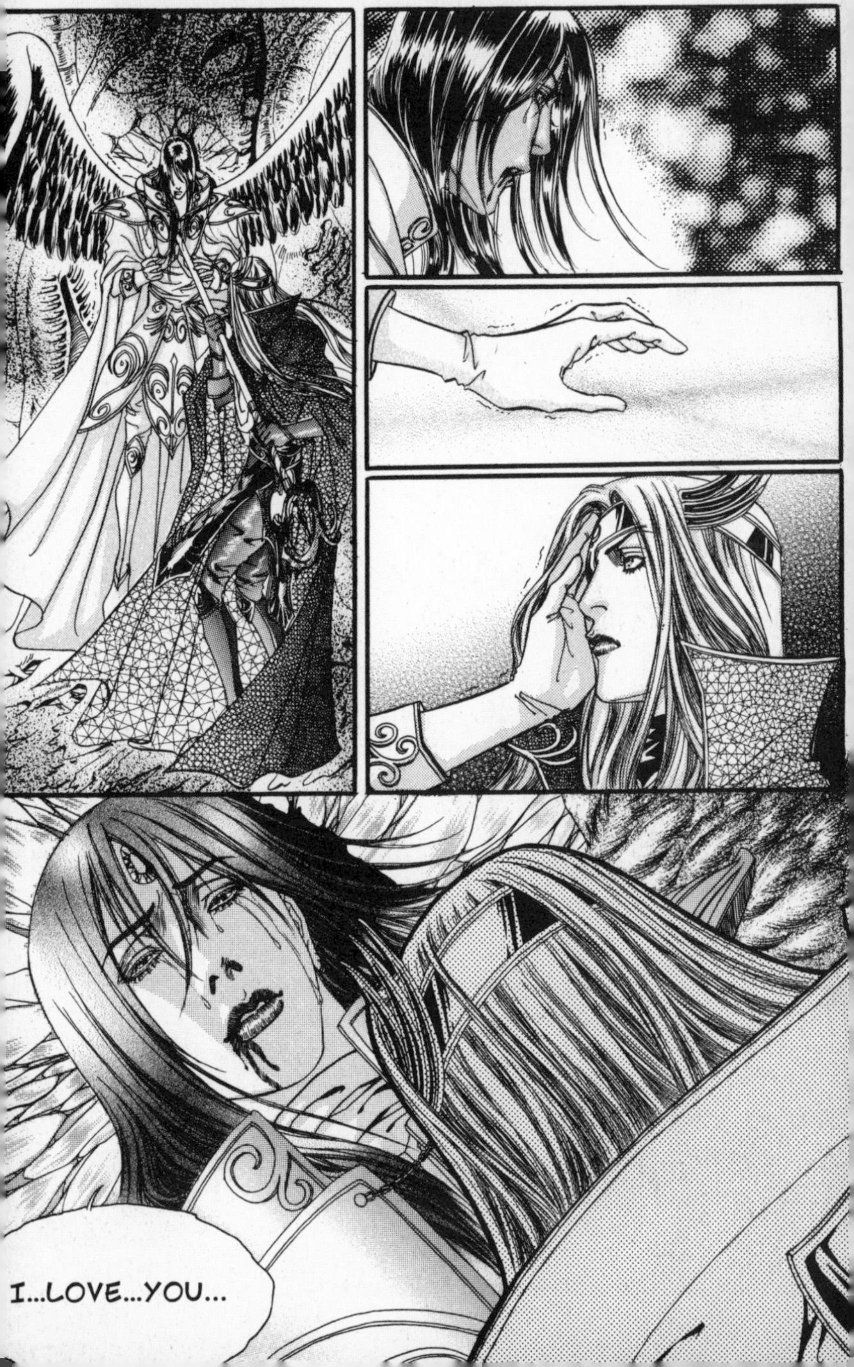
I...LOVE...YOU...

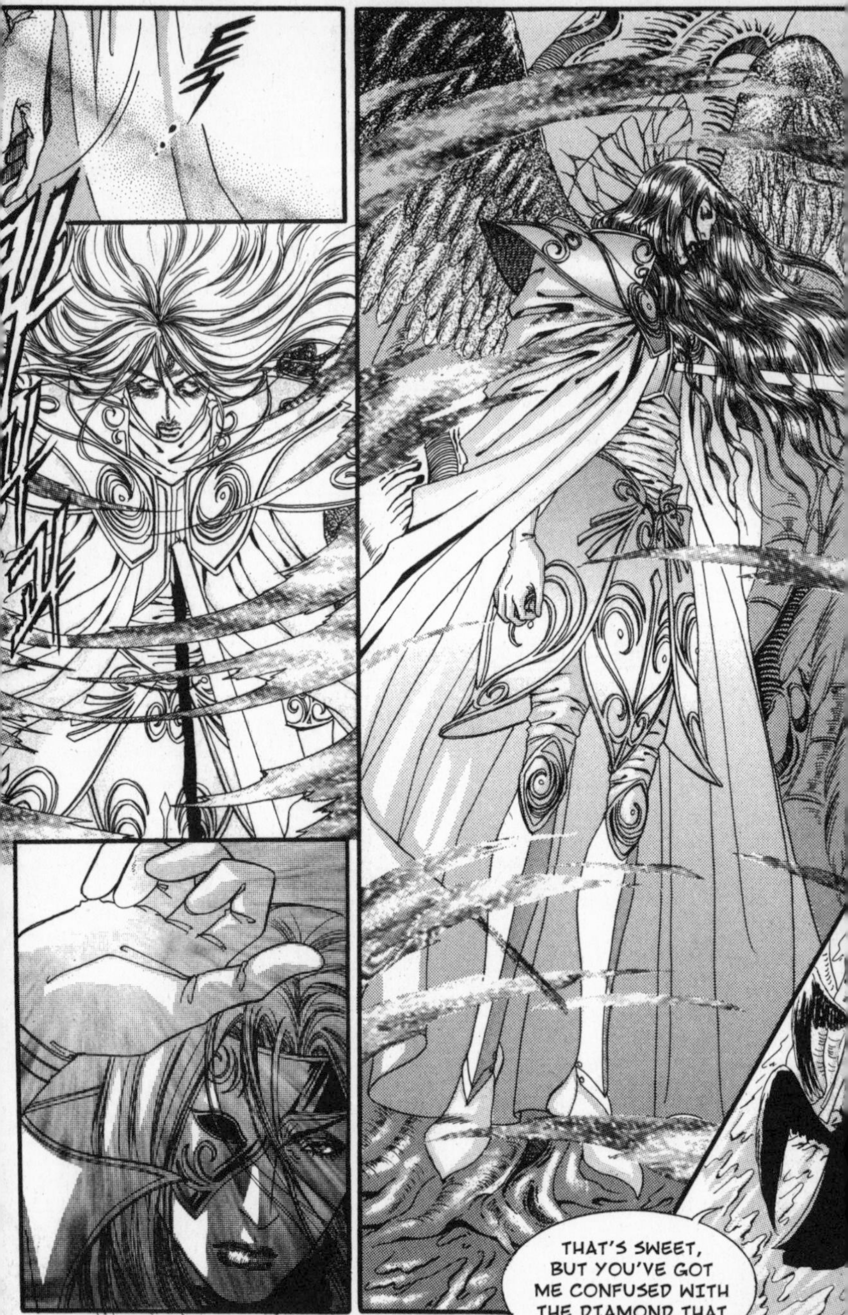
THAT'S SWEET, BUT YOU'VE GOT ME CONFUSED WITH THE DIAMOND THAT CARES.

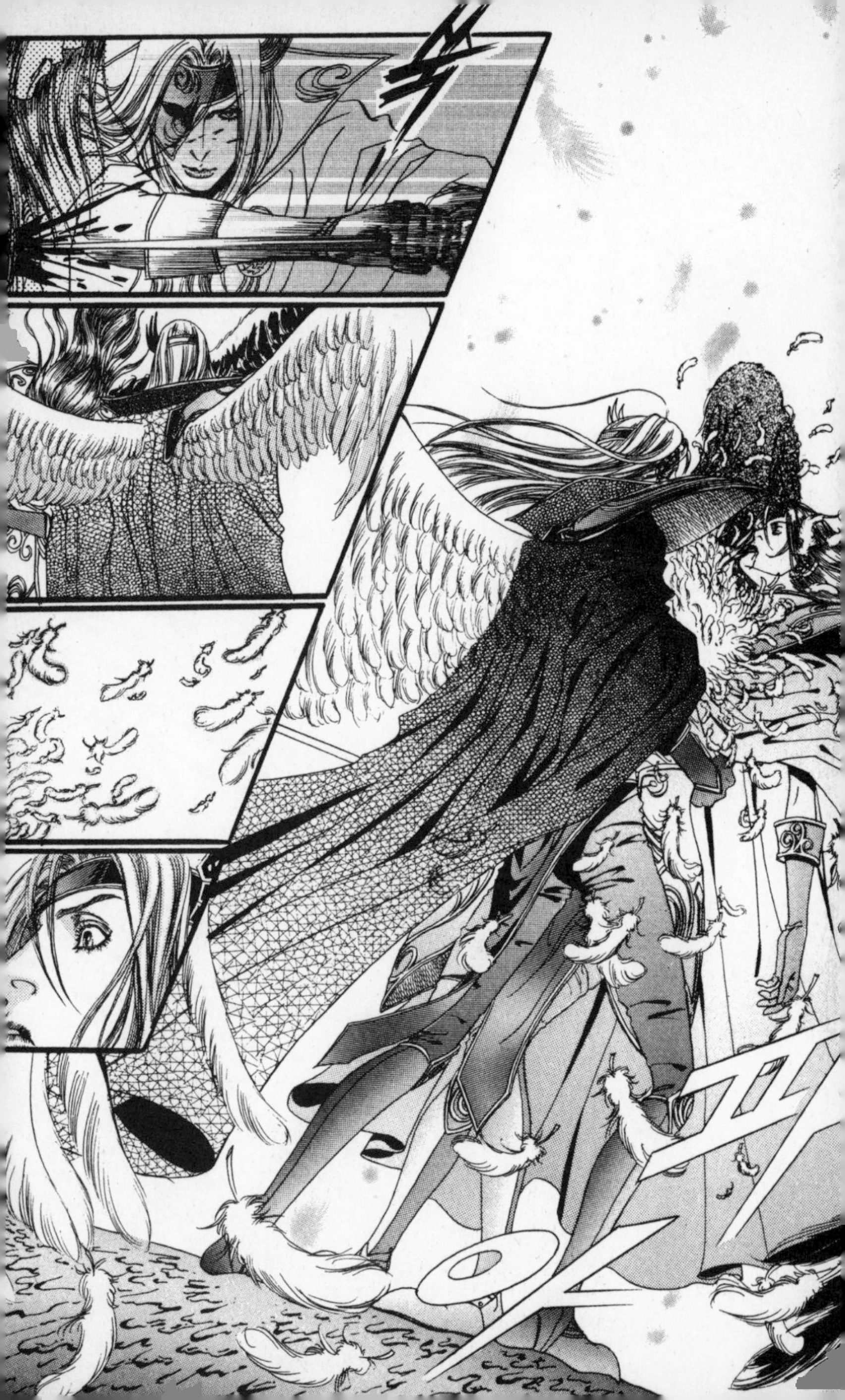

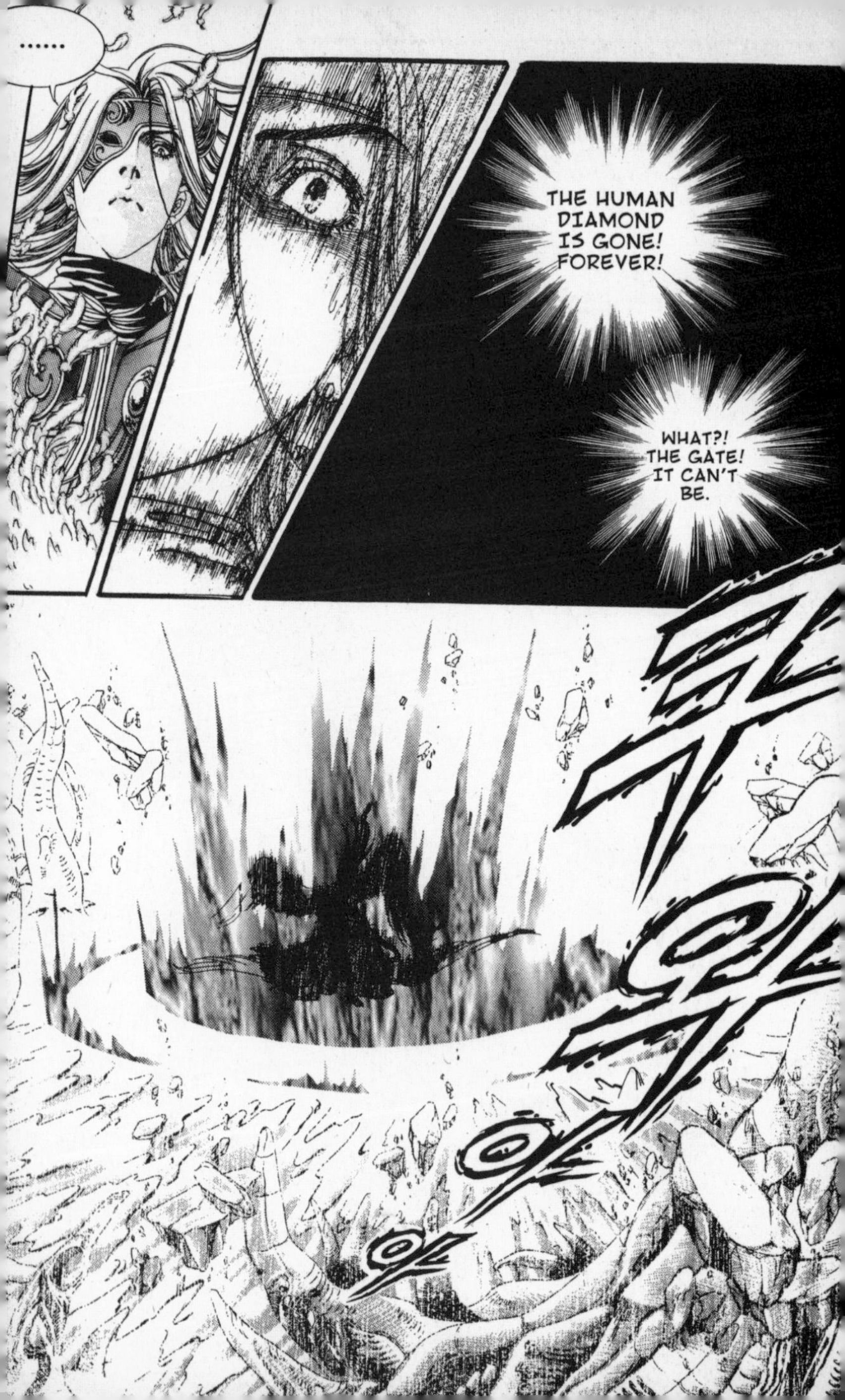
......
THE HUMAN DIAMOND IS GONE! FOREVER!
WHAT?! THE GATE! IT CAN'T BE.

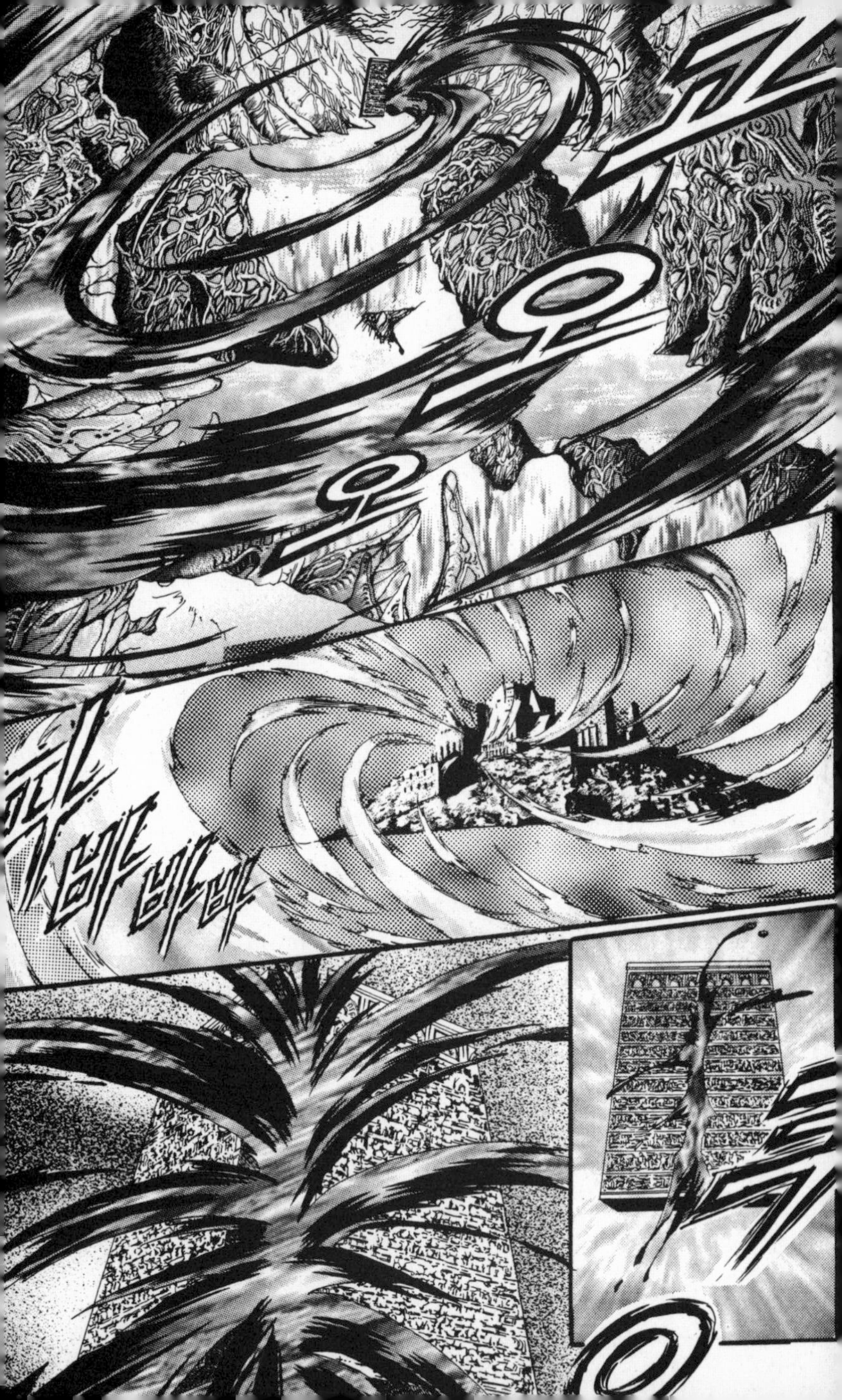

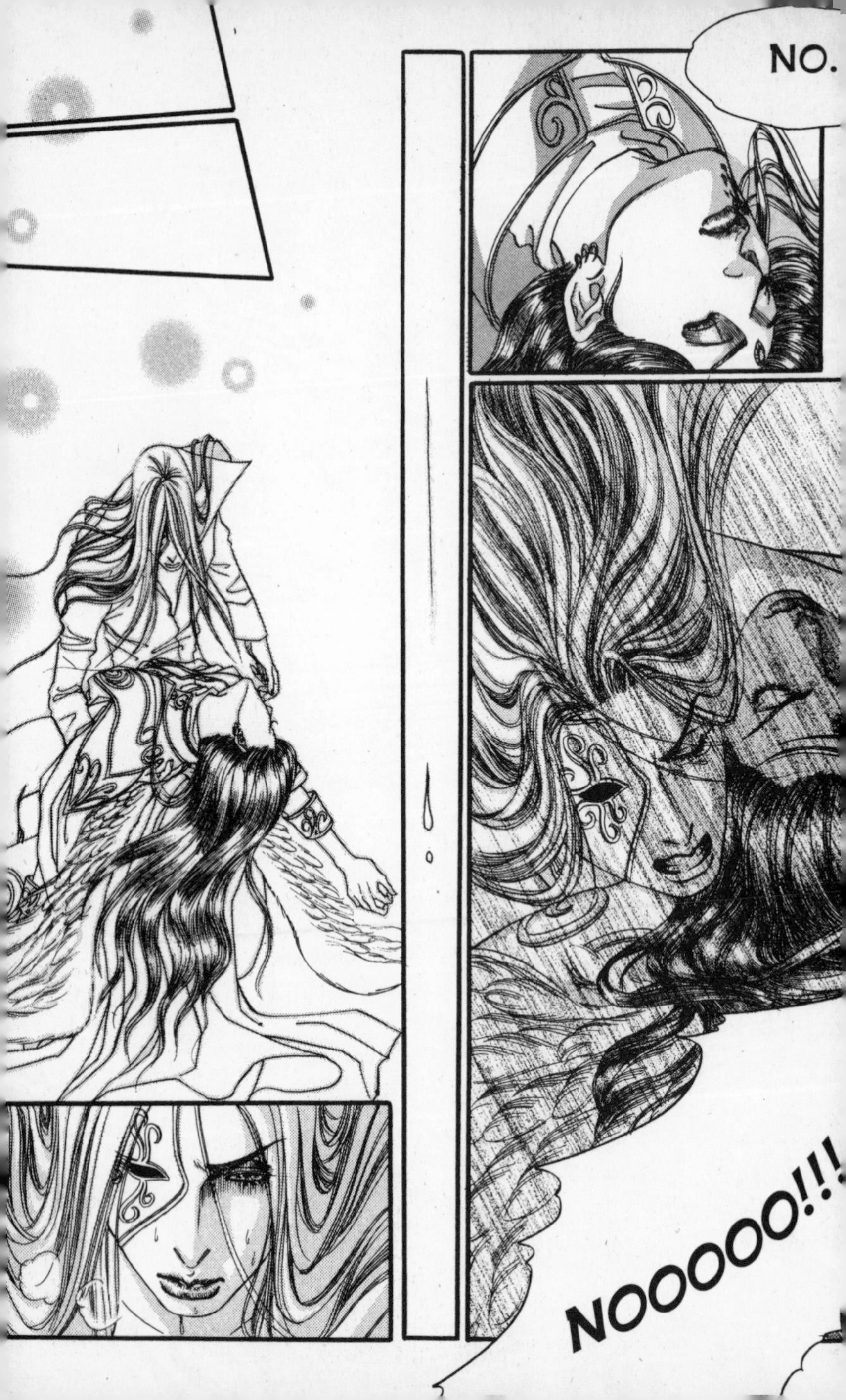
NO.
NOOOOO!!!

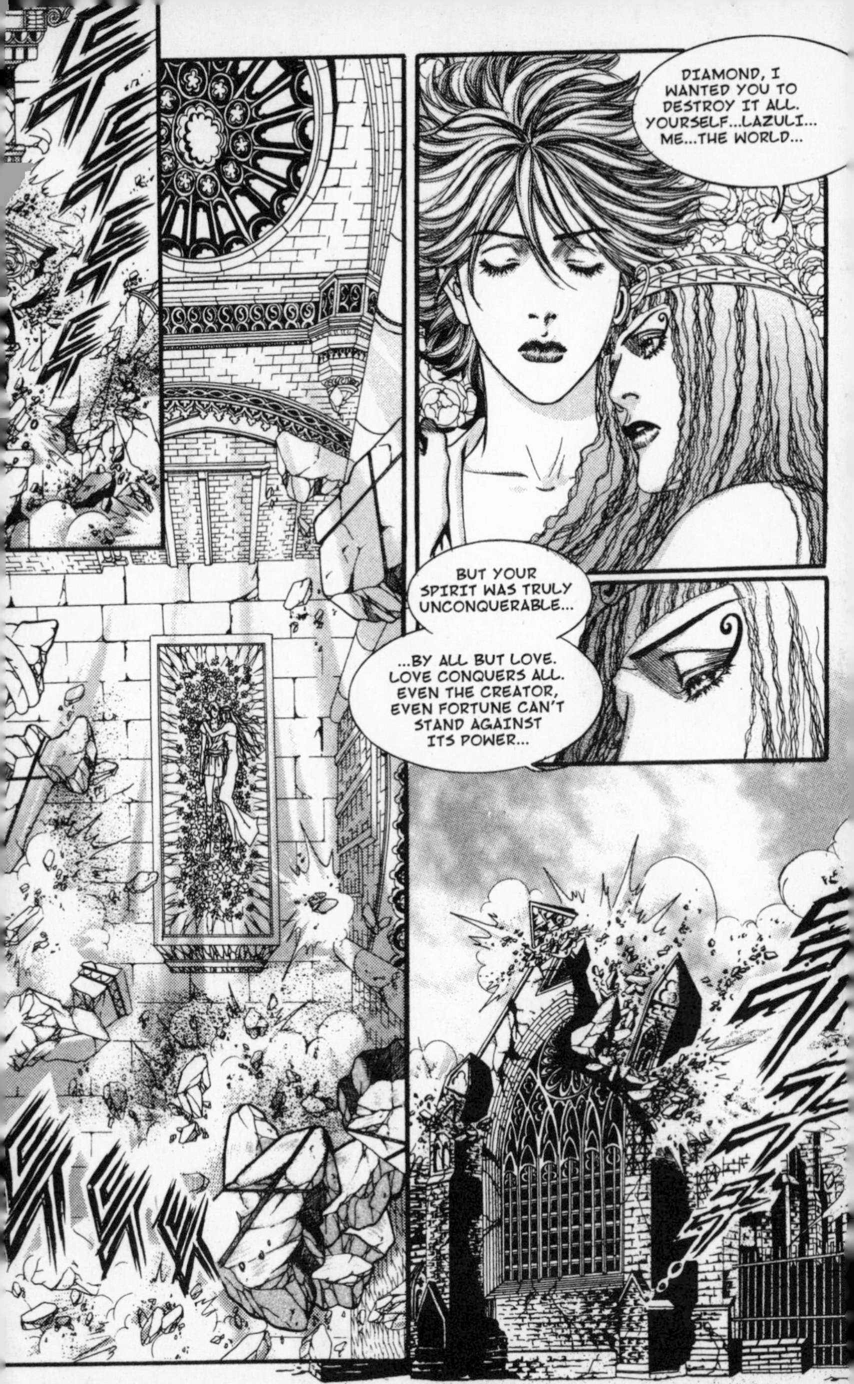
DIAMOND, I WANTED YOU TO DESTROY IT ALL. YOURSELF...LAZULI... ME...THE WORLD...
BUT YOUR SPIRIT WAS TRULY UNCONQUERABLE...
...BY ALL BUT LOVE. LOVE CONQUERS ALL. EVEN THE CREATOR, EVEN FORTUNE CAN'T STAND AGAINST ITS POWER...

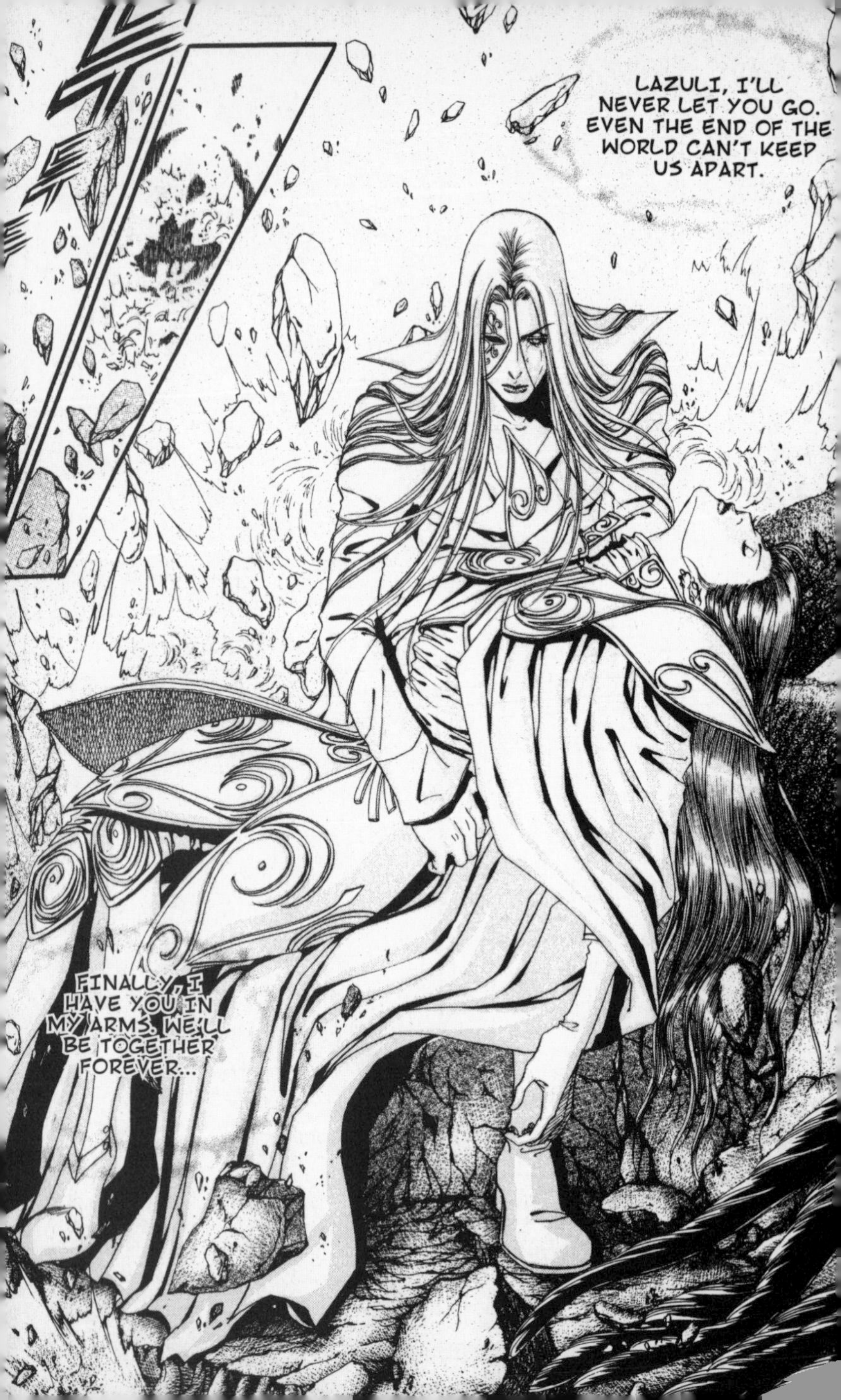
LAZULI, I'LL NEVER LET YOU GO. EVEN THE END OF THE WORLD CAN'T KEEP US APART.
FINALLY, I HAVE YOU IN MY ARMS. WE'LL BE TOGETHER FOREVER...

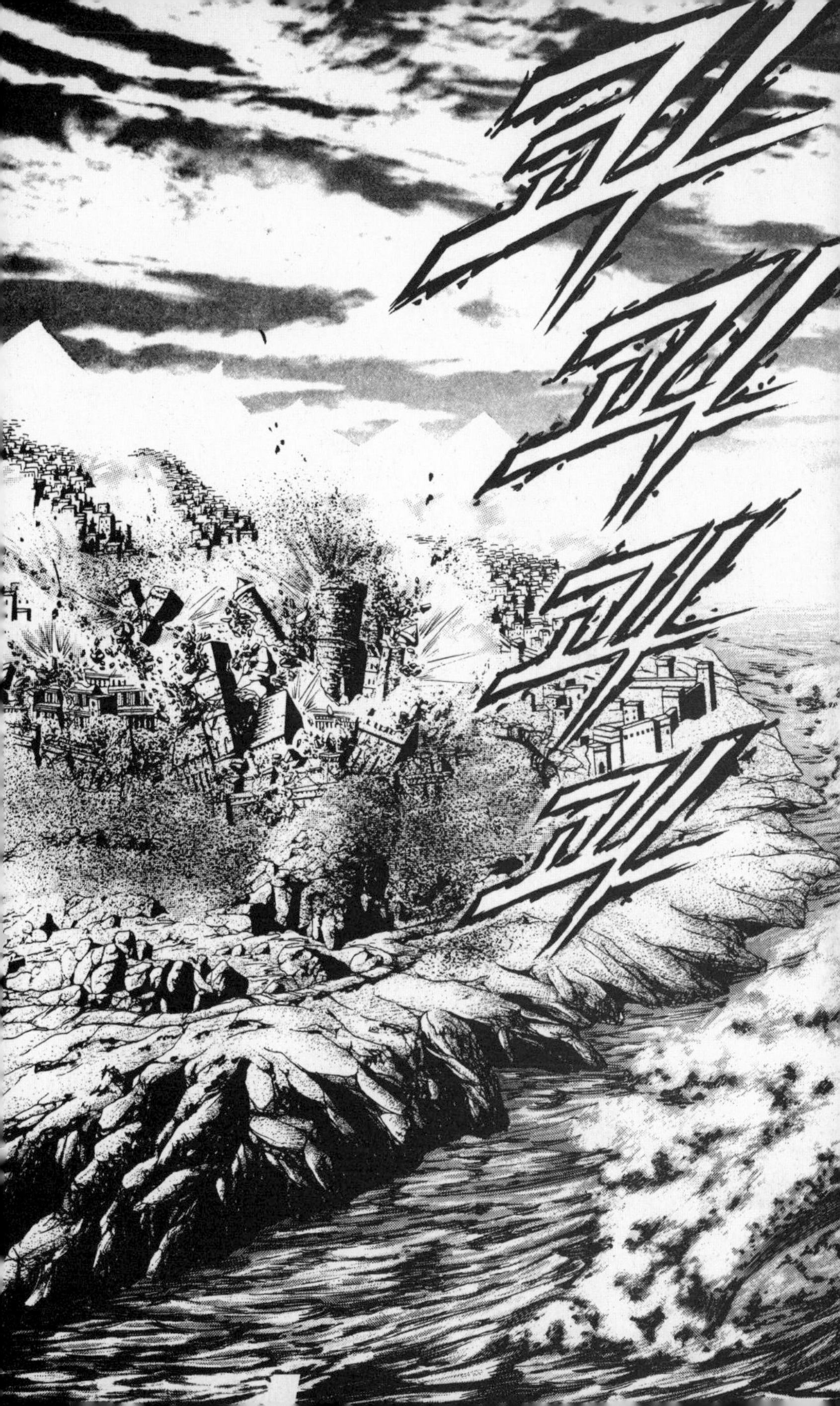

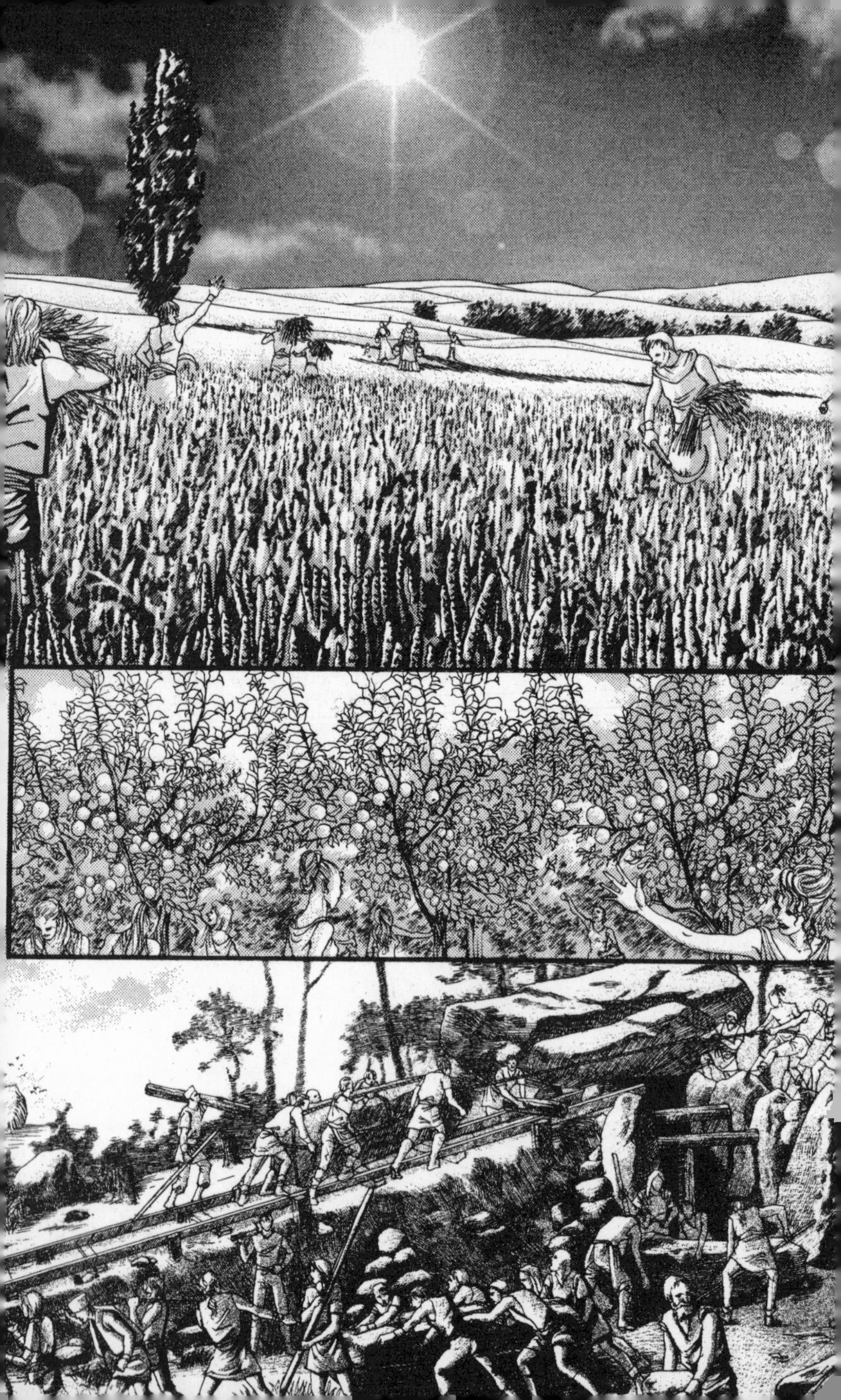

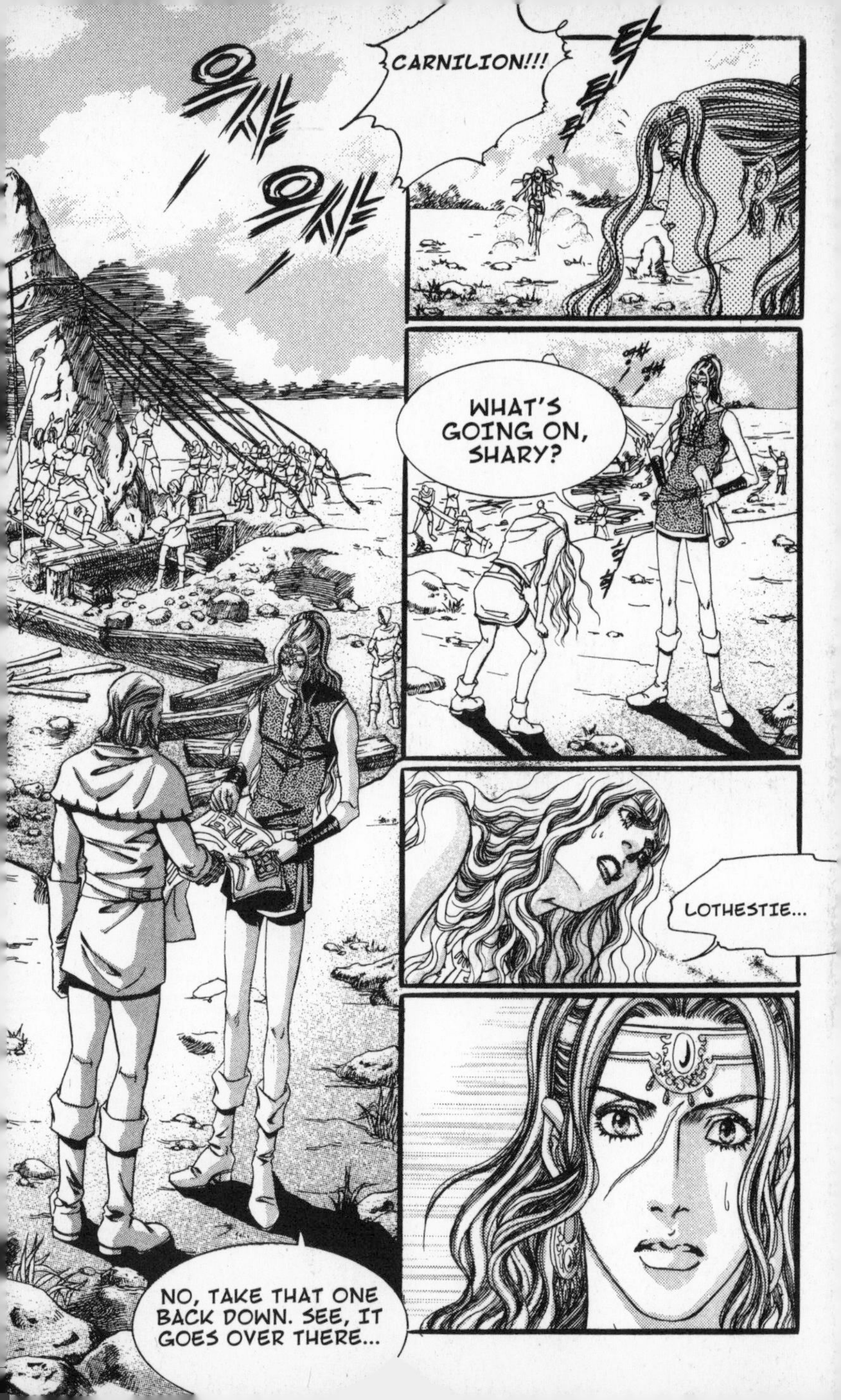

으샤 으샤
NO, TAKE THAT ONE BACK DOWN. SEE, IT GOES OVER THERE...
CARNILION!!!
WHAT'S GOING ON, SHARY?
LOTHESTIE...

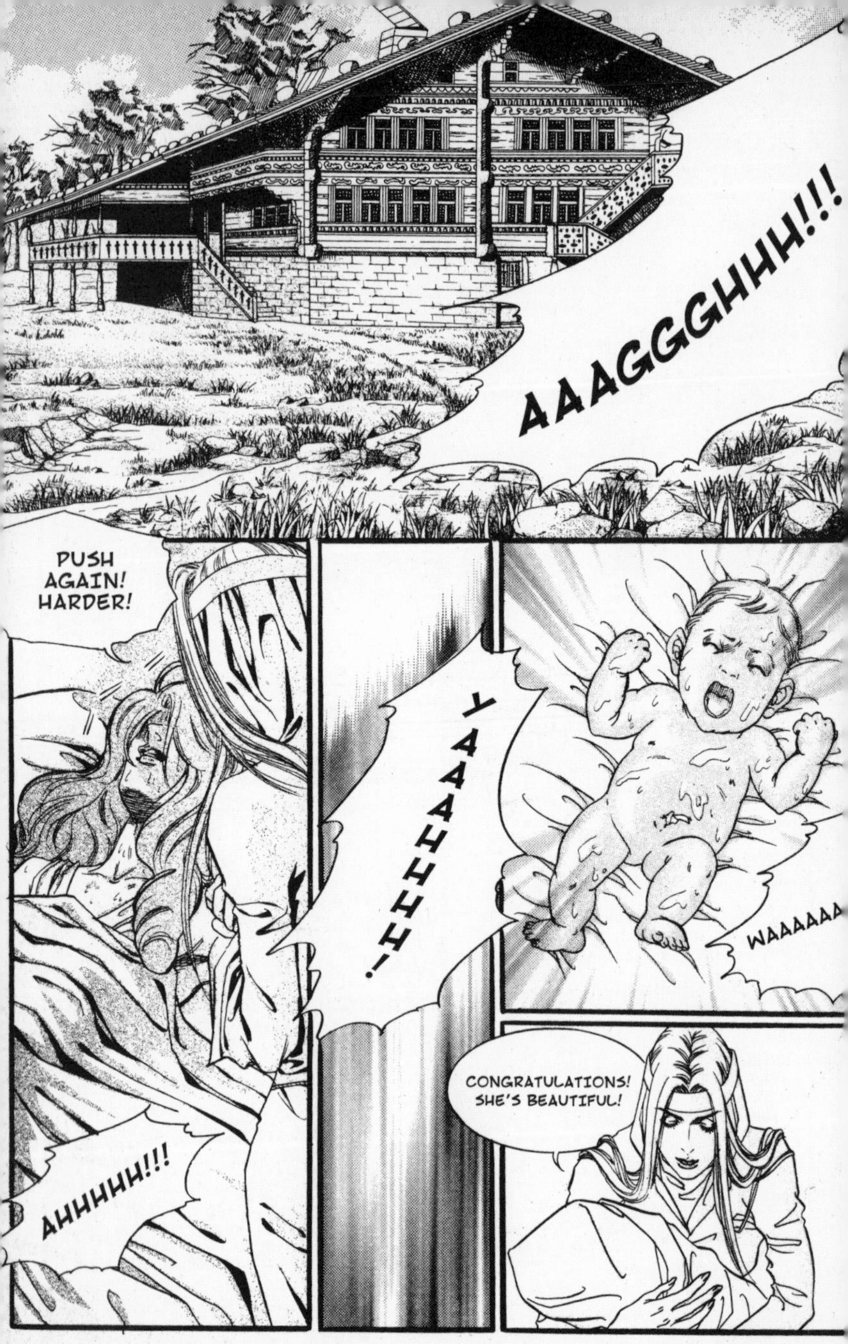

AAAGGGHHH!!!
PUSH AGAIN! HARDER!
AHHHHH!!!
YAAAAHHHHH!
WAAAAAA
CONGRATULATIONS! SHE'S BEAUTIFUL!

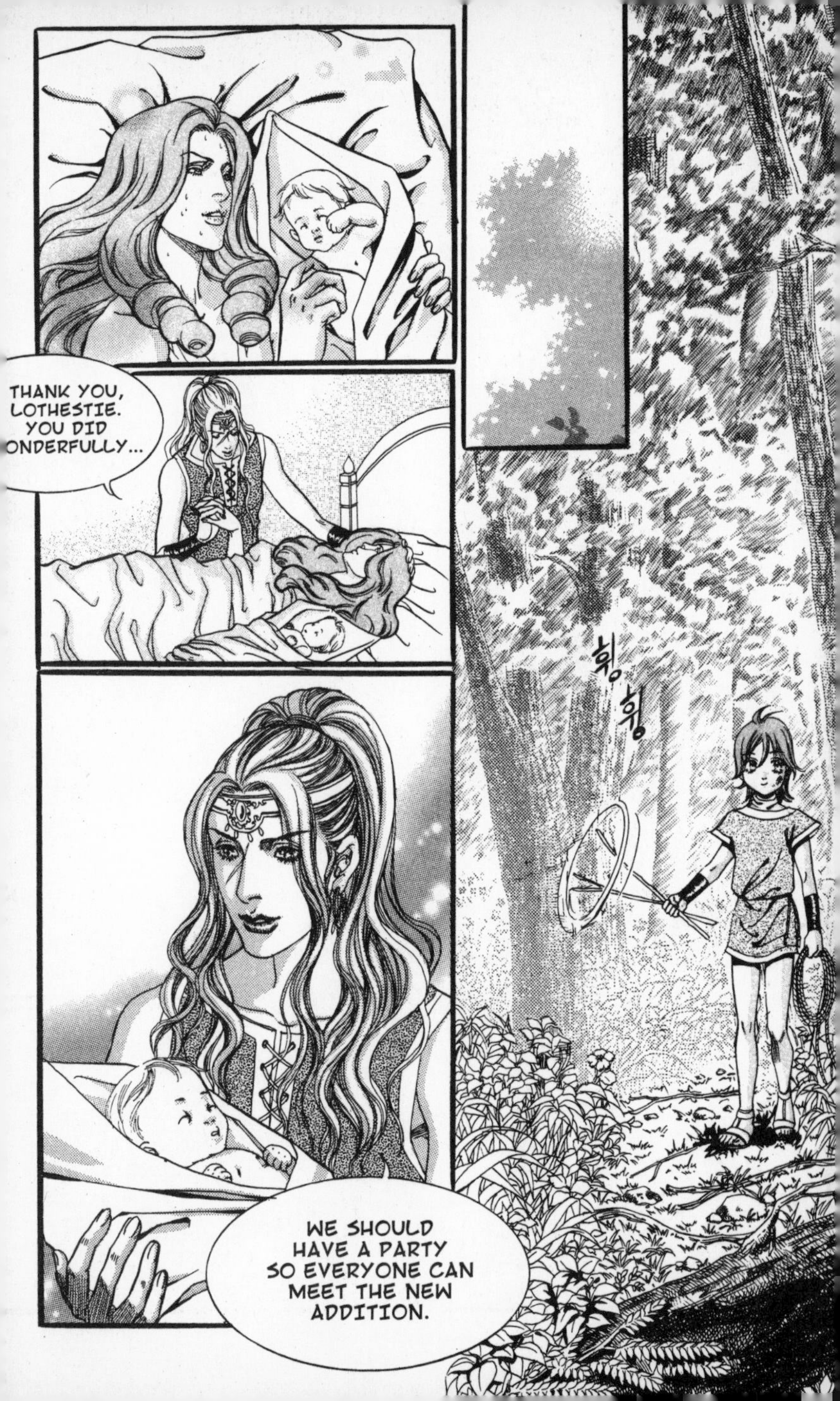
THANK YOU, LOTHESTIE. YOU DID ONDERFULLY...
휘잉 휘잉
WE SHOULD HAVE A PARTY SO EVERYONE CAN MEET THE NEW ADDITION.

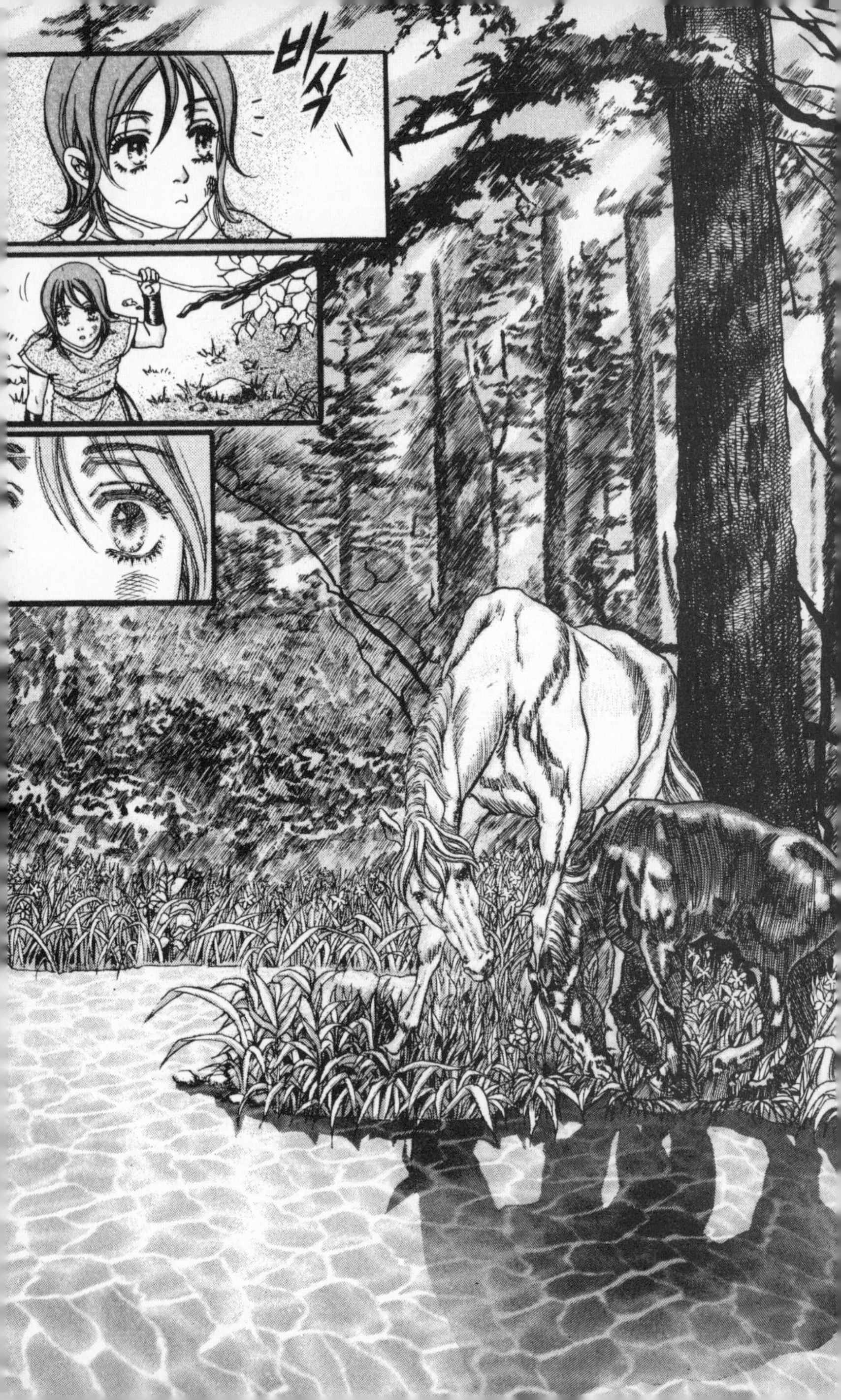
바삭

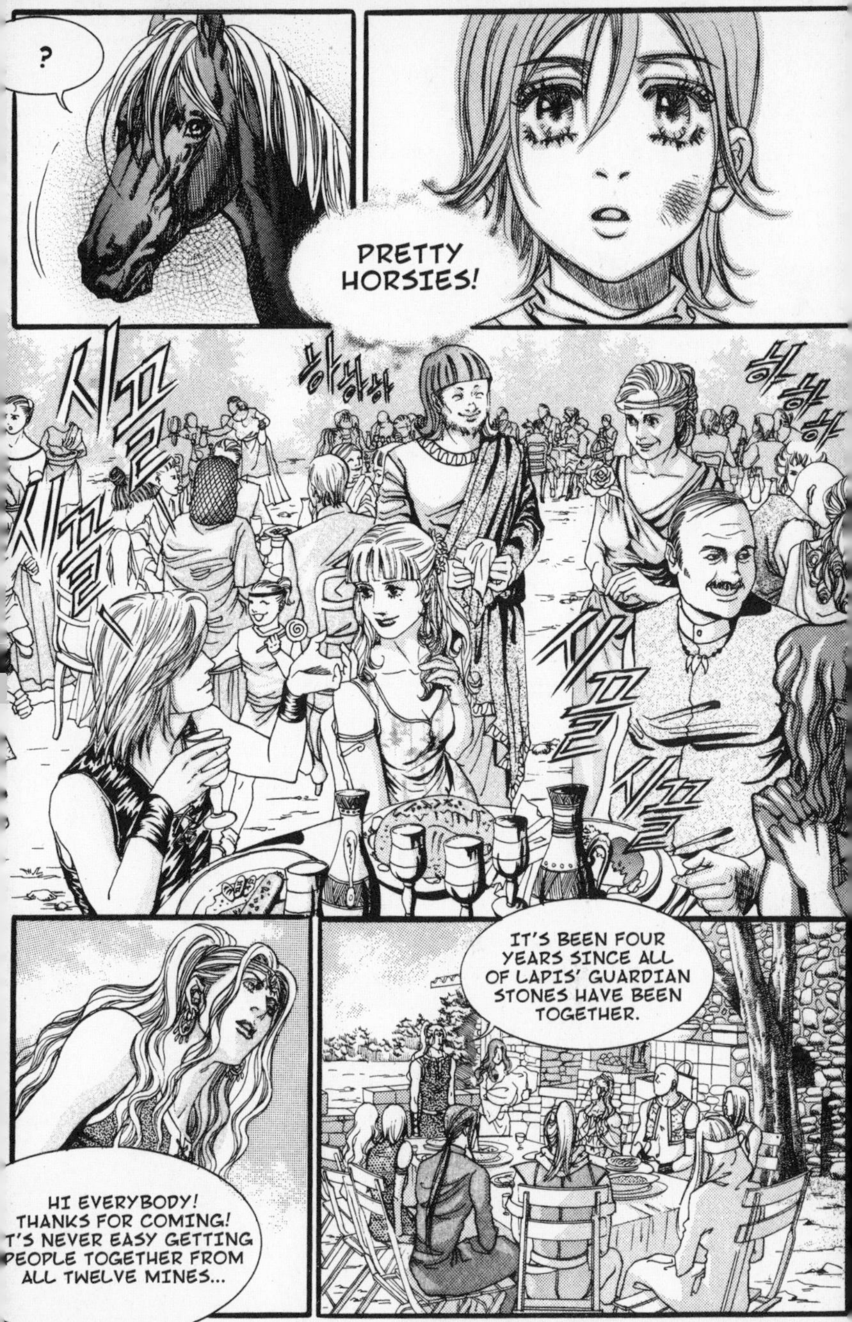
?
PRETTY HORSIES!
HI EVERYBODY! THANKS FOR COMING! T'S NEVER EASY GETTING EOPLE TOGETHER FROM ALL TWELVE MINES...
IT'S BEEN FOUR YEARS SINCE ALL OF LAPIS' GUARDIAN STONES HAVE BEEN TOGETHER.

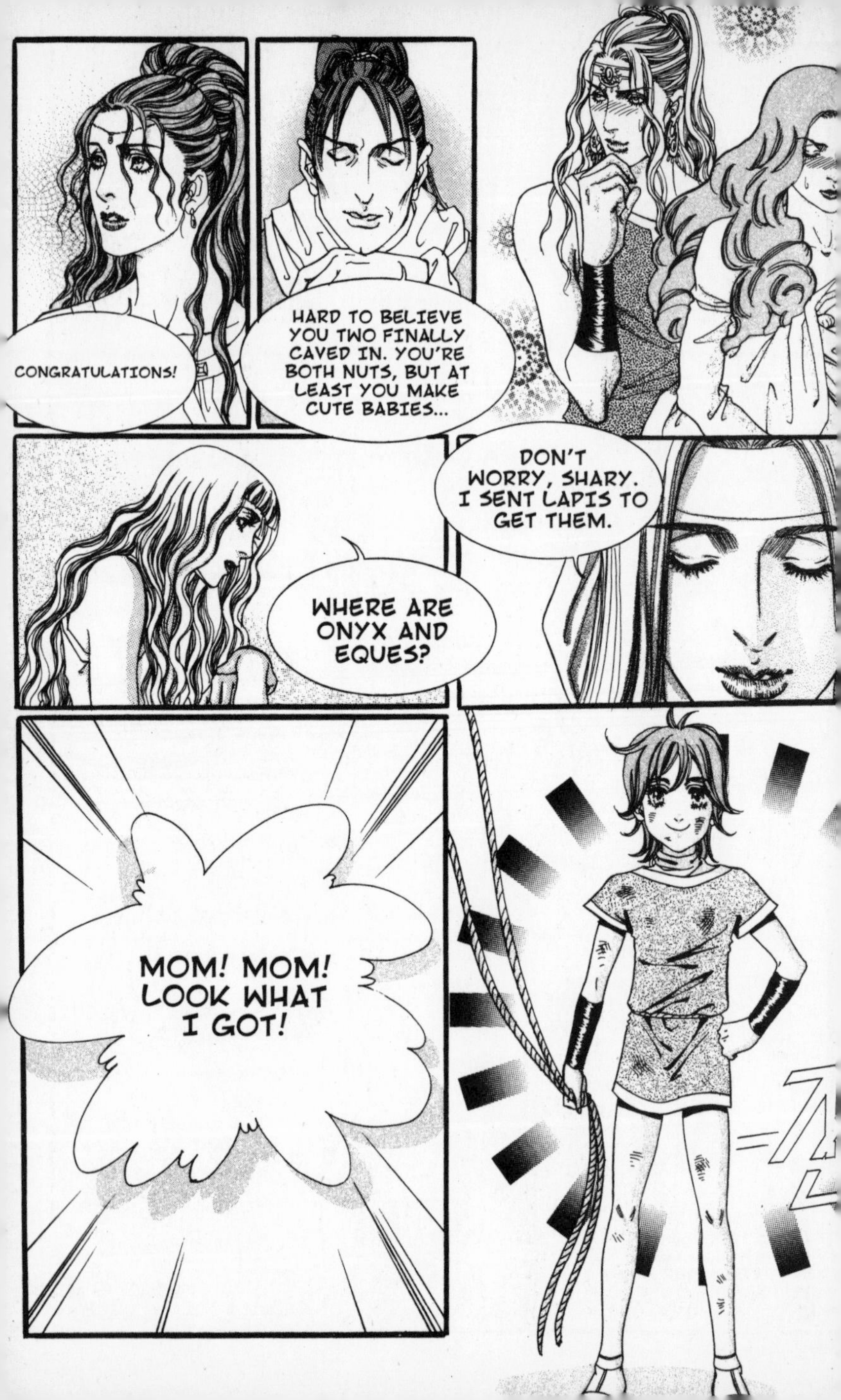
CONGRATULATIONS!
HARD TO BELIEVE YOU TWO FINALLY CAVED IN. YOU'RE BOTH NUTS, BUT AT LEAST YOU MAKE CUTE BABIES...
WHERE ARE ONYX AND EQUES?
DON'T WORRY, SHARY. I SENT LAPIS TO GET THEM.
MOM! MOM! LOOK WHAT I GOT!

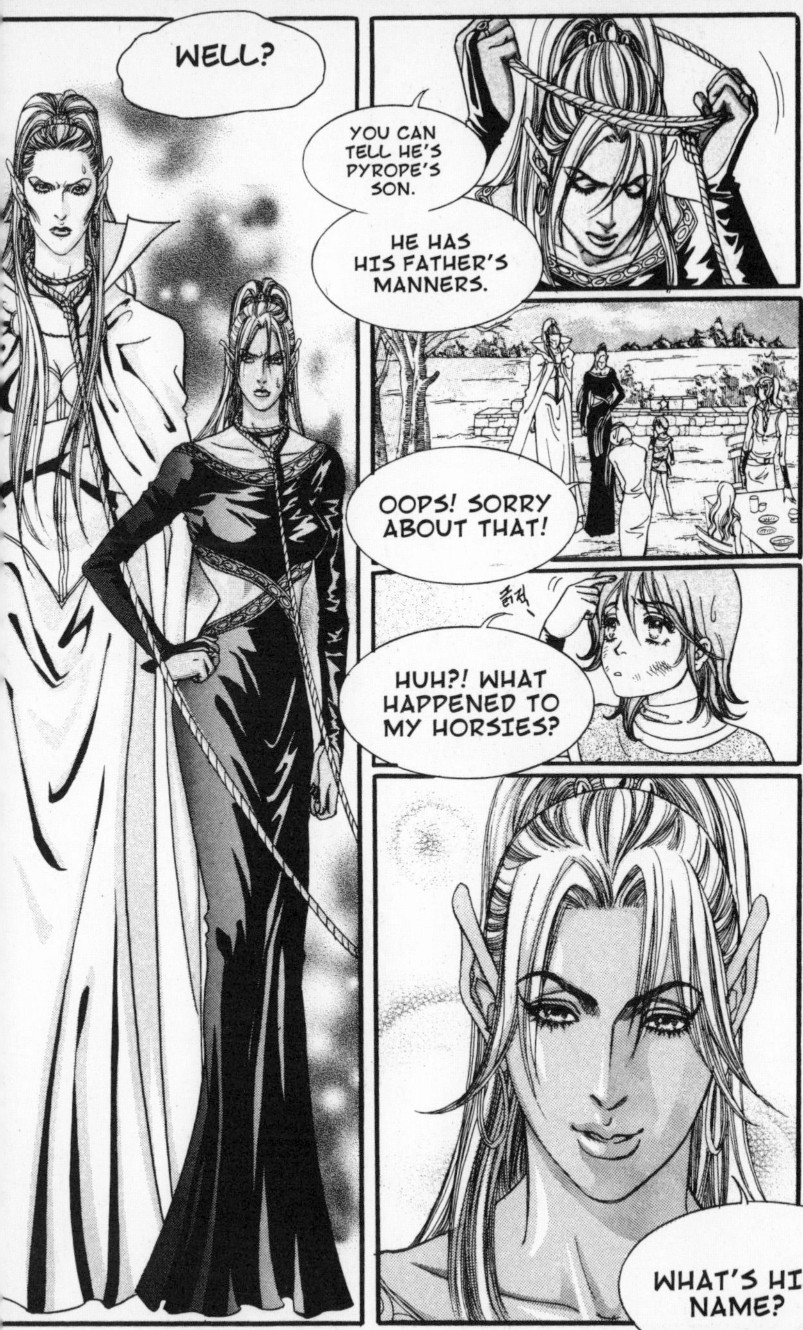
WELL?
YOU CAN TELL HE'S PYROPE'S SON.
HE HAS HIS FATHER'S MANNERS.
OOPS! SORRY ABOUT THAT!
HUH?! WHAT HAPPENED TO MY HORSIES?
WHAT'S HIS NAME?

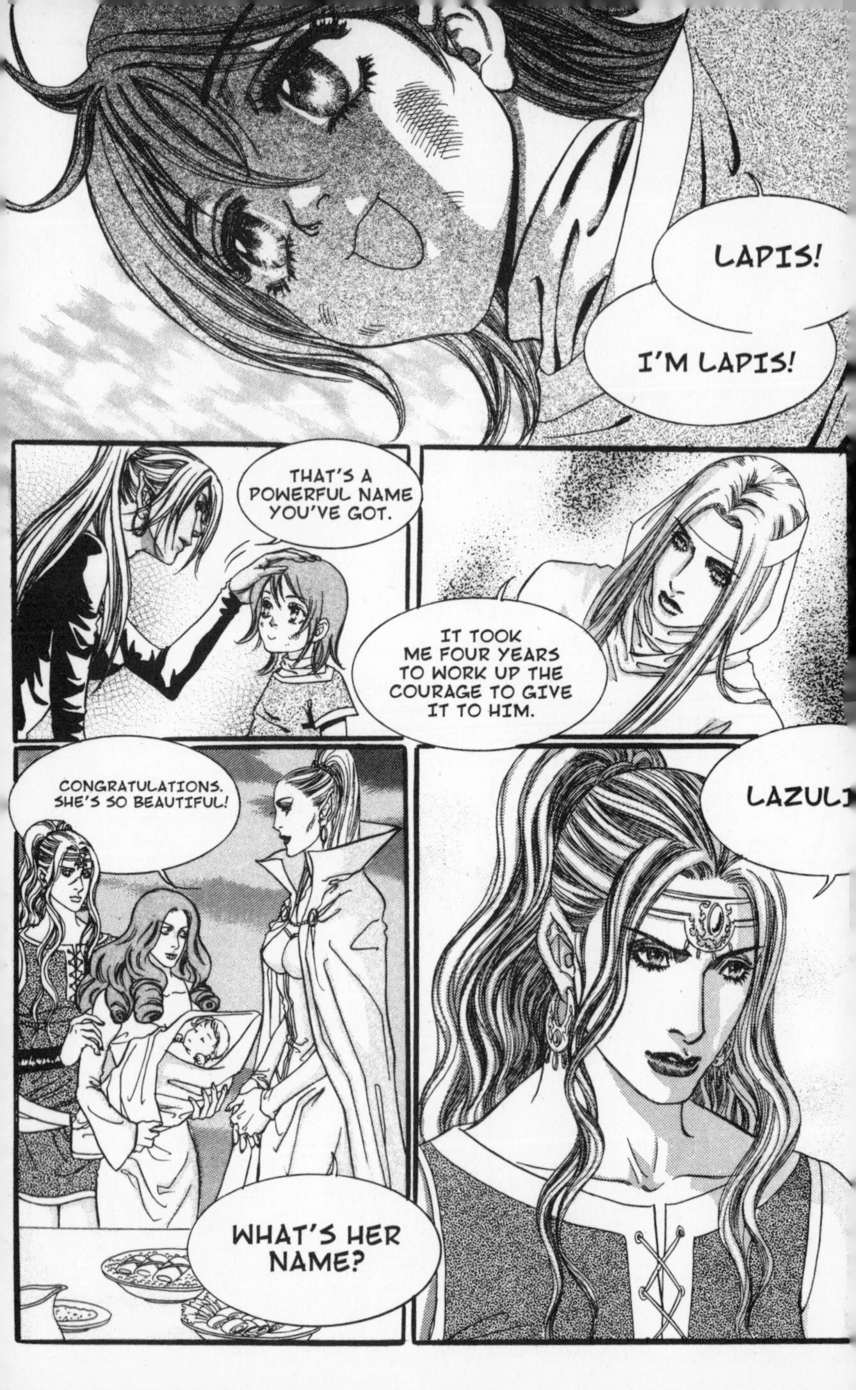
LAPIS!
I'M LAPIS!
THAT'S A POWERFUL NAME YOU'VE GOT.
IT TOOK ME FOUR YEARS TO WORK UP THE COURAGE TO GIVE IT TO HIM.
CONGRATULATIONS. SHE'S SO BEAUTIFUL!
WHAT'S HER NAME?
LAZULI

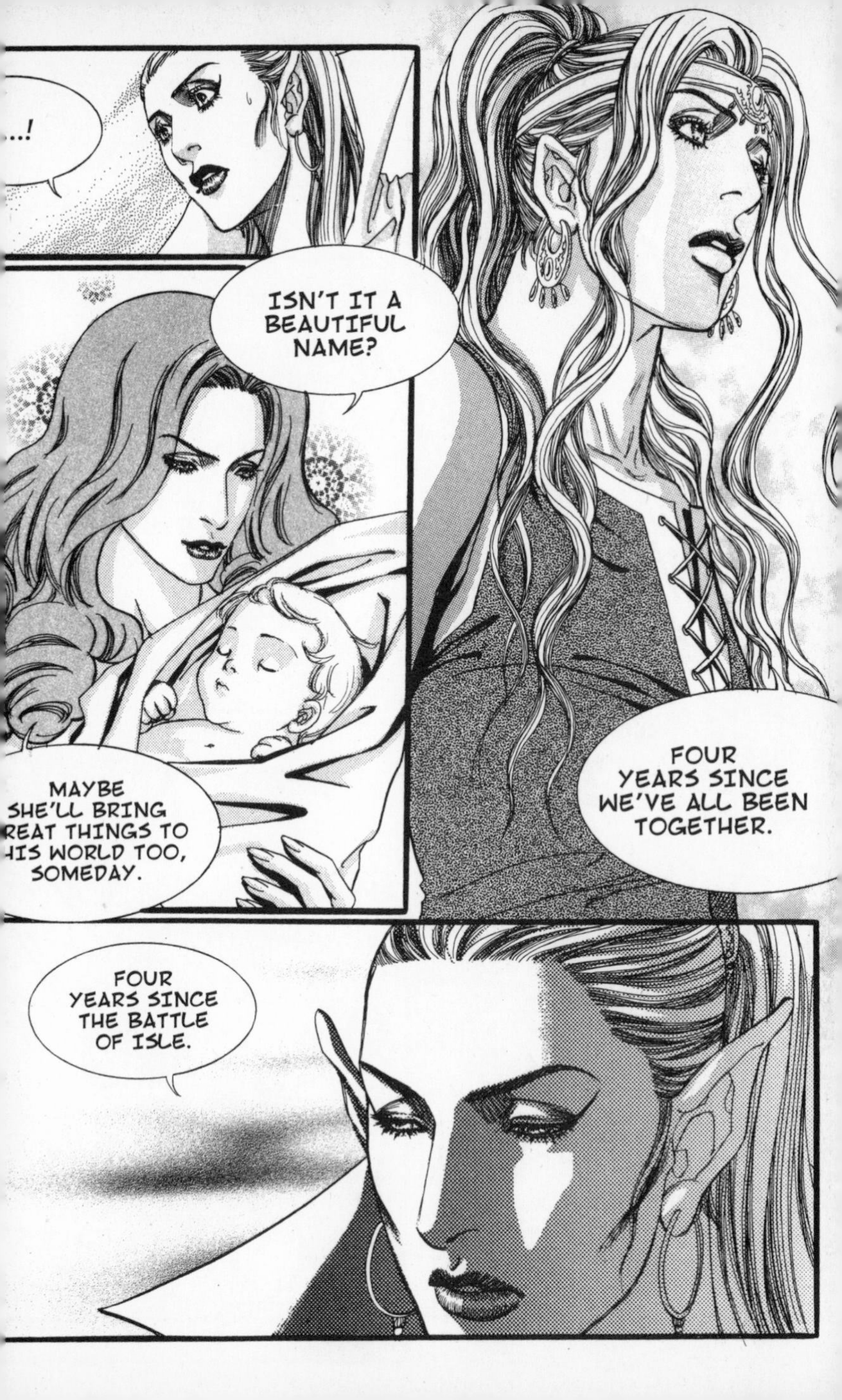
...!
ISN'T IT A BEAUTIFUL NAME?
MAYBE SHE'LL BRING REAT THINGS TO HIS WORLD TOO, SOMEDAY.
FOUR YEARS SINCE WE'VE ALL BEEN TOGETHER.
FOUR YEARS SINCE THE BATTLE OF ISLE.

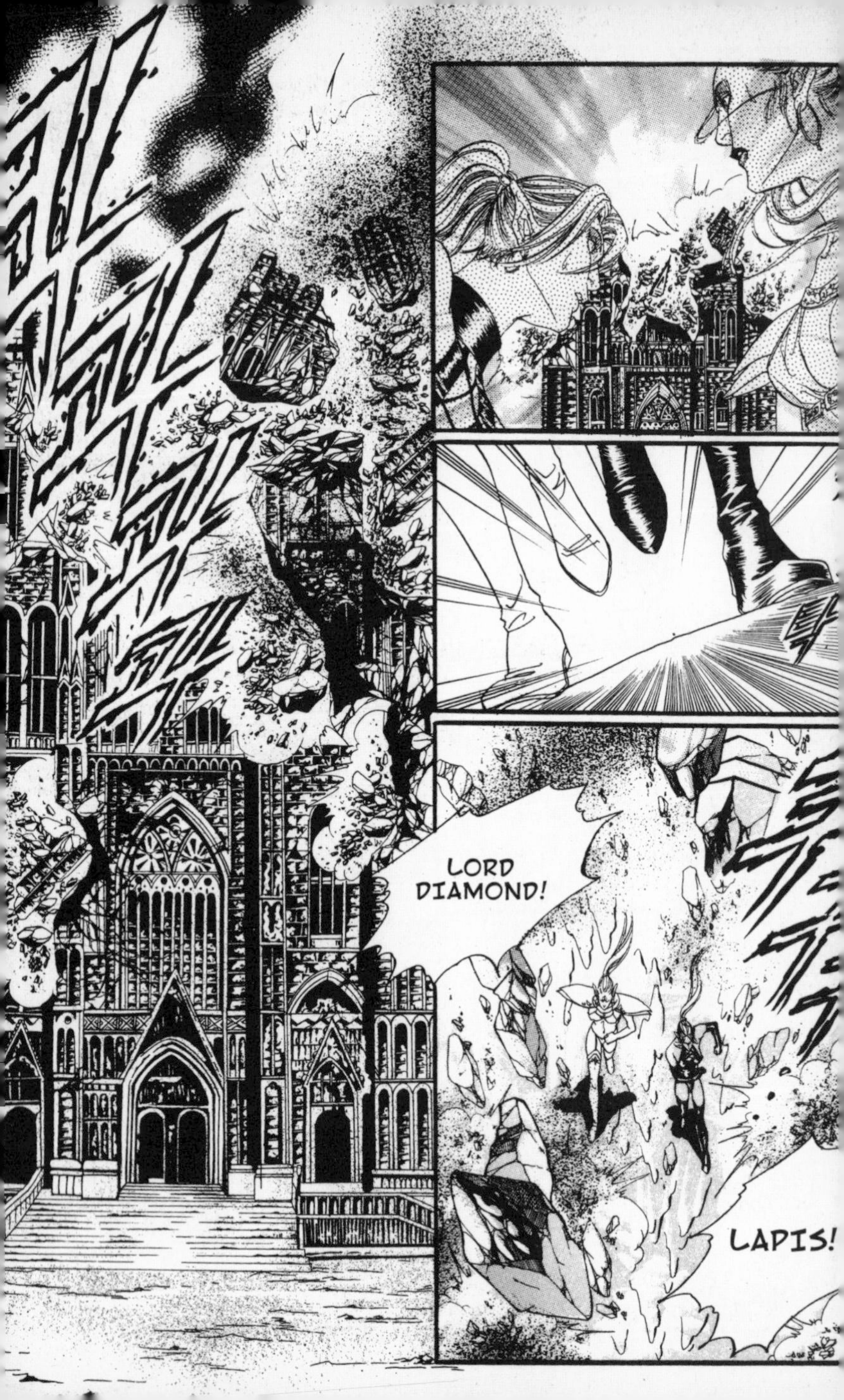
LORD DIAMOND!
LAPIS!

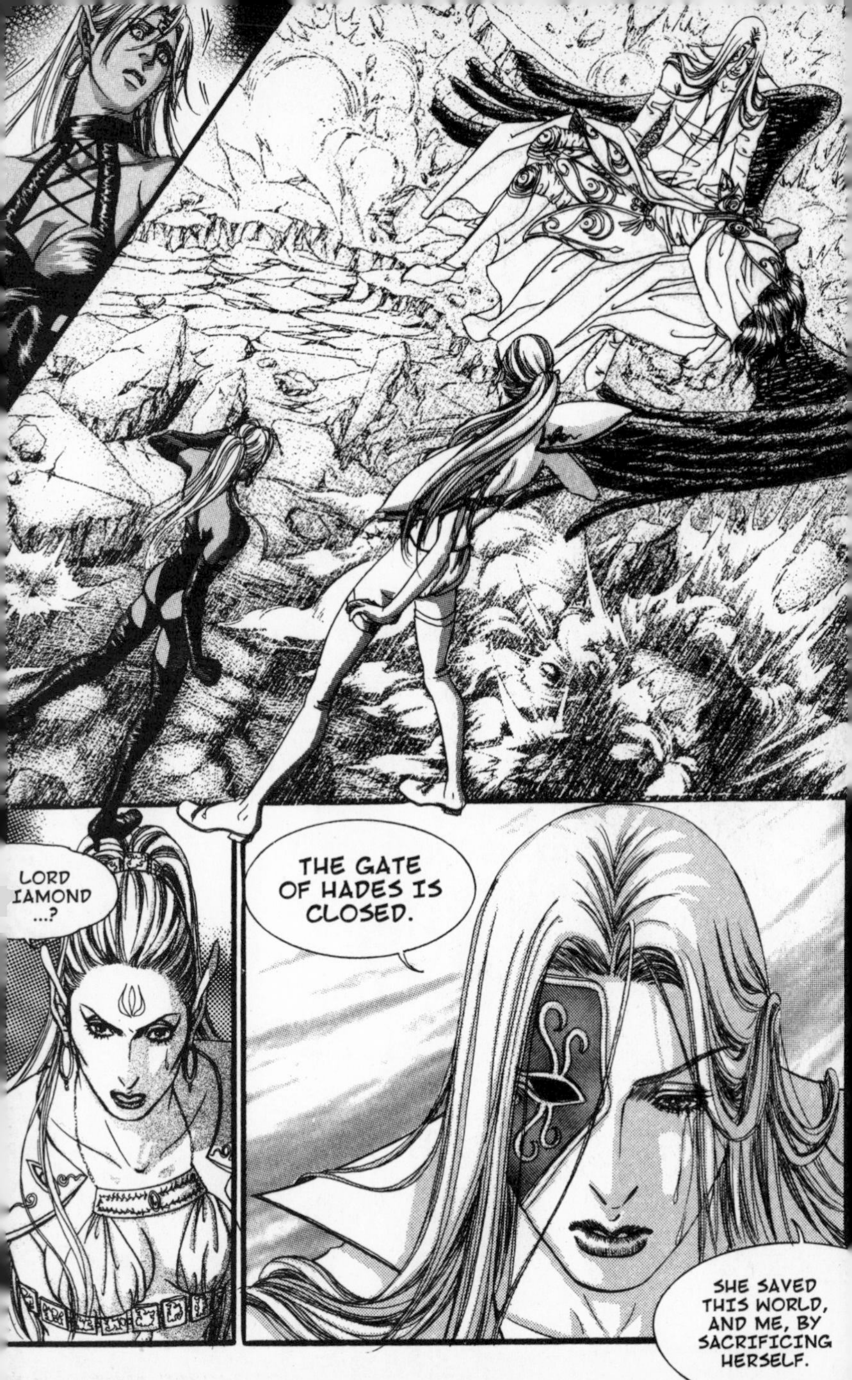
LORD IAMOND ...?
THE GATE OF HADES IS CLOSED.
SHE SAVED THIS WORLD, AND ME, BY SACRIFICING HERSELF.

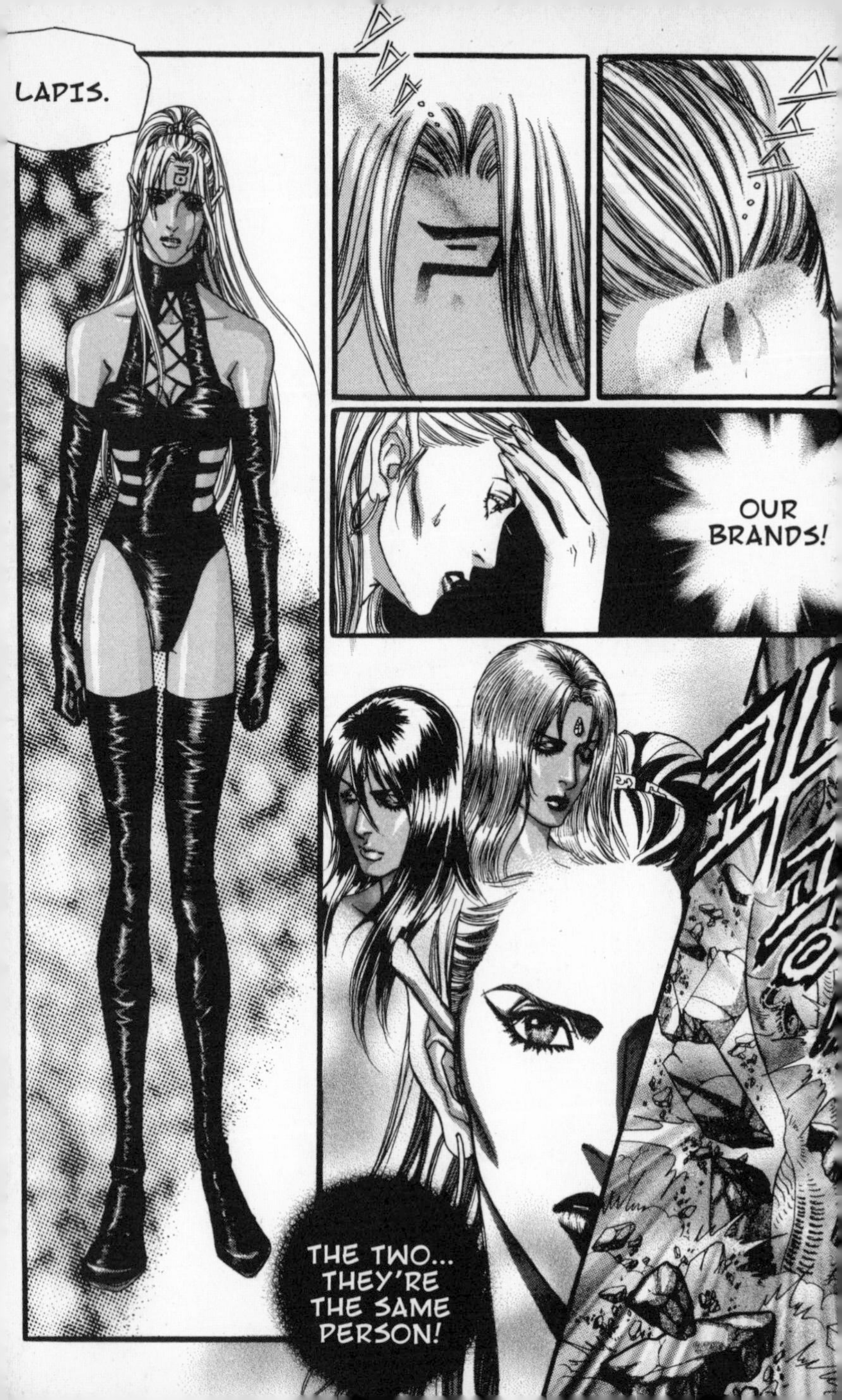
LAPIS.
OUR BRANDS!
THE TWO... THEY'RE THE SAME PERSON!

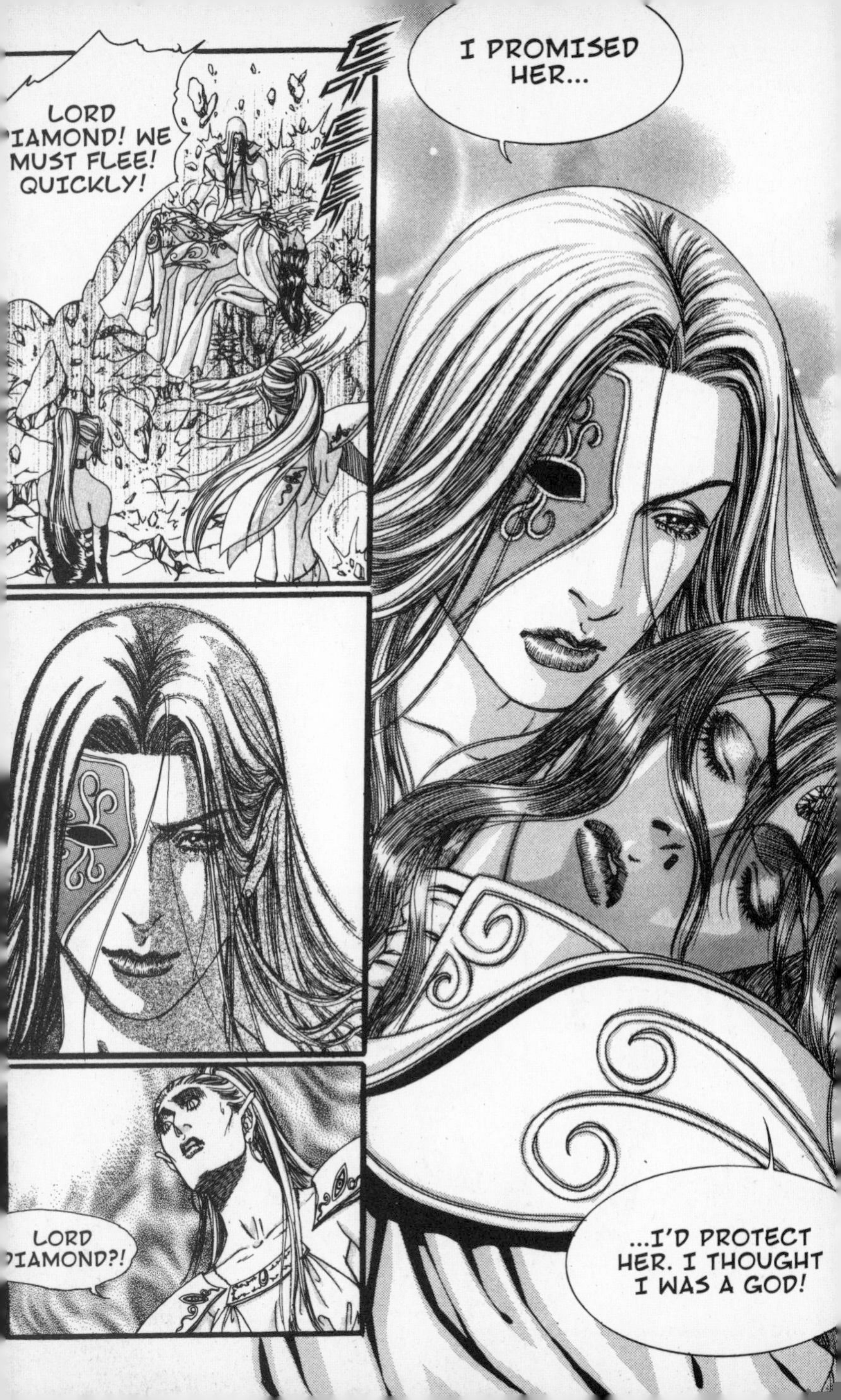
LORD
IAMOND! WE MUST FLEE! QUICKLY!
LORD
IAMOND?!
I PROMISED HER...
...I'D PROTECT HER. I THOUGHT I WAS A GOD!

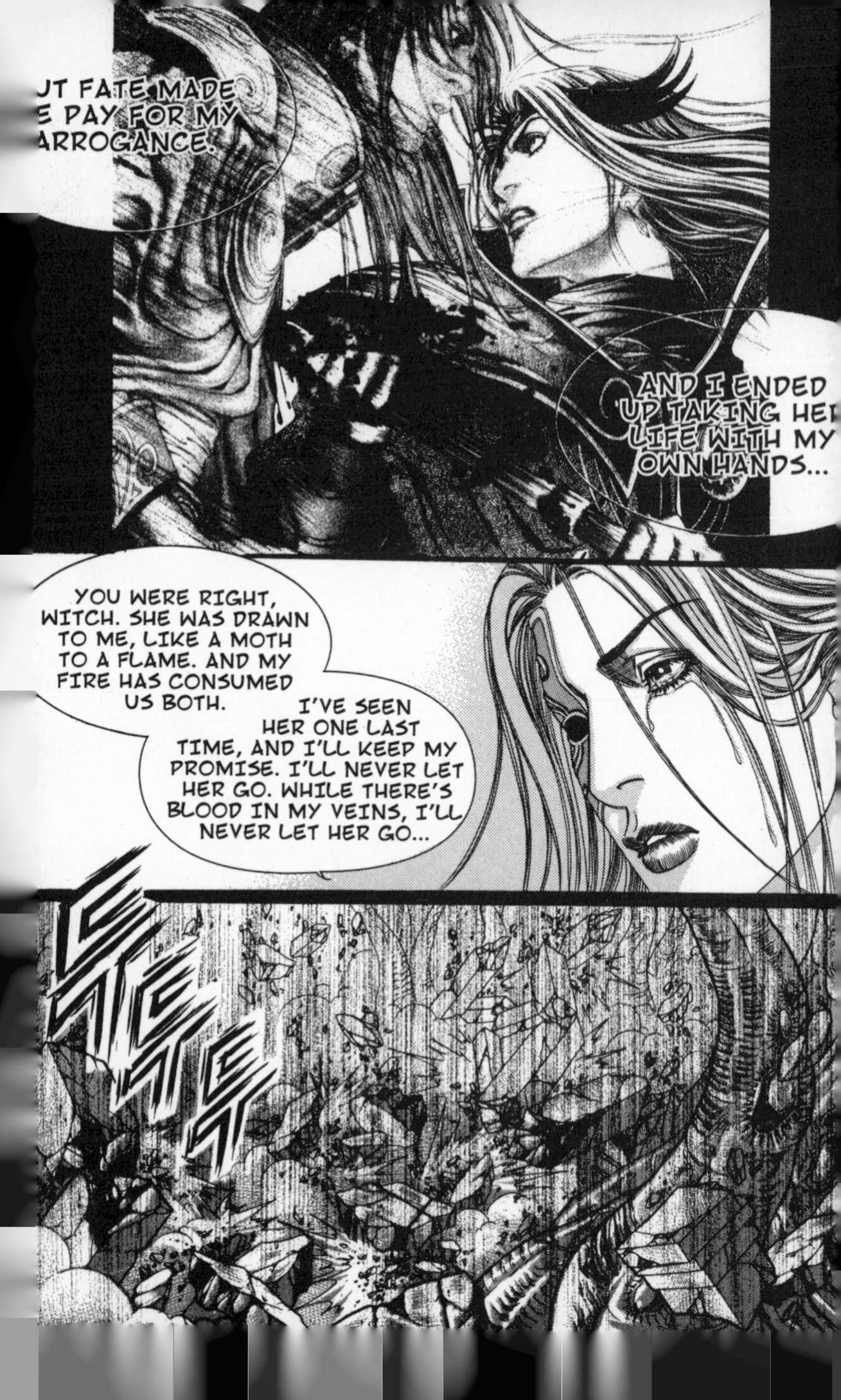
UT FATE MADE E PAY FOR MY ARROGANCE.
AND I ENDED UP TAKING HE LIFE WITH MY OWN HANDS...
YOU WERE RIGHT, WITCH. SHE WAS DRAWN TO ME, LIKE A MOTH TO A FLAME. AND MY FIRE HAS CONSUMED US BOTH.
I'VE SEEN HER ONE LAST TIME, AND I'LL KEEP MY PROMISE. I'LL NEVER LET HER GO. WHILE THERE'S BLOOD IN MY VEINS, I'LL NEVER LET HER GO...

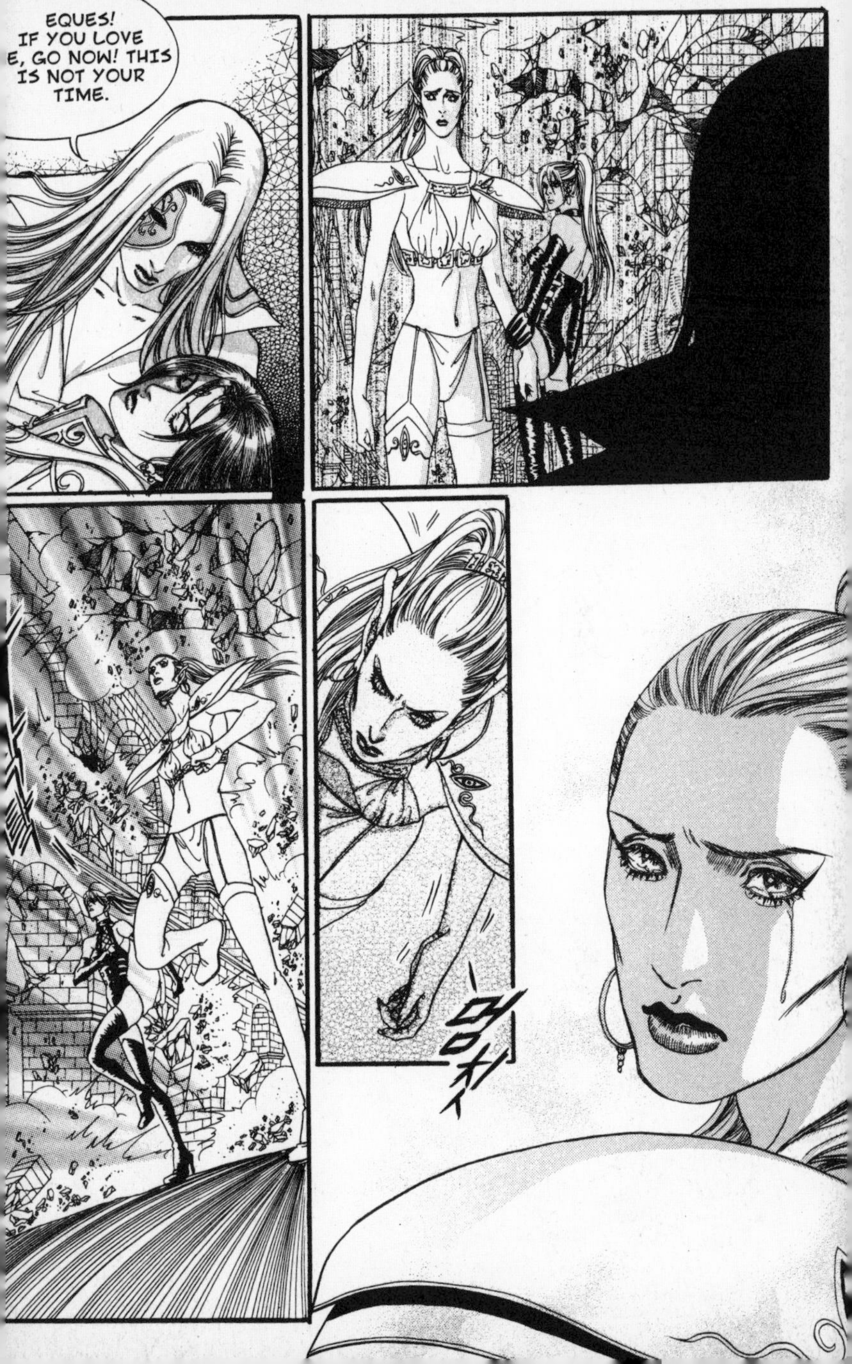
EQUES! IF YOU LOVE E, GO NOW! THIS IS NOT YOUR TIME.

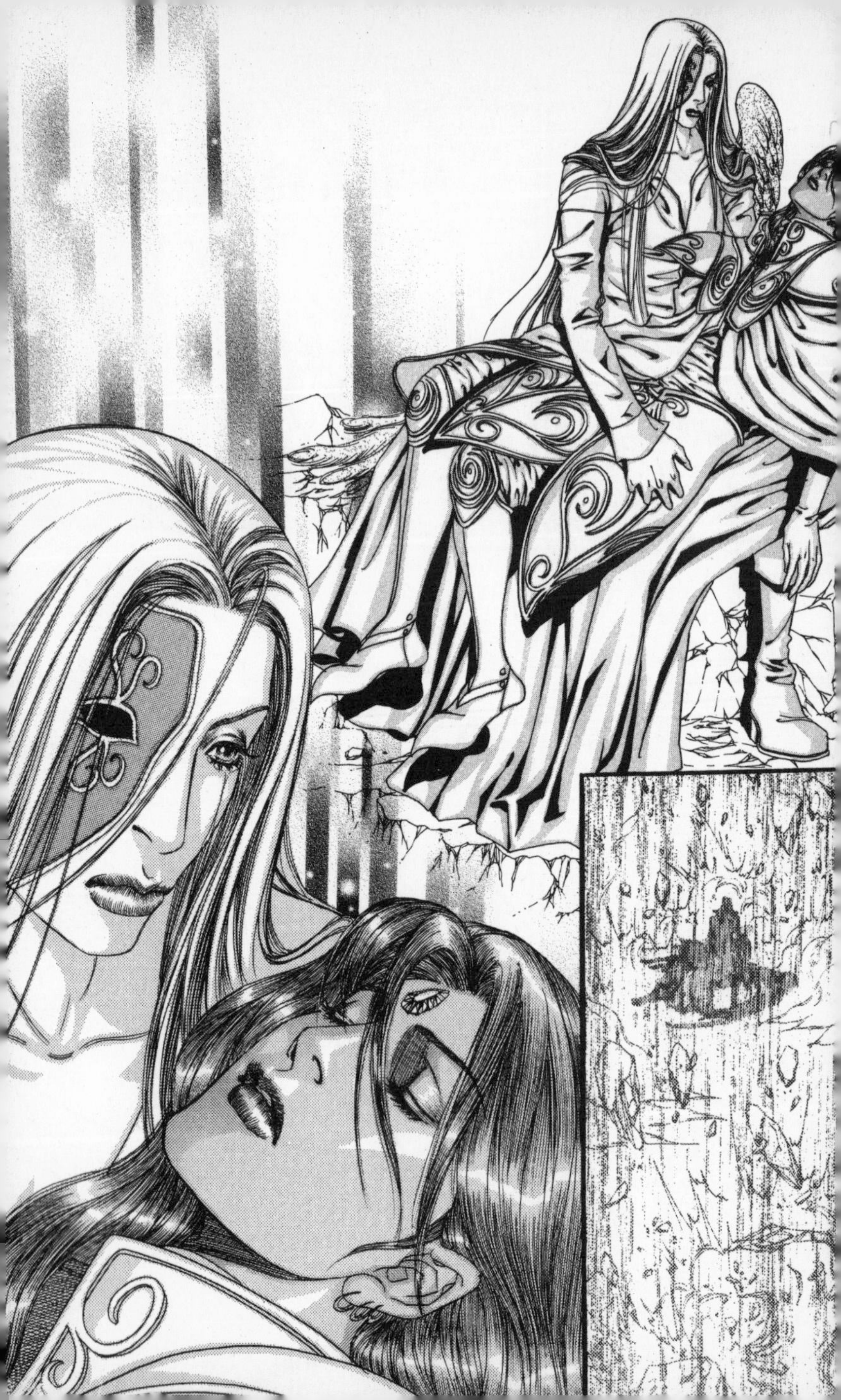

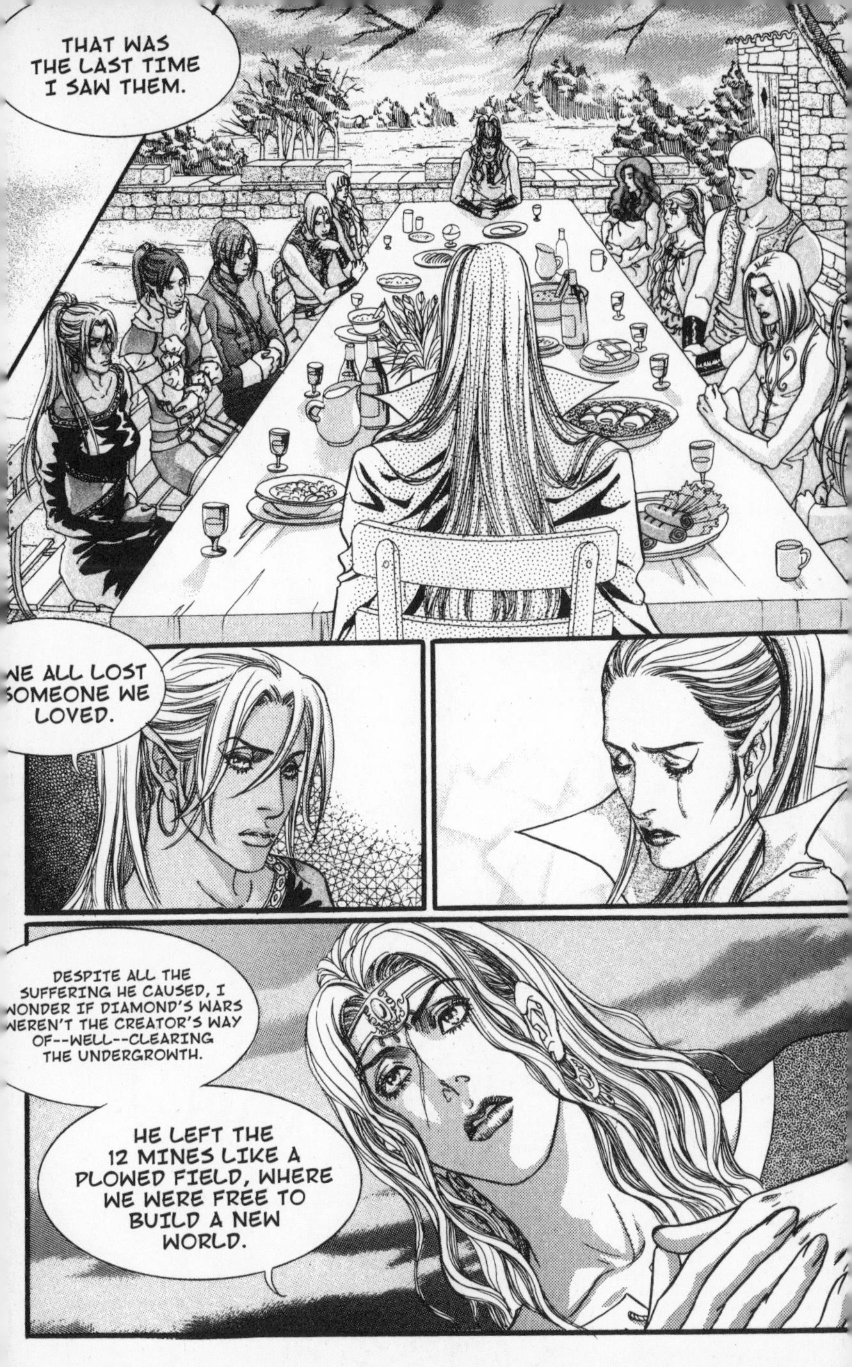
THAT WAS THE LAST TIME I SAW THEM.
WE ALL LOST SOMEONE WE LOVED.
DESPITE ALL THE SUFFERING HE CAUSED, I WONDER IF DIAMOND'S WARS WEREN'T THE CREATOR'S WAY OF--WELL--CLEARING THE UNDERGROWTH.
HE LEFT THE 12 MINES LIKE A PLOWED FIELD, WHERE WE WERE FREE TO BUILD A NEW WORLD.

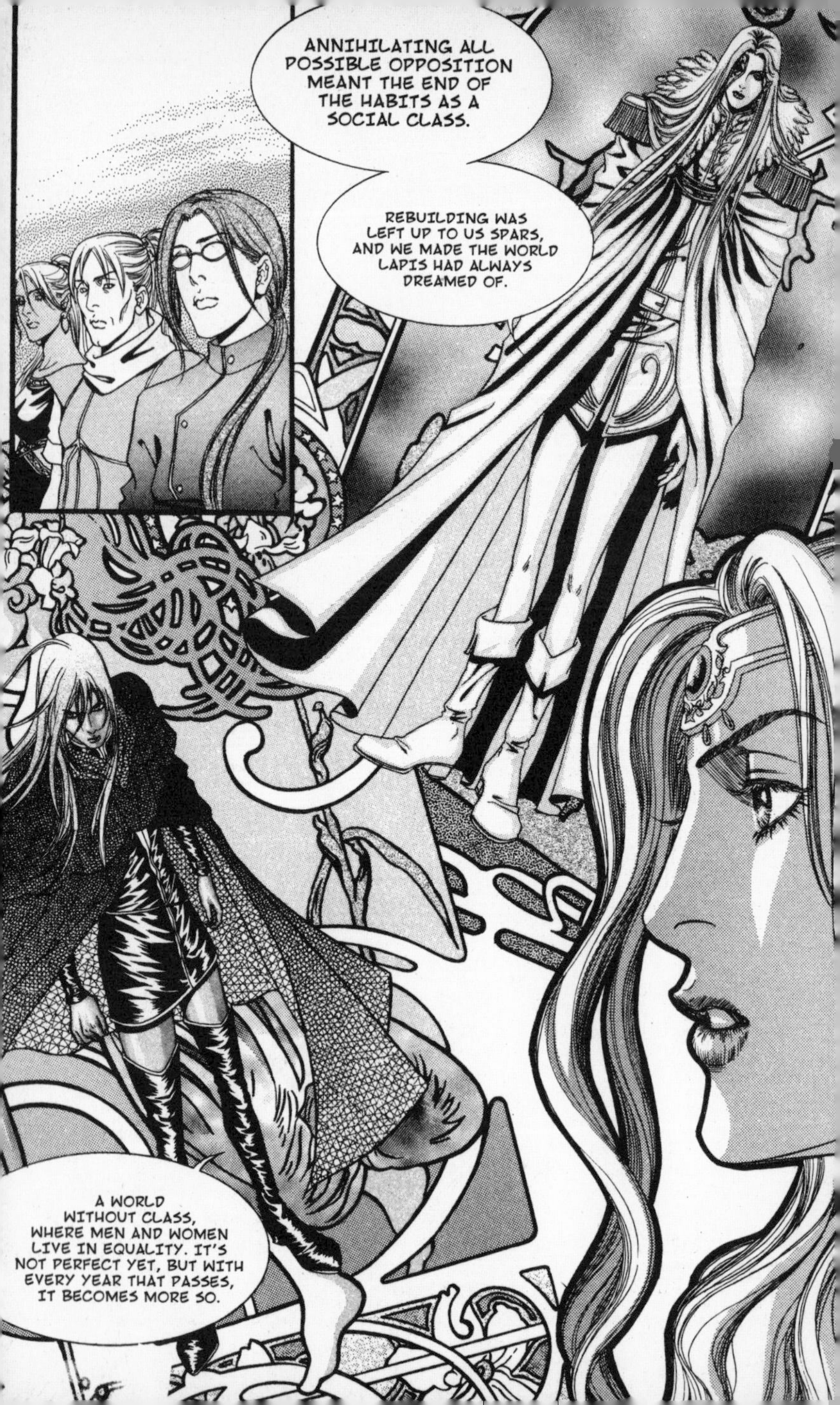
ANNIHILATING ALL POSSIBLE OPPOSITION MEANT THE END OF THE HABITS AS A SOCIAL CLASS.
REBUILDING WAS LEFT UP TO US SPARS, AND WE MADE THE WORLD LAPIS HAD ALWAYS DREAMED OF.
A WORLD WITHOUT CLASS, WHERE MEN AND WOMEN LIVE IN EQUALITY. IT'S NOT PERFECT YET, BUT WITH EVERY YEAR THAT PASSES, IT BECOMES MORE SO.

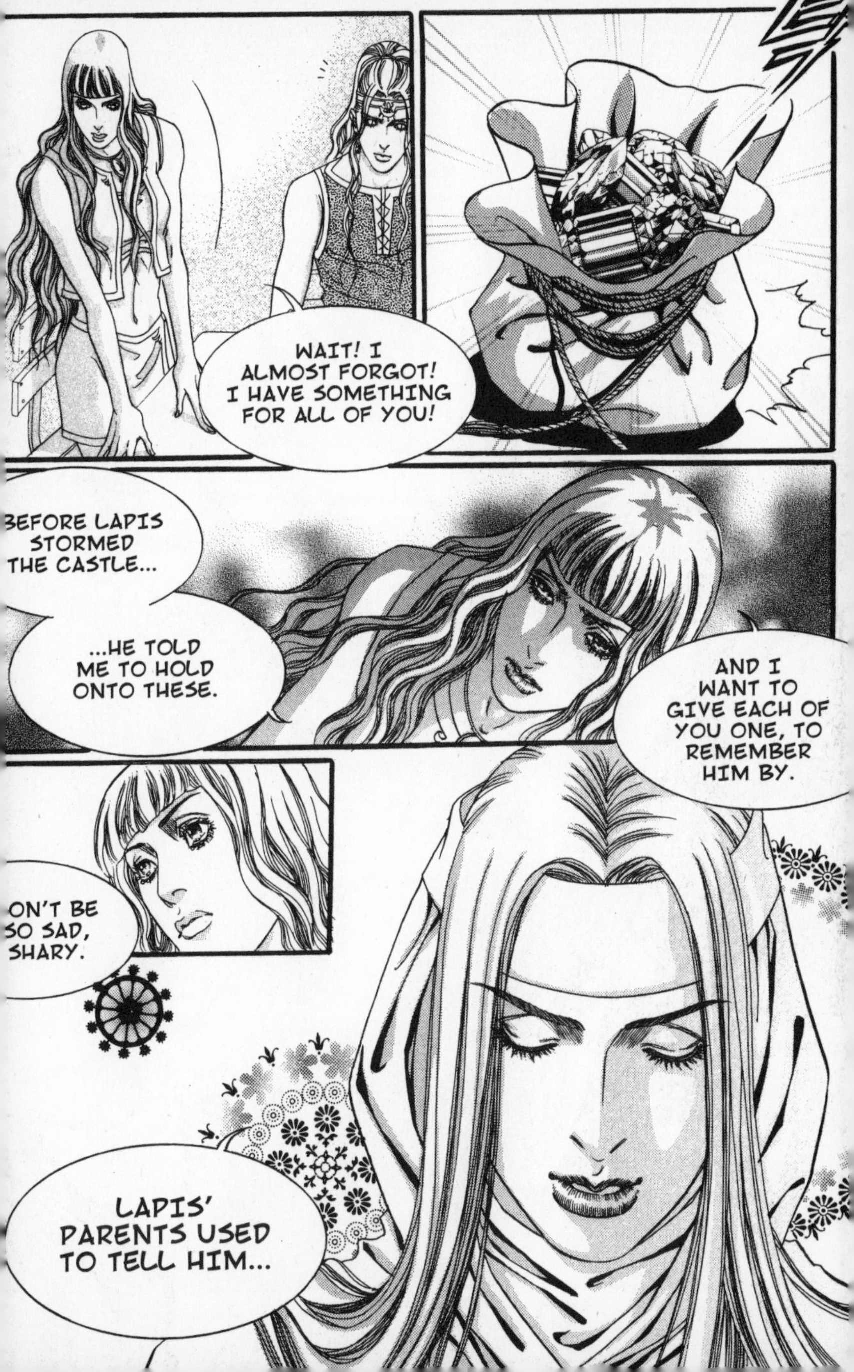
WAIT! I ALMOST FORGOT! I HAVE SOMETHING FOR ALL OF YOU!
BEFORE LAPIS STORMED THE CASTLE...
...HE TOLD ME TO HOLD ONTO THESE.
AND I WANT TO GIVE EACH OF YOU ONE, TO REMEMBER HIM BY.
ON'T BE SO SAD, SHARY.
LAPIS' PARENTS USED TO TELL HIM...

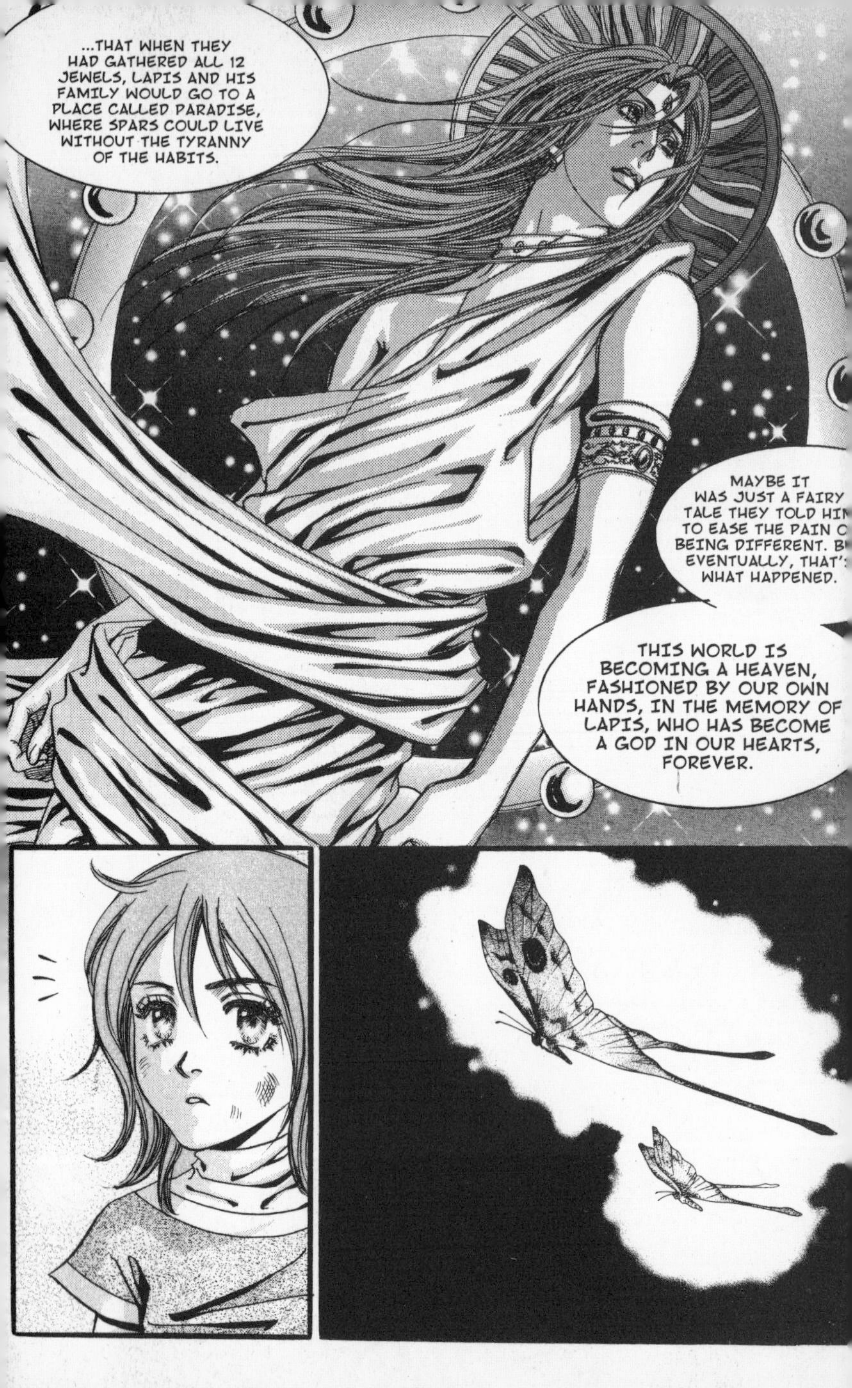
...THAT WHEN THEY HAD GATHERED ALL 12 JEWELS, LAPIS AND HIS FAMILY WOULD GO TO A PLACE CALLED PARADISE, WHERE SPARS COULD LIVE WITHOUT THE TYRANNY OF THE HABITS.
MAYBE IT WAS JUST A FAIRY TALE THEY TOLD HI TO EASE THE PAIN O BEING DIFFERENT. B EVENTUALLY, THAT' WHAT HAPPENED.
THIS WORLD IS BECOMING A HEAVEN, FASHIONED BY OUR OWN HANDS, IN THE MEMORY OF LAPIS, WHO HAS BECOME A GOD IN OUR HEARTS, FOREVER.

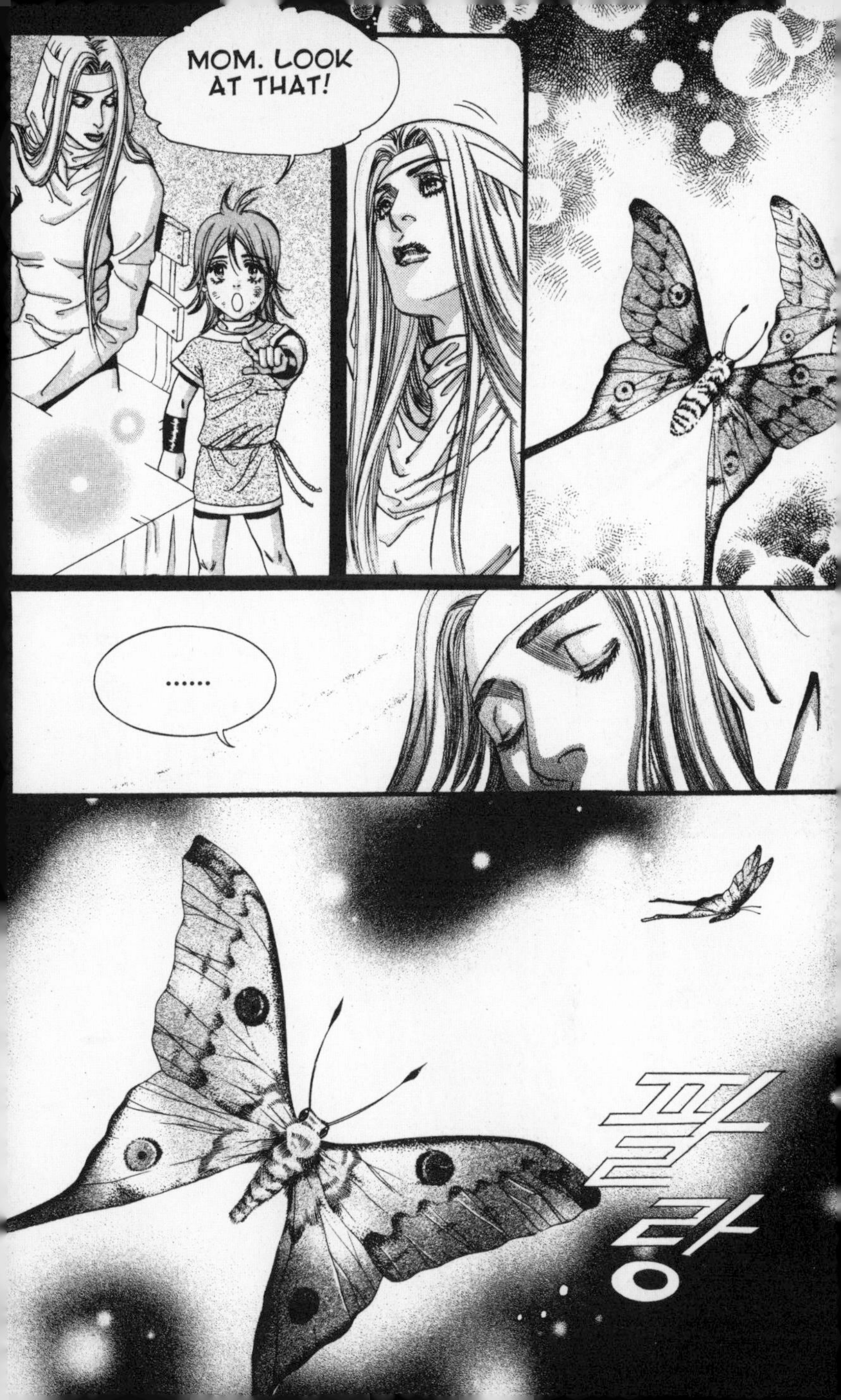
MOM. LOOK AT THAT!
......
파르랑

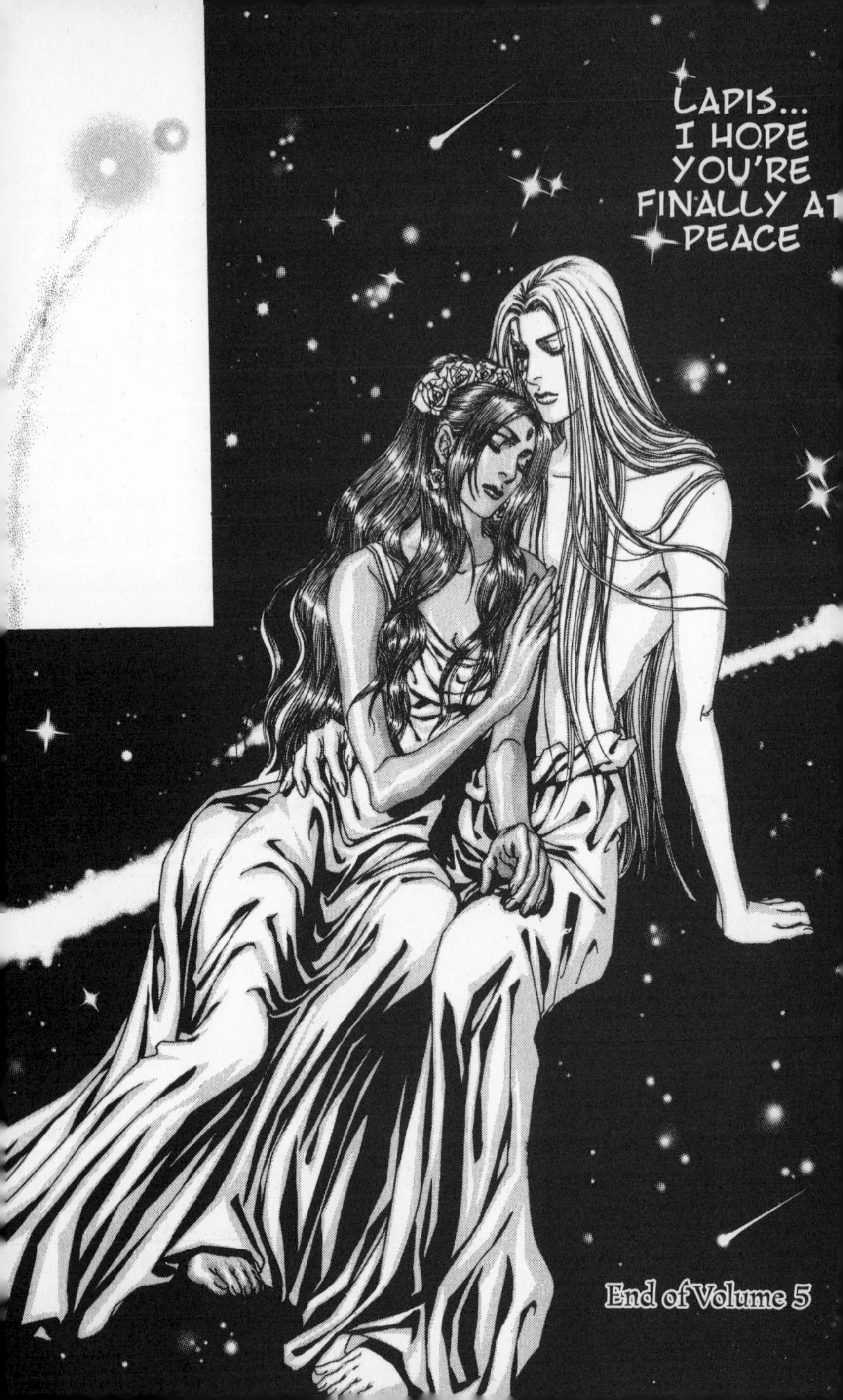
LAPIS... I HOPE YOU'RE FINALLY AT PEACE
End of Volume 5

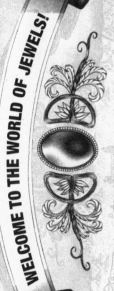

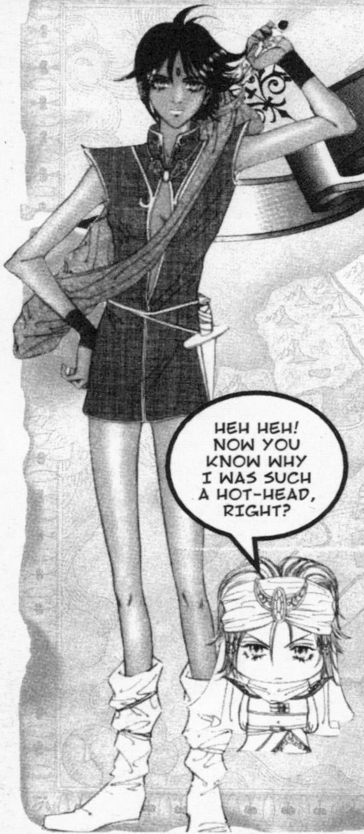
HEH HEH! NOW YOU KNOW WHY I WAS SUCH A HOT-HEAD, RIGHT?

WELCOME TO THE WORLD OF JEWELS!

GOD

Did you enjoy Les Bijoux? We're sorry, but this volume became the final chapter without much warning! I know you're curious about all the characters you didn't get to see much of, so I'll try to clear up some of the unsolved mysteries! These were some of the people we planned for Lapis to meet, and the places we wanted him to go:

People and places from *Les Bijoux*

MINE		
NAME		DOMINANT CHARACTERISTIC
1	NEIGE	SNOW
2	SOLEIL	SUN
3	SABLE	DESERT
4	LAC	LAKE
5	MER	SEA
6	ISLE	ISLAND
7	PLUIE	RAIN
8	CITE	CITY
9	SUMER	SEASHORE
10	MARSH	SWAMP
11	VOLCANO	VOLCANO
12	GLACE	ICE

KHODA (GOD) & KHODAPARAST (BELIEVERS)					
NAME/NAMESAKE			GUARDIAN GEM	NIRU (POWER WEAPON)	EYES AND HAIR
LAPIS	LAZULI	•	PERIDOT	SWORD THAT CONTROLS DARKNESS	BLACK
CARNILION	RUBY	♂	GARNET	LASH CONTROLLING FIRE AND BLOOD	RED
SILICA	GLASS	♀	QUARTZ	EARRING CONTROLLING WATER	BROWN
MORIAN	BLACK CRYSTAL	♂	LAZULI	BROOCH OF SECOND SIGHT	BROWN
TAIMAI	KALIUM	♂	AGATE	SHIELD CONTROLLING WIND AND SEA	BROWN
SHELL	CLAM	♀	PEARL	CHARM CONTROLLING LOVE	BROWN
RUTILE	SYNTHETIC RUTILE	♂	MALACHITE	FEATHER CONTROLLING LIGHTNING	BROWN
CUBIC	CUBIC ZIRCONIUM	♂	CHRYSOPRASE	INVISIBILITY HELM	CLEAR
LOTHESITIE	LODESTONE	♀	AMBER	WERE-TIGER GLOVE	BROWN
ADURA	MOONSTONE	♀	TOPAZ	MIRROR CONTROLLING DREAMS	PURPLE
SHARY	SARI	♀	AMETHYST	CLOAK OF MAGNETISM	BROWN
KIZETTE	BROWN COAL	♂	OPAL	BOOMERANG OF ILLUSION	BROWN

Q: HEY! HOW COME WE ONLY SAW LAPIS AND DIAMOND USE THE POWER OF THEIR STONES?

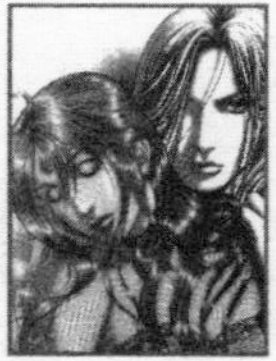

A: ORIGINALLY, THE PLAN WAS TO DEVELOP MORE OF THE CHARACTERS IN LES BIJOUX, BUT TO FINISH THE STORY IN THE NUMBER OF ISSUES WE DID, I HAD TO FOCUS ON LAPIS AND DIAMOND. EVERYONE ELSE MORE OR LESS GOT SHAFTED! I WOULD HAVE LOVED TO HAVE SHOWN YOU EACH OF THEIR ABILITIES! THE NEXT CHART IS SOMETHING THAT CHO EUNHA CAME UP WITH WHEN SHE FIRST WROTE *LES BIJOUX*.

CHARACTERS IN LES BIJOUX 2

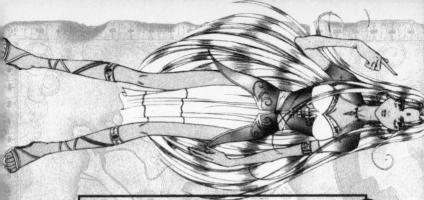

Q: DOES THE BOOK LES BIJOUX HAVE SAME STORY AS THE MANHWA?

A: THEY'RE SIMILAR, BUT THERE ARE SOME BIG DIFFERENCES.
FOR INSTANCE.
SHELL IS A WOMAN IN THE BOOK, BUT SHE TURNS OUT TO BE A BEAUTIFUL BOY IN THE MANHWA. I, PARK SANG-SUN, REVISED THE BOOK TO FIT INTO THE MANHWA FORMAT. IN THE BOOK, LAPIS BECOMES A GOD, BUT IN THE MANHWA, LAPIS IS MORE HUMAN, LIKE A MESSIAH. AREN'T THE DIFFERENCES THAT COME OUT WHEN TWO PEOPLE INTERPRET THE SAME TEXT INTERESTING?

MINE

	NAME	DOMINANT CHARACTERISTIC
1	NEIGE	SNOW
2	SOLEIL	SUN
3	SABLE	DESERT
4	LAC	LAKE
5	MER	SEA
6	ISLE	ISLAND
7	PLUIE	RAIN
8	CITE	CITY
9	SUMER	SEASHORE
10	MARSH	SWAMP
11	VOLCANO	VOLCANO
12	GLACE	ICE

KHAEN (TRAITORS)

NAME		EYES & HAIR	CHARACTERISTIC	NIRU (POWER)
DIAMOND	DIAMOND	CLEAR	COLD & CRUEL	SCEPTER OF SNOW
CARLSEDON	JADE	SUN	TYRANNY	SWORD OF THE SUN
PYROPE	GARNET	LIGHT	TYRANNY	AXE OF DESERT SANDS
RUBY	RUBY	BLOODY	LUSTFUL	CROWN OF WATERS
AQUAIRINE	BLUE JADE	WATER	ANDROGYNOUS	FAN OF THE SEA
EMERALD	EMERALD	DARK GREEN	COLD	SERPENT FLIES
JASPER	GREEN JADE	JADE	LUSTFUL	SWORD OF THUNDER
SINOFUN	YELLOW	CRYSTAL YELLOW	CUNNING	STAR SHAPED DARTS
SAPPHIRE	SAPPHIRE	BLUE	DETACHED	TYPHOON BROOCH
HEMATIN	HEMATITE	REDDISH PURPLE	CRUEL	HAMMER OF THE MARSH
ZIRCON	ZIRCON	PURPLE	CRUEL & BRAVE	VOLCANO FLAME
IVORY	IVORY	WHITE	GLOOMY	VEIL OF ICE

THE CHART ABOVE GIVES YOU AN IDEA OF WHAT WE LEFT OUT. IT COULD HAVE BEEN A REALLY LONG STORY! AND I'M REALLY SORRY THAT WE COULDN'T SHOW YOU EVERYTHING. PLEASE APPRECIATE THE MANHWA FOR WHAT IT IS, BECAUSE A LOT OF LOVE WENT INTO IT!

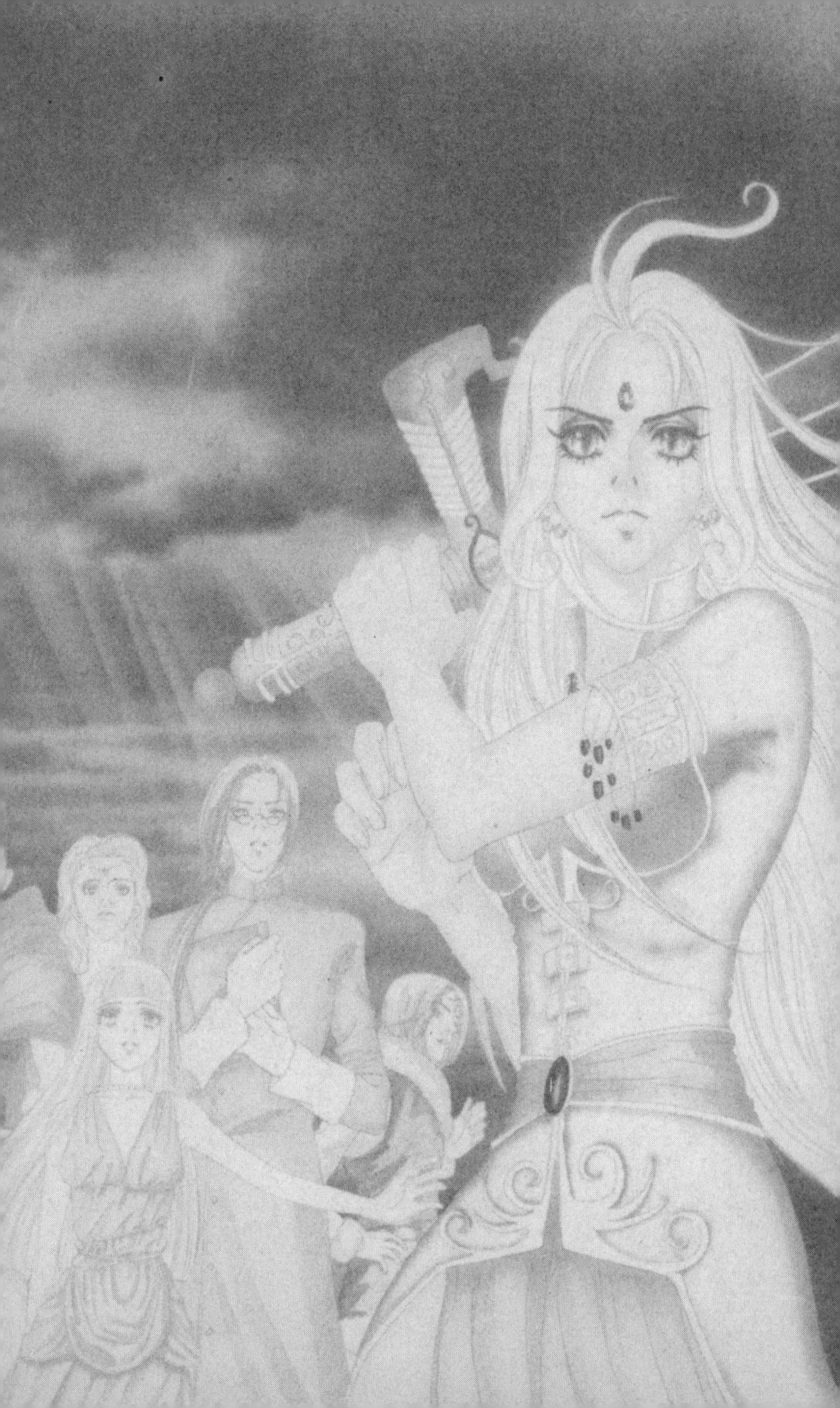

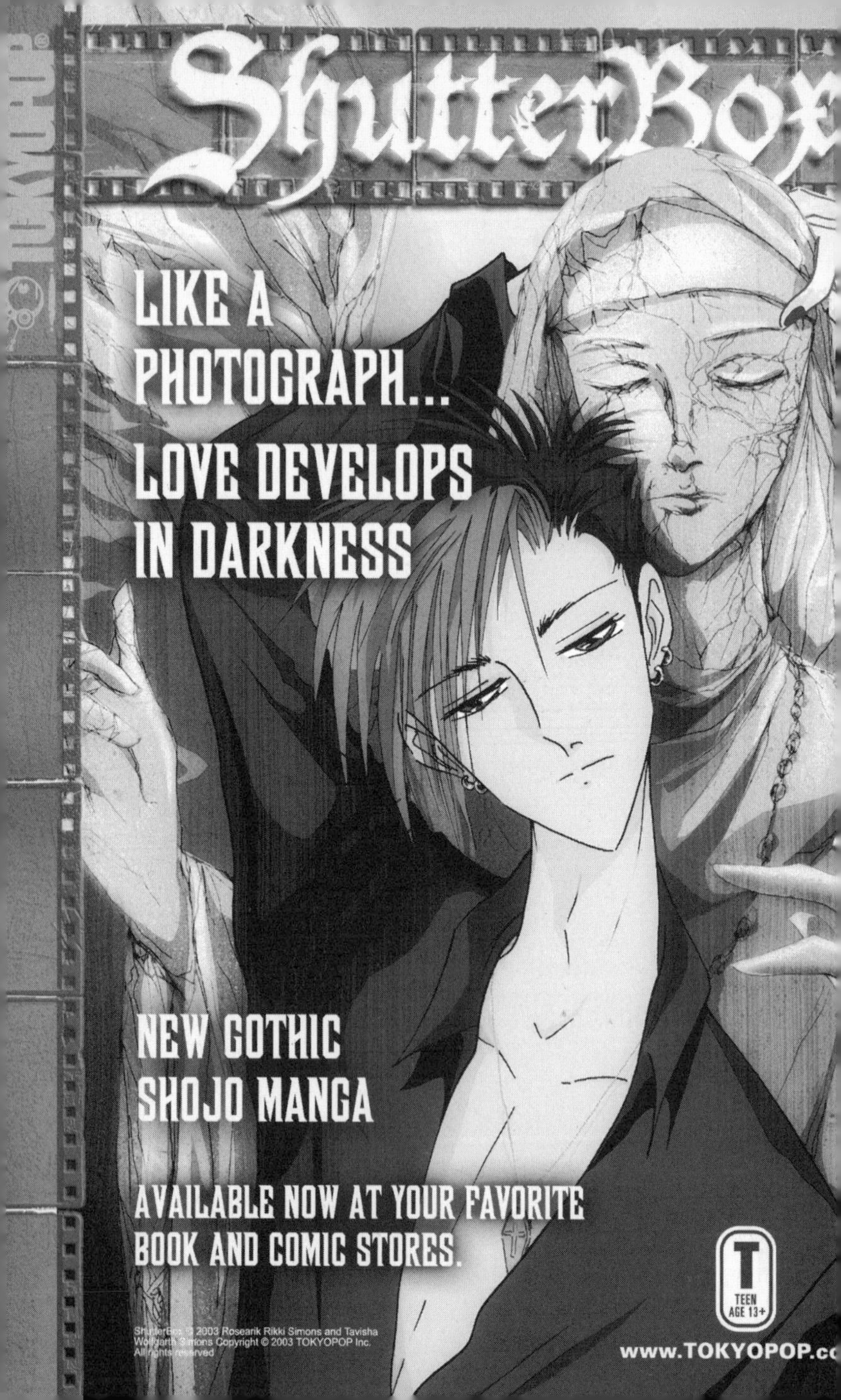
ShutterBox
LIKE A PHOTOGRAPH...
LOVE DEVELOPS IN DARKNESS
NEW GOTHIC SHOJO MANGA
AVAILABLE NOW AT YOUR FAVORITE BOOK AND COMIC STORES.
TEEN AGE 13+
ShutterBox © 2003 Rosearik Rikki Simons and Tavisha Wolfgarth Simons Copyright © 2003 TOKYOPOP Inc. All rights reserved
www.TOKYOPOP.co

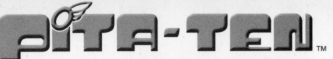

PITA-TEN™

By Koge-Donbo · Creator of Digicharat

The girl next door is
bringing a touch of heaven
to the neighborhood.

TOKYOPOP®

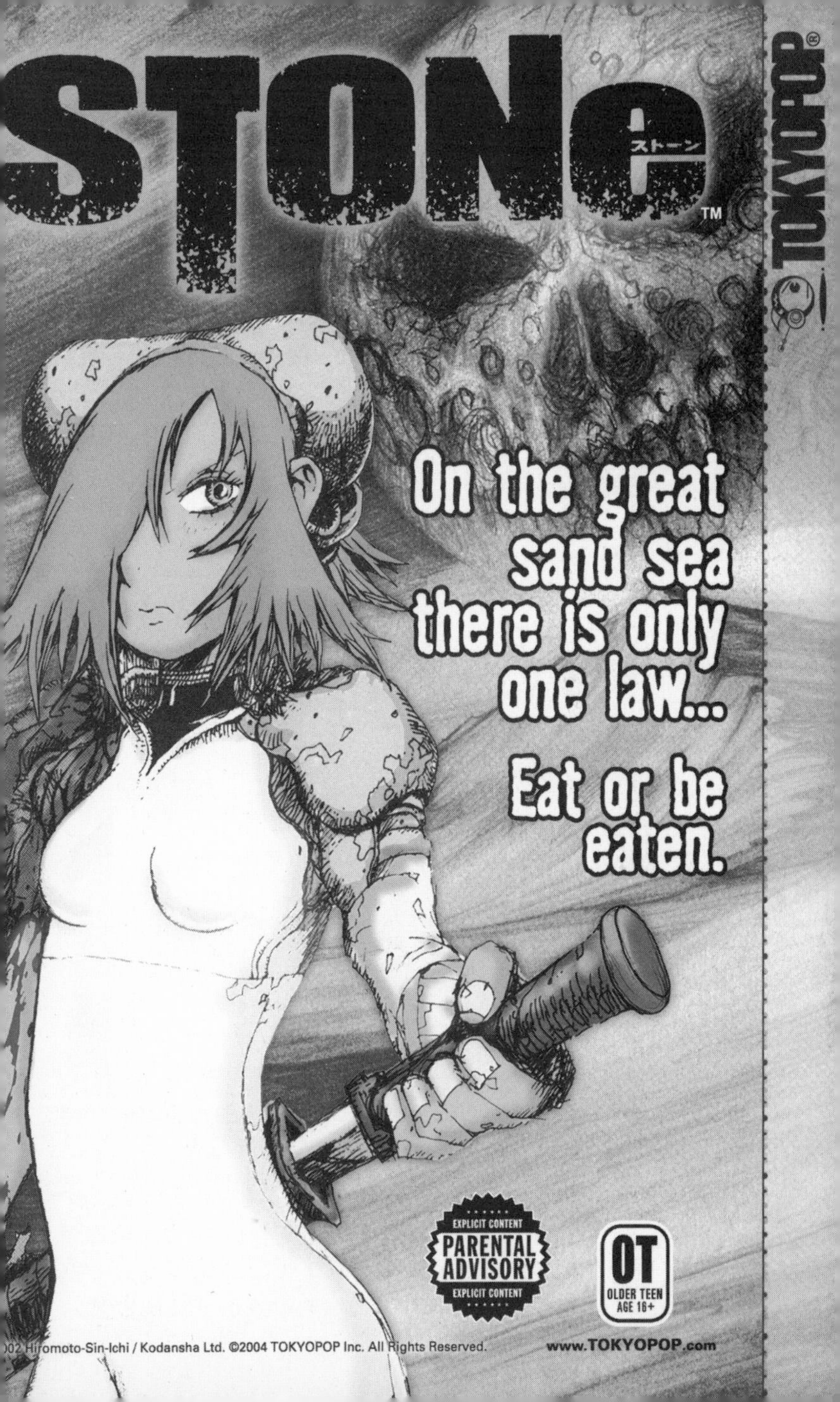

STONe
ストーン
TM
TOKYOPOP®
On the great sand sea there is only one law...
Eat or be eaten.
EXPLICIT CONTENT
PARENTAL ADVISORY
EXPLICIT CONTENT
OT
OLDER TEEN
AGE 16+
02 Hiromoto-Sin-Ichi / Kodansha Ltd. ©2004 TOKYOPOP Inc. All Rights Reserved.
www.TOKYOPOP.com

ALSO AVAILABLE FROM

MANGA

.HACK//LEGEND OF THE TWILIGHT
@LARGE
ABENOBASHI: MAGICAL SHOPPING ARCADE
A.I. LOVE YOU
AI YORI AOSHI
ANGELIC LAYER
ARM OF KANNON
BABY BIRTH
BATTLE ROYALE
BATTLE VIXENS
BOYS BE...
BRAIN POWERED
BRIGADOON
B'TX
CANDIDATE FOR GODDESS, THE
CARDCAPTOR SAKURA
CARDCAPTOR SAKURA - MASTER OF THE CLOW
CHOBITS
CHRONICLES OF THE CURSED SWORD
CLAMP SCHOOL DETECTIVES
CLOVER
COMIC PARTY
CONFIDENTIAL CONFESSIONS
CORRECTOR YUI
COWBOY BEBOP
COWBOY BEBOP: SHOOTING STAR
CRAZY LOVE STORY
CRESCENT MOON
CROSS
CULDCEPT
CYBORG 009
D•N•ANGEL
DEMON DIARY
DEMON ORORON, THE
DEUS VITAE
DIABOLO
DIGIMON
DIGIMON TAMERS
DIGIMON ZERO TWO
DOLL
DRAGON HUNTER
DRAGON KNIGHTS
DRAGON VOICE
DREAM SAGA
DUKLYON: CLAMP SCHOOL DEFENDERS
EERIE QUEERIE!
ERICA SAKURAZAWA: COLLECTED WORKS
ET CETERA
ETERNITY
EVIL'S RETURN
FAERIES' LANDING
FAKE
FLCL
FLOWER OF THE DEEP SLEEP, THE
FORBIDDEN DANCE
FRUITS BASKET

G GUNDAM
GATEKEEPERS
GETBACKERS
GIRL GOT GAME
GRAVITATION
GTO
GUNDAM SEED ASTRAY
GUNDAM WING
GUNDAM WING: BATTLEFIELD OF PACIFISTS
GUNDAM WING: ENDLESS WALTZ
GUNDAM WING: THE LAST OUTPOST (G-UNIT)
HANDS OFF!
HAPPY MANIA
HARLEM BEAT
HYPER RUNE
I.N.V.U.
IMMORTAL RAIN
INITIAL D
INSTANT TEEN: JUST ADD NUTS
ISLAND
JING: KING OF BANDITS
JING: KING OF BANDITS - TWILIGHT TALES
JULINE
KARE KANO
KILL ME, KISS ME
KINDAICHI CASE FILES, THE
KING OF HELL
KODOCHA: SANA'S STAGE
LAMENT OF THE LAMB
LEGAL DRUG
LEGEND OF CHUN HYANG, THE
LES BIJOUX
LOVE HINA
LOVE OR MONEY
LUPIN III
LUPIN III: WORLD'S MOST WANTED
MAGIC KNIGHT RAYEARTH I
MAGIC KNIGHT RAYEARTH II
MAHOROMATIC: AUTOMATIC MAIDEN
MAN OF MANY FACES
MARMALADE BOY
'MARS
MARS: HORSE WITH NO NAME
MINK
MIRACLE GIRLS
MIYUKI-CHAN IN WONDERLAND
MODEL
MOURYOU KIDEN: LEGEND OF THE NYMPHS
NECK AND NECK
ONE
ONE I LOVE, THE
PARADISE KISS
PARASYTE
PASSION FRUIT
PEACH GIRL
PEACH GIRL: CHANGE OF HEART
PET SHOP OF HORRORS
PITA-TEN

07.15.04T

ALSO AVAILABLE FROM ⦿TOKYOPOP®

LEGAL DRUG™

When no ordinary prescription will do...

FROM CLAMP CREATORS OF CHOBITS & TOKYO BABYLON